A SPIRIT OF SACRIFICE

A SPIRIT OF SACRIFICE

NEW YORK STATE
in the
FIRST WORLD WAR

AARON NOBLE, KEITH SWANEY, and VICKI WEISS

excelsior editions

Published by
STATE UNIVERSITY OF NEW YORK PRESS, ALBANY

© 2017 New York State Education Department, Albany, NY 12230

EXCELSIOR EDITIONS is an imprint of STATE UNIVERSITY OF NEW YORK PRESS
For information, contact
State University of New York Press, Albany, NY
www.sunypress.edu

Production and book design, Laurie D. Searl
Marketing, Fran Keneston

Library of Congress Cataloging-in-Publication Data

Names: Noble, Aaron, author. | Swaney, Keith, author. | Weiss, Vicki
(Victoria), author.
Title: A spirit of sacrifice : New York State in the First World War /
Aaron Noble, Keith Swaney, and Vicki Weiss.
Description: Albany : State University of New York Press, 2017. |
"Excelsior Editions." | Includes bibliographical references and index.
Identifiers: LCCN 2017000332 (print) | LCCN 2017028323 (ebook) |
ISBN 9781438467801 (e-book) | ISBN 9781438467788 (pbk. : alk. paper)
Subjects: LCSH: World War, 1914–1918—New York (State)
Classification: LCC D570.85.N4 (ebook) | LCC D570.85.N4 N63 2017 (print) |
DDC 940.3/747—dc23
LC record available at https://lccn.loc.gov/2017000332

10 9 8 7 6 5 4 3 2 1

Contents

Foreword

Americans live in the long shadow of World War I, in a world shaped by a hundred-year-old global conflict that is still reflected in our society, our culture, and our current events. From civil rights issues to international border crises, the Great War continues to influence our headlines and our choices. But unlike the stirring history of the Civil War or the heroic narrative of World War II, World War I is largely ignored, forgotten except as a simple predecessor to the massive destruction that followed a generation later.

The past, however, is more than prologue. Americans deserve to learn about the Great War if they want to understand our complex and fascinating country. New York played a particularly important part in World War I, an outsized role even for the Empire State. The remarkable story of New York from 1914 to 1919, at home and, after the United States declared war in 1917, on the war front, provides an important case study that expands our understanding not only of the Great War but also of its continued impact today.

The talented experts at the New York State Museum have assembled a fascinating exhibition, *A Spirit of Sacrifice: New York State in the First World War*, that showcases their unique collection of artifacts, documents, and artwork. Personal objects—from a New York doughboy's Enfield rifle to Father Duffy's extreme unction kit—heighten the humanity of this exhibit, but it is the posters that provide the backbone.

The World War I–era poster collection held by the New York State Library is second to none, as the *Spirit of Sacrifice* exhibition and this accompanying catalog demonstrate. New York artists, designers, and printers led the world in their stunning graphic designs. In 2017, their vibrant posters enthrall modern viewers, as they did one hundred years ago.

Many aspects of New York during the war find expression in these posters, from Wall Street and war bonds to Liberty Gardens and food preservation. Most people associate women working in war industry factories with World War II, but the 1940s' archetype of "Rosie the Riveter" had a mother, and she worked in a munitions factory during the Great War. Along with the suffragettes who marched up Fifth Avenue, these female industrial workers from New York challenged the status quo on gender roles.

In *A Spirit of Sacrifice*, the much-decorated Harlem Hellfighters (or Harlem Rattlers) of the 369th Infantry Regiment tell an inspirational civil rights story, juxtaposing harsh struggles, great achievements, and the introduction of modern jazz. Forty percent of New York City residents were foreign-born; the tension between national loyalty and individual rights speaks very clearly to us across the century. More servicemen hailed from New York than any other state, and more New Yorkers died in battle as well. Ultimately, it would be New York Harbor that welcomed the American Expeditionary Force home from the charnel-house battlefields of Europe.

A *Spirit of Sacrifice* tells this powerful history through a rich exhibition that extends our understanding of World War I way beyond New York. Congratulations to the curatorial team that assembled the compelling array of artifacts and artwork, expertly interpreted for all who visit the New York State Museum. It is a timely and generous contribution to the national commemoration of the World War I centennial, and an important example of public history at its best.

LIBBY H. O'CONNELL, PhD
U.S. World War I Centennial Commission

Message from
the Chancellor and the Commissioner

New York State and its citizens have played a major role in the United States's war efforts throughout history—from the Civil War to the present conflicts in Iraq and Afghanistan. An often overlooked war in American, and New York, history is World War I. No other state contributed more soldiers, supplies, and funds to the United States's efforts in World War I than New York State.

In the early twentieth century, New York State led the nation in population, wealth, and industry. Over half a million New Yorkers entered the military between 1917 and 1918. Thousands of companies employed New Yorkers at home to make equipment and weapons for soldiers. New York City's banks supplied millions of dollars in loans to the United States's allies during the war.

Although New Yorkers answered the call to war on the battlefield and the home front, its citizens were not all united, and many doubted the country's ability to fight in the war. Many New Yorkers were foreign-born, and there were uncertainties about where their loyalties truly lay.

A century later, we reflect on New York's role in World War I with an exhibition at the New York State Museum: *A Spirit of Sacrifice: New York State in the First World War*. As an educational institution under the State Education Department and the Board of Regents, the State Museum is charged with serving the lifelong educational needs of New Yorkers.

To accomplish this mission, the State Museum worked with its sister institutions— the New York State Library and New York State Archives—to feature objects from their world-class collections in the exhibition. The State Library owns one of the largest World War I poster collections in the nation, and more than seventy of these illustrated posters appear in the exhibition. It's an honor to share with the public these historical primary documents that reveal important messages without relying on much text.

A Spirit of Sacrifice also includes artifacts from cultural institutions and collections throughout the state—including the Rochester Historical Society, the Chemung County Historical Society, and the New York State Military Museum. The State Education Department is grateful to all lending institutions for helping to make this exhibition truly representative of the Empire State's role in World War I.

This exhibition is an opportunity for educators to teach our children and students about this pivotal event in New York and American history. Numerous themes of historic

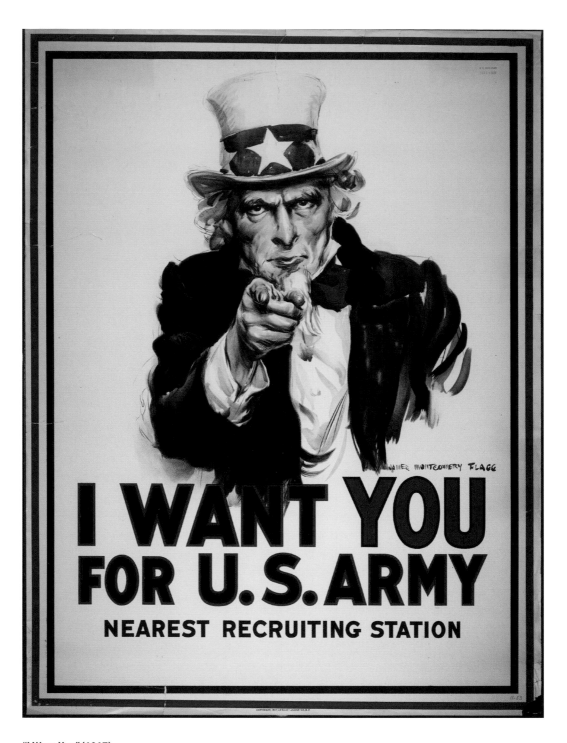

"I Want You" (1917).

Artist: James Montgomery Flagg; *Printer:* Leslie-Judge Co., New York; *Publisher:* United States Army;
Technique: Lithograph; *Dimensions:* 101 x 75 cm.

James Montgomery Flagg's recruiting poster featuring Uncle Sam became iconic of the call to arms during World War I. Flagg originally created the image for a July 1916 cover of Leslie's *Illustrated Weekly*.[1] Flagg was an early supporter of the Preparedness Movement. Over four million copies of the Uncle Sam poster were eventually printed. This particular poster was printed for use by the Albany, New York recruitment station located at 467 Broadway. Between April 1917 and November 1918, two million men volunteered for military service. New York State Library, Manuscripts and Special Collections.

1. "The Most Famous Poster," Exhibit: American Treasures at the Library of Congress, www.loc.gov/exhibits/treasures/trm015.html.

importance can be explored when studying World War I, including citizenship and civic duty, immigration, race and race relations, New York State's role as an industrial power, the rise and fall of empires, and the emergence of new economic systems. A teacher's guide is available to support educators in using the exhibition as a teaching tool. There is also an online version of the exhibition on the Museum's website for those unable to visit in person.

This exhibition also acknowledges the thousands of New Yorkers and Americans in the war who made the ultimate commitment to serve and keep the country safe. We thank all who serve in the military, past and present, for their honorable sacrifice and unmatched bravery in protecting this nation.

World War I was called "the war to end all wars," but citizens and service members alike would learn that it was not. Today there are no living veterans of World War I. We must rely on history to teach us. This exhibition is an opportunity for all New Yorkers and Americans to learn and reflect on the events of World War I and understand the impacts of the war in New York, the nation, and the world.

BETTY A. ROSA
New York State Board of Regents Chancellor

MARYELLEN ELIA
New York State Education Commissioner

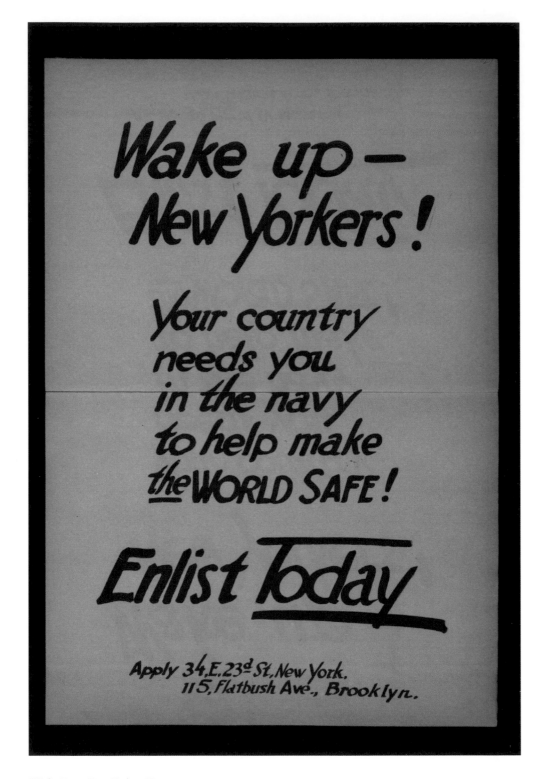

"Wake Up—New Yorkers!"

Artist: Unknown; *Printer:* Lutz and Scheinkman Inc. Litho., New York, New York; *Publisher:* United States Navy; *Technique:* Lithograph; *Dimensions:* 75 x 50 cm.

This 1917 recruiting poster targets New Yorkers to enlist in the U.S. Navy. Courtesy of the Library of Congress.

Acknowledgments

A *Spirit of Sacrifice* is an ambitious educational exhibition. The story of New York State's role in World War I is expansive and cannot be told through the collections of any single institution. The State Museum worked in close partnership with its sister institutions in the Office of Cultural Education: the New York State Archives and New York State Library. It is because of the unified mission of these institutions that we can bring together the comprehensive perspective on New York State's role in World War I.

As always, we are grateful for the continuing support of the New York State Board of Regents, the New York State Education Department, Board of Regents Chancellor Betty A. Rosa, and State Education Commissioner MaryEllen Elia.

This exhibition is a statewide story and benefits from materials from institutions throughout the state, reflecting the impact of the war on every community in New York. *A Spirit of Sacrifice* features posters from museums, libraries, and historical societies from across New York State, but it is not merely a poster exhibition. Rather, the exhibition is full of iconic artifacts, images, and information that together tell the story of New York State's essential role in World War I. In planning the exhibit, we reached out to other cultural institutions and historians and asked them to help broaden the story by loaning their objects and expertise. All responded with generosity and collegiality, and consequently all share in the ownership of the exhibition.

We are incredibly grateful for the encouragement and support of the National World War I Centennial Commission and especially Commissioners Libby O'Connell and Monique Seefried. The long list of other partners includes the following lending institutions and people: the Joseph Alteri Collection; the Albany Institute of History and Art; the Archives of American Art at the Smithsonian Institution; the Association of Public Historians of New York State; the Binghamton University Special Collections and University Archives; the Brandoline family; the Buffalo Transportation Pierce-Arrow Museum; the Chemung County Historical Society; the George Eastman Museum; the William F. Howard Collection; the Library of Congress; the Museum of American History; the National Archives and Records Administration; the National Park Service; the New-York Historical Society; the New York Public Library; the New York State Military Museum (Division of Military and Naval Affairs, Major General Anthony German, Adjutant General); the New York State Office of Parks, Recreation and Historic Preservation;

the New York Public Library; the Oneida County Historical Society; the Rochester Historical Society; the Schenectady County Historical Society; and the United States Army Center for Military History.

The realization of the exhibition, A Spirit of Sacrifice, also owes a tremendous debt to the efforts of our curatorial team: Aaron Noble, Vicki Weiss, and Keith Swaney, as well as Jill Cozzy, Robyn Gibson, and Jennifer Lemak. Neither the exhibition nor this catalog would have been possible without the efforts of our image researcher, Bridget Enderle, and museum photographer, John Yost. Additional thanks are owed to the entire staffs at the State Museum, State Library, and State Archives whose expertise, assistance, and guidance helped make the exhibition and this catalog a reality.

We are also grateful for the assistance of distinguished scholar Steven Jaffe. Steve reviewed and improved the text for the project through his insightful commentary. Last but certainly not least, we extend special thanks to James Peltz, Amanda Lanne-Camilli, and the professional staff at SUNY Press for their patience and guidance.

MARK SCHAMING
Deputy Commissioner of Cultural Education and
New York State Museum Director

BERNARD MARGOLIS
New York State Librarian

THOMAS RULLER
New York State Archivist

Introduction

"New York's pride is the pride of things done. Her leadership is no more due to her great wealth or her large population than to the patriotism of her citizens and the uses to which her wealth is put. In every war in which this country has engaged, she has shown a spirit of sacrifice that has made her preeminent among the States."

It was with these words that New York State governor Charles S. Whitman urged his fellow New Yorkers to purchase Liberty Bonds in support of the war effort on April 6, 1918.[1] In two sentences, Governor Whitman reminded New Yorkers and the nation that the Empire State once again led all others in the number of men, the amount of money, and the tonnage of materiel supplied to American forces during World War I. It was in this vein that the title for the New York State Museum's exhibition was selected. This was an exhortation to the people of New York to continue to sacrifice—through financing the war effort and through industrial production, agricultural output, and military service—as the people of the Empire State had in past conflicts; it was not, necessarily, an indication of the motivations behind New Yorkers for participation in the war effort. Because of the contemporary nature of the quotation, it does not have the benefit of historical hindsight over the ultimate failure and futility of World War I and its enduring legacy. Not only was the conflict not the "war to end all wars," but, in fact, it contributed greatly to the conditions that sparked a second and more deadly conflict just two decades later. What cannot be disputed, though, is that New York State surpassed all others during World War I in regards to men, money, and materiel provided to the war effort. The enormity of New York's role in the conflict cannot be overstated.

Governor Whitman's Proclamation of April 6, 1918.

New York State Archives, 13035-79.

James Sullivan served as the fourth New York State Historian from 1916 to 1923.

Following World War I, Sullivan and the New York State Office of Archives and History was tasked with compiling information for a history of the Empire State's role in the conflict. New York State Archives, A0412-78.

To convey the history on New York's role in World War I, the New York State Museum's exhibition, *A Spirit of Sacrifice: New York State in the First World War*, to which this book is a companion, relies primarily on the collections of the state's Office of Cultural Education—the New York State Museum, the New York State Library, and the New York State Archives. Included among these world-class collections are the nearly 3,600 posters of the Benjamin W. Arnold World War I Poster Collection at the New York State Library. World War I is frequently referred to as the golden age of poster illustration. As an advertising medium, posters had long been used for cultural

events such as the theater or the circus. During the conflict, poster artists were employed by governments on both sides to inspire the citizenry and convey important messages on a wide scale. In the United States, millions of copies of posters, often by some of the nation's leading illustrators, were printed to rally the nation to the war effort. Posters were appealing to government leaders and charitable organizations because their colorful images were easily understandable for passersby.[2] New York City, as the commercial capital of the country, played a critical role in the advertising and propaganda campaign during World War I. These graphically engaging posters were created during World War I by some of the most prominent graphic designers of the period from New York City, including James Montgomery Flagg, Charles Dana Gibson, and Edward Penfield. By interweaving the story of New York in the Great War and utilizing the tremendous array of artifacts of the New York State Museum collection within the pictorial history evinced by the posters of the era, the exhibition serves not simply as a display of poster art, but also as a more comprehensive examination of the primacy of the state's contributions to America's foray into World War I. *A Spirit of Sacrifice* conveys more fully than any other venue the collection of artifacts, images, and documents that show the breadth of New York State's efforts during World War I, from Buffalo to Albany and from Plattsburgh to Manhattan.

The museum's exhibition has profited from the rich collections of the New York State Library's Manuscripts and Special Collections Division and the New York State Archives. Both of these vast repositories contain an untold number of records from World War I era in addition to the artifacts that they provided. Thankfully, *A Spirit of Sacrifice* has greatly benefitted from the fact that the state of New York was very forward-thinking in its efforts to record its war history. In fact, within a month of the declaration of war on April 6, 1917, the New York State Historian, James Sullivan, was given the herculean task of documenting the state's contributions toward the ultimate goal of a definitive history of New York State in the Great War. Sullivan and his staff reached out to "historical and patriotic societies throughout the State, libraries, schools, colleges, and public officials of towns, villages, and cities" requesting their assistance in compiling the record of the war efforts in New York

State. Similarly, the New York State Library began work with libraries across the state to carry out a parallel effort.[3] In 1919, New York State amended its Education Law to establish local historians in every village, town, and city across New York State to help compile information about New York State's role in the war.[4] From these local historians, Sullivan sought service records of New Yorkers who served in the armed forces during the war, records of citizens who performed tasks for the war effort on the home front, information on New York State industry's role in the conflict, as well as photographs, letters, and other means of documenting the state's vast role in the conflict. Sullivan noted his limited success in collecting posters pertaining to the war effort, but acknowledged that "the State Library has made an excellent collection and all of the most important ones have been gathered and filed."[5] Nationally, James Sullivan served as the president of the National Association of State War History Organizations and helped guide the compilation of the history of the war across the country. Though they were never published, Dr. Sullivan's notes and files remain. This treasure trove of historical data can be found in the New York State Archives. Through intensive research using Dr. Sullivan's files and other collections within the archives, the New York State Museum has been able to more fully interpret New York State's role in World War I through the eyes of those who participated—both at home and overseas.

The exhibition also relies heavily on the records of the New York State Council of Defense. The extant archival records of the Council of Defense include letters, telegrams, minutes, reports, pamphlets, bulletins, and other administrative documents. These materials are preserved and made accessible by the New York State Archives, along with historical records of the other state agencies with which the council collaborated during World War I. In addition, the Archives holds over one million military service records of New Yorkers who served in World War I in the Army, Navy, and Marine Corps, and as nurses—which were compiled from records of the federal government by the New York State Bureau of War Records under the direction of the adjutant general. All told, the records in the State Archives tell the story of how the state's people and government responded to World War I on both the battlefield and the home front. In addition

"Wake Up, America! Civilization Calls" (1917).

Artist: James Montgomery Flagg; *Printer:* Hegeman Print, New York, New York; *Publisher:* Mayor's Committee (Wake Up America Day); *Technique:* Lithograph; *Dimensions:* 105 x 70 cm.

James Montgomery Flagg became arguably the most famous poster artist of World War I. In this poster titled, "Civilization Calls," the United States is depicted as Liberty asleep to the war raging. The poster was created for "Wake Up America Day" on April 19, 1917. In New York City and across the nation, parades and rallies were held in an effort to rally patriotic support for the United States's entry into World War I. Through his poster, Flagg urges his fellow Americans to rally to the defense of the Allied Cause. President Woodrow Wilson and others portrayed the conflict as a defense of civilization and a war to save democracy in an effort to rally public support to the war effort. By the thousands, New Yorkers responded to these calls both on the home front and overseas. New York State Museum Collection, H-1976.145.11.

James Montgomery Flagg (1877–1960).

Born in Pelham Manor, Westchester County, James Montgomery Flagg became one of the nation's leading illustrators. He attended the Art Students League of New York and studied in London and Paris. When the United States entered World War I, Flagg was working as a marketing illustrator. He created his most famous work in 1917 using his own face for Uncle Sam. Flagg was appointed New York State's official military artist by Governor Charles S. Whitman on June 19, 1917, in recognition of his "patriotic spirit in contributing, voluntarily, [his] abilities as an artist during this crisis, for the good of the State."[1] Flagg ultimately created forty-six poster designs for the war effort.[2]

1. Whitman, Charles Seymour, *Public Papers of Charles Seymour Whitman, Governor, 1915–1918*, vol. 3 (Albany: J. B. Lyon Company, Printers, 1919), p. 387.

2. Capozzola, Christopher, *Uncle Sam Wants You: World War I and the Making of the Modern American Citizen* (New York: Oxford University Press, 2008), p. 4.

to the museum's own research, the exhibition calls on the most recent external scholarship available to more fully tell New York State's story.

World War I is often overlooked, but it had major worldwide implications. The repercussions of World War I are still felt today in its centennial years. The borders of much of the modern world were drawn as a result of this conflict. The conflict is also significant for the failures that followed. The war was not the "war to end all wars," as President Wilson famously proclaimed. The harsh terms of the peace treaty that followed World War I created conditions that directly contributed to a second and more devastating world war only twenty years later. At home, both the state and the nation struggled to address the needs of millions of soldiers returning home from the horrors of the Western Front. As unprepared as the United States was in its entry into the war, the rapid cessation of hostilities and the capitulation of the Central Powers found the country equally unprepared for the peace that followed. Soldiers were left with inadequate benefits, limited prospects for employment, and struggling to cope with the wounds of war—both seen and unseen. A *Spirit of Sacrifice* attempts to explore these issues that followed the homecoming parades and victory celebrations.

New York's role in World War I was immense and far greater than could be fully told in any single volume or exhibition. James Sullivan in 1920 estimated that a published work on New York State during the Great War would encompass three volumes of 1,000 pages or more.[6] That being the case, A *Spirit of Sacrifice* broadly interprets the significant role played by the Empire State and its citizens during the conflict. No doubt, some elements of the story have been overlooked or perhaps not given their due. This should not be seen as minimizing the contributions of those individuals or detracting from the broader story. As is often the case, the exhibition went where the artifacts led. By interweaving the story of New York in war and utilizing artifacts within the pictorial history shown by the posters of the era, we present a comprehensive examination of how these issues were faced, and of the importance of the state's contributions to America's foray into the war.

1

The Empire State at War

As the nation commemorates the centennial of American participation in the First World War, historians across the country—and around the world—will revisit this oft-forgotten conflict and its significance to understanding our history today. With the global nature of the war that erupted in Europe in 1914 and into which the United States was drawn three years later, it is fair to question the significance of a museum exhibition or a book that focuses on the contributions of a single state. Given the scope of the conflict, how can a study of New York State's role in World War I add to the abundance of scholarship already available? The following examination of the enormous contributions of the Empire State to the American war effort will once again affirm that, in so many ways, the study of New York State history is, in fact, the study of American history. The story of New Yorkers during World War I mirrors those of other Americans from 1917 to 1918. What makes New York State's story unique, however, is the leading role that the state and its people played during this critical period—on both the battlefield and the home front. New York served as the site where critical questions were addressed pertaining to civic participation and protest; civil rights; race, ethnicity, and gender relations; and many other topics. The following chapters explore in depth how New York State answered the nation's call to arms and how these questions were addressed.

> I AM NEW YORK.
> . . . Because the war was fought for
> Right, I gave unsparingly my sons and
> my resources.
> And not until the last dollar of Victory is paid shall I call my
> task complete.
> —From "I Am New York and This Is My Creed" by Bruce Barton, 1919[1]

The opening of the Erie Canal in 1825 helped to propel the Empire State to its preeminent position. The state's business and political leaders solidified its standing over the remainder of the 1800s. New York City was the commercial and financial capital of the nation, and many of the country's leading manufacturers called New York State their home. During the American Civil War from 1861 to 1865, the Empire State contributed

"New York will see it through" (1918).

Artist: Unknown; *Printer:* Lutz and Scheinkman Inc. Litho., New York, New York; *Publisher:* Liberty Loan Committee, Government Loan Organization, Second Federal Reserve District; *Technique:* Lithograph; *Dimensions:* 55 x 80.5 cm.

This Liberty Loan poster was one of several variations printed that could be customized for a locality—in this case, New York. New York State Library, Manuscripts and Special Collections.

more men, money, and materiel in defense of the Union than any other state—and had correspondingly paid the highest cost in fathers, sons, and brothers lost, as well as in taxes paid and moneys donated. By the advent of the twentieth century, New York State remained unrivaled in the nation in regard to its population, industry, finance, and transportation networks. As the United States was drawn closer to being pulled into the war raging in Europe from 1914 to 1917, it was readily apparent to New York's civic, business, and political leaders that the Empire State would again be called upon to bear a tremendous burden in the conflict to come. As Governor Charles S. Whitman declared in his annual address to the legislature in January 1917, "no less than in 1776 and 1861, the Empire State [will be called to be] the sound and trustworthy keystone in the arch of national defense."[2]

Between April 2, 1917, and November 11, 1918, 518,864 New Yorkers entered military service. New Yorkers comprised more than 10 percent of the entire American Expeditionary Force (AEF). Consequently, New York State endured more casualties during the conflict, with 13,956 New Yorkers paying the ultimate sacrifice on the battlefields of France.

During World War I, New York State provided some of the most storied units, including the 165th Infantry Regiment of the 42nd "Rainbow" Division. The former 69th New York had earned fame as the "Fighting Irish" during the Civil War and retained both its Irish character and reputation in the trenches of the Western Front. The African American 369th Infantry Regiment, the "Harlem Hellfighters" (formerly the 15th Regiment of the New York National Guard), became one of the most decorated regiments of the war while fighting for the French Army; and the infamous "Lost Battalion" was part of the 77th "Liberty" Division comprised largely of draftees from New York City. New York's National Guard Division—the 27th—spearheaded the Allied breakthrough of the

New York's 7th Regiment departs for the war.

This September 11, 1917 photograph features the 7th Regiment, New York National Guard departing New York City for training at Spartanburg, South Carolina. Once federalized, the regiment became the 107th Infantry Regiment. Courtesy of the Library of Congress.

vaunted Hindenburg Line in the fall of 1918, but at tremendous cost. The heroism of New Yorkers during the war did not go unrecognized. New Yorkers earned eighteen of the 121 Medals of Honor awarded during the war, or thirteen percent of the total number of awards.

By the end of the war, there were more than 38,000 New York companies employing more than one million workers in wartime industry. Companies such as Remington Arms (Ilion), Eastman Kodak (Rochester), General Electric (Schenectady), and Alcoa (Massena), to name but a few, all contributed immensely to the production of weapons and equipment for the American and Allied war efforts. New York Harbor was central to America's role in France. Of the 2.1 million men in Europe during World War I, 1.65 million sailed from New York as did the bulk of the materiel needed to equip the AEF

New Yorkers played an equally important role on the home front. As the wealthiest state in the nation, New York contributed more in taxes to the war effort than any other state. New York City's banks supplied more than $2.5 billion in loans to cash-strapped Allied governments during the war—enabling the city to surpass London as the world's credit capital. New Yorkers purchased approximately one-third of the Liberty Bonds sold during the war, and the state's citizens proved immensely generous in their charitable giving between 1914 and 1918.

While New York's contributions surpassed those of all other states, its citizens were hardly united in their opinions about the conflict. These disagreements raised doubts about the nation's ability to fight this war, and called into question the loyalty of many of its citizens. These divisions needed to be overcome if the nation hoped to unite its citizens behind the war

3

effort. To achieve this goal, New York's Progressive leaders—Theodore Roosevelt, Charles Whitman, John Purroy Mitchel, and others—sought to mobilize millions of people of disparate backgrounds, social classes, races, and of both genders, and unify them in pursuit of a common goal. Using every means and media at their disposal—posters, film, newspapers, theater, and more—these political leaders attempted to mold public opinion in favor of the war.

Much of the language used to sway American opinion was based in the republican tradition of duty and obligation. According to historian Christopher Capozzola, Americans in 1917 associated these concepts with their relationship to the government. These "obligations were not just rhetorical flourishes," but rather were the customs and practices that enabled the nation's leaders to impel the nation to war.[3]

The central role occupied by New York State in terms of its industry, agriculture, and infrastructure,

as well as New York Harbor's position as the nation's most critical port, and New York City's position as the financial capital of the nation, made the Empire State a target for enemy activities. German agents and sympathizers planned and attempted numerous plots aimed to slow the supply of materiel to the Allied Armies in Europe. New York City remained a hotbed of German espionage efforts from 1914 until 1917.

In many cases, New York State became the laboratory where the nation's leaders sought to answer some of the most troubling questions arising out of the war: How could a diverse population of native-born whites, immigrants, African Americans, and men and women from dramatically different backgrounds and political leanings unify to fight a war an ocean away? How could this need for order, uniformity, and unity—which often required a suppression of dissent—be reconciled with the nation's democratic traditions and fundamental freedoms of speech and the press?[4] In

Anti-war rally in Union Square.

Prominent New York Socialist Party leader Cornelius Lehane speaks during an anti-war demonstration at Union Square in New York City on August 8, 1914. Socialists like Lehane argued that the "Capitalist War" in Europe pitted members of the working class—or proletariat—against one another. Courtesy of the Library of Congress.

New York, nearly 40 percent of the population was foreign-born. Many had arrived from motherlands now engaged in the European War—on both sides. Many initially favored their nation of birth. Other groups opposed American involvement based on conditions in their homelands. Many Irish Americans, for instance, were against American support of the Allies as a result of the continued British occupation of Ireland. Many Eastern European Jews had fled to New York City as a result of anti-Semitism in Russia. They refused to side with Czar Nicholas II and the Russian government as a result of its anti-Jewish pogroms and other policies.[5] It was concern over this diversity that Woodrow Wilson cited in support of American neutrality in 1914, when he stated that the United States must remain neutral in the European war, else "our mixed population would wage war on each other."[6] As overall American popular opinion began to shift against the Central Powers, the loyalty of immigrants from Germany and Austria-Hungary came under suspicion.[7] Former President Theodore Roosevelt famously declared that "there is no room in this country for hyphenated Americanism." Roosevelt and others feared that competing loyalties among immigrants would lead the nation to ruin.[8] Such fears lay at the foundation of the 100% American Movement, which had a significant following in New York during and after the war. In this vein, New York served as a proving ground in defining the relationship of these diverse immigrant communities with the government, with native-born New Yorkers, and their support (or perceived lack thereof) for the war effort.

Within the boundaries of the Empire State, advocates for the Preparedness Movement and others calling for American entry into the European War between 1914 and 1917 gave rise to the first citizens' military training camp at Plattsburgh. Additional camps would quickly follow across the country. At the same time, many of the leaders of the antiwar movement resided in New York City. The socialist and anarchist movements had found their most significant U.S. foothold in New York and many of the leading leftist intellectuals called Manhattan home. These groups argued that the war was caused by capitalist greed at the expense of the slaughter of the working classes in the trenches of Europe.[9]

New York was also the center of the burgeoning "New Negro" movement, particularly in Harlem.

Leaders in the African American community, such as W. E. B. Du Bois and James Weldon Johnson, resided in the city. Influential black newspapers and magazines, including the *New York Age* and *The Crisis,* were published in New York, giving voice to the growing civil rights movement and the emerging Harlem Renaissance to follow in the 1920s. The state's African American population was needed for the war effort, but New York's leaders had to reconcile the need for black patriotism with the social and economic injustices experienced by the African American community. [10]

As the chapters will show, New Yorkers did rally to support the war effort by sending their husbands, fathers, sons, and brothers to war. Thousands of women joined the effort as nurses and stenographers, but also as truck drivers and factory workers and volunteers for countless charitable organizations. New Yorkers struggled to answer many of the troubling questions raised by American entry into World War I. The results of these answers were decidedly mixed. New Yorkers demonstrated tremendous patriotism and unity, but often at the expense of freedom of speech and those who dissented. Immigrants and minorities fell under intense and largely unjust scrutiny and suspicion. The legacy of these results affected New York State and the nation far beyond the Armistice in November 1918.

The Power of Propaganda

During World War I, governments systematically employed visual propaganda on an unprecedented scale to mobilize millions of citizens for the war effort, to sway popular opinion about the conflict, and to unify support for the war. In New York and elsewhere, Progressive leaders demonstrated a willingness to use the press, public relations, and commercial art for wartime government purposes. Posters were an incredibly powerful weapon during World War I. Their visually stunning illustrations immediately conveyed important messages to passersby. A message that would normally be conveyed in a few paragraphs of text could be made immediately understandable through the use of the proper illustration.

"Enlist" (ca. 1916).

Artist: Fred Spear; *Printer:* Sacketts and Wilhelms Corporation, New York; *Publisher:* Boston Public Safety Committee; *Technique:* Photochemical print: Rotogravure, color; *Dimensions:* 82 x 58 cm.

Few posters more readily illustrate the power that posters of the era played in shaping the American people's outlook on World War I. Allied and pro-Allied propaganda in the United States targeted American popular opinion following the sinking of the British passenger liner *Lusitania* by German U-boats. This poster, alluding to the civilian casualties aboard the *Lusitania*, depicts a woman cradling an infant as both sink beneath the ocean's surface. Such graphic depictions were intended to inspire hatred towards the atrocities committed by Germany. New York State Library, Manuscripts and Special Collections.

"The Hun—his Mark" (1917).

Artist: James Allen St. John; *Printer:* Brett Lithograph Company, New York; *Publisher:* Treasury Department; *Technique:* Lithograph; *Dimensions:* 76 x 51 cm.

This poster was produced during the Second Liberty Loan drive from October 1 to 28, 1917. The bloody handprint is a clear and menacing allusion to the reported atrocities committed by the German Army and the danger a German victory would mean to the United States. Across the country, the war was now portrayed as a struggle between the democracies of the world and the "monster of autocracy." German victory, it was argued, would result in "the strangling of individual liberty" and that the "age-long struggle of the submerged masses of the world toward light and liberty is not only to be checked but rendered fruitless . . . that there shall be no right but the right of selfishness and the power to enforce it."[1] New York State Museum Collection, H-1976.53.4.

1. The Oneida County Home Defense Committee, "A Message on the War," June 1917, James Sullivan, Working Files for a Publication on New York in World War I, 1917–1925, New York State Archives Series A3166.

J. Allen St. John (1872–1957).

James Allen St. John was born in Chicago and studied at the Chicago Art Institute and the American Academy of Art.[1] St. John moved to New York City to continue his studies at the Art Students League of New York in 1898. He was employed by the *New York Herald* until 1906, when he traveled to Paris to study at the Académie Julian. In 1912, St. John returned to Chicago, where he continued his artistic career. During the war, the forty-seven-year-old St. John was too old to serve in the Army. He was subsequently recruited to design propaganda posters for the Division of Pictorial Publicity (DPP).[2]

1. Darracott, Joseph, ed., *The First World War in Posters* (New York: Dover Publications, 1974), page XX.

2. "J. Allen St. John" Biography, Pulptartists.com (http://www.pulpartists.com/StJohn.html).

"Remember Belgium" (1918).

Artist: Ellsworth Young; *Printer*: United States Prtg. and Lith. Co.; *Publisher*: Fourth Liberty Loan; *Technique*: Lithograph; *Dimensions*: 51 x 76 cm.

The German violation of Belgian neutrality in 1914 and reports of atrocities committed against Belgian civilians sparked widespread condemnation in the United States. Belgium had been "ravaged as no country . . . since Attila's day. To Germany treaties were naught. International law, humanity and morality were naught."[1] With American entry into the war in 1917, "Remember Belgium" became a rallying cry for the American war effort. New York State Museum Collection, H-1972.7.2.

1. The Oneida County Home Defense Committee, "A Message on the War," June 1917, James Sullivan, Working Files for a Publication on New York in World War I, 1917–1925, New York State Archives Series A3166.

"Must Children Die and Mothers Plead in Vain?"

Artist: Walter H. Everett; *Printer*: Sackett and Wilhelms Corporation, New York, New York; *Publisher*: Treasury Department; *Technique*: Lithograph; *Dimensions*: 102 x 75 cm.

The illustration for this poster features a mother clutching her child and reaching out for aid. The struggle of civilians in Europe was a popular theme in many of the propaganda posters of the era. New York State Museum Collection, H-1973.94.1 CC.

2

Poster Art in World War I

The First World War is frequently referred to as the golden age of poster illustration. During the conflict, poster artists were employed by governments on all sides to inspire the citizenry and convey important messages on a wide scale. In the United States, millions of copies of posters, often by some of the nation's leading illustrators, were printed to rally the nation to the war effort. Their visually stunning illustrations immediately conveyed important messages without relying on much text.

When the United States entered World War I, American public opinion was far from universally supportive of a declaration of war. George S. McMartin, chairman of the Jefferson County Home Defense Committee, wrote that, "Upon the declaration of War in April, 1917 . . . there was very little interest in war, and a very vague comprehension of the part that was to be played by this country in the War."[1] Shortly after the declaration, President Wilson established the Committee on Public Information (CPI). The primary purpose of this committee was to develop a plan to, quite literally, sell the war to a skeptical American public. Just six months earlier, Woodrow Wilson had won re-election to a second term on a platform of American neutrality. By April 1917, he needed to convince the nation to wholeheartedly support American intervention in a European war.[2] Under the leadership of Progressive publisher and Wilson ally George Creel, the CPI undertook the task of unifying the nation behind the war effort. For George Creel, the task was straightforward: The CPI needed to instill American public opinion with a "deathless determination" to see the war to a successful conclusion. To do so, the entire population had to be convinced that they had a common enemy—imperial Germany—and to commit to its defeat. When patriotic fervor proved insufficient, Creel and the CPI sought to instill hatred and suspicion of all things German.[3] American Progressives, particularly in New York State, included liberal journalists, social scientists, reformers, and politicians from across the major political parties, from Republican Theodore Roosevelt to Democrat Al Smith. Most Progressives embraced the idea that government power could be utilized to promote social reform and enhance American democracy by educating and "improving" its citizenry. It was this belief in the potential of government power to shape national opinion and behavior that led Progressive leaders to turn to journalists, publicists, and artists to assist the CPI in broadcasting the government's pro-war message to the population at large. Through much of the late nineteenth and early twentieth centuries, New York State—and New York City in particular—had emerged as a center of American Progressivism, and it was in New York that much of Creel's early energies and efforts were centered.

Creel recognized the importance that posters would play in shaping public opinion. He reached out to Charles Dana Gibson, president of the New York–based Society of Illustrators, to aid in the establishment of the Division of Pictorial Publicity (DPP) with Gibson as its head.[4] As the president of the Society of Illustrators, Gibson was in a unique position to lead this effort and to enlist many of the nation's best artists in the endeavor. The DPP reached out to artists nationwide to create posters for every facet of the war effort—recruiting, Liberty Bonds, conservation, etc. By appealing to the artists' patriotism and civic duty, the DPP frequently convinced these illustrators to work for free. By the time the DPP officially ceased operations in December 1918, more than 300 artists had created over 1,400 illustrations for the American government and philanthropic organizations from which millions of posters were printed in support of the war effort.[5]

Compared to the firing on Fort Sumter as the opening salvo of the American Civil War, or the Japanese surprise attack on Pearl Harbor on December 7, 1941, bringing the United States into World War II, the justifications for war in 1917 were far less tangible to the average citizen. Wilson's assertions of the right of freedom of the seas and the need to defend democracy against German militarism were subjects that did not immediately affect everyday life. In New York State, the average resident viewed American entry into the conflict as an event being driven by Washington, DC.[6] It was in this environment that Charles Dana Gibson and the Division of Pictorial Publicity went to work. The DPP was tasked with bringing the American population fully into support for the American war effort.

Hanging posters.

Elise Robert and Dorothy Kohn affix posters for the Second Liberty Loan drive to a building in Manhattan in 1917. Courtesy of the Library of Congress.

Frederick Strothmann (1879–1958).

Fred Strothmann was born in Philadelphia. He studied at numerous art schools, including the Carl Hecker Art School in New York City. As an adult, Strothmann settled in Flushing, Queens County, and worked as an illustrator for several New York City publications. He also worked as a portrait artist and genre painter.

"Beat back the Hun with Liberty Bonds" (1918).

Artist: Frederick Strothmann; *Printer:* Unknown; *Publisher:* Treasury Department; *Technique*: Lithograph; *Dimensions:* 76 x 51 cm.

Frederick Strothmann's "Beat back the Hun" poster became one of the most iconic images of World War I. Strothmann's illustration depicts a German soldier with bayoneted rifle dripping blood. The "Hun" is peering over a war-ravaged Europe and across the Atlantic Ocean toward the United States. During World War I, the term "Hun" was used by the Allied governments with the aim of "breeding, fostering, and engendering a fierce and unrelenting hatred against the German people …" who utilized "…any means to prosecute the business of wholesale human killing."[1] In addition to raising money for the Liberty Loan effort, the artists of the DPP were tasked with turning American public opinion against Germany and in favor of the Allied war effort. This poster was among the first created by the DPP. Following a request from the Liberty Loan Committee, the DPP received more than 50 designs from 48 artists.[2] This poster was one of ten selected by the Liberty Loan Committee, most of which depicted, as Strothmann's illustration did, the reported savagery of German soldiers. In the years since the war, much debate has arisen regarding the extent of German atrocities in Belgium. As early as 1914, some Americans did suggest that British accounts of German actions were exaggerated. Regardless of the accuracy, however, such reports became the primary narrative in American poster coverage and in the media. After April 1917, this image of the "Savage Hun" seemingly justified treatment of German Americans. New York State Museum Collection, H-1972.112.1 H.

1. Special Agent M.J. Driscoll to Chief Clerk C.L. Converse, July 13, 1919, Records of the Joint Legislative Committee to Investigate Seditious Activities (Lusk Committee), New York State Archives Series L0039, Investigative Subject Files, 1919–1920, Box 2, Folder 38.

2. Van Schaack, page 40.

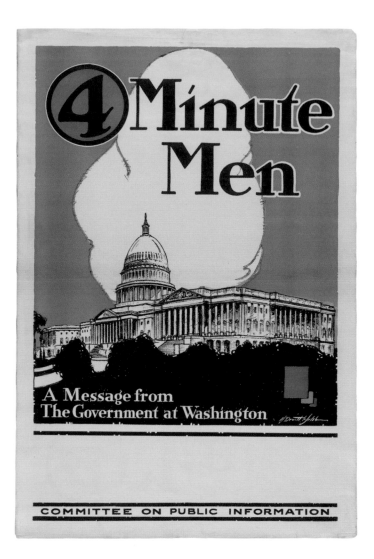

"4 Minute Men."

Artist: H. Devitt Welsh; *Printer*: Unknown; *Publisher*: Committee on Public Information; *Technique*: Lithograph; *Dimensions*: 105.5 x 70.5 cm.

The Four Minute Men were volunteer speakers who reported to the Committee on Public Information. Each speaker was tasked with giving four-minute presentations on topics pertaining to the American war effort, especially preparedness, universal military training, the sale of Liberty Bonds, and enlistment in the armed services. The length of the speeches was determined by the amount of time it took theater operators to change reels on the projectors for newly popular motion pictures—approximately four minutes.[1] New York State Library, Manuscripts and Special Collections.

> 1. Rawls, pages 137–138.

James S. Bryan.

Courtesy of the Rochester Historical Society.

James S. Bryan, Four-Minute Man
Rochester, Monroe County

James S. Bryan served on the home front with Company H, 2d Battalion, Home Defense League, from May 1917 to May 1919 in Rochester. He was an associate member of the Legal Advisory Board, City District Number 4, and a Four-Minute Man. Bryan

Horace Devitt Welsh (1888–1942).

Horace Devitt Welsh was born in Philadelphia in 1888. He studied under Thomas Anshutz at the Pennsylvania Academy of Fine Arts before pursuing a career as a painter, illustrator, and etcher. He was an active artist in both Philadelphia and New York City. During World War I, Welsh was an important member of the Division of Pictorial Publicity and the Committee on Public Information. In addition to designing posters, he served as the main point of contact for the CPI in Washington, DC, where he was a liaison with the heads of various governmental agencies to keep them informed of the capabilities of the DPP and its artists. Welsh was tasked with assessing the needs of these agencies and organizations in Washington and communicating them to Charles Dana Gibson at the DPP's headquarters in New York City for design.[1]

> 1. Rawls, pp. 150–53.

gave speeches at Rochester-area theaters and other public venues for all five Liberty Loan Drives. Following the Armistice, Bryan served on the Federal Board of Vocational Education for Disabled Soldiers and performed other welfare work to benefit returning soldiers.

The Benjamin Walworth Arnold and Cuyler Reynolds Poster Collections at the New York State Library

"Wow!" That word—or a variation thereon—is the expression of researchers and Office of Cultural Education staff when they see one or more of the New York State Library's 3,600-plus World War I posters. And this is the impact 100-year-old posters are having on a generation that has television screens that cover entire walls in their homes and can livestream concerts or virtually go down into the crystal caves of Mexico. Imagine the effect these posters had on people who got much of their information from the black-and-white print of newspapers and whose annual "big day" was the day the circus came to town!

With the outbreak of war in August 1914, European governments for the first time made a concerted effort to utilize visual propaganda—especially poster art—to sway the hearts and minds of their respective populations to ensure unified support for the war effort. When the United States entered the war in 1917, George Creel and the CPI looked to build on the examples established in Europe. Often, this went so far as to mimic (or even outright copy) designs from European poster artists on all sides.

Vibrant colors, heart-tugging or inspiring images, and cleverly crafted text just grab you. From the wide-eyed Statue of Liberty ordering YOU to buy a Liberty Bond "lest I perish" to the pain-filled image of a soldier kneeling on a battle field cradling the head of his fallen horse to the plucky call to "you and your 'pals'" to join the army to "bake [literally!] and break bread together;" to the black-and-white, text-only poster admonishing the reader to "Do Your Bit—Save the Pit" and not throw away those peach stones and walnut shells since they, ground up, could be used in gas masks and perhaps save the life of a soldier. (The State Library also has a German variation on "Save the Pit," which asks Germans to save fruit pits for the oil that can be squeezed from them! The German

poster boasts two peach pits, wearing straw boaters, strutting across the page like a vaudeville duo striding onto a stage.).

One interesting subset in the collection is sixteen posters designed by French children, which include the names and ages of several of the young artists. Another is several German posters, created after the war, sounding the alarm about the spread of Bolshevism from Russia into Germany. There are even several posters noting that since women were working alongside men in the war effort, the men should give them the vote. The men concurred with the women in New York State, giving them the franchise in November 1917.

The New York State Library has these posters mainly because of the forethought of two residents of Albany: Cuyler Reynolds, Albany city historian and the first curator of what is now the Albany Institute of History and Art; and Benjamin Walworth Arnold, who made his money in the family's lumber business and was an inveterate collector. In addition to posters of the Great War, Arnold collected birds' eggs, which he eventually donated to the New York State Museum, and plaster casts designed by sculptor John Rogers.

On April 2, 1917, President Woodrow Wilson appeared before a joint session of Congress and asked for a declaration of war against Germany. Congress declared war on April 6. Less than seven weeks later, on May 23, Cuyler Reynolds, realizing that posters and other ephemera related to the war would be useful "in the future for those studying the war period, and how the war was conducted," wrote a letter to Dr. James I. Wyer Jr., director of the New York State Library, asking him if the State of New York would be interested in receiving "a collection of articles relating to the Great War—after the war ends?" On May 24, Dr. Wyer wrote back that the library was "keenly interested . . . and, while unable to spend very much money in bringing such a collection together, will most heartily welcome any acquisition of material of this sort that may come to it through private generosity."[7]

By the middle of December, Reynolds had dropped off two boxes of "War Collection" material, consisting of "one thousand items." By February 1918 Reynolds had purchased a stamp that he was using "to show the State Library ownership of the War Collection of posters, placards, pamphlets, etc." that he was donating to the

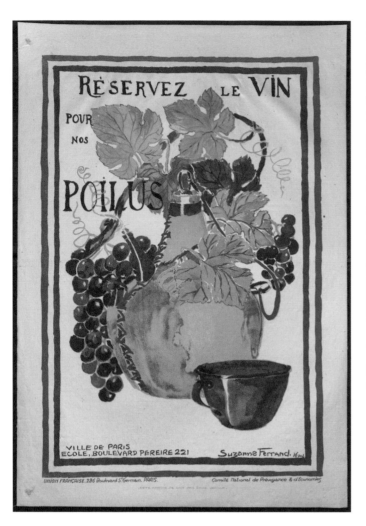

"Reservez le Vin pour nos Poilus" (Save Wine for Our Soldiers).

Artist: Suzanne Ferrand; *Printer:* Union Francaise, Paris;
Publisher: Comité National de Prévoyance et d'Économies;
Technique: Lithograph; *Dimensions:* 54 x 37 cm.

Beginning in 1916, the Comité National de Prévoyance et d'Économies organized a poster contest for school age children emphasizing conservation. This poster is one of sixteen in the collection of the New York State Library created by these French children during World War I. New York State Library, Manuscripts and Special Collections.

"Je Suis une Brave Poule de Guerre" (I am a fine war chicken).

Artist: G. Douanne; *Printer:* Union Francaise, Paris;
Publisher: Comité National de Prévoyance et d'Économies;
Technique: Lithograph; *Dimensions:* 59 x 38 cm.

As the war dragged on, supplies of food and other necessities were scarce. Rationing, conservation, and other measures were implemented in all the Allied nations. This was particularly true in France where much of the nation's arable land had become battlefields. The poster text reads, "Let's take care of the poultry" and "I am a good war chicken. I eat little and I produce a lot." The poster was signed by its 16-year-old artist, G. Douanne. New York State Library, Manuscripts and Special Collections.

library. Impressions of the stamp—which reads "THE GREAT WAR/NEW YORK STATE LIBRARY"—are still clearly visible on posters in the collection. In a letter to Wyer, he said he "found it necessary to designate the various items in this manner because . . . I expect to give [duplicates] to The Albany Institute, after selecting the better one for the State."

In the correspondence between Wyer and Reynolds, Reynolds frequently asks Wyer for some financial support in this effort and Wyer explains, again and

again, that the State Library cannot reimburse him for any of his expenses. One can feel the exasperation on Reynolds's part in his letter to Wyer of February 15, 1918: "If [in the past, New York State . . . has been willing to spend] as much as $15,000 for a collection of shells . . . also, spiders, eggs, etc., then the Great War demands at least some small share of attention."[8]

At the same time, while the State Library was not willing to pay for acquiring the posters, it did feel it had an obligation to pay to have a great many of them backed with muslin, which has, over the past 100 years, proven to be an excellent idea in that the posters with the backing are in much better condition than those without it.

By January 1920, Reynolds was anxious to move the posters he had collected to the library "soon 'in case of fire'" and suggested that the larger ones could be loaded on a stretcher—"an old, discarded closet door [would] serve the purpose"—to transport them quickly. He had sorted them by size and also by subject.

Benjamin Walworth Arnold, like Cuyler Reynolds, made an effort to collect posters related to the Great War. Arnold's contributions include the Australian posters, which, he said, had been sent to him by the chairman of the Australian Defense Committee, and the German posters, which he said were "produced during the first few months after the armistice when Germany desired to illustrate what might be possible under the influence of Bolshevik ideas." He also said he had secured most of the Russian posters "from small Russian stores and foreign banks in the populace quarters of New York City."[9]

By 1922 Arnold had indicated to Wyer that he was "not greatly interested in [the poster collection] anymore and [was] begin[ning] to feel that [it was] something of a white elephant on his hands" and would be willing soon to turn it over to the State Library. Small collections of posters were received from others. The Commissariat Général à l'Information et à la Propagande, Paris, France, sent twenty-three posters to the "New York State Library, as well as to other important Public Libraries in America." The State Library also received twenty-two posters in an exchange with the Maryland War Records Commission.[10]

A reporter, in a looking-back article, wrote in the *Albany Evening News* in 1930: "Day and night you are implored, adjured, advised, warned and commanded to save wheat, buy War Savings Stamps, join the Red Cross, subscribe to the YMCA, enlist in the Navy, get into the Marine Corps, tag your coal shovel, buy a Liberty Bond, remember the horrors of Prussianism, eat less butter, and otherwise do your innumerable bits to make the world safe for democracy."[11]

"Sammelt Obstkerne" (Collect Fruit Pits).

Artist: Gipkens; *Printer:* Dinse, Eckert and Co., Berlin; *Publisher:* Kriegsausschutz für Öle und Fette; *Technique*: Lithograph; *Dimensions*: 57 x 43 cm.

This wartime poster from Germany encouraged civilians to save their fruit pits. The pits were used in the manufacture of activated charcoal, which could then be used in gas masks for soldiers at the front. New York State Library, Manuscripts and Special Collections.

This imploring, adjuring, advising, warning, and commanding was done by posters. No Tweets; no YouTube videos; no emails; no ads on television; just posters. The collections of these works at the New York State Library and at repositories across the state and nation have created a lasting tribute to the artists and writers who created this magnificent legacy during the horrors of war.

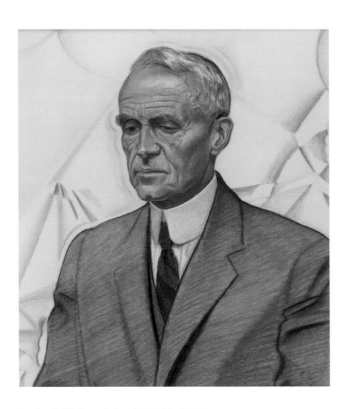

Benjamin Walworth Arnold (1865–1932).

This portrait of Benjamin Walworth Arnold was painted by Fritz Winold Reiss, ca. 1925. Courtesy of the Albany Institute of History and Art.

Cuyler Reynolds (1866–1934).

Courtesy of the Albany Institute of History and Art.

Benjamin W. Arnold of Albany was a successful entrepreneur in the lumber business in the mid- to late-nineteenth century. Arnold's company shipped lumber from all across the Great Lakes region via the Erie Canal. At Arnold's death in 1891, his son, Benjamin Walworth Arnold, inherited the family business. At the time of this transition, the lumber industry was in decline. The younger Arnold began diversifying the family's business interests, becoming president of the Duluth and Northern Minnesota Railroad and becoming involved in the banking industry in New York's Capital Region. During the war, Arnold became head of several home-front efforts, including the raising of liberty loans. Arnold resided in Albany until his death in 1932.

Cuyler Reynolds was born in Albany on August 14, 1866. He was educated at Albany Academy and at a boarding school in Catskill. Reynolds embarked on a career as a journalist and writer before becoming curator at the Albany Institute of History and Art. In 1899, Reynolds became the Institute's director, also serving as the unofficial Albany City Historian.[12] During World War I, Reynolds was instrumental in the development of the poster collections at both the New York State Library and the Albany Institute of History and Art.

Full-page Victory Loan advertisement, April 21, 1919.

Artist: Unknown; *Printer:* Albany Argus, Albany, New York; *Publisher:* Victory Liberty Loan Committee; *Technique:* Newsprint; *Dimensions:* 54 x 41 cm.

This full page advertisement featuring French Field Marshall Ferdinand Foch, commander of the Allied Armies in World War I, appeared in the *Argus* newspaper in Albany, New York, on April 21, 1919, advertising for the fifth and final Victory Liberty Loan. The ad space was contributed by Benjamin W. Arnold, a local banker and philanthropist. Arnold would later donate his extensive collection of World War I posters to the New York State Library. New York State Library, Manuscripts and Special Collections.

Murder of Austrian Archduke Franz Ferdinand and his wife, Sophie, in Sarajevo on June 28, 1914.

The Archduke was heir to the throne of the Austro-Hungarian Empire. His assassination sparked World War I. Courtesy of *Europeana, 1914–1918.*

Headline: Germany Declares War.

Courtesy of the Library of Congress, Chronicling America.

3

The War in Europe (1914–1917)

For decades, Europe's great powers—Great Britain, France, Germany, Russia, and Austria-Hungary—competed for supremacy. A naval and military arms race combined with an intricate system of alliances resulting in simmering tensions between European rivals. In June 1914, Austrian Archduke Franz Ferdinand was assassinated by a Serbian nationalist in Sarajevo. The death of the heir to the Austrian throne set in motion the series of alliances that drew the entire continent into war. Austria-Hungary blamed Serbia for the assassination and declared war on July 28. In response, Serbia's ally, Russia, declared war on Austria-Hungary. One by one, the nations of Europe were drawn into war by an array of treaties. Armies on all sides mobilized for what many believed would be a short war. On August 2, 1914, Europe was plunged into total war as Germany invaded Luxembourg and Belgium. The following day, Germany declared war on France. The German violation of Belgian neutrality brought Great Britain into the conflict in defense of Belgium. What had begun as a European conflict truly became a World War. Japan sided with the allies and seized German colonial territories in the Far East. Britain and France called on their colonies to send troops to the Western Front. Men from as far away as New Zealand, Australia, Canada, Senegal, and India would soon be in the trenches of France. Nor was the fighting limited to Europe. Rival forces battled one another in Southwest and East Africa and in the Middle East as well.

Expectations of a short and relatively bloodless war were soon shattered. After initial advances by the German Army, a stalemate developed on the Western Front. Both sides dug in and a series of trenches stretched over 1,000 miles from Switzerland to the English Channel. The horrors of modern warfare became visible for all to witness as nineteenth-century tactics of massed infantry charges collided with twentieth-century technologies such as the machine gun, artillery, and poison gas. During the Battle of the Somme, which raged from July to November, 1916, casualties on both sides totaled approximately 1,625,000.[1] During four years of fighting in the American Civil War from 1861 to 1865, Union and Confederate killed and wounded numbered roughly 1.1 million men.[2]

Across the Atlantic, the United States remained wary of becoming involved in a European conflict. American political leaders feared that the diversity of the nation's immigrant population would render the United States incapable of presenting the unified citizenry needed for a major war on the European continent.[3] The U.S. Army had fewer than 300,000 soldiers—dwarfed by the millions of men at arms across Europe—with no tested means to raise the necessary number of troops. To many Americans, the war in Europe was a distant affair. As one local historian in Rochester noted, "It never occurred to anyone in Rochester that because the Archduke of Austria was assassinated at Serajevo [sic] (in present-day Bosnia-Herzegovina) we ourselves would be drawn into the struggle eventually."[4] As the new realities of modern warfare emerged, stories of horror and carnage flooded the news. Reports of German savagery in Belgium and France inundated American newspapers,

drowning out journalists and others who questioned the accuracy of reports of German atrocities and their extent—and public perception slowly began to shift. Gradually, global events drew the United States closer to war.

In an effort to end the stalemate, Germany sought to utilize a new weapon, the submarine, to disrupt supplies to Great Britain, France, and Russia. During this period of unrestricted submarine warfare, hundreds of Allied vessels were sunk. In May 1915, the English-owned passenger ship *Lusitania* was torpedoed in the Atlantic, killing 1,198 people,

Belgrade.

This drawing depicts the raising of the Austro-Hungarian flag over Belgrade, the capital of Serbia. Austria's declaration of war against the Serbs had triggered a series of alliances that quickly drew the major European powers into a war across the entire continent. Courtesy of the Library of Congress.

including 128 Americans. The outrage in America forced the Germans to end the indiscriminate sinking of merchant vessels. Despite this, in 1916 President Woodrow Wilson won re-election on a platform of continued U.S. neutrality.

In March 1917, unrest in Russia culminated in revolution. With the country in chaos, the revolutionary Bolshevik government sought peace with Germany, freeing up thousands of troops to be used against Britain and France. As the war on the Western Front dragged on, the Germans again let loose their U-boats on Allied shipping, hoping to end the war before the United States could become involved. In addition, the German foreign secretary sent a secret telegram to the Mexican government guaranteeing German aid if Mexico would agree to go to war with the Americans. The message was intercepted and deciphered by British code breakers and subsequently leaked to the American government. The continued attacks on American merchant vessels by German U-boats forced President Wilson on April 2, 1917, to ask Congress for a declaration of war.

Germans in Flanders.

A German Army unit marches through a village in Flanders (Belgium) in the early weeks of the war. From the New York Public Library.

Belgian artillery outside of Antwerp in August 1914.

Courtesy of the Library of Congress.

Wounded French prisoners being escorted away from the front lines by German soldiers.

From the New York Public Library.

French Colonial troops from Algeria board trains heading to the front lines.

Courtesy of the Library of Congress.

Sikh soldiers from India served with the British Army in France.

Courtesy of the Library of Congress.

A German artillery depot on the Western Front.

From the New York Public Library.

German infantry advance along the Eastern Front in Russia in 1914.

From the New York Public Library.

A German cavalry regiment occupies a Russian castle in Russian-governed Poland.

At the start of the conflict, modern-day Poland was divided among the German, Russian, and Austro-Hungarian Empires. From the New York Public Library.

U-boat.

In the hopes of preventing needed war materiel from reaching the Allies and thereby breaking the stalemate that had developed on the Western Front, Germany employed the use of submarines against merchant vessels. Courtesy of the Library of Congress.

A German U-boat sets sail on patrol from a German port.

From the New York Public Library.

British soldiers, casualties of a German gas attack, are led away from the front lines after the Second Battle of Ypres, April 18, 1915.

In the second offensive against Ypres, the German Army introduced the use of poison gas. Over 10,000 Allied troops were affected. Nearly half died from the effects of the gas.[1] The Allies withdrew from Ypres on May 25. Courtesy of the Imperial War Museum, London.

1. "The Second Battle of Ypres, 1915," FirstWorldWar.com: A Multimedia History of World War One, www.firstworldwar.com/battles/ypres2.htm, accessed March 2016.

German troops in the trenches along the Aisne River in France.

Courtesy of the Library of Congress.

German troops repairing barbed wire entanglements in front of the trenches along the Western Front in France.

Courtesy of the Library of Congress.

British soldiers in the trenches during the Battle of the Somme (July 1–November 18, 1916).

In five months of fighting along the Somme, there were 613,000 Allied and 650,000 German casualties. The Allies succeeded in advancing only seven miles.[1] Courtesy of the Imperial War Museum (Wikimedia Commons).

1. "The Battle of the Somme, 1916," FirstWorldWar.com: A Multimedia History of World War One, http://www.firstworldwar.com/battles/somme.htm, accessed March 2016.

Headline: Somme Costs 3,450 Men a Day.

Courtesy of the Library of Congress, Chronicling America.

Soldiers man a barricade in St. Petersburg.

In March 1917, revolution erupted in Russia. On March 15, Czar Nicholas II abdicated the throne in favor of a provisional government. His abdication was followed by months of unrest before the Bolsheviks under Vladimir Lenin seized power in October, sparking a civil war between "Red" communist forces and their "White" opposition. On March 3, 1918, Russian and Germany signed the Treaty of Brest-Litovsk, formally ending the war on the Eastern Front and freeing thousands of German troops to be moved to the West. Courtesy of the Library of Congress.

German Army *Pickelhaube* (spiked helmet).

The *Pickelhaube* helmet was an iconic element of German Army uniforms during World War I. The *Pickelhaube* was not well suited to the conditions of trench warfare. The helmet's leather offered no protection from shrapnel. In addition, the prominent spike made the helmet's wearer a target for opposing sharpshooters and snipers. Eventually, the *Pickelhaube* was replaced with steel helmets. New York State Museum Collection, H-1987.73.6.

German M1908 Spandau machine gun, sled mounted.

The *Machinengewehr* or machine gun quickly became one of the most effective weapons of the war. This German sled-mounted MG 08 heavy machine gun was designed to be maneuvered by four infantry soldiers. As such, it was cumbersome for use in an attack, but deadly in an entrenched defensive role. New York State Museum Collection, H-1977.200.1.

German Army *Stahlhelm* (steel helmet).

The Imperial German Army replaced the iconic *Pickelhaube* beginning in 1916 with steel helmets. The *Stahlhelm* design became distinctive of German military forces through both World Wars. New York State Museum Collection, H-1977.200.3.

M98 German Mauser rifle with bayonet.

The M98 bolt-action Mauser rifle was the primary service weapon of the Imperial German Army during World War I. The weapon used a 5-round clip-loaded magazine. The rifle was highly accurate, but its length was not well suited to the close-quarters nature of trench warfare. New York State Museum Collection, H-1977.200.7 and H-1977.200.11 A.

German Army belt buckles, medals, and insignia.

New York State Museum Collection H-2012.23.39-.47.

German Army machine gunner's breastplate.

German machine gunners often used steel plating in addition to the steel helmet to guard against enemy fire. New York State Museum Collection, H-1977.200.4.

German Army gas mask, ca. 1917.

This gas mask was issued to soldiers in the Imperial German Army. The mask is constructed of a rubber-coated fabric. Some variations were also made of leather. The filter canister attaches at the mouth of the mask. New York State Museum Collection, H-1987.73.7 A-B.

Roth–Steyr M1907 pistol with holster.

The Roth–Steyr M1907 was the principal sidearm of the Austro-Hungarian armed forces during World War I. New York State Museum Collection, H-1978.137.6 A-C.

German Army canteen.

New York State Museum Collection H-1977.200.13.

French Army gas mask.

The French gas mask varies greatly from the English—and later American—versions and lacks a charcoal filter canister. This mask was issued to American Field Service Ambulance Driver Charles McArdell, who drove ambulances for the French Army. Courtesy of the Joseph Alteri Collection.

Belgian Army Adrian helmet.

Private Collection.

British Army steel helmet.

The British Mark I steel helmet was first developed in 1915 and is often called a Brodie Helmet after its designer. This style of helmet was adopted by the U.S. Army as the Model 1917 Helmet. Private Collection.

French Colonial Infantry Adrian helmet.

New York State Museum Collection.

French colonial troops.

Senegalese infantry soldiers march through a village in France wearing helmets similar to the one shown here. French colonial forces from Africa served alongside French soldiers in the trenches of the Western Front throughout the war. Courtesy of the Library of Congress.

British .303 caliber Enfield rifle.

Private Collection.

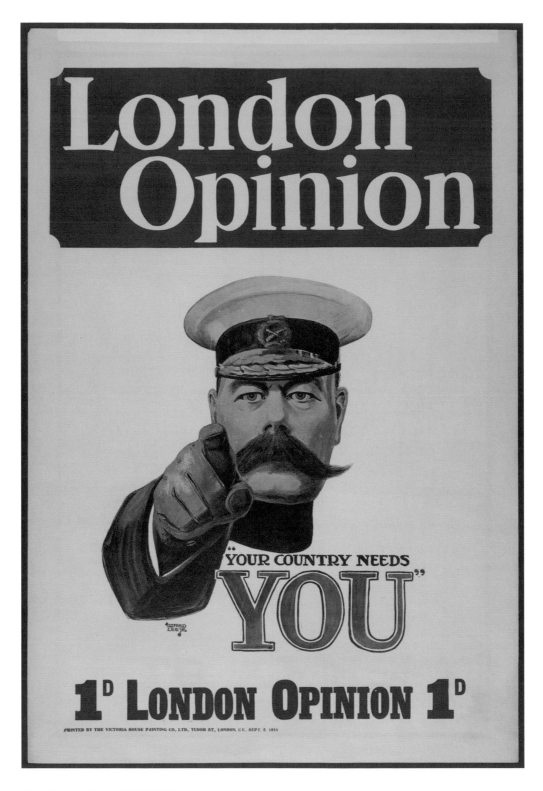

"Your Country Needs YOU" (1915).

Artist: Alfred Leete; *Printer:* London Opinion; *Publisher*: London Opinion; *Technique:* Lithograph; *Dimensions:* 74 x 50 cm.

This British recruiting poster depicts British Secretary of State for War, Lord Herbert Kitchener. This poster was likely an inspiration for James Montgomery Flagg's iconic Uncle Sam recruiting poster. Courtesy of the Library of Congress.

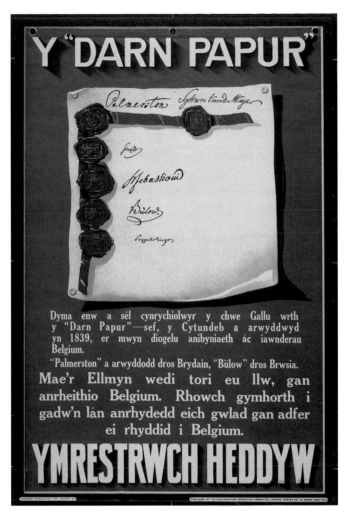

"The 'Scrap of Paper' " (December 1914).

Artist: Unknown; *Printer:* Johnson, Riddle and Co. Ltd., London, England; *Publisher:* Parliamentary Recruiting Committee; *Technique:* Lithograph; *Dimensions:* 74 x 47.5 cm.

New York State Library, Manuscripts and Special Collections.

"Y 'Darn Papur' " (The "Scrap of Paper") (December 1914).

Artist: Unknown; *Printer:* Johnson, Riddle and Co. Ltd., London, England; *Publisher:* Parliamentary Recruiting Committee; *Technique:* Lithograph; *Dimensions:* 72 x 47.5 cm.

At left: This British recruitment poster titled, "Scrap of Paper" features an image of the signatures and seals of Great Britain, France, Prussia, Austria-Hungary, Russia, and The Netherlands from the 1839 Treaty of London. The treaty guaranteed Belgian neutrality and committed Britain to come to its defense in the event of an invasion. It was under this treaty that Great Britain entered World War I following Germany's attack on Belgium in August 1914.[1] The title is derived from a statement made by German Chancellor Theobald von Bethmann-Hollweg in reference to the treaty and Britain's demand that Germany honor its terms in 1914.[2] *At right:* The same poster was also printed in Welsh. Great Britain, with its empire extending around the globe, called on all of its subjects during World War I. New York State Library, Manuscripts and Special Collections.

1. Joll, James, *The Origins of the First World War* (New York: Pearson Education Limited, 1992), pages 100–101.

2. "Theobald von Bethmann-Hollweg, FirstWorldWar.com: A Multimedia History of World War One (http://www.firstworldwar.com/bio/bethmann.htm).

"The Empire Needs Men!" (1915)

Artist: Arthur Wardle; *Printer:* Straker Brothers Ltd., London, England; *Publisher:* Parliamentary Recruiting Committee; *Technique:* Lithograph; *Dimensions:* 73.5 x 50 cm.

As a stalemate set in along the Western Front in 1914, Great Britain turned to its colonies for men to fight. What had begun as a European conflict truly became a World War as soldiers from across the globe were brought to France to defend the British Empire. Courtesy of the Library of Congress.

"Which picture would your father like to show his friends?"

Artist: Harry J. Weston; *Printer:* Unknown; *Publisher:* New South Wales Recruiting Committee; *Technique:* Lithograph; *Dimensions:* 77 x 50 cm.

In this Australian recruiting poster, the artist implies that failure to enlist in the armed forces would result in familial disgrace. New York State Library, Manuscripts and Special Collections.

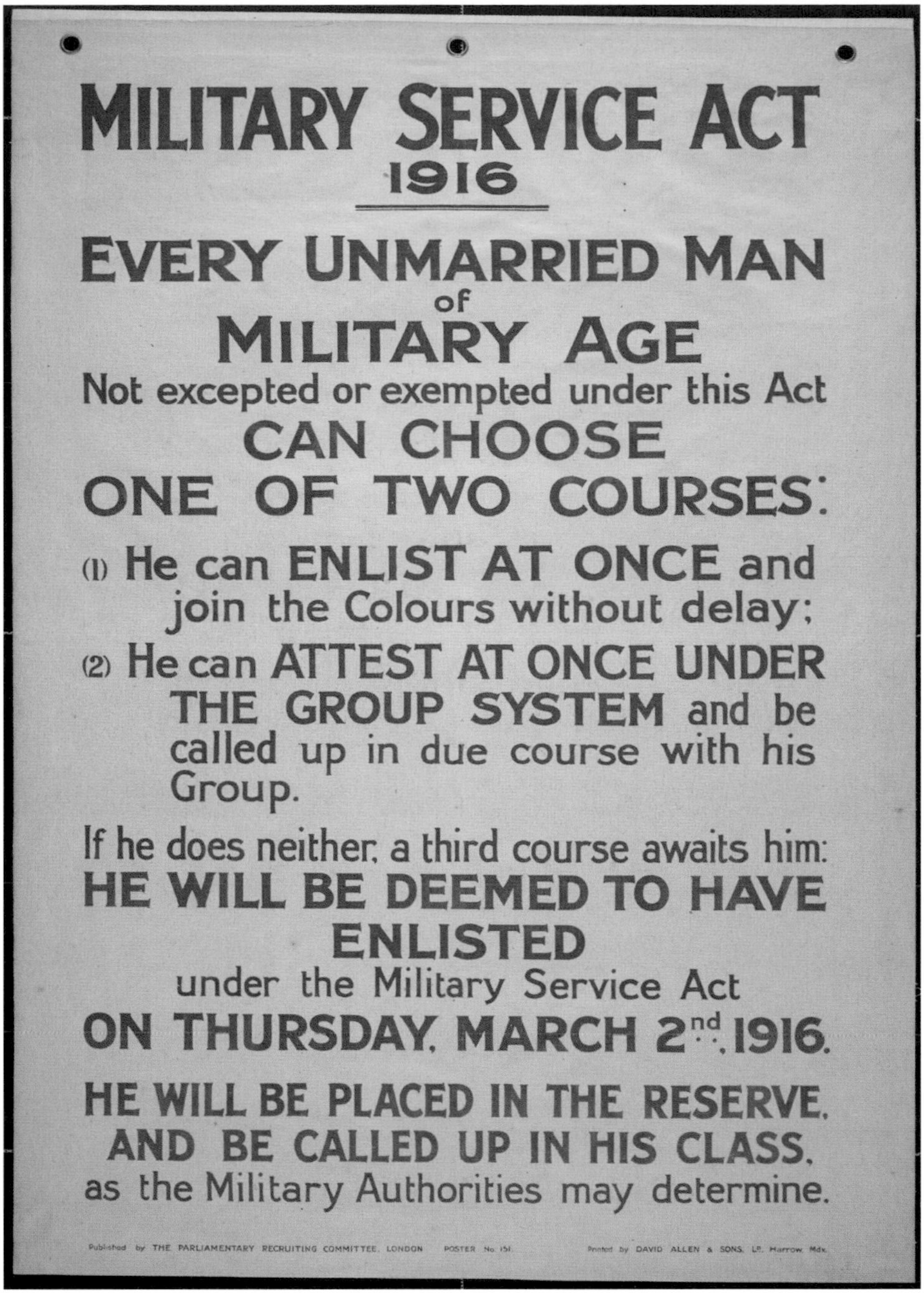

MILITARY SERVICE ACT
1916

EVERY UNMARRIED MAN
of
MILITARY AGE
Not excepted or exempted under this Act
CAN CHOOSE
ONE OF TWO COURSES:

(1) He can **ENLIST AT ONCE** and join the Colours without delay;

(2) He can **ATTEST AT ONCE UNDER THE GROUP SYSTEM** and be called up in due course with his Group.

If he does neither, a third course awaits him:
HE WILL BE DEEMED TO HAVE ENLISTED
under the Military Service Act
ON THURSDAY, MARCH 2nd, 1916.

HE WILL BE PLACED IN THE RESERVE, AND BE CALLED UP IN HIS CLASS,
as the Military Authorities may determine.

Published by THE PARLIAMENTARY RECRUITING COMMITTEE, LONDON   POSTER No. 151   Printed by DAVID ALLEN & SONS, Ld., Harrow Mdx.

Military Service Act broadside (1916).

Artist: None; *Printer:* David Allen and Sons, Ltd., Harrow, Middlesex, England; *Publisher:* Parliamentary Recruiting Committee; *Technique:* Unknown; *Dimensions:* 74.5 x 49 cm.

Voluntary enlistment in the British Army came to an end as the Military Service Act of 1916 took effect. The law specified that single men from age 18 to 41 were liable to be conscripted for military service. A second act in May 1916 extended the liability to married men. With the enactment of universal conscription, the need for persuasively illustrated recruitment posters subsided. Text-filled posters were used to disseminate information rather than as a tool to encourage enlistment.[1] Illustrative posters calling on civilians to contribute to the war effort continued. New York State Library, Manuscripts and Special Collections.

1. Keitch, Charlie, "First World War Recruitment Posters," The Imperial War Museums (http://www.iwm.org.uk/learning/resources/first-world-war-recruitment-posters), accessed February 1–3, 2016.

"Join the 148th Battalion."

Artist: Unknown; *Printer:* J.J. Gibbons, Limited; *Publisher:* 148th Overseas Battalion, Canadian Expeditionary Force, McGill University C.O.T.C.; *Technique:* Lithograph; *Dimensions:* 106 x 69.5 cm.

This recruitment poster features a wounded soldier at the front calling for men at home to enlist. The text reads: "Why be a mere spectator here when you should play a mans part in the real game overseas?" The smoke emanating from the soldier's rifle depicts a hockey game being played in a crowded arena on the home front. New York State Library, Manuscripts and Special Collections.

"On les aura!" (We will get them).

Artist: Jules Abel Faivre; *Printer:* Devambez, Imp., Paris, France; *Publisher:* 2nd National Defense Loan; *Technique:* Lithograph; *Dimensions:* 111 x 78.5 cm.

Featuring a French *poilu* (soldier) and the slogan *On les aura!* (We will get them), this poster for the 2nd National Defense Loan encouraged French citizens to subscribe to the loan effort in 1916. This loan drive was the least successful of the four initiated by the French government and came after the horrors on the battlefield at Verdun and at the Battle of the Somme where one million French soldiers were killed or wounded between July and November 1916. After two years of fighting, the French population was growing fatigued and disillusioned with the war. In response, the government turned more and more to posters as propaganda. New York State Library, Manuscripts and Special Collections.

Alsace Libérée.

Artist: Béatrix Grognuz; *Printer:* Unknown; *Publisher:* Comité National de Prévoyance et d'Économies; *Technique:* Lithograph; *Dimensions:* 55 x 37 cm.

Beginning in 1916, the *Comité National de Prévoyance et d'Économies* organized a poster contest for school-age children. This poster by 16-year-old Béatrix Grognuz reads, "March 1, 1871 to March 1, 1918. In liberated Alsace, young girls willingly make sacrifices to hasten the liberation of the part of Alsace still annexed. Follow their example." The poster, dated March 1918, refers to the loss by France of the territories of Alsace and Lorraine to Prussia following the Franco-Prussian War (1870–1871). Prussian victory in the conflict resulted in the unification of Germany into a single state under the Prussian monarch. The loss of territory was seen as a national disgrace in France and was one of the simmering tensions that exploded into war in 1914. New York State Library, Manuscripts and Special Collections.

"Pour la Liberté du Monde" (For the Liberty of the World) (1917).

Artist: Sem; *Printer:* Devambez, Imp., Paris, France; *Publisher:* Banque Nationale de Credite; *Technique:* Lithograph; *Dimensions:* 116.5 x 75 cm.

This poster for a 1917 War Loan drive in France suggests to the viewer the attitude of many in the French population by the third year of the war. As battlefield casualties mounted, the French people were again being called on to subscribe funds to pay for the war effort. Many had, by this point, given all that they could. The winter of 1916–1917 was extremely cold. Civilians and soldiers alike suffered from shortages of food and coal. Many were fed up with a war with no end in sight.[1] Soldiers in the trenches were mutinying against their conditions. Many refused to go on the offensive and into the slaughter of No Man's Land. The poster depicts the Statue of Liberty visible on the horizon. Lady Liberty, a gift of the French people to the United States in 1876, is being called upon to save the "liberty of the world." By 1917, the United States had entered the war and France was desperate for the influx of American soldiers and money into the conflict.[2] The poster artist is seemingly imploring the people of France to hold on just long enough for America to come to their aid. New York State Library, Manuscripts and Special Collections.

1. Winter, Jay and Blaine Baggett, *The Great War and the Shaping of the 20th Century* (New York: Penguin Books, 1996), page 209.

2. "Pour la liberté du monde. Souscrivez à l'emprunt national à la Banque Nationale de Crédit," Bibliothèque Numerique Mondial (http://www.wdl.org/fr/itcm/4613/), accessed February 3, 2016.

"The More Money, the More Shells!"

Artist: Chepstov; *Printer:* Unknown; *Publisher:* Printed in Petrograd, Russia; *Technique:* Lithograph; *Dimensions:* 106.5 x 71 cm.

This Russian war loan poster depicts Russian artillerymen on the battlefield above the slogan, "The More Money, the More Shells!" New York State Library, Manuscripts and Special Collections.

"Zeichnet vierte Österreicheische Kriegsanleihe" (Subscribe to the
Fourth Austrian War Loan).

Artist: Adolph Karpellus; *Printer:* K.u.k. Hofl. J. Weiner, Wien, Austria;
Publisher: Österrechishe Landerbank; *Technique:* Lithograph;
Dimensions: 94 x 62 cm.

This poster for the Fourth Austrian War Loan features a soldier in Renaissance-
period dress carrying the banner of the Hapsburg Empire. The illustration
attempts to recall a time when the Austro-Hungarian Empire was at its
political and military peak. New York State Library, Manuscripts and Special
Collections.

"Zeichnet 8. Kriegsanleihe" (Subscribe to the 8th War Loan) (1918).

Artist: K. Sterrer; *Printer:* Unknown; *Publisher:* Wiener Bankverein (Austrian
Bank Association); *Technique:* Lithograph; *Dimensions:* 94 x 62 cm.

Poster for the 8th Austrian war loan drive. New York State Library, Manuscripts
and Special Collections.

"Zeichnet Kriegsanleihe!" (Buy War Loans!)

Artist: Paul Gerd; *Printer:* Unknown; *Publisher:* Zeitung der 10. Armee; *Technique:* Lithograph; *Dimensions:* 86 x 58 cm.

This poster for a German war loan drive depicts a man doing battle with a lion—a common symbol of the British Empire. The man has the lion pinned and is preparing to swing a death blow with his sword. New York State Library, Manuscripts and Special Collections.

"Was England Will!" (What England Wants!) (1918).

Artist: Egon Tschirch; *Printer:* Selmar Bayer, Berlin; *Publisher:* Unknown; *Technique:* Lithograph; *Dimensions:* 97 x 65 cm.

This poster depicts hundreds of British planes bombing a German factory. Fighting a war on two fronts, many German posters depict the fear of the nation being overrun by the Allied Powers. New York State Library, Manuscripts and Special Collections.

The New York Press, May 8, 1915.

On May 7, 1915, a German U-boat sank the British Cunard passenger liner *Lusitania*, killing 1,198 civilians, including 128 Americans. Germany was forced to suspend unrestricted submarine attacks following American outrage over the event. Courtesy of the New York State Library, Manuscripts and Special Collections.

4

Prelude to U.S. Involvement

Reports of German atrocities in Belgium and France generally turned American public opinion against the German Empire. Though a majority of Americans were sympathetic to the Allied cause, most favored President Wilson's policy of neutrality.[1] At the same time, nearly 30 percent of New York State's population, or more than 2.7 million state residents, were listed as foreign-born in the census of 1910. The largest of these immigrant populations were Russians (558,952), Italians (472,192), Germans (436,874), and Irish (367,877). Large numbers of British, Austrian, and Hungarian immigrants also lived in the state. More than one million of these émigrés were young men of fighting age. These populations thus became fertile ground for recruitment by their warring homelands.[2] Regardless of which belligerent nation they came from, the large population of immigrants from Europe in the state watched events in Europe with great attention.[3]

At the outset of the war, Great Britain had instituted a blockade of German ports enforced by the Royal Navy. American merchant ships attempting to enter German ports were instead directed to British harbors for inspection. Though the Wilson administration protested the British measure, American ships readily complied with the Royal Navy's directives. Germany responded with a counterblockade utilizing its U-boat fleet. On numerous occasions, American merchant ships were targeted by German submarines. Between May 1, 1915, and April 6, 1917, at least twenty American-flagged vessels were either damaged or sunk by enemy action. While the German Navy often gave the merchant vessels warning before sinking the ships, more than seventy American seamen were killed in torpedo attacks on merchant shipping.[4] The most significant incident of German submarine attacks on civilian shipping vessels occurred on May 7, 1915, when a British-owned passenger liner, the *Lusitania*, was sunk, killing over 1,000 civilians, including more than 120 Americans. While newspaper editorials shifted solidly in favor of the Allies, American policy remained unchanged.[5]

Despite America's official neutrality, many New York businesses quickly aligned themselves with the Allied cause. In Manhattan, J. P. Morgan Company became the official purchasing agent for England, France, and Russia, signing contracts on behalf of the belligerents for weapons and ammunition.[6] At Remington Arms, headquartered in Ilion, New York, Chairman of the Board Marcy Dodge was appalled by the German violation of Belgian

Buffalo newspapers.

These newspapers from Buffalo, Erie County, highlight the deterioration of relations between the United States and the German Empire. The March 26, 1917, *Buffalo Express* notes that the city's National Guardsmen had been recalled from the Mexican border and that President Wilson ordered the Navy to increase recruitment. The *Buffalo Evening Times* from that same day notes the arrival of the first armed American merchant ship in an English port. New York State Museum Collection, H-1995.20.1574.1–.2.

New York financier J.P. Morgan (left) stands alongside 1st Viscount Haldane, Richard B.S. Haldane, and Sir Kenneth W. McKenzie in 1913.

Morgan's close ties to British officials led to his early support for the Allied war effort. Courtesy of the Library of Congress.

neutrality. While supporting the country's official policy of neutrality, he was unable to remain impartial. Personal politics aside, Dodge was quick to jump at the unanticipated economic windfall. When approached by the Allied powers to manufacture rifles for their armies, Remington Arms eventually contracted to manufacture more than two million weapons for France, England, and Russia between 1914 and 1917.[7] In total, Remington Arms received the majority of Allied munitions contracts between 1914 and 1917. One contract with the Russian government placed the cost for each Moisin-Nagant rifle produced at $3,000 in 1915.[8] This is equivalent to more than $50,000 each in 2015 real value.[9]

By the summer of 1914, the United States economy had been dipping into recession. The influx of capital from the European combatants helped to slow the slide, but it was not until American entry into the war in 1917 that the economy fully rebounded.[10]

While President Wilson recognized that the participation of American businesses and banks in the war effort could compromise the nation's neutrality, he also recognized the economic necessity of putting Americans back to work as a result of Allied investment in the economy.[11] Despite American neutrality, the war in Europe propelled the New York economy as businesses geared up to supply the warring armies. New York City's financial district became the credit capital of the world, and approximately 75 percent of all war materiel shipped across the Atlantic came from New York Harbor.[12]

New Yorkers Divided

While former President Theodore Roosevelt and General Leonard Wood advocated for "preparedness" and often urged American entry into the European war on the Allied side, several highly visible segments of the population in New York opposed the war or favored the Central Powers. Outside of citizens of German and Austrian descent, who supported their mother countries at the outset of the conflict, many Irish Americans opposed U.S. support for Britain, which continued to occupy Ireland. Many East European Jews advocated against siding with the anti-Semitic government of Tsar Nicholas II of Russia.

Because of its large population of immigrants, New York became visible in the struggle and debate over America's potential entry into the war. The divisions within New York society and across the nation needed to be overcome if the nation hoped to rally its citizens behind the war effort.

American Isolationism

Even after Europe was plunged into total war in 1914, isolationist sentiment in the United States pressured the government to stay out of the conflict. This policy of neutrality and isolationism has strong precedents in American history. American presidents frequently adhered to George Washington's parting advice—to avoid entangling alliances—to maintain American neutrality in European wars. When war consumed that continent in 1914, Woodrow Wilson and American political leaders asserted that America would not choose sides. Many feared that American entry into the war would damage the economy and argued that the nation was not prepared to fight a global war. Citing the freedom of the seas, Wilson declared that it was the nation's intention to continue to trade with both the Allied and the Central powers.

In 1916, President Woodrow Wilson campaigned for re-election on a platform of nonintervention. World events would eventually force him to abandon this policy and ask for a declaration of war against Germany.

Anti-war rally at Union Square (1914).

Attendees of this anti-war rally at Union Square in Manhattan called for the United States government to remain neutral in the conflict on the European Continent. While events gradually drew the nation towards entry into the war, American public opinion remained deeply divided even after President Wilson's declaration in April 1917. Courtesy of the Library of Congress.

"We Have no Quarrel with the German People. We Have no Feeling Toward Them but One of Sympathy and Friendship." (Woodrow Wilson) 2181

Campaign pin.

This campaign pin was created in support of Woodrow Wilson's re-election campaign in 1916 on a promise of continued peace and prosperity for the United States. During the election of 1916, Wilson ran against former Republican New York State Governor Charles Evans Hughes. The Republican platform was significantly more pro-Allies than that of the Democrats, though Hughes never argued for America's full entry into the war in Europe. Rather, he argued that American involvement was needed to defend the nation's rights to freedom of the seas against the German U-boat menace.[1] While Hughes carried New York State, President Wilson was reelected by more than half a million votes nationwide.[2] New York State Museum Collection, H-1976.224.58.

1. Sullivan, James, ed. *History of New York State, 1523–1927*, Volume V (New York: Lewis Historical Publishing Company, Inc., 1927), page 1816–1817.

2. Sullivan, James, ed. *History of New York State,* Volume V, page 1817.

Postcard.

In 1916, Woodrow Wilson campaigned for re-election on a platform of continued neutrality. This unused postcard features a photograph of President Wilson atop a message of friendship and goodwill towards Germany. Six months after winning re-election, Wilson went before Congress to ask for a declaration of war against Germany. New York State Museum Collection, H-1969.66.1496.

Songsheet, "I Didn't Raise My Boy to Be a Soldier."

This song, first published by Leo Feist of New York City in 1915, became a hit across the United States.[1] The anti-war sentiment was popular among pacifists and isolationists who opposed American involvement in the European war. From the New York Public Library.

1. 1915 Top 40 Songs (http://playback.fm/charts/top-100-songs/1915/); "1915 in Music" (https://en.wikipedia.org/wiki/1915_in_music#Hit_recordings), accessed April 1, 2016.

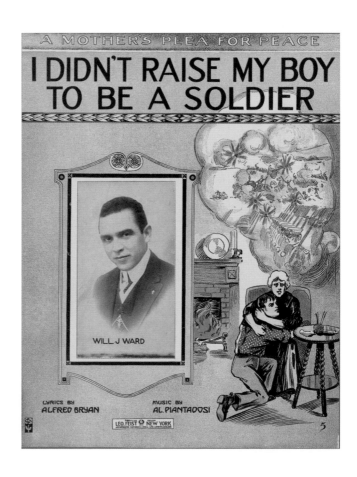

Pacifism in New York

As war raged in Europe, a significant number of American pacifists urged the Wilson administration to avoid American involvement at any cost. Many of the pacifist organizations were founded along religious grounds, whose tenets included "religious injunctions against killing" and prohibited military service.[13] Others objected on political or moral grounds. Many of the most vocal pacifist and antiwar groups were organized or headquartered in New York City, including the Carnegie Endowment for International Peace, led by former New York senator, secretary of state, and Nobel Peace Prize recipient Elihu Root,

Nicholas Murray Butler, ca. 1915.

Columbia University President Nicholas Murray Butler played a crucial role in convincing Andrew Carnegie to provide money to establish the Carnegie Endowment for International Peace. He was a founding member of the Endowment and succeeded Root as president in 1925. For his work advocating international peace, Butler was a co-recipient of the Nobel Peace Prize with Jane Addams in 1931.[1] Courtesy of the Library of Congress.

1. "Nicholas Murray Butler," *C250 Celebrates Columbians Ahead of their Time* (http://c250.columbia.edu/c250_celebrates/remarkable_columbians/nicholas_butler.html), accessed November 10, 2016.

Elihu Root, 1916.

Elihu Root was a former U.S. Senator from New York State (1909–1915), Secretary of War (1899–1904), and U.S. Secretary of State (1905–1909). Root received the Nobel Peace Prize in 1912. He served as the first president of the Carnegie Endowment for International Peace.[1] Courtesy of the Library of Congress.

1. Carnegie Endowment for International Peace..

and Columbia University president Nicholas Murray Butler. The Endowment was founded in 1910 with $10 million from industrialist and philanthropist Andrew Carnegie, and chartered to "hasten the abolition of war, the foulest blot upon our civilization."[14]

Many prominent New Yorkers lent their voices to the pacifist movement in the early years of World War I, including Rabbi Stephen S. Wise, the most prominent Jewish leader of the New York–based American Union Against Militarism (AUAM).[15] Wise and other Progressives criticized the American Preparedness Movement and its militaristic and nationalistic rhetoric, arguing they were incompatible

Rabbi Stephen S. Wise, ca. 1910.

As a leading Rabbi in New York City, Stephen S. Wise was an early member of the American Union Against Militarism. By 1917, however, Wise and other pacifists came to view defeat of the German Empire, which they blamed for the start of the war, as the surest way to achieve their goals and became advocates of American entry into the conflict. Courtesy of the Library of Congress.

with democracy.[16] The AUAM had been successful in limiting U.S. intervention along the Mexican border following Pancho Villa's raids into New Mexico in 1916, and sought to prevent American involvement in the European conflict as well.[17]

As public opinion in the United States began to turn against Germany and American involvement appeared increasingly likely, many pacifist organizations in New York shifted their stance. They came to blame the war on Germany and argued that Prussian militarism was the most significant obstacle to global peace. Pacifist leaders began to assert that American entry into the war was, in fact, the most necessary measure to achieve their stated goal of abolishing war. Allied victory, they claimed, would bring peace on American terms as outlined by President Wilson. [18] Rabbi Wise's conversion to this line of thought was one of the biggest blows to the organized pacifist movement in the United States.[19] In a sermon to his congregation titled "The World War for Humanity,"

Wise argued that Germany had forced the United States to the brink of war and that militarism must be defeated.[20] When America entered the war in April 1917, public perception of pacifists dramatically changed. No longer were these organizations viewed as advocates of international peace and cooperation, but rather, were linked with draft evaders, socialists, anarchists, and other opponents of the war.[21] Those who favored pacifism were immediately painted as "of disloyal or treasonable character."[22]

Preparedness Movement

Americans viewed with horror the slaughter being wrought on the Western Front on a seemingly industrial scale. There was little appetite in the United States to take a side in the war. Despite repeated submarine attacks and the loss of American lives, many continued to believe that the conflict was a European affair and that the United States would not become involved. In his second annual message to Congress on December 8, 1914, President Wilson addressed the issue of America's preparedness for war: "It is said in some quarters that we are not prepared for war. What is meant by being prepared? Is it meant that we are not ready upon brief notice to put a nation in the field, a nation of men trained to arms? Of course we are not ready to do that; and we shall never be in time of peace. . . . We never have had, and while we retain our present principles and ideals we never shall have, a large standing army."[23]

Former President Roosevelt was particularly critical of President Wilson and American neutrality. In

New York Yankees drilled by Sergeant Gibson.

Preparedness even found its way into the national pastime. Here, members of the New York Yankees practice military drills prior to a baseball game at the New York Polo Grounds in early 1917. Courtesy of the Library of Congress.

Cornell University Cadet Corps, ca. 1914.

Cornell University was founded under federal funding provided by the Morrill Land Grant Act of 1862. As part of this act, these universities were required to provide military training to their students. The lessons of the American Civil War had made clear the need for a well-trained reserve corps of officers for the Army.[1] Thus, when Cornell opened in 1868, all students were required to train for two years with the Cornell University Corps of Cadets.[2] These colleges and universities became a cornerstone of General Leonard Wood and the Preparedness Movement. Beginning in 1913, students from the various cadet corps were invited to attend summer training camps commanded by Regular Army officers in order to better prepare them for military service.[3] This tunic belonged to George Corby, Cornell University Class of 1918. New York State Museum Collection, H-1972.76.56.

1. Perry, Ralph Barton. *The Plattsburg Movement: A Chapter of America's Participation in the World War* (New York: E.P. Dutton and Company, 1921), page 4–5.

2. "Cornell Founding and the Morrill Act," Cornell University ROTC (http://www.goarmy.com/rotc/schools/cornell-university/history.html), accessed March 30, 2016.

3. Perry, pages 11–20.

Cornell University Cadet Corps members study a three-dimensional model of trench fortifications.

Courtesy of the Library of Congress.

a speech at Kansas City, Missouri, in May 1916, Roosevelt decried, "It is not righteous to fail to fight on behalf of assailed righteousness. Such a course probably means sheer cowardice, and certainly means moral surrender."[24] He lambasted what he called the "broomstick preparedness" of the Wilson administration, which he asserted had taken few steps to prepare for the eventuality of war in 1915 and 1916.[25] Ever the astute politician, however, Roosevelt understood that Americans were not prepared to enter a war across the Atlantic. During the presidential campaign of 1916, he advocated a policy of national preparedness in which the nation would prepare to go to war should it become necessary. Roosevelt championed civilian military training—a concept that would take form at Plattsburgh, New York—and increased military spending. While President Wilson ultimately won re-election in 1916, Roosevelt's Preparedness Movement gained a wide following, particularly among young, college-educated men in New York City and across the Northeast.

Leslie's Uncle Sam.

Illustrator James Montgomery Flagg was a proponent of the Preparedness Movement. He originally created his iconic "Uncle Sam" for the cover of *Leslie's Illustrated Weekly Newspaper* of July 6, 1916, with the title, "What are YOU doing for Preparedness?" Once the United States entered the war, the illustration was repurposed for use as a recruiting poster and became arguably the most famous image of the war. Courtesy of the New York State Library, Manuscripts and Special Collections.

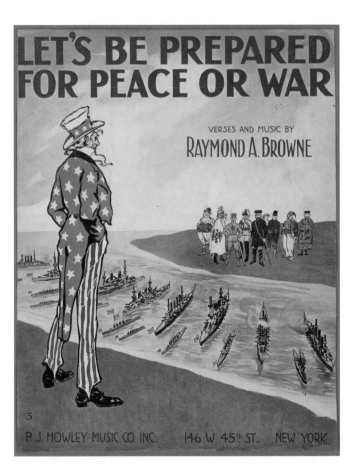

Sheet music, "Let's Be Prepared for Peace or War."

This song, published in 1916 by P.J. Howley Music Co. of New York, was composed by Raymond A. Browne. The lyrics were written in support of the growing Preparedness Movement in the nation and argue that " . . . no one knows the hour when foes may gather at our gates, [a]nd put the curse of war upon our own United States." While the song's author hopes that war can be avoided, he advocates for a strong army and navy so that the nation is prepared in the event of war. From the New York Public Library.

"Give Your Vacation to Your Country" (1916).

Artist: C.B. Falls; *Printer:* Unknown; *Publisher:* Unknown;
Technique: Lithograph; *Dimensions:* 18 x 12.75 cm.

This flyer was distributed on college campuses across the northeast in the spring of 1916. The poster advertisement was created for a series of summer preparedness camps to be held across the nation. The slogan, "Give Your Vacation to Your Country" was first used in recruitment for the Plattsburgh training camp in 1915.[1] From the New York Public Library.

1. "Give Your Country Your Vacation," *The Crimson* (Cambridge: Harvard Univerity, June 4, 1918) (http://www.thecrimson.com/article/1918/6/4/give-your-country-your-vacation-pit/), accessed March 30, 2016.

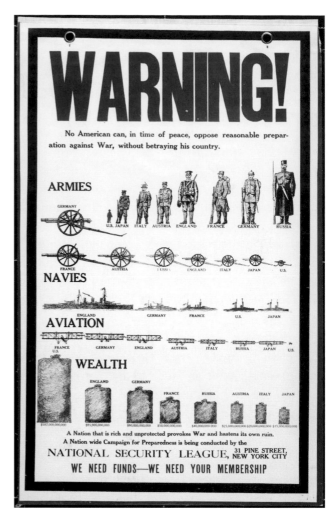

"Warning! No American can, in time of peace, oppose reasonable preparation against War."

Artist: Unknown; *Printer:* Unknown; *Publisher:* National Security League;
Technique: Lithograph; *Dimensions:* 52 x 32 cm.

This poster graphically compares American military preparedness with that of Japan, Italy, Austria, England, France, Germany, and Russia. The images depict the nation's military as significantly smaller than any of the other nations. Advocates of the Preparedness Movement called for an increase in the nation's military. New York State Library, Manuscripts and Special Collections.

"National Preparedness."

Artist: Unknown; *Printer:* Unknown; *Publisher:* Rochester Branch of the Woman's Section for National Preparedness.

This placard was used by members of the Rochester Branch of the Woman's Section for National Preparedness in an effort to garner support for their advocacy efforts for the movement. Organizations such as the one in Rochester argued for increased military training in preparation for possible American involvement in the European war. Courtesy of the Rochester Historical Society.

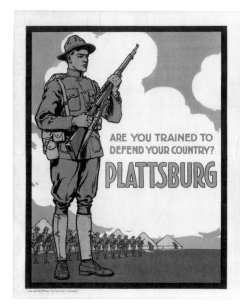
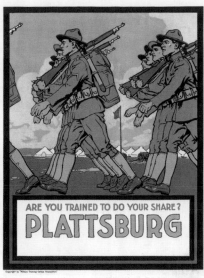

"Are You Trained to Defend Your Country?" (1915).

Artist: Unknown; *Printer:* Unknown; *Publisher:* Unknown; *Technique:* Lithograph; *Dimensions:* 68.5 x 155 cm.

Following the sinking of the *Lusitania* and other German provocations, former President Theodore Roosevelt and others criticized President Wilson's policy of neutrality. Roosevelt became an advocate for the Preparedness Movement, which sought to ready the nation's citizens for a war that seemed unavoidable.

In the summer of 1915, the first citizens' military training camp was held at Plattsburgh, New York, to train college students and young, business professionals in basic military drill and tactics. The "Plattsburg Movement" as it came to be known was spearheaded by Army Chief of Staff General Leonard Wood. Attendees were expected to finance their own way to the camp and were not to receive any compensation for their time at Plattsburgh. According to General Wood, the purpose of the Plattsburgh camp and others like it was to "increase the present inadequate personnel of the trained military reserve of the United States by a class of men from whom, in time of a national emergency, a large proportion of the commissioned officers will probably be drawn . . ."[1] Men for the camps were primarily recruited from the society and business elite in New York and other northeastern cities.

When the camp opened, 1,300 men—many from New York's young business and professional class—signed up. The following summer, 16,000 attended the camp at Plattsburgh and similar camps nationwide. These training camps were so popular that admittance to them became quite difficult. By the spring of 1917, James Husted Jr., son of New York Congressman James Husted Sr., telegraphed his father from school at Yale requesting assistance in obtaining three high-profile recommendations in order to be admitted to the upcoming Plattsburgh camp.[2] For those without political connection, admittance was more difficult. These camps taught the men the basic skills needed by officers in the United States Army. When war was declared, many graduates of Plattsburgh became officers in the new National Army. New York State Museum Collection, H-1977.139.1.

1. Perry, page 2.

2. Husted, James W., Jr., Telegram to Father, April 23, 1917. The Husted Family Papers, 1853–1943, New York State Library, Manuscripts and Special Collections, SC23259.

Diploma.

This certificate verifies that Robert E. Coppinger had completed the military training camp at Plattsburgh on August 8, 1916. New York State Library, Manuscripts and Special Collections.

The American Field Service

More than 1,200 young Americans volunteered to serve as ambulance drivers in France. The American Field Service (AFS), as it became known, reached a height of 2,000 volunteers, including 474 young men from New York State. Many were recruited from college campuses across New York State and the Northeast. By the time the United States entered the war, AFS drivers had transported more than 500,000 soldiers from the front lines. Members of the AFS reported the horrors of war back to the United States and helped to transform public opinion about the conflict. In 1918, the drivers of the AFS were absorbed into the United States Army.

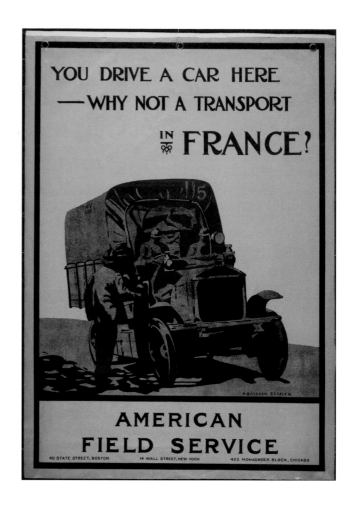

"You Drive a Car Here—Why Not a Transport in France?"

Artist: H. Blyleven Esselen; *Printer:* Unknown; *Publisher:* American Field Service; *Technique:* Lithograph; *Dimensions:* 69 x 49 cm.

This recruitment poster seeks American volunteers to serve as ambulance drivers in France. New York State Library, Manuscripts and Special Collections.

American Field Service.

Group photograph of American volunteer ambulance drivers from the American Field Service in France. Courtesy of the Library of Congress.

Charles McArdell in front of an AFS Ambulance.

The AFS camp that Charles McArdell was stationed at was located twenty-five miles from the front-line trenches. According to one letter home, McArdell notes ambulances were "rushing to the front continuously and the roar of the big guns can be heard distinctively at this point." Courtesy of the Joseph Alteri Collection.

Charles V. McArdell (1894–1957), Syracuse, Onondaga County

Charles McArdell and thirty-one other Syracuse University students volunteered with the American Field Service as ambulance drivers shortly after the American declaration of war in 1917. The group—all of whom were either current or recent graduates—had attempted to volunteer for the American Army, but were turned away because the United States was preparing to implement the wartime draft and had suspended voluntary enlistments. McArdell and the other members of the Syracuse University Ambulance Unit departed for France on August 22, 1917, and arrived at Bordeaux on September 9. The men were initially stationed in Paris before moving to a camp closer to the front lines. The members of the

ambulance unit continuously transported wounded soldiers from the front lines to hospitals in the rear. The drivers of the unit frequently found themselves in the trenches and often had to traverse No Man's Land to reach the wounded. During the war, Charles McArdell was stricken during a gas attack, but survived. The effects left his vision impaired and he wore glasses the remainder of his life.

Upon the arrival of the American Expeditionary Forces in France, the Syracuse University Ambulance Unit was absorbed into the U.S. Army as Army Ambulance Service Section Unit 622. All thirty-two members of the Syracuse unit survived the war and returned safely to Syracuse to a hero's welcome.

Dog tag and wallet.

Dog tag issued to Charles McArdell and a leather wallet given to members of the AFS. This wallet features a French flag and Rooster—a national symbol of France—on the front. The interior is stamped, "AMERICAN FIELD SERVICE / DERNIER NOEL DE LA GUERRE (Last Christmas of the War) / DECEMBRE 1918." These wallets were given as gifts to the volunteer ambulance drivers of the American Field Service by the French government. Courtesy of the Joseph Alteri Collection.

Canteen.

This canteen was carried by Charles McArdell during his service in World War I. Courtesy of the Joseph Alteri Collection.

German *Pickelhaube* and *Stahlhelm* helmets, unit label insignia, belt buckles, and gas mask.

These items were picked up by Charles McArdell on the battlefields of the Western Front. Courtesy of the Joseph Alteri Collection.

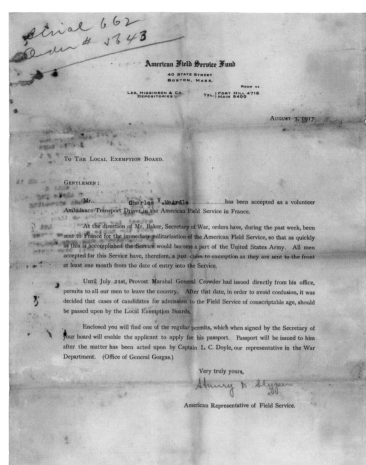

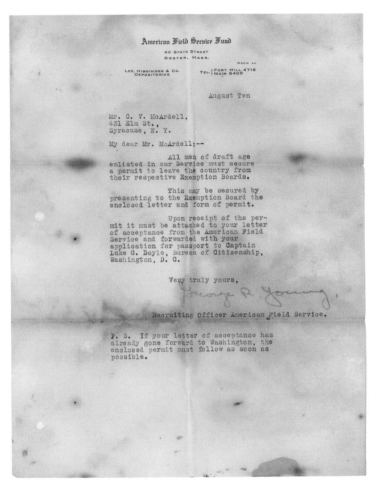

Letter, August 3, 1917.

This letter on AFS stationery informed Charles McArdell of his acceptance in the American Field Service. The accompanying permit exempted him from draft eligibility. When the American Expeditionary Force arrived in France, most ambulance drivers of the AFS were absorbed into the United States Army. Courtesy of the Joseph Alteri Collection.

Line of ambulances on the Western Front.

Courtesy of the Joseph Alteri Collection.

Ambulances in ruins of a village.

Courtesy of the Joseph Alteri Collection.

Enlistment in Foreign Armies

While the U.S. government remained neutral when World War I broke out in August 1914, thousands of American citizens chose to serve with foreign armies. It is estimated that upwards of 75,000 Americans served under foreign flags during World War I.[26] Their service in foreign armies is an often-forgotten part of a conflict that engaged millions of soldiers from around the world. With its proximity to the Canadian border, New York State contributed more men to foreign enlistment than any other state in the nation.[27] Approximately 200 Americans served in the French Foreign Legion. Tens of thousands enlisted in the Commonwealth Forces of the British Empire—mostly in Canada—and hundreds volunteered as pilots in the Lafayette Escadrille. An unknown number probably volunteered for service in the armies of the Central Powers as well. Much of this recruitment of Americans was intentional, particularly by the British. In September 1914, Winston Churchill, First Lord of the British Admiralty, declared, "Nothing will bring American sympathy along with us so much as American bloodshed in the field."[28] In Rochester, 1,100 Belgians departed to defend their native lands, as did 27 Dutch immigrants.[29]

Many of the immigrant populations living in New York State viewed the war as an opportunity for their homelands to gain independence from the empires that ruled them. This was particularly true of Americans of Polish descent. Poland in 1914 was divided between the Russian, German, and Austro-Hungarian empires. Many Poles dreamed of an independent Poland. These "White Falcons," as they referred to themselves, sought to enlist in the Polish Army in exile being raised in France. Most crossed the border into Canada to enlist. In Rochester, 258 men left the city for service with the Polish Army prior to American entry into the war.[30]

While many young men enlisted to fight for their native lands, others saw the war as a grand adventure. In an October 1914 letter to his mother, American expatriate Alan Seeger wrote, "I have always thirsted for this kind of thing, to be present always where the pulsations are liveliest. Every minute here is worth weeks of ordinary experience."[31]

Whatever their motivation, the decision made by these young men carried inherent risks, and not only those associated with the battlefield. President

Donato Di Russo.

Italian American Donato Di Russo returned to his native land to serve in the Italian Army. He was killed in action on June 30, 1916. Like most of the young men who left the peace and security of the United States to fight in World War I between 1914 and 1917, very little is known about Donato Di Russo. New York State Archives, A0412-78.

Wilson's declaration of neutrality made it a criminal offense to enlist in the service of any of the warring nations. Since shortly after the American Civil War, the United States government had viewed service in a foreign army as grounds for loss of naturalization.[32] By 1914, there was significant concern that the participation of American citizens in a European War could create tensions between the United States and a belligerent of the war. As a consequence, these young Americans also risked the loss of their American citizenship under the Expatriation Act of 1907, which declared that Americans could relinquish citizenship if they took actions deemed to have the "intention of relinquishing United States nationality." In 1914, it was uncertain whether the Wilson administration would determine that enlistment in foreign armies showed this intent.[33]

German reservists marching on Broadway.

This photograph captured a parade of German Army reservists marching down Broadway in New York City in 1914. The men carried both the U.S. and Imperial German flags during their march. While American public opinion tended to favor the Allies, many others remained loyal to their homelands of the Central Powers at the outset of the conflict. Courtesy of the Library of Congress.

German Americans enlisting at the German Consulate in New York City as part of German mobilization in 1914.

Courtesy of the Library of Congress.

American volunteers for the French Foreign Legion in Paris, France, in 1914.

Ninety Americans, including New York native Alan Seeger, joined the Legion prior to America's involvement in 1917. Of these men, 38 were killed and the other 52 were each wounded at least one time.[1] Courtesy of the Library of Congress.

1.Ward, Gary. "Engaged in Glory Alone: Yanks in French Foreign Legion Were First to Fight," *VFW* Magazine, Vol. 102, No. 1, September 1914, page 36.

French reserves.

French reservists returning to their homeland aboard the steamship *La Lorraine*, which departed New York Harbor on August 5, 1914. Courtesy of the Library of Congress.

Legionnaire 2nd Class Alan Seeger.

Alan Seeger (June 22, 1888–July 4, 1916) in his Foreign Legion uniform. From *The Literary Digest History of the World War* by Francine Whiting Halsey, page 243.

Legionnaire Alan Seeger (1888–1916)
French Foreign Legion

It was not only unknown immigrants such as Donato Di Russo who left the United States to fight in World War I. Numerous prominent Americans also determined to fight for the Allies. Among them was Alan Seeger, an American poet living in Paris when war broke out in 1914. Born in New York City in 1888, he was educated at Harvard University and settled in Greenwich Village, New York City, in 1910 before moving to the Latin Quarter in Paris. On August 24, 1914, Seeger enlisted in the French Foreign Legion. As an American citizen, Seeger and other foreigners were prohibited from joining the French Army. Seeger, like many young men, saw the war as a chance for adventure and envisioned it as a romantic endeavor. Seeger eagerly awaited his "bapteme de feu"—baptism by fire.[34] The realities of warfare, however, quickly became clear to even the most idealistic soldiers. By December, Seeger wrote of the experience of the average soldier: "Exposed to all the dangers of war, but with none of its enthusiasms or splendid élan, he is condemned to sit like an animal in its burrow and hear the shells whistle over his head and take their little daily toll from his comrades."[35] Alan Seeger was killed near Belloy-en-Santerre, France, during the Battle of the Somme on July 4, 1916.[36] In his final letter on June 28, 1916, Seeger wrote a friend, "We go up to the attack tomorrow. This will probably be the biggest thing yet. . . . I will write you soon if I get through all right. If not, my only earthly care is for my poems."[37] Perhaps his most famous poem, "Rendezvous," was published after his death in 1917 per his request.

> I have a rendezvous with Death
> At some disputed barricade,
> When Spring comes back with rustling shade
> And apple-blossoms fill the air—
> I have a rendezvous with Death
> When Spring brings back blue days and fair.
>
> It may be he shall take my hand
> And lead me into his dark land
> And close my eyes and quench my breath—
> It may be I shall pass him still.
> I have a rendezvous with Death
> On some scarred slope of battered hill,
> When Spring comes round again this year
> And the first meadow-flowers appear
>
> God knows 'twere better to be deep
> Pillowed in silk and scented down,
> Where love throbs out in blissful sleep,
> Pulse nigh to pulse, and breath to breath
> Where hushed awakenings are dear . . .
> But I've a rendezvous with Death
> At midnight in some flaming town,
> When Spring trips north again this year.
> And I to my pledged word am true,
> I shall not fail that rendezvous.
>
> —"Rendezvous" by Alan Seeger

"Britishers, You're Needed."

Artist: Lloyd Myers; *Printer:* Allen Frank and Co., New York, New York; *Publisher:* British and Canadian Recruiting Mission; *Technique:* Lithograph; *Dimensions:* 103 x 70 cm.

This poster was printed by a New York–based print company for British and Canadian recruiters. The poster's message was readily apparent to the passerby. As the stalemate developed along the Western Front in Europe, the British Army was in need of men to fill its rapidly expanding ranks. In addition to its colonial dominions, the British government sought to recruit British expatriates and other sympathetic Americans to the Allied Cause. New York State Library, Manuscripts and Special Collections.

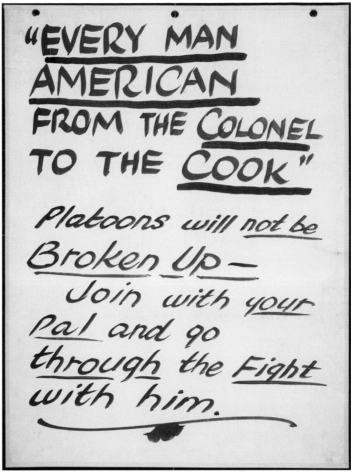

"For Immediate Service Drafts of Americans Officered by Americans."

Artist: None; *Printer:* Unknown; *Publisher:* Canadian Expeditionary Force; *Technique:* Lithograph; *Dimensions:* 107 x 71 cm.

The 213th Overseas Battalion was raised in Toronto, Ontario, in 1916. It was one of several units in the "American Legion" of the Canadian Expeditionary Forces. 35,000 members of the Canadian Expeditionary Force listed their place of birth as the United States. New York State Library, Manuscripts and Special Collections.

"Every Man American from the Colonel to the Cook."

Artist: None; *Printer:* Unknown; *Publisher:* Canadian Expeditionary Force; *Technique:* Lithograph; *Dimensions:* 70.5 x 52 cm.

A second recruitment poster for the Canadian Expeditionary Force's 213th Overseas Battalion, which emphasizes the American origins of the unit. New York State Library, Manuscripts and Special Collections.

Private Walter C. Duncan.

Courtesy of the Rochester Historical Society.

Private Walter C. Duncan
Canadian Expeditionary Force

Walter Duncan's family moved to Rochester when he was one year old. Duncan graduated from the city's Number 14 Public School. Upon graduation, he was employed by the Eastman Kodak Company, but left to work in Chicago. He returned to Rochester to enlist from home. He tried first to enlist in the United States Army, but was refused. He then opted to join the Canadian Army. Duncan entered the service on January 15, 1917, at the age of thirty, as a private. He was assigned to Company H, 3rd Battalion, Canadian Infantry. He received basic training at Toronto, Ontario. While in training there he received word that his father was dying, but as his outfit was soon to embark overseas he was not allowed to go home. His unit departed Canada on March 23, 1918. Duncan's father died while he was at sea. He was in training at Whitley Camp, Surrey, England, when he was taken ill. He was sent to the hospital on June 29, 1918. He died of pneumonia at General Hospital Number 12, Bramshott, England, on July 3, 1918, and was buried in Bramshott Parish Churchyard, Grave Number 1352, alongside his fellow Canadian and English soldiers. Three days after Private Duncan was taken ill, his company went into combat.

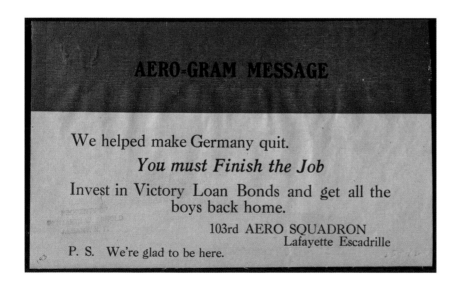

Aero Gram Message, 103rd Aero Squadron, Lafayette Escadrille: "We helped make Germany quit."

The Lafayette Escadrille was a squadron composed mostly of American pilots who fought for the French Army. The squadron was originally formed in April 1916 as the *Escadrille Americaine*, but soon changed its name to the Lafayette Escadrille following complaints from the German government. 265 Americans served in the squadron, which was transferred to the U.S. Army as the 103rd Aero Squadron upon American entry into the war. New York State Library, Manuscripts and Special Collections.

American pilots of the Lafayette Escadrille.

Courtesy of the Library of Congress.

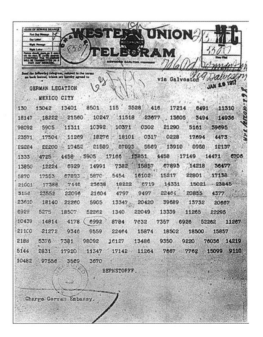

Zimmerman Telegram.

Fearing America's entry into the war, in January 1917, the German foreign secretary sent a secret telegram to the Mexican government guaranteeing German aid if Mexico agreed to go to war with the United States. Germany would assist Mexico in reclaiming its former territories of Texas, New Mexico, and Arizona. British code-breakers intercepted the note and leaked the contents to the U.S. government on March 1. Courtesy of the Library of Congress.

Declaration of War

By early 1917, tensions between the United States and the German Empire reached a tipping point. The stalemate on the Western Front prompted Germany to announce resumption of unrestricted submarine warfare in the hopes of so disrupting the flow of supplies across the Atlantic as to choke the Allied war effort into submission.[38] The move infuriated President Wilson, who called on the Germans to end their offensive to no avail. The release of the Zimmerman Telegram and Germany's offers of an alliance with Mexico proved to be the final straw. On April 2, 1917, Woodrow Wilson stood before a joint session of the United States Congress and asked for a declaration of war against the German Empire.

"Polacy! Kościuzko i Pulaski walkczyli za wolność Polski i innych narodów! Idźmy w ich ślady!" (Poles! Kosciuszko and Pulaski fought for the Liberty of Poland and Other Nations! Follow Their Example).

Artist: W.T. Benda; *Printer:* Stacyja No. 27/Rekutacyjna, St. Paul, Minnesota; *Publisher:* Unknown; *Technique:* Lithograph; *Dimensions:* 103 x 68 cm.

When the war began, Poland did not exist as an independent nation. By 1914, Poland had been divided between the Russian, German, and Austro-Hungarian empires. Because of its location, much of the most severe fighting on the Eastern Front took place on Polish territory. In 1916, the German government announced the creation of the Kingdom of Poland, a puppet state allied to the Central Powers. When Russia signed the Treaty of Brest-Litovsk, Germany and Austria received all of Poland's territory. When the United States entered the war in April 1917, Polish nationalists seized upon President Woodrow Wilson's call for self-determination—the right of all national and ethnic groups in Eastern Europe to be given the opportunity to create their own independent nations—and actively worked towards Polish independence. While it is not explicitly stated, it is likely that this poster was generated towards this end. Towards the end of the war, a Polish Army was established in France under the command of General Jósef Haller.[1] This Army recruited "Polish Legions" from the diaspora across Europe and the United States. The figures of Kosciuszko and Pulaski, two Polish officers who voluntarily fought for the American cause during the Revolution, would have resonated among both immigrants and native born Americans in the U.S. Some 4,000 Polish residents of New York joined the Polish Legion, approximately twenty percent of the 25,000 American Poles to do so.[2] Following the Armistice in 1918, the Polish Army returned to Poland where it fought for Polish independence and helped to halt the advance of the Bolsheviks into Europe.[3] New York State Library, Manuscripts and Special Collections.

1. Ruskoski, David Thomas, "The Polish Army in France: Immigrants in America, World War I Volunteers in France, Defenders of the Recreated State in Poland." Dissertation, Georgia State University, 2006, pages 73–75 (http://scholarworks.gsu.edu/history_diss/1), accessed April 7, 2016.

2. Sullivan, James. Working files for a publication on New York in World War I, 1917–1925. New York State Archives, Series A3166.

3. Ruskoski, pages 88–90.

W. T. Benda (1873–1948).

Wladislaw Teodor Benda was born in Posen, Germany (modern-day Poland). He studied art at Kraków College of Technology and Art and the School of Fine Art in Vienna, Austria. He immigrated to the United States in the late-nineteenth century, eventually settling in New York City in 1902, where he continued his studies at the Art Students League of New York. Benda joined the Society of Illustrators in 1907 and became an American citizen in 1911. During World War I, Benda created numerous poster designs for the Division of Pictorial Publicity, but also for the Polish Army in France. After the war, Benda remained in the United States and was employed as an artist and illustrator in New York City.

"Czechoslovaks! Join Our Free Colors."

Artist: Vojtech Preissig; *Printer:* Unknown; *Publisher:* Czechoslovak Recruiting Office, New York City; *Technique:* Lithograph; *Dimensions:* 92.75 x 64.75 cm.

A recruitment poster for the Free Czechoslovakian Army. Like Poland, the nation of Czechoslovakia (today, the nations of the Czech Republic and Slovakia), did not exist, but rather was divided between the German and Austro-Hungarian empires. This poster was printed by the Czechoslovak Recruiting Office in New York City. Thousands of foreign born New Yorkers returned to Europe to defend their homelands. 3,000 Italians from Rochester returned to Italy. Statewide, the number was likely closer to 10,000.[1] New York State Museum Collection, H-1976.147.22.

1. Sullivan, Series A3166.

Vojtech Preissig (1873–1944).

Vojtech Preissig was born in Austria-Hungary in what is today the Czech Republic. After studying in Prague and Paris, Preissig immigrated to the United States. After arriving in New York City, Preissig taught at the Art Students League and at Columbia University.[1] He eventually moved to Boston, where he became the director of the Department of Printing and Graphic Arts at the Wentworth Institute. He returned to newly independent Czechoslovakia in 1931.[2]

1. "Extension Teaching Announcement," Columbia University Bulletin of Information, 1916–1917, page xiii.

2. Darracott, page xx.

Wilson before Congress.

On April 2, 1917, President Woodrow Wilson addressed a joint session of Congress to ask for a declaration of war against Germany. Congress formally declared war on April 6. Courtesy of the Library of Congress.

Wilson's Declaration.

Artist: None; *Printer:* Unknown; *Publisher:* The New York American; *Technique:* Lithograph; *Dimensions:* 59.5 x 48 cm.

This poster features a bust portrait of President Wilson and the full text of his speech to Congress on April 2, 1917. The poster is an example of the ways in which information was disseminated to the American public in order to rally opinion in favor of war with Germany. New York State Library, Manuscripts and Special Collections.

"Proclamation of War."

Artist: None; *Printer:* Cheltenham Press; *Publisher:* Unknown; *Technique:* Lithograph; *Dimensions:* 90 x 60.5 cm.

Citing Germany's use of unrestricted submarine warfare among other causes, President Wilson asked Congress to declare war on Germany on April 2, 1917. Wilson painted the conflict as a battle between autocracy and democracy. In leading the nation into "the most terrible and disastrous of all wars," President Wilson asserted that the United States was fighting to "make the world itself at last free." On April 6, 1917, Congress responded with a declaration of war. New York State Library, Manuscripts and Special Collections.

Proclamation!

To the Citizens of New York:

Upon just grounds and after long and patient forbearance, the President and the Congress of the United States have declared that by the act of the autocratic government which rules in the Empire of Germany war exists between the two countries, and the free people of America are about entering into the great World Conflict. Millions of the people of this city were born in the countries engaged in this great war. No part of the earth is without its representatives here.

I enjoin upon you all that you honor the Liberty which so many of you have sought in this land, and the free self-government of the American Democracy in which we all find our opportunity and individual freedom, by exercising kindly consideration, self-control, and respect to each other and to all others who dwell within our limits, that you one and all aid in the preservation of order and in the exercise of calm and deliberate judgment in this time of stress and tension.

There will be some exceptional cases of malign influence and malicious purpose among you, and, as to them, I advise you all that full and timely preparation has been made adequate to the exigency which exists for the maintenance of order throughout the City of New York; and, for the warning of the ill-disposed, I quote the Statute of the United States which is applicable to all residents enjoying the protection of our laws whether they be citizens or not: "Whoever owing allegiance to the United States levies war against them or adheres to their enemies giving them aid or comfort within the United States or elsewhere is guilty of treason." The punishment prescribed by law for the crime of treason is death or at the discretion of the court imprisonment for not less than five years and a fine of not less than $10,000. All officers of the police have been especially instructed to give their prompt and efficacious attention to the enforcement of this law.

John Purroy Mitchel
MAYOR.

"To the Citizens of New York."

Artist: None; *Printer:* Unknown; *Publisher:* The City of New York; *Technique:* Lithograph; *Dimensions:* 46 x 30 cm.

This proclamation was signed by New York City Mayor John Purroy Mitchel, exhorting the people of the city to rally to the war effort. Mitchel was a staunch supporter of the Preparedness Movement and universal military service. He was defeated for re-election just prior to the declaration of war by John F. Hylan. Mitchel joined the Army Air Service and was killed in a training accident in July 1918. New York State Library, Manuscripts and Special Collections.

"Together We Win."

Artist: James Montgomery Flagg; *Printer:* W.F. Powers Co., Litho., New York, New York; *Publisher:* United States Shipping Board; *Technique:* Lithograph; *Dimensions:* 98 x 71 cm.

This poster by James Montgomery Flagg features a sailor, a laborer, and a soldier marching arm in arm above the slogan "Together We Win," emphasizing the notion that the United States needed to mobilize both militarily and industrially for the conflict. The war effort ultimately required the total participation of all elements of American society. New York State Library, Manuscripts and Special Collections.

5

"Follow the Flag"

American Entry into the War

When President Wilson declared war in April 1917, the United States was completely unprepared for a global war. The U.S. Army numbered only 200,000 soldiers, and the weapons, ammunition, and materiel needed to fight a modern war were in short supply. Before America could affect this "war to end all wars," the nation needed to mobilize on an unprecedented scale. Former president Theodore Roosevelt, a critical opponent of Woodrow Wilson, lamented that "the army we had gathered in the cantonments had neither the rifles, the machine-guns, the cannon, the tanks, nor the airplanes which would have enabled them to make any fight at all against any army of any military power."[1] One of Roosevelt's allies in Congress, Republican Representative James W. Husted of Peekskill, lamented that the United States had "somewhat neglected the military arts—too much to suit the views of many of us; she is confessedly unready to meet, on equal terms at the start, forces fully trained and equipped with all the instruments of modern warfare."[2] Before the American Army could make an impact on the Western Front, the nation would have to address these deficiencies. Even the sharpest critics of Wilson's lack of preparedness noted that "America aroused to arms in a righteous cause is a power which will make her enemies tremble."[3] To effect this power, the nation wanted to expand its armed forces to four million.

New York State was uniquely poised to take a leading role in the American war effort. As the most populous state in the nation, New York was again called on to provide a greater share of the fighting men to the country's armed forces as tens of thousands of men joined the New York National Guard or enlisted in the U.S. Army, Navy, or Marine Corps. As a manufacturing and financial center, New York's industrial productivity focused on producing the weapons and materiel needed for the American Expeditionary Forces and providing the money needed to pay for the war effort. By the end of the war, the Empire State would lead all others in the numbers of soldiers, tonnage of supplies, and money raised to support America's efforts. The state's extensive rail and canal systems provided the means to transport large quantities of supplies for shipment overseas via the Port of New York. New York Harbor became the nation's leading port through which the vast majority of men and goods would ship to Europe.

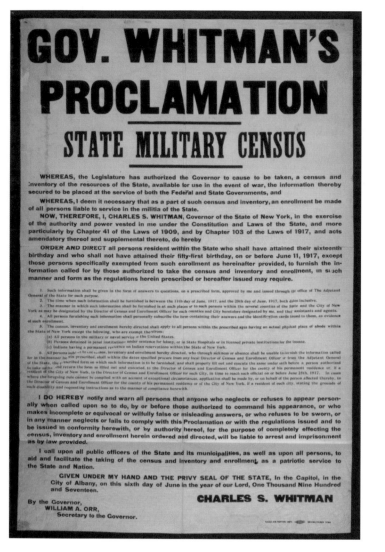

Whitman's Proclamation.

Among the many duties the New York State Council for Defense was tasked to oversee was the implementation of a statewide military census.. Courtesy of the Library of Congress.

New York's citizens plunged into the war effort. News of the declaration of war resulted in mass meetings, rallies, and parades across New York State. In Albany, more than 600 young men immediately enlisted. Jamestown, in Chautauqua County, established a home relief and defense committee.[4] For many, service in the war was a grand crusade or an opportunity for adventure. Despite three years of news about the carnage occurring in Europe, many young men were thrilled at the opportunity for service. Basil Elmer of Ithaca, Tompkins County, in a letter to his parents, encouraged them to "[b]e happy for me in the great adventure. The whole thing is teeming with excitement and romance that occasionally I thrill at the thought of it and long to get at it. It is a wonderful game."[5]

As men joined the military, women joined the industrial and agricultural labor force as never before. Across the state, companies that had already begun production of goods for European armies began filling contracts for equipment to be used by American soldiers. Industries that had not already done so shifted to the production of war materials. By the end of the conflict, New York State held the largest number of defense contracts of any state; it had contributed 518,864 of its citizens to military service, serving in all branches. This was the largest contribution of men from any state.[6]

Governor Charles Whitman appointed a five-member State Council of Defense to ensure that the military, industrial, agricultural, and transportation resources of the state were fully utilized and directed toward the war effort.[7] On May 6, 1917, Whitman ordered the New York National Guard to be increased by 10,000 soldiers, which was accomplished by mid-July. On July 10, President Wilson ordered all state National Guard members into federal service. In August, the 40,780 officers and men of the New York National Guard departed the state for training at Spartanburg, South Carolina.[8] In Buffalo, 50,000 people gathered to bid farewell to their hometown soldiers.[9] Similar scenes were repeated across the state.

For a period, dissent and antiwar views were subsumed by a wave of patriotic fervor. In this atmosphere, the Division of Pictorial Publicity produced a myriad of recruiting posters for the U.S. military. These posters, while artistically diverse, generally reflected the themes of teamwork and unity, masculinity, and loyalty to the flag.

The New York State Council of Defense

Less than a month after President Woodrow Wilson declared war on Germany, the U.S. Council of National Defense began to urge the states to form their own defense councils to support the work of the federal government in mobilizing resources and manpower for the war effort. On May 4, 1917, the New York State Legislature passed an act to organize the State Council of Defense. The council was to be responsible for making "all investigations and plans for efficient coordination and cooperation of the military, industrial, agricultural and commercial resources of the state in time of war," and for creating "relations which render possible immediate concentration and utilization of state resources for military purposes." The council oversaw the organization and coordination of the civilian as well as military population, and its oversight encompassed transportation systems, hospital and medical services, industry, volunteer organizations, and the registration and supervision of aliens. Persons employed by the council were deemed to be in the military service of the state. This practice was repeated again at the local level as many counties in the state adopted local defense organizations.

Governor Whitman was chairman, William A. Orr was secretary, and Joseph H. Wilson was auditor of the Council of Defense. Other members appointed in May of 1917 included Frank M. Williams, the state engineer and surveyor; William W. Witherspoon, the superintendent of public works; Charles S. Wilson, the commissioner of agriculture; and Charles H. Sherrill, who became adjutant general in September of 1917 on the resignation of Louis W. Stotesbury. The membership of the council reflected the notion that preparing the state for war meant not only amassing men and materiel for the war effort, but organizing and coordinating civilian efforts on the home front to ensure that each citizen's work could be utilized most effectively in defense of the nation.

The council controlled expenditures made from appropriations voted in 1917 for general mobilization of New York State's resources, for a food supply commission, and for a military census. Detailed plans for taking a military census—which counted hundreds of thousands of persons in the state, including the illiterate and non–English speaking—and mobilizing the state's resources were worked out by the adjutant general's office through twelve divisions within a Resource Mobilization Bureau.[10] For each of these divisions there was a corresponding subcommittee that operated in each county of the state under the direction of the county home defense committee. Since the county functioned as the basic unit for

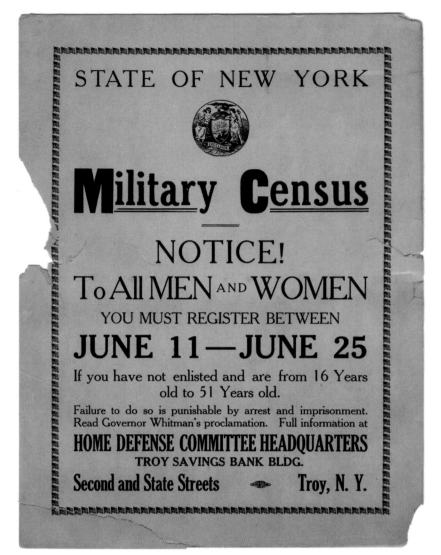

Broadside for military census in Rensselaer County.

The State Legislature on March 29, 1917 authorized Governor Whitman to carry out a census to identify the state's military resources. The census included the registration of all men and women between the ages of 16 and 50. When Congress enacted the Selective Service System, the state forwarded the names of 2,917,909 New York men to Washington. New York State Archives, A0412-78.

mobilization of the state's resources during wartime, the home defense committees oversaw such vital home-front activities as food production and conservation; efficient transportation of materials across the state; and enrollment for home defense of men not eligible for National Guard duty.

In addition to their close cooperation with the state Council of Defense, the county committees worked with the federal government in a number of efforts to mobilize manpower and resources during World War I. Such efforts included the promotion

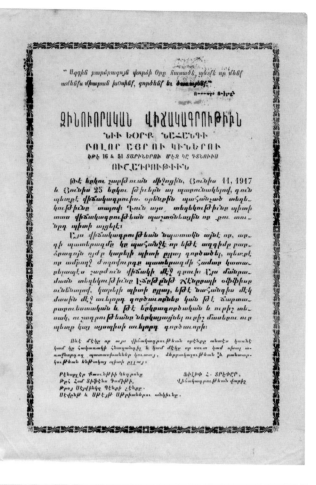

Censimento Militare
STATO DI NEW YORK

---◄·◄═◊═►·►---

Italiani dai 16 ai 51 anni!

Vi si partecipa che dal giorno 11 al 25 corr. Giugno, si fara' un censimento generale di tutte le persone fra l' eta' dei 16 ai 51 anni, residenti in America.

Tutti dovrete rispondere con sincerita' alle domande che vi saranno fatte dalle persone incaricate per il censimento che verranno in casa vostra.

Questo censimento si fa per verificare la forza di questa grande Nazione, affinche' con le vostre informazioni, pienamente dettagliate, l' Aiutante Generale dello Stato, potra' portare la sua attenzione su quelle sezioni in bisogno, qualunque avanzo di mano d' opera, di fornimenti industriali, agricoli ed altro.

Ogni famiglia e' caldamente pregata di accogliere le persone che si presentano con dignita' e rispetto.

Nessuno deve sottrarsi a questo obbligo sacrosanto emanato dal Governatore, e tutti coloro che trascureranno, o si rifiuteranno di conformarsi alla legge, o daranno risposte od informazioni false, per intralciare o traviare il lavoro delle autorita', saranno soggetti allo arresto ed indi condannati alla pena del carcere.

Philip H. Draper
Direttore del Censimento.

Sede della Rensselaer County
Home Defense Committee.
Troy Savings Bank Building,
Corner Second and State Sts., Troy, N. Y.

Foreign language broadsides for the military census.

These broadsides for the state's military census were printed in numerous languages including Italian, Armenian, and German. These foreign language broadsides highlight the fact that New York State had become one of the most diverse places in the world by 1917, largely due to the number of immigrants who came to this country through the Port of New York. During the war, this diversity would provide newly arrived Americans an opportunity to serve their adopted country, but also raised many serious challenges for both the state and for various minority groups. New York State Archives, A0412-78.

Enrollment card.

This enrollment card was issued to James Husted of Peekskill, Westchester County, to verify that Husted had complied with New York State's Military Census. New York State Library, Manuscripts and Special Collections.

of Liberty Loan bonds; education of homemakers on food conservation efforts as part of United States Food Administration director Herbert Hoover's food conservation pledge and "cleanup campaign;" collection of the federal income tax; and the work of the federal exemption and enlistment boards. Overall, the relationship of the county committees with the state Council of Defense and the federal government reflected the idea that direct channels of communication and organizational hierarchy—between all three levels of government—were critical to massing a united effort of military and civilian resources.

At a meeting on November 29, 1918, the council decided that the wartime emergency for which it was created had ended with the Armistice, and that it would conclude its activities on December 15, 1918. Two branches of its work continued: the Bureau of Americanization, under the State Education Department; and the Division of Information, which continued to handle requests from the federal government for publicity on activities regarding federal reconstruction programs and to keep the county defense committees advised of its work. The Bureau of Americanization worked to promote civic engagement through the promotion of literacy and fluency in the English language. While the bureau was ostensibly tasked with providing literacy services to all New Yorkers, its efforts very early on looked to the state's many immigrants for whom English was not a primary language.[11] The state's Reconstruction

Commission recommended solutions for problems associated with demobilization of soldiers and other difficulties pertaining to New York's return to a peacetime footing. The law that abolished the council took effect in March of 1919, and it required that all of the "books, papers and documents" of the council be turned over to the adjutant general's office.

Such efforts highlighted the growing cooperation of government agencies at all levels. The functions of these agencies were frequently coordinated and consolidated to meet the needs of the war effort. Thus, while state and federal government leaders and the Committee on Public Information continued to espouse a spirit of voluntarism in a war that pitted democracy against authoritarianism, wartime needs led to a significant expansion of "big government" into previously untouched aspects of daily life. In this manner, the recruitment posters, such as Flagg's "I Want You!" poster, stood at odds with the implementation of the Selective Service Act. Whereas fewer than 10 percent of Union soldiers during the Civil War were conscripted, in World War I more than 70 percent were draftees.[12] Through the efforts of the Committee for Public Information and the Division of Pictorial Publicity, government officials worked to create a sense of civic obligation to serve.[13]

The Call to Arms

> [W]e are prouder still to have a share in a greater cause than any that has called forth a great or small people to war.
>
> —Lieutenant Harold W. Mitchell, Sanitary Squad No. 1, Division 41, AEF[14]

As the nation prepared for war, the United States looked to expand its armed forces from a peacetime level of fewer than 200,000 to four million men at arms. Unlike in previous conflicts in American history, the U.S. Army did not seek to utilize volunteer regiments raised by individual states to increase the size of its military force. Following Congress's declaration of war, the federal government worked to establish a Selective Service Plan to meet the nation's manpower needs. As a result, relatively few enlistments were recorded for April and May of 1917.[15] Thousands of New Yorkers volunteered for service with the state's National Guard as it was brought up to wartime strength for federal service. Millions more

PROCLAMATION

State of New York

Executive Chamber

WHEREAS, On the fifteenth day of July the troops of our National Guard will be, by proclamation of the President, taken over into the Federal service of the United States, and sent out of the State to Federal concentration camps, and

WHEREAS, There will shortly also be taken into the Federal service by means of the operation of the Military Conscription Law our State's quota of men for the United States' Army;

NOW, THEREFORE, I, Charles S. Whitman, Governor of the State of New York, do appoint

SUNDAY, JULY FIFTEENTH

as a day upon which all our people, of whatever religion or creed, shall repair to their houses of worship and offer up prayer to Almighty God on behalf of our gallant young manhood now about to go forth to battle in a most righteous cause in the armies of our beloved Nation, discharging thus their duty as worthy descendants of our ancestors who, while gaining for us our liberty, acknowledged in their Declaration of Independence their firm reliance on the protection of Divine Providence.

GIVEN under my hand and the Privy Seal of the State at the Capitol in the city of Albany this tenth day of July in the year of our Lord one thousand nine hundred and seventeen.

By the Governor:

Secretary to the Governor.

National Guard proclamation.

In this proclamation, Governor Charles S. Whitman honored the men of the New York National Guard as they prepared to enter federal service. New York State Archives, A13035-79.

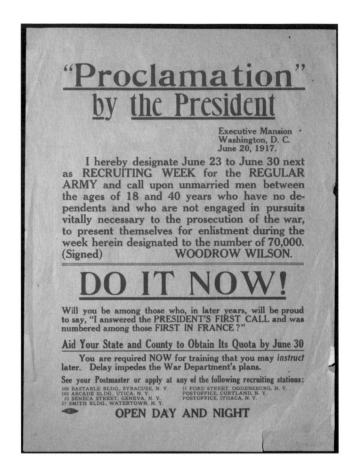

Proclamation, June 20, 1917.

Artist: None; *Printer:* Unknown; *Publisher:* Unkown; *Technique:* Lithograph; *Dimensions:* 31 x 23 cm.

This text-only broadside includes a proclamation from President Wilson designating June 23 to 30, 1917, as "Recruiting Week" for the U.S. Army. The poster identifies New York State recruitment stations at Syracuse, Geneva, Watertown, Ogdensburg, Cortland, and Ithaca. New York State Library, Manuscripts and Special Collections.

registered for the draft when the new Selective Service Plan was enacted in May. In total, more than 500,000 New Yorkers would respond to the nation's call to arms.

On August 5, 1917, President Wilson ordered the state's National Guard to depart for federal military service. The previous month, Governor Charles S. Whitman had issued a proclamation honoring the men in the New York National Guard as the state's

"gallant young manhood" prepared to "go forth to battle in a most righteous cause." On August 15, the state's guardsmen departed for war.

> When I filled out my application, I chose the old 69th—because it and I were Irish.
> —Corporal Martin J. Hogan, Company K, 165th Infantry[16]

Opportunity for Men

outside of the draft age

To Fight In France

with

New York's Volunteers

the

27th U. S. Army Division

MEN WANTED

Between the Ages of 18 to 21, and 31 to 40 for

All Branches of the Service

Infantry, Artillery, Engineers, Machine Gun and Signal Corps Batallions
Ammunition Train, Hospital Orderlies, Military Police, Etc.

Vacancies are being rapidly filled

ENLIST TODAY!

At Recruiting Headquarters, 27th Division, U.S.A., 721 Fifth Avenue, N. Y.

Phone, Plaza 1888

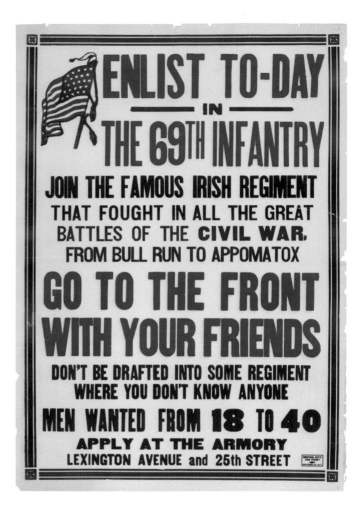

27th Division recruiting poster.

Artist: None; *Printer:* Unknown; *Publisher:* New York National Guard;
Technique: Lithograph; *Dimensions:* 63.5 x 48.25 cm.

Anticipating American entry into the war, Governor Charles Whitman and the State Legislature authorized increased funding and recruitment for the New York National Guard in January 1917. In his call for additional Guardsmen, Whitman assured the population that the measure was "not because I want war, but because I want peace."[1] When war was declared, New York was one of the only states with a full National Guard Division ready to be sent to France. Many assumed that the New York Division would be the first National Guard unit shipped overseas. Political leaders in Washington worried about the political ramifications if New York's National Guardsmen were to be sent *en masse*. Newton Baker, Woodrow Wilson's Secretary of War, worried that New Yorkers would object to their sons being the only ones sent first, and that other states would see it as preferential treatment for the Empire State.[2] For this reason, the War Department authorized the formation of the 42nd Division. New York's contribution to the Rainbow Division was to be the 69th Infantry Regiment. The New York State National Guard Division was designated the 27th Division on July 20, 1917. When it sailed for France, the 27th numbered 991 officers and 27,114 enlisted men. New York State Museum Collection, H-1975.185.3.

1. Flick, pages 292–293.

2. Harris, Stephen L., *Duffy's War: Fr. Francis Duffy, Wild Bill Donovan, and the Irish Fighting 69th in World War I* (Washington, DC: Potomac Books, Inc., 2008), page 32.

69th New York recruiting poster.

Artist: None; *Printer:* Empire City Job Print; *Publisher:* New York National Guard; *Technique:* Lithograph; *Dimensions:* 102 x 71 cm.

Organized in New York City in the 1850s, the 69th Regiment was composed of Irish Americans, many recently arrived from their homeland. The unit served with distinction throughout the U.S. Civil War and earned the nickname "The Fighting Irish." When the 69th Infantry was brought to wartime strength, the regiment's composition went from 85 percent Irish to 50 percent. The regiment's chaplain, Father Francis Duffy, stated that the men of the 69th were, "Irish by adoption, Irish by association, or Irish by conviction."[1] Many of the Irish-born soldiers in the regiment were less than enthusiastic about America's alliance with Great Britain, which continued to occupy Ireland. Many members of the 69th were or had been staunch Irish nationalists and supporters of Irish independence.[2] New York State Museum Collection, H-1984.78.1.

1. Harris, *Duffy's War*, page 36.

2. Harris, *Duffy's War*, pages 19–20.

"Recruits Wanted, 15th Regiment New York Guard."

Artist: Unknown; *Printer:* Unknown; *Publisher:* New York National Guard; *Technique:* Lithograph; *Dimensions:* 94 x 66 cm.

After the United States entered the war in 1917, Harlem's 15th New York was the first regiment in the state to reach wartime strength.[1] The regiment's commander, Colonel William Hayward, hoped the 15th would be selected as New York's contribution to the newly formed 42nd "Rainbow" Division.[2] The 15th departed New York City for initial training at Camp Whitman, near Poughkeepsie, Dutchess County, on May 13, 1917.[3] In addition to basic training, the regiment was assigned to patrol critical infrastructure, including the New York City aqueducts and railroads. Soon thereafter the men were sent to federal training at Camp Wadsworth in Spartanburg, South Carolina, with the rest of the New York National Guard. Racial tensions in both South Carolina and Camp Mills on Long Island prompted the movement of the regiment to France. Thus, the 15th was the first New York unit to arrive overseas. Despite poor treatment of black units such as the 15th, tens of thousands of African Americans enlisted in the armed forces. New York State Museum Collection, H-1975.185.4.

1. Harris, Stephen L. *Harlem's Hell Fighters* (Dulles, VA: Potomac Books, Inc., 2003), page 91.

2. Harris, page 81.

3. Sammons, Jeffrey T. and John H. Morrow Jr. *Harlem's Rattlers and the Great War: The Undaunted 369th Regiment and the African American Quest for Equality* (Lawrence, KS: University of Kansas Press, 2014), page 131.

"Some Backing."

Artist: James Montgomery Flagg; *Printer:* Unknown; *Publisher:* Unknown; *Technique:* Lithograph; *Dimensions:* 104.25 x 54.75 cm.

This recruiting poster by James Montgomery Flagg was produced for the New York Guard. The New York Guard was a home defense force established in 1917 to replace the National Guard units that had entered federal service during the war. The New York Guard was comprised almost completely of boys and men outside of draft age—younger than 18 or older than 45 years of age—or men whose physical handicaps prevented service in the Army but was not so limiting as to prevent service on the home front. By the end of the war, the New York Guard consisted of 22,000 officers and men stationed across New York State guarding critical infrastructure, factories, and public utilities.[1] New York State Museum Collection, H-1978.182.1.

1. Berry, Brigadier General Charles W., The Adjutant General, *Annual Report of the Adjutant General for the year 1919* (Albany: J.B. Lyon Company, 1921), pages 3–4.

"Join the Irish '300' for France with 69th Regiment" (1917).

Artist: Unknown; *Printer:* Unknown; *Publisher:* 69th Regiment, U.S. Army;
Technique: Lithograph; *Dimensions:* 49.5 x 38 cm.

This recruitment poster for the 69th Regiment of the New York National Guard prominently celebrates the regiment's Irish heritage. New York State Library, Manuscripts and Special Collections.

"Only the Navy Can Stop This" (ca. 1917).

Artist: William Allen Rogers; *Printer:* *New York Herald*, New York, New York;
Publisher: United States Navy Publicity Bureau; *Technique:* Lithograph;
Dimensions: 64 x 49 cm.

This U.S. Navy recruitment poster features a German soldier wearing the iconic *Pickelhaube* helmet and brandishing a bloody saber as he wades through the water, which washes over the bodies of women and children. For three years, reports of German U-boat attacks on civilian shipping had gradually transformed American public opinion against Germany. The poster's slogan implies that without a strong American Navy, continued German attacks against the United States would be inevitable.

The fear of the U-boat threat became readily apparent to New Yorkers on June 2, 1918, when a New York–bound passenger vessel, the *Carolina*, was sunk in New Jersey coastal waters, along with two cargo ships and three schooners. German submarines laid mines near channels into New York Harbor and cut telegraph cables disabling communication between New York and Europe. While the harbor itself was protected by an underwater net of steel cable and a small fleet of gunboats and submarine chasers, the menace of Germany's U-boats lay just over the horizon.[1] New York State Museum Collection, H-1977.141.1.

1. Jaffe, pages 209–210.

William Allen Rogers (1854–1931).

Born in Springfield, Ohio, William Allen Rogers studied at Worcester Polytechnic Institute (Worcester, Massachusetts) and Wittenburg College in Ohio, though he never graduated. In 1873, Rogers moved to New York City and was hired as an illustrator for the *Daily Graphic*. He worked for *Harper's Weekly* and the *New York Herald* as well.[1] He completed what is arguably his most famous illustration in 1904—his depiction of Theodore Roosevelt and his "Big Stick Diplomacy." As a member of the Society of Illustrators, Rogers was recruited to provide artwork for the war effort in 1917.

1. "Artist Biography: William Allen Rogers (1854–1931)," Smithsonian Libraries (http://www.sil.si.edu/ondisplay/caricatures/bio_rogers.htm), accessed April 1, 2016.

"Here he is, Sir" (ca. 1917).

Artist: Charles Dana Gibson; *Printer:* Latham Litho. and Ptg. Co., Brooklyn, New York; *Publisher:* United States Navy; *Technique:* Lithograph; *Dimensions:* 104.5 x 70 cm.

A U.S. Naval recruiting poster. In the image, an anxious mother is offering her son to a reassuring Uncle Sam for service in the U.S. Navy. New York State Library, Manuscripts and Special Collections.

Charles Dana Gibson (1867–1944).

Charles Dana Gibson was born in Roxbury, Massachusetts. As a young man, he exhibited significant artistic talent and was enrolled in the Art Students League in New York City by his parents. Gibson remained in New York, where he worked as an illustrator for numerous publications, including *Life* magazine, *Harper's Weekly*, and *Collier's*. He is perhaps most famous for his "Gibson Girls" drawings of the late-nineteenth and early-twentieth centuries. These drawings helped "define" beauty in American advertising until well after World War I. During the war, Gibson, who was the president of the Society of Illustrators, headed the Division of Pictorial Publicity, a quasigovernmental agency that facilitated the production of propaganda posters for the Committee on Public Information.

Military service abstract for Humphrey Bogart.

At age 18, Humphrey Bogart enlisted in the United States Navy on May 28, 1918. He received his basic training at the U.S. Naval Training Camp at Pelham Bay Park, New York and served aboard the U.S.S. *Granite State*. The U.S. Navy facility at Pelham Bay was one of several training camps established across New York State during World War I. New York State Archives, B0808-85.

Humphrey Bogart, ca. 1940.

After the war, Bogart moved to Hollywood, California, and became an internationally famous film star. Courtesy of Wikimedia Commons, originally published by the *Minneapolis Tribune*.

"Follow the Flag" (1917).

Artist: James Henry Daugherty; *Printer:* Carey Print Lith., New York, New York; *Publisher:* United States Navy; *Technique:* Lithograph; *Dimensions:* 106.75 x 71.25 cm.

U.S. Navy Recruiting Poster. More than 25,413 New Yorkers served in the United States Navy during the war with an additional 48,068 men and 2,329 women serving in the Naval Reserve. Courtesy of the Rochester Historical Society.

James Henry Daugherty (1889–1974).

James Henry Daugherty was born in North Carolina and spent his early childhood in Indiana and Ohio before settling in Washington, DC. There, he studied at the Corcoran School of Art and later traveled to London for further study. Daugherty's career focused primarily on the illustration of children's books but, during World War I, he joined fellow illustrators in producing propaganda posters for the Division of Pictorial Publicity.

"Tell That to the Marines!" (1917).

Artist: James Montgomery Flagg; *Printer:* Unknown; *Publisher:* United States Marine Corps; *Technique:* Lithograph; *Dimensions:* 101.75 x 76.25 cm.

Recruiting poster, U.S. Marine Corp. New York State Museum Collection, H–1976.145.4.

"Go Over the Top with U.S. Marines."

Artist: John A. Coughlin; *Printer:* Unknown; *Publisher:* U.S. Marine Corps Recruiting; *Technique:* Lithograph; *Dimensions:* 70 x 52 cm.

This U.S. Marine Corps recruiting poster depicts a Marine carrying a Vickers machine gun in the foreground as he and his comrades emerge from a trench and go "over the top." Volunteers are directed to enlist at the Marine Corps Recruitment Office at 8 North Water Street in Rochester, Monroe County. Courtesy of the Rochester Historical Society.

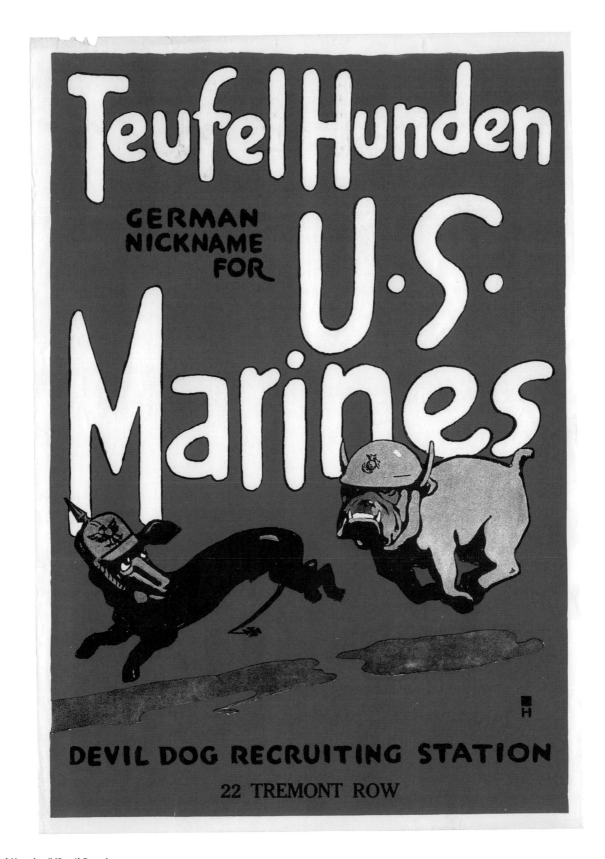

"Teufel Hunden" (Devil Dogs).

Artist: H; *Printer:* Unknown; *Publisher:* U.S. Marine Corps Recruiting; *Technique:* Lithograph; *Dimensions:* 63.5 x 48.25 cm.

This recruiting poster highlights the German nickname given to U.S. Marines during the fighting in World War I—*Teufel Hunden,* or Devil Dogs. New York State Museum Collection, H-1979.111.8..

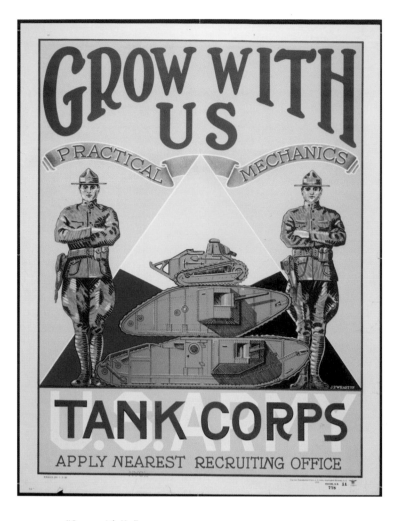

"Grow with Us."

Artist: J.P. Wharton; *Printer:* Engineer Reproduction Plant, Washington, DC; *Publisher:* United States Tank Corps; *Technique:* Lithograph; *Dimensions:* 63 x 48 cm.

The U.S. Army's fledgling Tank Corps not only needed operators for its tanks, but skilled mechanics capable of keeping them operating in the field. New York State Library, Manuscripts and Special Collections.

"Treat 'em Rough!"

Artist: August Hutaf; *Printer:* National Printing and Engraving Co., Chicago, New York, St. Louis; *Publisher:* United States Tank Corps; *Technique:* Lithograph; *Dimensions:* 103.5 x 68 cm.

This poster seeks recruits for the United States Army Tank Corps, which was established in September 1917. The fledgling Tank Corps was eventually to number 2,000 light tanks and 200 heavy tanks. By the time of the Armistice, 8 heavy and 21 light battalions had been raised. The British had introduced tanks in combat in September 1916 during the Battle of the Somme. While the new weapons did not immediately break the stalemate along the Western Front, many American officers foresaw the potential of the tank on the battlefield.[1] It was not until World War II that the tank became a decisive weapon in combat. New York State Library, Manuscripts and Special Collections.

1. Wilson, Captain Dale E., *The American Expeditionary Forces Tank Corps in World War I: From Creation to Combat*, A Thesis Submitted in Partial Fulfillment of the Requirements for the Masters of Arts Degree in History, College of Arts and Sciences (Philadelphia: Temple University, 1988), pages 8–10.

"Join the Black Toms."

Artist: W.F. Hoffman; *Printer:* Unknown; *Publisher:* United States Army Tank Corps; *Technique:* Lithograph; *Dimensions:* 63.5 x 48.25 cm.
New York State Museum Collection, H-1976.147.12.

1. Wilson, pages 8–10.

Men wait to register for the draft outside of the Bahnsen and Roeloffs grocery store in Manhattan on June 5, 1917.

Courtesy of the Library of Congress.

The Draft

On May 18, 1917, Congress passed the Selective Service Act authorizing the president to increase the size of the United States military via a draft (compulsory enlistment). When President Wilson declared war, the U.S. Army numbered fewer than 200,000 soldiers with an additional 181,000 in the National Guard. By 1918, 2.8 million men had been drafted into service. The draft was suspended following the Armistice in November 1918.

In New York State, local boards were established in cities and towns across the state and headed by prominent local business or civic leaders.[17] These local boards reported to nine district boards, who in turn answered to Colonel Franklin S. Hutchinson of Rochester, who was appointed the draft executive for New York State.[18] Following the first registration day on June 5, 1917, 1,035,000 New York men registered

for the draft. In the two registrations that followed, an additional 1,476,000 made themselves eligible to be drafted into military service.[19]

Exemption boards were established throughout the state to adjudicate cases where men were physically or mentally unfit for military service. Draftees could also request exemption in cases where they had dependents such as wives, children, or aging parents.[20] Unlike in the draft during the Civil War, the Selective Service Act did not permit the purchase of substitutes or replacements. A person's wealth was no longer enough to avoid military service; rather it would "touch all homes without partiality or differentiation."[21] New York City would supply one whole Army division—the 77th—and New Yorkers from across the state would serve in newly formed National Army divisions composed entirely of drafted soldiers.

Elmira draft.

A group of men stand outside the draft headquarters in Elmira, Chemung County, reviewing the list of local men drafted into military service. Courtesy of the New York State Archives, A0412-78.

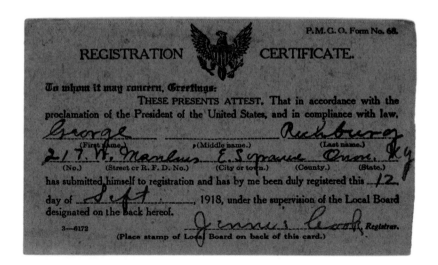

Draft registration card.

Selective Service registration card for George Richburg of East Syracuse, Onondaga County. The Selective Service Act established a decentralized system of registration and conscription. Much of the responsibility for the draft fell to state governments and local draft boards. The draft initially called for men between the ages of 21 and 31. By September 1918, the age range was expanded to 18 to 45. New York State Museum Collection, H-1970.107.38.

Selective Service registration certificate.

Enrollment card for John Shield of Erie County. On June 5, 1917, ten million young men voluntarily enrolled for the draft. This response eased the memories of the draft riots that had occurred during the Civil War in 1863. New York State Museum Collection, H-1972.18.3.

Orders No. 2.

October 4, 1917, orders for the organization of a parade of draftees in Albany. New York State Museum Collection, H-1977.90.50.

NATIONAL ARMY MEN'S THIRD ESCORT PARADE.

ALBANY, N. Y., *October 4, 1917.*

ORDERS,
No. 2.

I. The column for the street parade on Saturday, October 6, 1917, as escort to the members of the National Army will be composed as follows:

Detachment of Albany Mounted Police.
Marshal and Staff.

1st DIVISION, in order as stated.
Col. Adrian W. Mather, commanding; 1st Lieut. William L. Gillespie, Aide.
Stahler's Band.
Provisional Company, 10th Infantry, N. Y. Guard.
Ladies representing the Red Cross, carrying a large American flag.
Semi-Military organizations.
Uniformed Civic organizations.

2nd DIVISION, in order as stated.
Ben. V. Smith, commanding; Frank D. Sargent, Aide.
St. Vincent's Drum and Fife Corps.
Arab Patrol, Cyprus Temple, A. A. O. N. M. S.
Kiwanis Club.
Civic organizations, (Clubs, Societies, etc.)
Civilians, not organized.
Drafted men, not called.

3rd DIVISION, in order as stated.
Theodore C. Hailes, commanding; Major Harry S. Richmond, Aide.
Wendell's Band.
The Adjutant General of the State and State Officials.
Officials of Albany County and of the Cities of Albany, Cohoes and Watervliet.
Albany County Home Defense Committee and Chairman.
District Boards of Albany County.
National Army Men called for service.

II. The 1st Division will form on Maiden lane, with its right at Eagle street.
The 2nd Division will form on the south side of Washington avenue above Eagle street, with its right at Eagle street.
The 3rd Division will form on Eagle and Elk streets, with its right at Pine street.
The Marshal and staff will take position, in front of the 1st Division, on Eagle street opposite Maiden lane.

Armband.

This armband was given to drafted men before they were inducted into the Army and issued uniforms. New York State Museum Collection, H-1987.1.23.

Photograph of draftees wearing armbands.

This photograph from Westfield, Chautauqua County, shows local draftees wearing armbands similar to the one displayed above. Courtesy of the New York State Archives, A0412-78.

Military service abstract for Irving Berlin.

Irving Berlin was born Israel Baline. He immigrated to the United States from Russia in 1893. Berlin was drafted into the United States Army in New York City on May 8, 1918. Already an emerging star before entering the Army, Berlin gained fame as one of the nation's leading musical composers and songwriters after the war. New York State Archives, B0808-85.

Irving Berlin with his wife, Ellin Mackay.

Courtesy of the Library of Congress.

Draftees arrive at Camp Upton.

The photograph is entitled "Mustering Recruits, Camp Upton, L.I.N.Y." The camp, located in Suffolk County, Long Island, was the muster point for thousands of draftees from New York City, including members of the newly formed 77th Division. 73,000 New York draftees passed through the camp, which was opened in 1917 upon American entry into the war and closed in 1921. New York State Museum Collection, H-2014.12.38.2.

Sheet music, "Yip-Yip-Yaphank!"

"Yip Yip Yaphank" was a musical revue composed by Irving Berlin while a U.S. Army recruit at Camp Upton, Long Island. Camp Upton was situated in Yaphank, Suffolk County. After initial performances at the camp, the production was staged in New York City to raise money for additional construction at Upton. From the New York Public Library.

Service flag.

This service flag hung in the Staten Island home of Peter Schaming, who served in the 106th Infantry Regiment, 27th Division, American Expeditionary Force. Service flags, like this one, indicated that a household had a loved one in military service. The blue stars on the white field corresponded to the number of family members on active duty. A gold star denoted a serviceman or woman who had been killed in service to the nation. New York State Museum Collection, H-2007.7.1.

Service flag.

This large service flag was flown in front of the Rapid Hose Fire Company in Kingston, Ulster County, for two members of the volunteer fire company who were in military service during World War I. New York State Museum Collection, H-2016.13.4.

To Them
that Star Stood for One Hundred
per cent American Soldier.
The Best Soldiers make the Best
Citizens.

"To Them That Star Stood for One Hundred percent American Soldier."

Artist: Captain Gordon Grant, United States Army; *Printer:* Unknown; *Publisher:* Unknown; *Technique:* Lithograph; *Dimensions:* 35 x 28 cm.

This poster features an older couple gazing at a service flag. These flags were immediately recognizable to Americans on the home front during World War I. New York State Library, Manuscripts and Special Collections.

Medal.

This medal was presented "For the Mothers of Men at War from Albany County." It was issued at a ceremony at the Executive Mansion on October 26, 1918, by Mrs. Charles S. Whitman, the wife of New York's Governor. New York State Museum Collection, H-1987.28.72.

Gordon Grant (1875–1962).

Gordon Grant was born in San Francisco in 1875. He studied in Scotland and London before returning to San Francisco in 1895. The following year, he moved to New York City, where he worked as an illustrator for the *World* and the *Journal*. He served as an artist-correspondent covering the Boer War in South Africa (1899–1902). In 1907, he joined the 7th Regiment of the New York National Guard and served with the unit on the Mexican border in 1916. A foot injury prevented him from serving with the 27th Division in the American Expeditionary Force. Instead, Grant was stationed in Washington, DC, with the rank of captain. While serving, he provided numerous posters for the war effort.

Slackerism

The term "slacker" was commonly used throughout the war to describe any individual who avoided military service or employment in support of the war effort. In cities across New York and the nation "Slacker Raids" rounded up any men in a given area suspected of being of military age. The American Protective League and other groups were instrumental in assisting the federal government develop extensive lists of "slackers."

When the Selective Service Act was first announced in April 1917, married men were thought to be exempted from the draft. This led to a marked increase in applications for marriage licenses across New York State.[22] In Buffalo alone, the Marriage License Bureau at City Hall issued 100 licenses before noon in a single day.[23] Ultimately, however, marital status did not exempt a man from military service, though nearly 92 percent of married men did receive deferments in the first draft.[24]

On September 14, 1918, more than 60,000 men were detained in New York City during one of the largest slacker raids of the war. Fewer than 500 of these proved to be men who were actually evading the draft.

> [W]e have got to fight to protect our country and I know that you would not want a slacker.
> —Alton Clark, April 15, 1918[25]

Slackers.

In this photograph, a U.S. soldier inspects the paperwork of a passing civilian to ensure he has enrolled for the draft. Slacker raids and other measures were implemented throughout New York State and the nation to compel compliance with the Selective Service Act. From *U.S. Official Pictures of the Great War* (Washington, DC: Pictorial Bureau, 1920), New York State Museum Collection, H-1971.113.11.

"Will You Let Them Fight It Out Alone?"

Artist: Unknown; *Printer:* The Telegram Publishing Co., Holyoke, Massachusetts; *Publisher:* U.S. Army Recruiting; *Technique:* Lithograph; *Dimensions:* 46 x 39 cm.

American recruitment efforts relied not only on the patriotism of its citizens, but also on a process of "voluntary coercion" in which military service was not only a civic duty, but failure to serve lent an aura of disgrace to a man and his family.[1] New York State Library, Manuscripts and Special Collections.

1. Capozzola, pages 21–36.

"Rivets Are Bayonets."

Artist: J.E. Sheridan; *Printer:* Thomsen-Ellis Co., Baltimore, Maryland; *Publisher:* United States Shipping Board;
Technique: Lithograph; *Dimensions:* 96 x 63 cm.

American posters during the war emphasized the important role played by workers on the home front as being equally critical to the war effort as soldiers on the battlefield. By equating industrial production with military service, civic and business leaders sought to tie workers' efforts to the Allied victory. Courtesy of the Library of Congress.

6

"On the Job for Victory"

New York's Contributions on the Home Front

Fighting for democracy is a pretty abstract cause when you get lonesome or homesick but a tangible proof of the backing and sacrifice of the people back home can be appreciated by every soldier whether he appreciates the grandeur of the cause or not.
—Lieutenant Harold W. Mitchell, Sanitary Squad No. 1, Division 41, AEF[1]

Virtually no aspect of life on the home front was unaffected by America's entry into World War I. The conflict transformed the American economy. The United States became a leading creditor nation to the Allied cause. While the United States had maintained its policy of neutrality between 1914 and 1917, several companies in New York had already begun to transition to wartime production to supply the Allied powers with munitions and equipment. When the U.S. finally entered the war in 1917, American industrial production and agricultural output had become critical to the beleaguered Allies. New York joined the nation's industries in a rush to bring the economy to a wartime footing. While the nation was slow to prepare for the war in Europe, many were confident that "she can get ready quicker than any nation on earth, and, in the end, the business ability, inventive genius, energy, and manhood, which have made our country the greatest in industrial achievement can win the greatest war of history."[2] In cities from Buffalo, to Binghamton, to Albany, factories were rapidly adapted to the production of war materiel and, in many instances; new plants were constructed to meet the needs of the war effort.

New York State agricultural production was increased and placed under the supervision of the State Food Supply Commission to respond to the food emergency in Europe and to provide for the men in military service. Programs for food conservation were held throughout the state. Hoarding of food and fuel was banned and some items were rationed.

As men were drafted into military service, so too were workers in New York State conscripted into the war effort. On May 11, 1918, Governor Whitman issued a "Work or Fight" proclamation requiring that all able-bodied men between the ages of eighteen and fifty who were not in military service be employed in an occupation "useful" to the war effort.[3] Men were required to register with the State Industrial Commission and could be assigned jobs if necessary. Law enforcement across New York State was tasked with enforcing these new "anti-loafing" regulations. Between 1918 and 1919, the New York State Police recorded seventy-nine arrests for loafing, with fifty-six convictions in 1918 and four in 1919.[4]

ON THE JOB FOR VICTORY

UNITED STATES SHIPPING BOARD   EMERGENCY FLEET CORPORATION

"On the Job for Victory."

Artist: Jonas Lie; *Printer:* The W.F. Powers Co., New York; *Publisher:* United States Shipping Board, Emergency Fleet Corporation; *Technique:* Lithograph; *Dimensions:* 75 x 98 cm.

The New York State shipbuilding industry witnessed a rapid expansion during World War I as the need for increased shipping to transport vast numbers of troops and massive quantities of materiel to Europe were needed. New York State Museum Collection, H-1975.107.5.

The transport of freight along the state's railroads and canals was taken over by the federal government to facilitate the movement of men and materiel to the ports for transport to Europe.[5] The New York Telephone Company and all telephone and telegraph lines in New York and across the nation were placed under the control of the postmaster general. The New York Port of Embarkation (NYPOE) was established as a distinct Army command to facilitate the transport of troops and war materiel from the Port of New York to overseas service. NYPOE oversaw three transient camps for troops on Long Island to house thousands of soldiers on their way to Europe. The NYPOE was also in command of subports at Boston, Baltimore, and Philadelphia.

Charitable organizations—many headquartered in New York City—had been responding to the humanitarian disaster that was occurring in Europe since the start of the war in 1914. Established organizations, including the American Red Cross, the Salvation Army, the YMCA, and the YWCA, raised money and sent volunteers overseas. Newly established charities were formed to meet the needs created by the war as well. New York's generous response totaled nearly $3 million in 1914 alone.[6] With America's entry into the war, these organizations expanded their services to the care of America's soldiers, sailors, and Marines.

World War I left New York State's economy booming. By the end of the war, more than 38,000 New York companies were employing more than one million workers in wartime industry. Agricultural output had dramatically increased. While the nation dipped into a short economic recession immediately after the war, the effects of the war on the New York economy would not fully end until the start of the Great Depression in October 1929.[7]

As with the recruitment posters for the military, the work of the Division of Pictorial Publicity for the war effort on the home front featured the unifying themes of loyalty, teamwork, and working toward the common good to rally the nation's citizenry to support all facets of the war effort.

> The men who remain to till the soil and man the factories are no less a part of the army that is in France than the men beneath the battle flags.
> —President Woodrow Wilson, Proclamation 1370, May 18, 1917

> The citizenship of a country is worthless unless in a crisis it shows the spirit of the two million Americans who in this mighty war have come forward to serve . . . and of the other millions who would now be beside them overseas if the chance had been given them.
> —Theodore Roosevelt, 1919[8]

The New York Stock Exchange, July 31–November 28, 1914

As the crisis in Europe intensified, the New York Stock Exchange (NYSE) was ordered to close on July 31, 1914, as European investors rushed to liquidate their holdings in the United States markets before war erupted in Europe. As these foreign investors withdrew from the market, prices began to fall and American investors became nervous.[9] The NYSE was already in the midst of a marked decline and many feared a panic on Wall Street as a result of the war in Europe.[10] Such a mass exodus of funds from the American exchanges threatened to push the United States further into economic recession.[11] The NYSE finally reopened on November 28, 1914, though the exchange would not fully return to anything approaching normal levels of trade until April 1915.[12] This four-month hiatus remains the longest period in its history that the NYSE has shut down.

The New York Stock Exchange (1913).

This image of the New York Stock Exchange is from a postcard postmarked 1913. New York State Museum Collection, H-1983.159.573.

The nation's economy was further shaken by a significant rise in inflation during the war years as access to and ability to trade gold on world financial markets was significantly diminished. Fluctuations in the value of gold led to inflation in the United States. The American Federal Reserve was unable to control the impact of the conflict on inflation, which rose over 20 percent between 1914 and American entry into the war in 1917. The gold standard was never able to regain its pre-war levels.[13] By 1933, the United States ceased valuing the dollar against the gold standard.

The measures taken by New York's financial industry and government leaders were deemed necessary to

Run on German bank in New York City.

New Yorkers line up outside a German American bank in Manhattan in early August 1914. Many feared that the outbreak of war in Europe would trigger economic turmoil across the Atlantic and sought to remove their assets from many European-owned institutions. Courtesy of the Library of Congress.

industry was already a leading contributor to the Allied cause with companies such as Remington Arms having been involved in producing munitions for the various armies. The declaration of war in April 1917 brought all of New York State industry into the war effort. In July 1915, the Wilson administration established the Navy Consulting Board, which was tasked with reviewing the state's industries. The board issued a report "on the possibilities of their use in case of war."[18] Savage Arms in Utica began producing machine guns for the U.S. Army. Lackawanna Steel and Curtiss Aeroplane Company in Erie County both received significant government contracts. Bausch and Lomb in Rochester produced optical equipment for the military. Eastman Kodak in Rochester, General Electric in Schenectady, and Alcoa's plant in Massena, St. Lawrence County, also shifted to wartime production. New York State

prevent a "ruinous collapse" of the American economy.[14] By many estimates, these actions staved off the worst effects of the war on the nation's economy.

In addition to the stock market, New York's financial industry provided some of the greatest assistance to the Allied nations prior to American entry into the war. New York banks lent Great Britain and France $2.5 billion. Prior to 1917, the German government also secured several smaller loans in New York City.[15] The New York Exchange reached a new peak in 1916 as investors sought to take advantage of profits being made by American companies selling goods to Europe. This surge continued following America's entry into the war in 1917. As a result of World War I, New York City surpassed London as the world financial capital.[16]

Made in New York

Beginning in 1914, New York industry found itself flooded with orders for war materials from all belligerent nations in Europe. Between August 1914 and April 6, 1917, New York companies had earned approximately $2.5 million in the production of arms, munitions, and other equipment.[17] New York State

War contract analysis blueprint, 1918.

This blueprint, created by the New York State Defense Council's Division of Information, shows nationwide distribution of companies holding contracts for war production. The drawing clearly illustrates New York State as the undisputed leader. By the time of the Armistice in November 1918, 38,000 New York State companies were producing for the war effort. New York State Archives Collection, A4242 78.

Oakley Chemical Company.

African American workers at the Oakley Chemical Company factory in New York City manufacturing artillery shells for the war effort during World War I. Beginning in 1910, thousands of African Americans moved from the South to industrial centers in the North, as well as to the Midwest and Western states in search of better paying jobs and increased opportunity. New York State, as the most industrialized state of the time, was a prime destination for many of these black workers. With the marked reduction in immigration from Europe as a result of the war in 1914, labor shortages in northern industry increased. The Great Migration, as it came to be known, saw a period of acceleration during the war years as wartime jobs in New York factories afforded African Americans roles in the workforce that had before been closed to them.[1] Courtesy of the Library of Congress.

1. Williams, Chad, "African Americans and World War I," *Africana Age: African and American Diasporan Transformations in the 20th Century*, online exhibition (Schomburg Center for Research in Black Culture, New York Public Library), http://exhibitions.nypl.org/africanaage/essay-world-war-i.html, accessed November 14, 2016.

"The Biggest Gun in the War for Democracy."

Artist: Unknown; *Printer:* Unknown; *Publisher:* National Industrial Conservation Movement, New York, New York; *Technique:* Lithograph; *Dimensions:* 63 x 47 cm.

In this poster, Uncle Sam is shown firing a cannon labeled, "American Industry." The gun is shooting supplies and munitions to waiting Allies in Europe. The United States' entry into World War I not only meant an infusion of fresh troops on the battlefield, but the might of the nation's industrial strength being brought into the war effort. New York State Museum Collection, H-1973.5.7 J.

industries manufactured a wide range of goods and materiel for both the American and Allied war efforts between 1914 and 1918.

New York companies became some of the most sophisticated manufacturers of the new mechanized weapons of war—aerial cameras, machine guns, trucks, airplanes, gas masks, gyroscopes for torpedoes, and more. In Rochester alone, more than 100 companies were manufacturing goods for the war effort. In addition to Eastman Kodak and Bausch and Lomb, the city became the "ordnance center for the whole state," manufacturing more than 40,000 Lewis machine guns, 500,000 rifles, 1,300 75mm artillery pieces, as well as munitions and other materiel. By the time of the Armistice, Rochester companies held over $300 million in government military contracts.[19]

The rise in industrial demand coincided with a decrease in available manpower as men were needed for the rapidly expanding armed forces. This labor shortage resulted in increased opportunities for women. By war's end, women would comprise a significant percentage of the state's industrial labor force.

Every man put on French soil increases the need of ships to supply and feed him.
—Lieutenant Basil Beebe Elmer,
December 24, 1917[20]

"Not Just Hats Off to the Flag, But Sleeves Up for It!"

Artist: A.H. Palmer; *Printer:* Alpha Litho. Co., Inc., New York, New York; *Publisher:* U.S. Army Ordnance Department; *Technique:* Lithograph; *Dimensions:* 105 x 69 cm.

As New York State's industry mobilized for the World War, the need for skilled labor was nearly as great as the Army's need for soldiers. Skilled machinists and other laborers could be deemed exempt from the draft if their work was critical to the war effort. The need for factory labor also opened up new employment opportunities for women. New York State Library, Manuscripts and Special Collections.

REMINGTON ARMS COMPANY
ILION, HERKIMER COUNTY

When war erupted in August 1914 in Europe, Remington Arms Company was flourishing as a manufacturer of civilian sporting rifles. Save for a few government contracts for ammunition, the company did not manufacture military firearms. As the need for weapons by

"Go Over the Top with the Tank That Will Win the War!" (1918).

Artist: Phifer; *Printer:* Unknown; *Publisher:* National Association of Manufacturers, New York, New York; *Technique:* Lithograph; *Dimensions:* 63 x 47 cm.

American industrial might is again the focus of this poster illustration. In this depiction, American industry is rolling over "Disloyalty," suggesting that labor strife and discord were being overcome through patriotic effort. New York State Museum Collection, H-1977.146.2.

the Allied powers rose, Britain, France, and Russia all turned to Remington. Production rose dramatically in Ilion, leading to a massive expansion of the company's factory there. Employment rose from 1,200 in 1914 to 15,000 in 1917.[21] Demand quickly exceeded capacity and the company constructed new plants in Bridgeport, Connecticut, and a cartridge factory in Hoboken, New Jersey.

With America's entry into the war, Remington was virtually the only American manufacturer with the capacity to arm the rapidly growing American Army. By the end of the war, the company had manufactured nearly 70 percent of all the rifles used by the AEF and over 50 percent of the small-arms ammunition used by the United States and its allies.[22]

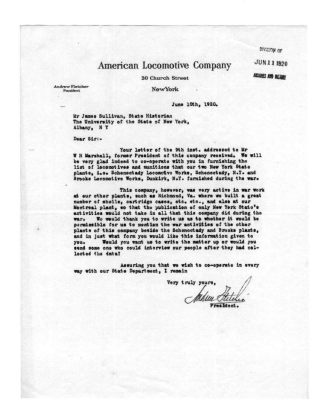

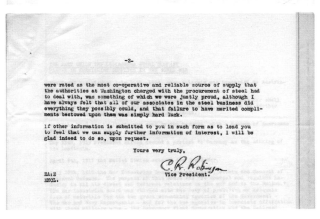

Sampling of Letters: American Locomotive Company (Schenectady County), Lackawanna Steel Company (Erie County), National Biscuit Company (New York County), and Welch Grape Juice Company (Chautauqua County).

In 1919, New York State Historian Dr. James Sullivan was tasked with compiling a history of New York in the World War. Though the work was never completed, these correspondence from industries across New York State document their contributions to the war effort. New York State Archives, A3166-78.

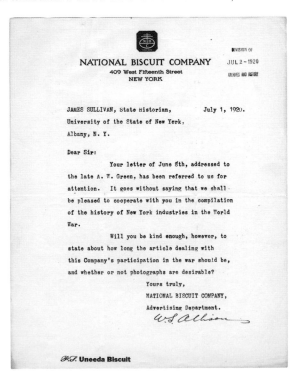

Collapsible bucket, Abercrombie and Fitch Co. (Manhattan, New York County).

This bucket was manufactured by the Abercrombie and Fitch Company for use by the United States Army. It was used during World War I by Major George Corby of Company L, 161st Infantry Regiment. The company was originally founded in 1892 as an outfitter of hunting and sporting goods, though today it is primarily known for its clothing lines. New York State Museum Collection, H-1972.76.60.

Mirror, Defiance C-W Corporation (Rochester, Monroe County).

This mirror was made from polished steel and was marketed as "unbreakable." The packaging contains instructions for mailing the mirror to soldiers serving in the AEF. New York State Museum Collection, H-1972.76.131.

World War I War Service shipbuilding badge.

This shipbuilder's badge, number 37106, was issued at the Bethlehem Shipyard on Staten Island during World War I. New York State Museum Collection, H-1991.59.10.

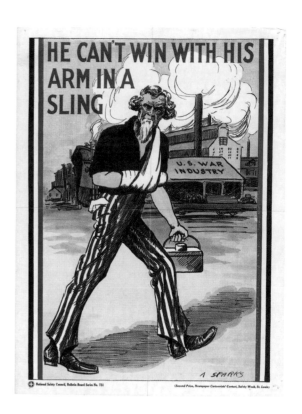

"He Can't Win with His Arm in a Sling."

Artist: A. Sparks; *Printer:* Unknown; *Publisher:* National Safety Council; *Technique:* Lithograph; *Dimensions:* 56 x 40.75 cm.

The call to arms strained the nation's labor reserves. As more men entered military service, the strain on industry was dramatic. The United States undertook campaigns to emphasize the need for safety in the work place as a means to conserve productive labor. New York State Museum Collection, H-1992.19.71.

"Think Safety!"

Courtesy of the Rochester Historical Society.

EAST MAIN STREET, SHOWING REMINGTON ARMS & AMMUNITION COMPANY, ILION, N. Y.

Workers at Remington Arms.

World War I–era postcard image of workers at the bustling Remington Arms factory. The factory operated around the clock in order to keep up with production needs. New York State Museum Collection, H-1980.50.3.

Plant of Remington Arms & Ammunition Co., Ilion, N. Y.

Remington Arms Company, ca. 1917.

New York State Museum Collection, H-1980.50.4.

Imperial Russian Mosin-Nagant rifle, 1917.

In 1915, the Imperial Russian government contracted with Remington Arms for one million Mosin-Nagant rifles and one hundred million rounds of ammunition. This rifle bears the royal crest of Tsar Nicholas II, and the Remington Arms manufacturer's stamp.

In 1917, revolution swept across Russia. The Tsar was deposed and eventually executed by Bolshevik revolutionaries as civil war erupted. With nobody to take delivery of the contracted rifles, Remington faced financial catastrophe until the American government purchased 600,000 of these rifles. Some were used to train American soldiers before embarkation to France. The U.S. government also equipped American forces being sent to Russia in 1918 and to equip the White Russian Army at Vladivostok to combat the Bolsheviks.[1] New York State Museum Collection, H- 1975.163.1.

1. Hatch, 224.

By the mid-1880s, the U.S. government had established Watervliet Arsenal as the sole manufacturing facility for large cannon for both the Army and Navy. Production at the arsenal was slow to increase in the years leading up to the war, and in fact, decreased in 1916—a sign of the country's lack of preparation for war.

In addition to continued production of cannons for the Army and Navy, the Watervliet Arsenal undertook experimentation to develop a "balloon gun" in 1916 and 1917. This weapon was an early version of anti-aircraft artillery intended to defend the United States against potential airborne attacks from German zeppelins or airplanes.[23] The Arsenal was also tasked with establishing a Cannon Relining School to train soldiers in the Army's ordnance department how to repair and refit artillery at ordnance depots in France. Coursework alternated between classroom lessons and hands-on experience in the factories at the Arsenal. The first unit of 123 men arrived with the American Expeditionary Forces in May 1918 and the second in September.[24]

During World War I, the Arsenal constructed numerous large-bore cannons for coastal defense and naval warships as well as smaller cannons to be used by American field artillery. In 1918 alone, Watervliet manufactured 465 cannons.[25]

"The American Enfield," U.S. Army rifle, model 1917.

The U.S. Army in 1917 had approximately 700,000 Model 1903 Springfield Rifles in all of its arsenals. The planned expansion of the Army called for 4 million men to be trained, equipped, and sent to Europe. No manufacturer could meet this demand. Remington, however, suggested modifying the British Enfield rifles the company was manufacturing to accommodate the .30 caliber American ammunition. The bore of the rifle's barrel was increased slightly and the length of the magazine was increased to accommodate the slightly longer American cartridges.[1] The "American Enfield" was adopted by the U.S. Army as the U.S. Rifle, Model 1917. By December of that year, Ilion was producing 3,000 of the M1917 rifles each day.[2] The majority of American soldiers in the AEF were ultimately issued the Model 1917 rifle.[3] New York State Museum Collection, H-1971.78.1.

1. Shields, Joseph W., Jr., *From Flintlock to M1* (New York: Coward-McCann, Inc., 1954), page 161.

2. Hatch, 224.

3. Shields, page 165.

Edward Buyck (1888–1960).

Edward Buyck was born in Bruges, Belgium. As a young student, he studied at the Royal Academies in both Bruges and Antwerp, Belgium, and finally at the École des Beaux Arts in Paris. When the German Army invaded Belgium in 1914, Buyck sent his family to safety in England while he joined the Belgian Army. He was wounded and discharged from military service. After rejoining his family in England, Buyck immigrated to the United States and eventually arrived in Albany. When the United States entered the war in 1917, Buyck put his artistic talents to use for the war effort, creating several posters in the Capital Region. After the war, Buyck married Mary Willard Vine and settled in Slingerlands, Albany County. During the 1930s, Edward Buyck continued as an active artist in New York's Capital Region.

"Brain and Brawn."

Artist: Edward Buyck; *Printer:* Burleigh Litho. Co., Troy, New York; *Publisher:* U.S. Army Ordnance Department, Watervliet Arsenal; *Technique:* Lithograph; *Dimensions:* 94.5 x 62 cm.

This poster was printed to recruit workers for the Watervliet Arsenal. Recruitment and retention of skilled laborers became a serious problem at the arsenal. As a federal facility, Watervliet's wages were significantly lower than private munitions companies working on government contracts. This made it very difficult for the Arsenal to recruit and retain skilled laborers. By July 1918, the rate of turnover at the Watervliet Arsenal was over 60 percent and the average worker stayed less than two months.[1] New York State Museum Collection, H–1975.85.6.

1. Swantek, page 158.

Dutch Coppersmith.

Artist: Edward C. Buyck; *Technique:* Oil on canvas; *Date:* 1932
New York State Museum Collection, H-1972.101.1.

It ain't the individual or the army
as a whole,
BUT the everlastin' TEAM WORK
of every bloomin' soul.

Kipling

"Learn to Make and Test the Big Guns."

Artist: Charles Buckles Falls; *Printer:* Engineer Reproduction Plant, Washington, DC; *Publisher:* U.S. Army Recruiting; *Technique:* Lithograph; *Dimensions:* 48.5 x 63 cm.

A U.S. Army recruiting poster for the Ordnance Department. Mechanics and skilled laborers were desperately needed by Watervliet Arsenal and other units of the Army Ordnance Department in order to manufacture and maintain artillery and equipment in France. New York State Library, Manuscripts and Special Collections.

"Team Work."

Artist: Edward Buyck; *Printer:* Burleigh Litho. Co., Troy, New York; *Publisher:* U.S. Army Ordnance Department, Watervliet Arsenal; *Technique:* Lithograph; *Dimensions:* 88.5 x 61 cm.

This poster depicts factory workers manufacturing a cannon in the foreground and soldiers using a cannon in the background. In 1887, Watervliet Arsenal became the nation's only manufacturing facility for large-bore artillery for both the United States Army and Navy. The Arsenal is often referred to as "America's Cannon Factory" so the visual reference would be instantly recognizable to viewers in New York's Capital Region. New York State Museum Collection, H-1968.52.6.

SAVAGE ARMS COMPANY
UTICA, ONEIDA COUNTY

The Savage Arms Company was founded in Utica in 1895 by Arthur W. Savage. The company primarily manufactured a line of sporting rifles for the first two decades of its existence. Savage Arms supplied more than 70,000 Lewis machine guns to the British Army at the beginning of the war.[26] Upon America's entry into the conflict, the company was contracted to manufacture Lewis machine guns for the U.S.

Army.[27] As with Remington Arms and other firearms manufacturers, Savage needed to manufacture the Lewis guns with minor modifications to enable the weapon to fire American 30-06 cartridges rather than the British .303 caliber. During the war, the company grossed almost $25 million for the manufacture of the Lewis machine gun, employing thousands of workers in Oneida County.[28]

EASTMAN KODAK COMPANY
ROCHESTER, MONROE COUNTY

The Eastman Kodak Company was heavily involved in wartime contracts with the U.S. Army and Navy during World War I. The company began developing aerial cameras for use in airplanes in 1915. By 1916, Kodak was testing two models with the Navy.[29] In October 1917, Eastman Kodak introduced the K-1, the first U.S. military aerial camera. In addition to manufacturing cameras and film for the Army Signal Corps and Airplanes, Eastman Kodak assisted in experimentation with camouflaging ships and improving periscopes, and in the development of nonflammable paints and varnishes.[30]

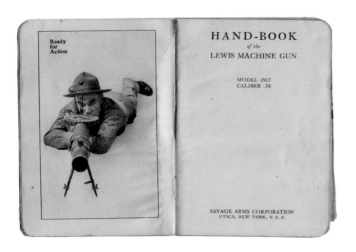

Savage Arms Company.

This image featuring an American soldier firing a Lewis machine gun was produced by the Savage Arms Company of Utica, and published in its handbook for the Lewis machine gun. During the war, the company's Utica factory manufactured Lewis machine guns for the American Army.[1] Courtesy of the Oneida County Historical Society.

1. Swinney, page 1443.

Magazine advertisement.

This advertisement for the Savage Arms Corporation highlights the fact that the company was producing the Lewis machine gun for use by the armed forces of seventeen Allied nations as well as the U.S. Army. By its own estimate, the company had produced 100,000 for use during World War I. Courtesy of the Oneida County Historical Society.

Mounted camera.

A member of the U.S. Army Air Service is featured in this photograph with an aerial camera mounted to the side of his training aircraft. Courtesy of Harry S. Truman Library and Museum.

The U.S. Army School of Aerial Photography

In late 1917, Eastman Kodak president George Eastman volunteered to set up a school of aerial photography in Rochester to train airmen in the method of taking aerial photographs, developing film, and interpreting the imagery. The U.S. Army School of Aerial Photography opened at Kodak Park in March 1918 and offered courses on aerial photography and camera repair. Between March and December 1918, the school graduated 1,995 students from its photography class and an additional 182 trained in camera repair. Given the importance of aerial photography in the planning of military operations during World War I, many consider the school to be one of the most important wartime activities in the city of Rochester.[31]

F and S Aero Camera Model A-1. Folmer and Schwing Division of Eastman Kodak Company, Gift of W. W. Rogers.

The F and S Model A-1 camera was used by the U.S. Army and Navy Air Service during World War I. A handheld plate camera, it could be fitted with the Graflex Magazine holder with twelve exposures. The Hawk-Eye Aero lens that it came with was one of the first photographic lenses manufactured by Eastman Kodak Company. Courtesy of the George Eastman Museum.

Eastman Kodak letter.

This letter from Eastman Kodak Company to New York State Historian James Sullivan was in response to his efforts to compile information on New York State industry during World War I and briefly describes the company's efforts during the conflict. New York State Archives Collection, A3166-78.

DIVISION OF
JUN 12 1920
ARCHIVES AND HISTORY

EASTMAN KODAK COMPANY
ROCHESTER, N.Y.
June 10, 1920.

Mr. James Sullivan,
University of the State of New York,
Albany, N. Y.

My dear Sir:

Mr. Eastman has handed me your letter of June 9th, and I wish to say that we will be very glad indeed to co-operate with you so far as possible.

Our manufacturing work here connected with the war consisted of furnishing the non-inflammable varnish used on airplane wings, photographic goods for general use, aerial cameras for use by observers, lenses for gun-sights and an attachment for the Lewis Gun, whereby men in the aviation schools fought each other by taking photographs of each other instead of with bullets. In addition our Research Department was very active in the matter of assisting in camouflage for ships and in the experimental work in connection with colloidal fuel.

We don't know how much of a "story" you want, but if you will let us know about this, and also let us know whether or not it would be interesting for you to have any photographs of our aerial cameras and of the Lewis Machine Gun attachment, we will undertake to get out something that will be satisfactory to you.

Yours very truly,

Advertising Manager

PLEASE ADDRESS REPLY TO ADVERTISING DEPARTMENT.

Pierce-Arrow army trucks at Broadway Auditorium assembled for trip to New York.

This photograph features trucks manufactured by the Pierce-Arrow Motor Car Company during World War I. The company became one of the largest manufacturers of trucks for the army during the war with production surpassing the manufacture of passenger cars. Pierce-Arrow not only manufactured 2- and 5-ton trucks for the American Army, but also for the allied British and French governments.[1] From Daniel J. Sweeney's *The History of Buffalo and Erie County in the World War, 1914–1919* (City of Buffalo: Committee of the One Hundred, 1919), page 66.

1. "The War Years," The Pierce-Arrow Society (www.pierce-arrow.org/history/history3.php), accessed April 5, 2016.

PIERCE-ARROW MOTOR CAR COMPANY
BUFFALO, ERIE COUNTY

The George N. Pierce Company was established in the 1870s and quickly became a noted manufacturer of bicycles. In 1901, the company produced its first automobile, for demonstration at the Pan-American Exposition in Buffalo. In 1908, the company became the Pierce-Arrow Motor Car Company and specialized in the manufacture of luxury automobiles. With America's entry into World War I, Pierce-Arrow— like many industries in New York and across the nation—retooled for the war effort. The company shifted from luxury car production to the manufacture of trucks for use by the U.S. military. During the war, Pierce-Arrow employed nearly 10,000 men and women.[32]

ALUMINUM COMPANY OF AMERICA (ALCOA)
MASSENA, ST. LAWRENCE COUNTY

Chemists first discovered how to extract aluminum ore in 1825, but it was not until 1889 that a cost-effective method for doing so was finally developed. Soon thereafter, aluminum production in Europe and the United States exploded. Because of its utility, aluminum was used in the manufacture of a wide range of goods prior to World War I, including power transmission lines, electrical wiring, internal combustion engines, and the emerging airplane industry.[33] Alcoa, headquartered in New York City, opened its plant in Massena, St. Lawrence County, in 1903. The company was the only manufacturer of pig aluminum in the United States in 1914. As a result, Alcoa was called on to produce enough aluminum for

Aluminum cable.

Alcoa's factory in Massena became the leading source for aluminum wire and cable used by the United States and Allied navies during the war.[1] New York State Museum Collection, H-2015.36.2.

1. McCombs, page 61.

Meat can and canteen, 1918.

This meat can and canteen was produced from aluminum processed by Alcoa at the company's Massena plant. During World War I, the U.S. Quartermaster Corps contracted for canteens and meat cans to be manufactured by five companies, including Alcoa. These canteens were manufactured using the specifications that Rock Island Arsenal developed in 1914.[1] New York State Museum Collection, H-2015.36.1 A-C and H-2015.36.3 A-C.

1. "World War I Field and Mess Equipment," U.S. Army Center for Military History, http://www.history.army.mil/html/museums/messkits/Field_Mess_Gear(upd_Jul09).pdf, accessed May 17, 2016.

the United States and the Allies between 1914 and 1918.[34] In addition, Alcoa produced a wide variety of finished aluminum products. Because Alcoa had a virtual monopoly on the aluminum industry, the company's president, Arthur Davis, worked directly with the War Industries Board (WIB) to set the price of aluminum throughout the war years.[35] This emerging government-private cooperation of Alcoa and other New York companies with the WIB again highlights the degree to which government expansion and oversight occurred during the war.

When war broke out, the company shifted to the production of military equipment. With aluminum imports from Europe suspended, Alcoa saw rapid growth from 1915 to 1918, though profits were restricted by tight governmental price controls. Alcoa's nationwide production of aluminum increased from 109 million pounds in 1915 to 152 million in 1917.[36] By the time the United States entered the war, 90 percent of Alcoa's manufacturing was for military equipment, including mess kits, dog tags, vehicle parts, and aluminum powder for high explosives.[37] The company also became the leading manufacturer of dirigible airships for the Navy.[38] Despite the company's best efforts, demand from the Allied armies began to outpace production. At Massena, Alcoa worked with both the American and Canadian governments to ensure uniform water supply from the St. Lawrence River to increase the plant's production capacity in 1918.[39]

GENERAL ELECTRIC
SCHENECTADY, SCHENECTADY COUNTY

The General Electric Company in Schenectady was heavily involved in the war effort in the production of searchlights, turbines, motors, airplane compasses, radio tubes, and many other items.[40] Among the most important work being done at GE was work on a device to help detect German U-boats.

Taffrail log, ca. 1918.

This instrument was used to determine a vessel's speed and distance traveled. "Taffrail" refers to the railing at the stern of the ship where the log was mounted when it was in use. Taffrail logs, such as these, were used by the U.S. Navy throughout the war. New York State Museum Collection Accession, H-1975.139.5 A-E.

GE alternator.

As the first corporate research laboratory in the nation, the company's facilities in Schenectady were already heavily involved in electronic and radio research and manufacturing when war was declared. In 1918, General Electric unveiled an alternator that helped enable leaders in Washington, DC, to communicate with the Allies and the American Expeditionary Forces in France. Courtesy of the Library of Congress.

A Curtiss JN training plane in flight.

The Curtiss-built "Jenny" was the most common training aircraft for the fledgling U.S. Army Air Service. From the New York Public Library.

CURTISS SCHOOL *of* AVIATION

Buffalo, N. Y.   Hammondsport, N. Y.
Newport News, Va.   Miami, Fla.   San Diego, Cal.
Under Aviation Section, United States Army, Supervision

CURTISS AEROPLANE AND MOTOR COMPANY
BUFFALO, ERIE COUNTY,
AND HAMMONDSPORT, STEUBEN COUNTY

The Curtiss Aeroplane Company was established in 1916 in Hammondsport. With the outbreak of World War I, orders for Curtiss aircraft increased dramatically. The company headquarters relocated to Buffalo. During the war, Curtiss became the nation's largest aircraft manufacturer. The company employed 18,000 workers in Buffalo and 3,000 in Hammondsport. Curtiss Aeroplane and Motor Company manufactured 10,000 airplanes during the World War.

"Curtiss School of Aviation" (1917).

Artist: E.W. Pirson; *Printer:* Unknown; *Publisher:* Curtiss Aeroplane Company, Buffalo, NY; *Technique:* Lithograph; *Dimensions:* 97 x 65 cm.

Recruitment poster for the Curtiss School of Aviation. Company founder Glenn Curtiss initially opened the flying school in 1915 and established schools across the United States and in Toronto, Canada. The schools instructed many pilots who went on to become military pilots during World War I. When the United States entered the war in 1917, the U.S. Army took over operations of the school to train pilots for the Army Air Service. New York State Library, Manuscripts and Special Collections.

Curtiss Aero and Motor Corporation training school.

Female employees of the Curtiss Aeroplane and Motor Corporation assemble aircraft wing floats. Courtesy of the U.S. Naval History and Heritage Command.

LOWE, WILLARD AND FOWLER
ENGINEERING COMPANY
COLLEGE POINT, QUEENS COUNTY

Lowe, Willard and Fowler was an aircraft engineering firm founded at College Point in Queens County in 1915. During World War I, the company was contracted to manufacture the Curtiss HS-2L flying patrol boat, the Martin NBS-1 bomber, and the Douglass DT-2 torpedo plane. By 1924, however, the company had declared bankruptcy. Despite its short lifespan, the company made significant contributions to the American war effort.

"Men Wanted To Build Aeroplanes" (1917).

Artist: E.W. Pirson; *Printer:* Unknown; *Publisher:* Curtiss Aeroplane Company, Buffalo, NY; *Technique:* Lithograph; *Dimensions:* 62 x 49 cm.

Recruitment poster for the Curtiss Aeroplane Company's Buffalo factory. As military contracts for aircraft rapidly increased, the need for skilled labor became critical. New York State Library, Manuscripts and Special Collections.

Tacking wings.

A worker at Lowe, Willard and Fowler tacks fabric to the frame of an airplane's wing. Courtesy of the Library of Congress.

Lowe, Willard and Fowler Factory.

Airplanes under construction at Lowe, Willard and Fowler's College Point factory. Courtesy of the Library of Congress.

Plane veneer.

Workers apply veneer to a plane's fuselage. Courtesy of the Library of Congress.

Bausch and Lomb
Rochester, Monroe County

By 1914, technology in warfare had advanced to such a degree that armies and navies around the world relied on optical equipment to increase the range capabilities of their military forces. Periscopes, binoculars, aerial cameras, searchlights, gun sights, and a myriad of other pieces of equipment required the use of specialized optical lenses.[41] Until the outbreak of war in 1914, the United States military relied on optical glass manufactured in Europe, especially Germany. Rochester's Bausch and Lomb Optical Company had begun production of optical glass in 1912 and by 1917 was the only manufacturer producing lenses sufficient for the needs of the military. The company manufactured virtually every range finder used by the U.S. Army and Navy during the war and by November 1918 was producing 3,500 binoculars each week.[42]

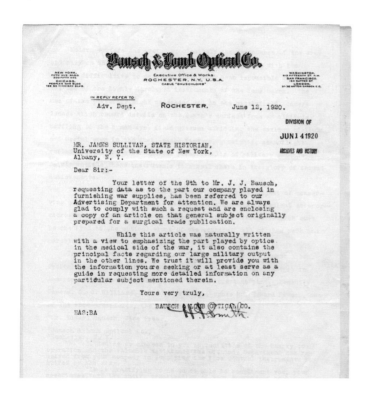

Letter, H. Smith to James Sullivan, State Historian, June 12, 1920.

The letter was sent to New York State Historian James Sullivan from Bausch and Lomb Optical Company along with an article on the company's involvement in the war effort. Bausch and Lomb produced nearly 70 percent of all the optical glass used by the American military in gun sights, periscopes, binoculars, and telescopes during World War I. In 1917, the company produced 40,000 pounds of glass for the war effort.[1] New York State Archives, A3166-78.

1. Flick, page 349.

"Will You Supply Eyes for the Navy?"

Artist: Gordon Grant; *Printer:* Sacketts and Wilhelms Corp., New York, New York; *Publisher:* U.S. Navy; *Technique:* Lithograph; *Dimensions:* 72 x 51 cm.

This World War I poster called for donations of binoculars for the U.S. Navy to help combat the U-boat threat. Prior to the war, the United States imported the majority of lenses used in binoculars and other optical devices. Despite the best efforts of manufacturers such as Bausch and Lomb in Rochester, American factories could not produce lenses in the quantity needed to supply binoculars to the hundreds of ships being placed into service during the war.[1] The call was issued by then-Assistant Secretary of the Navy and future New York State Governor Franklin Delano Roosevelt. In Rochester, Roosevelt recruited George Eastman, president of the Eastman Kodak Company to coordinate the government's request for binoculars, telescopes, spy glasses, and other navigational equipment.[2] New York State Library, Manuscripts and Special Collections.

1. New York State Council of Defense Records, Administrative and Correspondence Files, 1917–1918, New York State Archives Series A4242.

2. Finding Aid, Eastman House Museum Archives, 1981:1702.

Endicott-Johnson's National Guardsmen.

This 1916 photograph of Endicott-Johnson employees, who were part of the New York National Guard's 1st Artillery Regiment, was likely taken before the men deployed to the Mexican border in 1916. Courtesy of the Special Collections, Preservation, and University Archives, State University of New York at Binghamton.

ENDICOTT-JOHNSON COMPANY
BINGHAMTON, BROOME COUNTY

The Endicott-Johnson Corporation was originally formed in 1854 as the Lester Brothers Boot and Shoe Company. In 1890, it was purchased by the founder of the Endicott Shoe Company of Dedham, Massachusetts, Henry Bradford Endicott, who partnered with the Binghamton-born factory foreman, George F. Johnson.[43] During World War I, the company manufactured the vast majority of boots for the U.S. Army. At its peak shortly after the war, Endicott-Johnson employed nearly 20,000 people.[44]

NEW YORK'S MEATPACKING INDUSTRY

The meatpacking industry in New York State was spurred by the proliferation of railroads in the state in the nineteenth century. Many of the largest plants were centered in New York City, and in cities across the western part of the state.[45] During World War I, many of New York's meatpacking plants were contracted to process and can meats for use by American troops in the United States and in the AEF[46]

The process of canning foods was invented in the late-eighteenth century and gained popularity during the nineteenth century. Canning became the preferred method for preserving foods because it allowed food to be preserved with minimal loss of nutritional value.[47] The process was popular for military purposes because it increased the portability of foodstuffs badly needed by soldiers in the front lines.

Box, ca. 1920, Jacob Dold Packing Co., Buffalo, Erie County.

This wooden box from the Jacob Dold Packing Company in Buffalo was used to distribute canned meats from the factory. Boxes similar to this would have been used for shipment to soldiers in the AEF. New York State Museum Collection, H-1992.24.1.

1915 photograph of the Tobin Meatpacking Company factory in Rochester, Monroe County.

New York State Museum Collection, H-2010.19.2.8.

Trimming meat at the Dold Packing Plant, Buffalo, New York, 1917.

The American war effort during World War I did not solely involve large corporations such as Remington Arms or Eastman Kodak, but included small business contractors such as Dold. Across New York State companies of all sizes produced goods for the U.S. Army. New York State Archives, A3045-78.

"Back our girls over there."

Artist: Clarence F. Underwood; *Printer:* Unknown; *Publisher:* YWCA; *Technique:* Lithograph; *Dimensions:* 71.25 x 53.5 cm.

YWCA poster for the United War Work Campaign, 1918. This advertising encouraged women to enter the work force to support the war effort. New York State Museum Collection, H-1975.85.1.

Women in the Workforce

According to former New York State Historian Alexander Flick, "The part played by New York girls and women in winning the World War was more pronounced than has commonly been recognized. In addition to their services as war nurses, many of them performed helpful tasks through the YWCA, the Salvation Army, and other agencies. . . . They worked on the farms . . . and in the factories and mills."[48] The dual forces of fewer men in the workforce and the need for increased production for the war effort gave women unprecedented opportunities in jobs that had traditionally been closed to them. While World War I did not bring a dramatic rise in the number of women in the labor force, the conflict did result in a shift of women into industrial production. Women made up approximately 14 percent of workers in wartime industries in New York State.[49] By 1920, that percentage had increased to 25.2 percent.[50] Women were also afforded greater opportunities in white-collar positions such as office clerks, stenographers, and bookkeepers. This increase was offset by decreases in women working in more traditional occupations such as seamstress and housekeeper. Groups such as the Young Women's Christian Association (YWCA) raised money and helped to recruit workers to the war effort.

"For Every Fighter a Woman Worker."

Artist: Adolph Treidler; *Printer:* Unknown; *Publisher:* YWCA; *Technique:* Lithograph; *Dimensions:* 76 x 50.75 cm.

This iconic poster from the war illustrates the new role played by women in traditionally male-dominated industries. New York State Museum Collection, H-1973.94.1 Z.

Female worker at Watervliet Arsenal.

This 1917–1918 photograph features a woman worker driving an electrical cart at the U.S. Army's Watervliet Arsenal. Courtesy of the Library of Congress.

Adolph Treidler (1886–1981).

Born in Westcliff, Colorado, Adolph Treidler moved to New York City to study under artist Robert Henri after graduating the California School of Design in San Francisco. Beginning in 1908, Treidler illustrated for *McClure's*, *Harper's*, and *Collier's* magazines, and the *Saturday Evening Post*, among others. During the war, he created posters for Liberty Bonds and military recruitment. Many of his posters featured American women in industry. After the war, Adolph Treidler worked on marketing campaigns for Buffalo's Pierce-Arrow Motor Car Company.

Magazine advertisement, Pierce-Arrow Motor Car Company.

This magazine ad for the Pierce-Arrow Motor Car Company was designed by Adolph Treidler. New York State Museum Collection, H-1979.73.15.

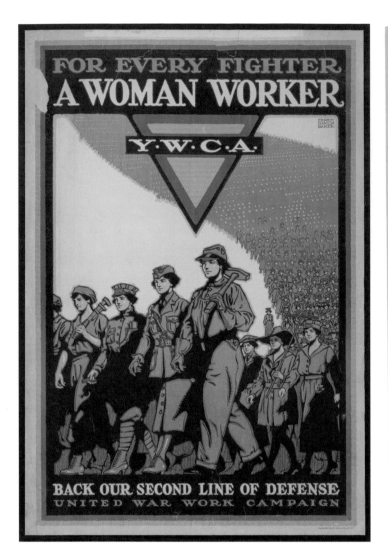

"For Every Fighter a Woman Worker."

Artist: Ernest Hamlin Baker; *Printer:* United States Printing and Litho. Co.;
Publisher: Young Women's Christian Association; *Technique:* Lithograph;
Dimensions: 105 x 69 cm.

Organizations like the Young Women's Christian Association sought to improve
the conditions of and care for the young women answering the nation's call
during the war as well as the soldiers. The YWCA raised funds towards these
efforts. New York State Library, Manuscripts and Special Collections.

"Every Girl Pulling for Victory."

Artist: Edward Penfield; *Printer:* Unknown; *Publisher:* United War Work
Campaign; *Technique:* Lithograph; *Dimensions:* 71.25 x 56 cm.

Under the direction of the DPP, poster artists emphasized the need to have all
of American society working towards the war effort. The important role played
by women was a common theme in many World War I posters. New York State
Museum Collection, H-1973.94.1 I.

"Stenographers! Washington needs you!"

Artist: Roy Hull Still; *Printer:* Prudential Litho. Co, New York; *Publisher:* U.S. Employment Office; *Technique:* Lithograph; *Dimensions:* 76.25 x 52 cm.

The war effort opened increased opportunities for women to work in office and clerical positions, such as stenographers, but also in roles and positions traditionally dominated by men. New York State Museum Collection, H-1976.147.9.

"Stenographers Wanted."

Artist: None; *Printer:* Unknown; *Publisher:* Gun Division of the Ordnance Department; *Technique:* Lithograph; *Dimensions:* 62.5 x 48 cm.

The war brought unprecedented employment opportunities for women. Wartime jobs also frequently paid these female workers more money than their pre-war counterparts. New York State Library, Manuscripts and Special Collections.

Frances Johanna Raetz.

Courtesy of the Rochester Historical Society.

Frances Johanna Raetz

Frances Johanna Raetz was born and raised in Rochester, New York. She attended Public School Number 18 and graduated from Public School Number 13. She was a member of St. Thomas's Episcopal Church in Rochester and was a teacher in the Sunday school. Raetz was employed by the Bell Telephone Company in Rochester for six years. During the war, Raetz entered government service as a clerk and typist and was sent to Washington, DC, on September 22, 1918. She was there only two weeks when she contracted influenza. Frances Raetz died of pneumonia on October 5, 1918, in Washington. She was buried in Mt. Hope Cemetery, Rochester, on October 10, 1918.

"Stand Behind the Country's Girlhood."

Artist: W.T. Benda; *Printer:* Unknown; *Publisher:* YWCA; *Technique:* Lithograph; *Dimensions:* 75 x 50 cm.

With women increasingly asked to assume male jobs in factories across New York State and the nation, new challenges and concerns emerged. In Ilion, New York, whose pre-war population was soon dwarfed by the influx of workers to the Remington Arms Company, a large proportion of these new workers were young women from farms across central New York State. At Ilion, the YWCA opened and operated a recreation hall to provide entertainment and recreational opportunities for these women. While organizations like the YWCA sought to provide recreational opportunities for women in newly emerging factory jobs, their efforts were motivated in part by fears that the new freedoms and mobility afforded to women during wartime might also lead to increases in premarital sex and even prostitution. New York State Library, Manuscripts and Special Collections.

"For Girls Must Work That Men May Fight."

Artist: M.B.; *Printer:* Unknown; *Publisher:* Young Women's Christian Association; *Technique:* Lithograph; *Dimensions:* 77 x 56 cm.

This YWCA poster encourages women to volunteer for the war effort in order to free up men to enter military service. A female in nurse's uniform is pictured within the blue triangle of the YWCA. New York State Museum Collection, H-1973.94.1 H.

"We Are Ready to Work Beside You."

Artist: Unknown; *Printer:* Unknown; *Publisher:* Unknown; *Technique:* Lithograph; *Dimensions:* 103.5 x 73 cm.

The contributions of women to the war effort in industry and agriculture, as nurses, and in the innumerable charitable campaigns led by women, resulted in increased support for the suffrage movement in the United States. This contributed to both the passage of woman's suffrage in New York State in 1917, and to the passage of the 19th Amendment to the Constitution in 1920.[1] Following the war, New York Governor Al Smith called upon the New York State Legislature to ratify the Nineteenth Amendment, arguing that women had earned the right to vote as a result of "their heroic conduct in the great crisis through which we have so recently passed."[2] New York State Library, Manuscripts and Special Collections.

1. Ellis, pages 391–392.

2. Sullivan, Volume V, page 1821.

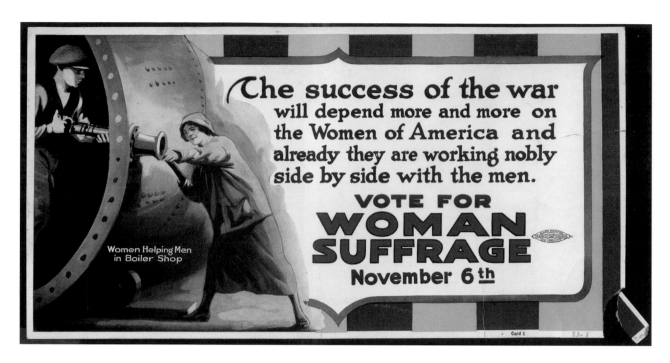

Women Helping Men in Boiler Shop

The success of the war will depend more and more on the Women of America and already they are working nobly side by side with the men.

VOTE FOR WOMAN SUFFRAGE November 6th

"The Success of the war will depend more and more on the Women of America."

Artist: Unknown; *Printer:* Unknown; *Publisher:* Unkown; *Technique:* Lithograph; *Dimensions:* 28 x 53.5 cm.

In his speech before Congress on April 2, 1917, President Wilson proclaimed that the United States was entering the World War, " . . . to fight thus for the ultimate peace of the world and for the liberation of its peoples, the German peoples included: for the rights of nations great and small and the privilege of men everywhere to choose their way of life and of obedience. The world must be made safe for democracy. Its peace must be planted upon the tested foundations of political liberty."[1] It was this rationale that was seized upon by woman suffragists, African American leaders, and other disenfranchised groups in their struggles for equal rights after 1917. In New York State, the suffrage movement received a tremendous boost when voters approved woman's suffrage in November 1917. As one of the largest states in the nation, the success of the movement in New York provided crucial momentum for the push nationwide.[2] New York State Library, Manuscripts and Special Collections.

1. Wilson, Woodrow. Joint Address to Congress Leading to a Declaration of War Against Germany, April 2, 1917, National Archives Collections (http://www.archives.gov/historical-docs/todays-doc/?dod-date=402).

2. Capozzola, pages 106–107.

ENROLLING FOR WAR AT SUFFRAGE HDQ'RS

Woman Suffrage Party.

Female suffragists posed for this 1917 photograph at the Woman Suffrage Party headquarters in New York City. The leaders of the organization had gathered to symbolically enlist the movement in the United States's war effort. The suffragists highlighted the critical role played by women in factories and on farms as a significant justification for amending the state constitution to give women the right to vote in New York in November 1917. While many within the Suffragist Movement supported the war effort, not all did. World War I became one of several issues to divide suffragists in New York and across the nation.[1] The war also became a rallying point for the anti-suffrage movement as the slogan "Bullets, not ballots" advocated the need for women to lay aside their quest for suffrage in order to "just be women backing up the men in every phase of fighting the war."[2] Courtesy of the Library of Congress.

1. Chatfield, page 1922–1923.

2. Capozzola, page 106.

"Food Will Win the War":
Agricultural Production and Conservation

After three years of war, food supplies were desperately short in Europe. American production was called on to feed the Allied nations. American farm production was critical not only to American and Allied troops overseas, but to the civilian populations in Europe. By the time war was declared, the United States already supplied 90 percent of the wheat consumed in Great Britain. A poor wheat crop in 1915–1916 exacerbated the need for the United States to both increase production and decrease consumption. This placed an extraordinary burden on American civilians in lower economic classes, who were already struggling with the rising cost of food.

On May 5, 1917, Herbert Hoover was appointed to lead the U.S. Food Administration and to implement rationing and conservation of food in the United States. Americans were asked to limit consumption of wheat, meat, and eggs. In New York State, Governor Whitman established the New York State Food Commission to oversee conservation efforts in the state.[51] Much of the effort in New York State focused on increasing production by New York farms. This was accomplished through a variety of educational campaigns to inform the state's farmers about the most productive seed grains and how to increase the supply

Herbert Hoover, head of the U.S. Food Administration, outside of the agency's headquarters in New York City.

Courtesy of the Library of Congress.

"America, the hope of all who suffer."

Artist: John Greenleaf Whittier; *Printer:* Strobridge Litho. Co.; *Publisher:* United States Food Administration; *Technique:* Lithograph; *Dimensions:* 91.5 x 142.25 cm.

The U.S. Food Administration was tasked with implementing a system of rationing and conservation of food in the United States. The government was initially hesitant about enforcing a mandatory rationing system, preferring instead to rely on the patriotic voluntarism of the American people. When this proved ineffective in conserving sufficient amounts of foodstuffs, stricter policies were put into place. New York State Museum Collection, H–1976.149.14.

"The Spirit of '18."

Artist: William McKee; *Printer:* Forbes, Boston, Massachusetts;
Publisher: United States Food Administration;
Technique: Lithograph; *Dimensions:* 76.25 x 51 cm.

In this poster, the artist alludes to the image of fife, drum, and flag bearer of the "Spirit of 1776" by replacing those items with bushel basket, wheat sheaf, and fruit crate, to imply that agricultural production was a patriotic duty and that the United States was needed to feed the world. New York State Museum Collection, H-1975.176.1.

of eggs and milk. State farm experiment stations and agricultural colleges were tasked with preventing and controlling plant diseases and pests. The commission also assisted with loans for struggling farmers, provided tractors and mechanized equipment to be lent to farms to improve crop yields, and gave assistance with shipping products to be sent overseas.[52]

The efforts of the State Food Commission and New York State farmers resulted in a marked increase in agricultural production statewide between 1917 and 1918. According to the commission's final report in 1919, grain crop acreage increased 10 percent. The yield per acre was expected to be significantly greater as "the farmers have also paid unusual attention this year to the preparation of the soil, fertilization, and the selection of seeds."[53] The spring harvest of 1918 produced nine million bushels of wheat and two million bushels of rye. Oat production increased 15 percent to more than sixty million bushels (fifteen million bushels more than was produced in 1917). Farmers also reported an increase of over 30 percent in the number of pigs being raised on New York farms.[54] More than 33,000 cows were being milked daily.[55] In 1918, New York State was once again listed by the U.S. Department of Agriculture as a leader in wheat production alongside the Midwestern states.[56] The efforts of New York State's agricultural industry were a crucial component in the nation's efforts to feed American soldiers and the people of Europe during the war.

> To fail to utilize our land to produce its greatest yield would harm only ourselves and would benefit only our enemy. As loyal sons of America and patriotic citizens, we must do our utmost for the common good of all.
> —Governor Charles S. Whitman,
> March 14, 1918

> We must produce not only our usual supplies of food, but we must feed a large part of the world.
> —Governor Charles S. Whitman,
> March 14, 1918

Man plowing a field.

This photograph from the records of the New York State Military Training Commission features a man plowing a field with the assistance of two horses. While agriculture in New York and across the nation became increasingly mechanized in order to meet the needs of the war effort, many small farmers still relied on traditional technologies such as walking plows. New York State Archives, A4436-78.

Plow, Syracuse Chilled Plow Company (ca. 1900).

The chilled-iron plow manufactured by Syracuse Chilled Plow Company was very popular among farmers in the northeastern United States. These plows worked extremely well in the region's gravelly soil. In 1911, the company was purchased by the John Deere Company. Plows of this type were still in use on farms across New York State during World War I. Walking plows were a frequent feature in poster art of the era. While plows such as this were still frequently used by farmers in New York State, the need for increased farm production during World War I resulted in a concerted push towards mechanization in the agricultural industry. By 1918, the New York State Food Commission made seventy state-owned tractors available for rental by small farms in order to increase the acreage under production. The distribution of tractors coincided with those areas where farm labor shortages were most acute.[1] The state also took measures to encourage privately owned tractors to be placed in almost continuous operation by renting their use to neighboring farms. The State Food Commission also established twenty tractor schools to educate farmers on how to use the modern machines.[2] New York State Museum Collection, H-1983.89.3.

1. New York State Food Commission, page 17.

2. New York State Food Commission, page 19.

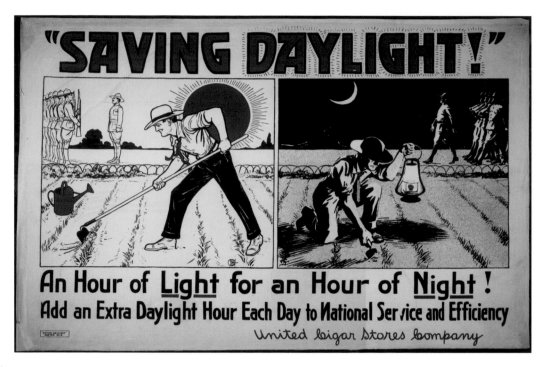

"Saving Daylight!"

Artist: N.B.H.; *Printer:* Unknown; *Publisher:* United Cigar Stores Company; *Technique:* Lithograph; *Dimensions:* 96 x 53 cm.

In 1918, Congress instituted daylight savings time in the United States to aid the war effort by providing more daylight to farmers in the fields. The measure was repealed following the war before being re-implemented in 1942. New York State Library, Manuscripts and Special Collections.

"Saving Daylight!"

Artist: Unknown; *Printer:* Unknown; *Publisher:* United Cigar Stores Company; *Technique:* Lithograph; *Dimensions:* 71.25 x 48.25 cm.

As this poster indicates, the idea behind daylight savings time was to increase the number of productive daylight hours, particularly for agricultural production, by 100 million hours for the entire U.S. population. New York State Museum Collection, H-1976.149.1.

"Sow the Seeds of Victory!" (1918).

Artist: James Montgomery Flagg; *Printer:* Unknown; *Publisher:* National War Garden Commission; *Technique:* Lithograph; *Dimensions:* 84 x 56 cm.

This poster encouraging the creation of war gardens was designed by artist James Montgomery Flagg. New York State Library, Manuscripts and Special Collections.

Bryant Park war garden.

Two young boys and a man study informational notices at a demonstration war garden at Bryant Park, 42nd Street and Fifth Avenue, in New York City. Courtesy of the Library of Congress.

War Gardens

War gardens were introduced to the American population in 1917 as a means of lessening the pressure on the food supply caused by rationing. These gardens were intended to increase American food production without adding strain to American farms already suffering from a labor shortage. Under guidance from the National War Garden Commission, the New York State Food Commission worked with cities, towns, and factory owners to organize war gardens across the state. Utilizing a model developed in Watertown, Jefferson County, each municipality established a war garden committee, which in turn nominated an experienced "practical gardener" for each district, ward, or factory. These gardeners and their assistants were given "general charge of the gardening operations" in their respective areas. The town, city, or factory owners would assume the cost for plowing and tilling of the available vacant land and purchasing fertilizer and seeds. Volunteers were then assigned plots to undertake cultivation.[57]

War gardens were considered a civic duty and were used to boost morale on the home front. Over five million gardens were planted nationwide. In New York State, such efforts helped to increase agricultural production by an estimated 30 percent.[58]

"Liberty Sowing the Seeds of Victory."

Artist: Frank Vincent DuMond; *Printer:* Unknown; *Publisher:* National War Garden Commission; *Technique:* Lithograph; *Dimensions:* 94 x 56 cm.

The poster advocated for participation in the national campaign for war gardens. New York State Museum Collection, H-1976.149.16.

"Raised 'em Myself" (1919).

Artist: Anonymous; *Printer:* American Lithographic Co., New York, New York; *Publisher:* United States School Garden Army, Bureau of Education, Department of the Interior; *Technique:* Lithograph; *Dimensions:* 76 x 51 cm.

Under the leadership of Charles Lathrop Pack, the National War Garden Commission encouraged citizens to help the war effort by growing their own food crops at home. Cities, towns, schools, and factories allotted plots of land for use as war gardens. The commission provided informational literature and seeds to help novice gardeners. New York State Museum Collection, H-1975.85.4.

Frank Vincent DuMond (1865–1951).

Frank Vincent DuMond was born in Rochester, Monroe County. DuMond was interested in drawing and illustration from a young age and was employed in Rochester creating illustrations for a sign-painting business. After high school, he moved to New York City in 1884 and studied at the Art Students League. To pay for his education, DuMond worked as an illustrator for the *Daily Graphic* newspaper. He was eventually hired by *Harper's Weekly*, *Century*, and *Scribner's* as well. He studied in Paris at the Académie Julian in the early 1890s, where he became immersed in the Art Nouveau impressionist movement of the era. After returning to the United States, DuMond was active in the art community across the nation, organizing several art exhibitions. As a member of the Society of Illustrators, he contributed illustrations to the Division of Pictorial Publicity for use in various posters during World War I.[1]

1. "Frank Vincent DuMond papers, 1866–1982," Archives of American Art, Smithsonian Institution (http://www.aaa.si.edu/collections/frank-vincent-dumond-papers-7453), accessed January 25, 2016.

"Can Vegetables, Fruit, and the Kaiser Too" (1918).

Artist: J. Paul Verrees; *Printer:* Unknown; *Publisher:* National War Garden Commission; *Technique:* Lithograph; *Dimensions:* 52.5 x 36 cm.

Canning as a means to preserve foodstuffs was strongly encouraged. Food preservation demonstrations took place statewide. "Canning kitchens" were established in cities across the state in Buffalo, Binghamton, Solvay, Saratoga Springs, New York City, and White Plains. These efforts led to an estimated 500 million quarts of fruits and vegetables being preserved each year.[1] New York State Library, Manuscripts and Special Collections.

    1. Flick, page 331.

Handbill, "Can Vegetables, Fruit, and the Kaiser Too" (1918).

Artist: J. Paul Verrees; *Printer:* Unknown; *Publisher:* National War Garden Commission; *Technique:* Unknown; *Dimensions:* 23 x 16 cm.

This handbill was created for distribution to American civilians by the National War Garden Commission. This two-color printed piece used the poster image designed by artist J. Paul Verrees. The U.S. government encouraged civilians to grow "War Gardens" to reduce their reliance on food items needed for the war effort. In addition to growing their own foodstuffs, Americans were prompted to can food in order to prolong its freshness. Jarring and canning food in their homes helped to reduce the burden on the food canning industry, thereby freeing those products for shipment to the soldiers of the AEF.[1] New York State Museum Collection, H-1992.19.97.

    1. Stoller-Conrad, Jessica, "Canning History: When Propaganda Encouraged Patriotic Preserves," National Public Radio, August 3, 2012 (http://www.npr.org/sections/thesalt/2012/08/02/157777834/canning-history-when-propaganda-encouraged-patriotic-preserves), accessed January 22, 2016.

Leonebel Jacobs (1883–1967).

Leonebel Jacobs spent her early years living abroad in Peking, China. Much of her early portrait work centered on the people of China. After returning to the United States, Jacobs settled in New York City. She became a renowned portrait artist and painted portraits of U.S. President Herbert Hoover, author Ayn Rand, and many of New York society's elite.

"Win the Next War Now."

Artist: Leonebel Jacobs; *Printer:* F.M. Lupton, Publisher, Inc., New York, New York; *Publisher:* National War Garden Commission; *Technique:* Lithograph; *Dimensions:* 40.75 x 28 cm.

New York State Museum Collection, H-1976.34.1.

Canning kitchen, New York City.

Women at a canning kitchen in New York City during the war. Similar kitchens were established across the state in an effort to preserve food. Courtesy of the Library of Congress.

CANNING DEMONSTRATIONS
Convention Hall Every Thursday and Friday, 2:30 p.m.
Mechanics Institute Daily at 2:30 p.m.
WOMEN INVITED—NO CHARGE

The Monroe County Home Defense Committee

"Preserve."

Artist: Carter Housh; *Printer:* Unknown; *Publisher:* Monroe County Home Defense Committee; *Technique:* Lithograph; *Dimensions:* 103 x 70 cm.

This poster advertises canning demonstrations at the Mechanics Institute (present-day Rochester Institute of Technology) in Rochester. Courtesy of the Rochester Historical Society.

As with the state's industries, wartime shortages in labor threatened New York's ability to produce crops in quantities sufficient for the war effort. The Food Commission was tasked with recruiting the labor necessary to enable New York State's farmers to not only maintain, but to increase production. By October 1918, the commission had assigned 9,840 men and 3,849 women to more than 4,600 farms across the state.[59] Despite its best efforts, the New York State Food Commission was never able to provide all of the manpower requested by New York's farmers. This was due in large part to the fact that the farmers could not compete with the wages being offered in factories manufacturing goods for government contract.[60]

The shortage of available labor on New York State farms created yet another employment opportunity for women in New York State during the war. The New York State Food Commission employed eight women farm-labor specialists to recruit women to farm work. Most of the recruits were college

"The Girl on the Land Serves the Nation's Need."

Artist: Edward Penfield; *Printer:* The United States Printing and Lithograph Co., New York; *Publisher:* YWCA/Land Service Committee; *Technique:* Lithograph; *Dimensions:* 63 x 76 cm.

This recruitment poster for women farm laborers again emphasizes the role that women played in agricultural production during the war. New York State Library, Manuscripts and Special Collections.

"Get Behind the Girl He Left Behind Him."

Artist: Unknown; *Printer:* Guenther American Lithographic Co.; *Publisher:* New York State Land Army Committee; *Technique:* Lithograph; *Dimensions:* 75 x 50 cm.

The Women's Land Army (WLA) was patterned after an organization of the same name in Great Britain. It was established in 1917 and organized in 42 states, including New York. The organization's mission was to recruit and place women into agricultural roles being vacated by men entering military service. The WLA helped to ensure that the women who volunteered received equal pay as their male counterparts and to guarantee an eight-hour work day. Nationwide, more than 20,000 women—most of whom came from cities and towns—were brought to farms during World War I. New York State Library, Manuscripts and Special Collections.

students, teachers, stenographers, clerical workers, and industrial workers, mostly from cities or suburban towns.[61] According to the commission's final report, the duty of these specialists was not only to recruit female workers, but to "show the farmers how they can employ women."[62] After passing a rigorous physical examination, the women were trained in various agricultural jobs and practices. Recruits were then assigned to farms either singly or as part of larger units. Female farm laborers were limited to an eight-hour working day and a fifty-four-hour work week.[63] The women drove tractors, cared for livestock, and worked as general farmhands.[64]

NEW YORK STATE BOYS' WORKING RESERVE (FARM CADET PROGRAM)

New York State officials feared that the loss of manpower on the state's farms could result in a severe food shortage. Governor Charles Whitman sought to encourage the enrollment of New York's youth population into the agricultural program of the Boys' Working Reserve. Patterned after a federal program of the same name, the New York State Boys' Working Reserve encouraged boys who, although not old enough to serve in the military, could provide the labor necessary to maximize food production on New York farms. By June 30, 1918, there were nearly 7,000 young men participating in the program.[65]

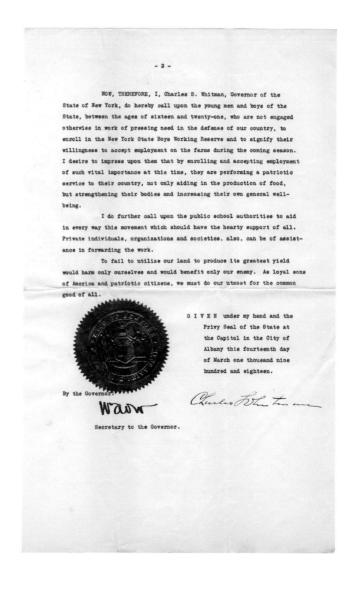

Boys' Working Reserve Proclamation.

Governor Charles S. Whitman's Proclamation establishing the Boys' Working Reserve. New York State Archives, 13035-79.

"Fight World Famine."

Artist: Unknown; *Printer:* Thomas Ellis Co., Baltimore, MD and New York, New York; *Publisher:* U.S. Employment Service; *Technique:* Lithograph; *Dimensions:* 69 x 46.5 cm.

With 4 million men entering military service, the United States found itself facing a significant shortage of labor for both industry and agriculture. The U.S. Department of Labor announced the formation of the Boys' Working Reserve to enlist boys between the ages of 16 and 21 and direct their efforts to needed industrial and agricultural endeavors. New York State Library, Manuscripts and Special Collections.

"Farm to Win 'Over There'."

Artist: Adolph Treidler; *Printer:* Government Printing Office, Washington, DC; *Publisher:* U.S. Department of Labor, U.S. Boys' Working Reserve; *Technique:* Lithograph; *Dimensions:* 100 x 75 cm.

This recruitment poster for the U.S. Boys' Working Reserve features the silhouette of a boy behind a walking plow. The boys were paid between $6 and $9 per week.[1] New York State Library, Manuscripts and Special Collections.

    1. New York State Food Commission, page 116.

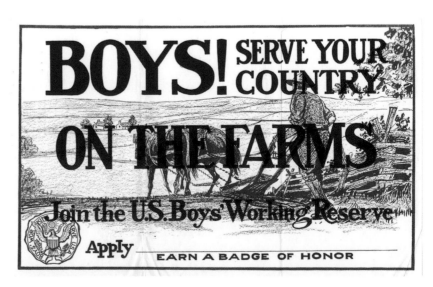

"Farm for Freedom."

Artist: None; *Printer:* Unknown; *Publisher:* United States Boys' Working Reserve; *Technique:* Lithograph; *Dimensions:* 28 x 21.75 cm.

Recruitment poster for the U.S. Boys' Working Reserve program, ca. 1917–1918. New York State Archives, A4436-78.

New York State Food Commission pamphlet, March 1918.

The Farm Cadet Program of the New York State Boys' Working Reserve Program allowed high school age boys to enroll as farm cadets either on a family farm or on another farm in the state. In total, 18,627 farm cadets helped to plant, cultivate, and harvest crops on New York State farms. New York State Archives, A0226-78.

"Boys! Serve Your Country on the Farms."

Artist: Unknown; *Printer:* Government Printing Office, Washington, DC; *Publisher:* U.S. Boys' Working Reserve, Department of Agriculture; *Technique:* Lithograph; *Dimensions:* 17.75 x 27.75 cm.

Recruiting poster for the New York Farm Cadets program, ca. 1917–1918. The program sought to lessen the strain that World War I put on state agriculture by sending urban school-children to work on farms. New York State Archives, A4436-78.

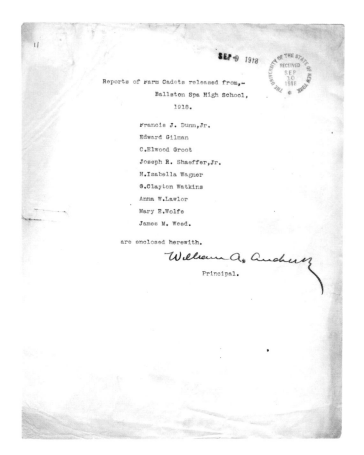

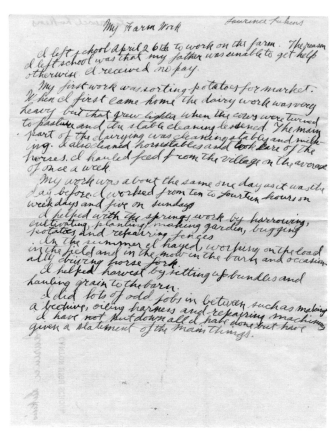

Cadet essays for the New York State Boys' Working Reserve Program.

Hundreds of boys and girls between the ages of 16 and 21 volunteered for the Boys' Working Reserve. These young men and women provided invaluable labor in industries stricken by loss of manpower as more and more men were drawn into military service. New York State Archives, A3112-77.

CONSERVATION

Herbert Hoover was reluctant to institute a strict system of rationing at the outset of the war, preferring instead to appeal to Americans' sense of patriotic duty.[66] The U.S. Food Administration offered lessons in canning and preservation and suggested substitutes for needed foodstuffs such as wheat, meats, eggs, and dairy products. In August 1917, Congress passed the Food and Fuel Control Act, which granted Hoover the authority to fix prices, license distributors, encourage increased agricultural production, and prevent hoarding or profiteering from food items. The program also instituted "Meatless Tuesdays" and "Wheatless Wednesdays" in an effort to promote conservation.[67]

"Get Behind Our Soldiers, Sailors, and Our Allies" (1917).

Artist: Rienecke Beckman; *Printer:* Sackett and Wilhelms Corp., New York, New York; *Publisher:* United States Food Administration; *Technique:* Lithograph; *Dimensions:* 28 x 53.5 cm.

The U.S. Food Administration was tasked with the rationing and conservation of food in the United States. Americans were asked to limit consumption of wheat, meat, eggs, and other items. New York State Museum Collection, H-1975.72.8.

U.S. Food Administration headquarters.

The New York City headquarters for the U.S. Food Administration was located on Broadway near Columbus Circle. Courtesy of the Library of Congress.

"Fighting with Food."

Artist: None; *Printer:* J.B. Lyons Company, Albany, New York; *Publisher:* New York State Food Commission; *Technique:* Lithograph; *Dimensions:* 70 x 55 cm.

This poster advertises conservation exhibits and demonstrations sponsored by the New York State Food Commission at the 1917 State Fair in Syracuse, Onondaga County. New York State Library, Manuscripts and Special Collections.

"Selection, Preparation, Preservation."

Artist: None; *Printer:* Unknown; *Publisher:* New York State Food Supply Commission; *Technique:* Lithograph; *Dimensions:* 50 x 37 cm.

This poster was produced by the New York State Food Supply Commission, headed by Commissioner of Agriculture Charles S. Wilson. The commission was replaced in October 1917 by the New York State Food Commission. Both bodies worked with the United States Food Administration to ensure that New York State was contributing its quota to the supply of food needed by the U.S. military and the European Allies.[1] New York State Library, Manuscripts and Special Collections.

    1. Flick, pages 328–329.

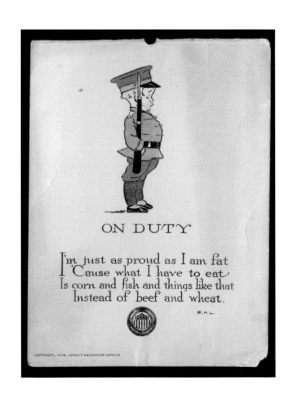

"On Duty."

This card was distributed by the U.S. Food Administration to encourage citizens to consume less meat and wheat in order to conserve supplies for the U.S. and Allied armies. New York State Library, Manuscripts and Special Collections.

Come in

Be Patriotic
sign your country's
pledge to save the food

U.S. FOOD ADMINISTRATION

Description, page 41. Photograph of a poster 21 by 29 inches, in color. Suggested for use in "Food and War Facts." Copies may be obtained from State Food Administrator

Paul Stahr (1883–1953).

Paul Stahr was born in New York City. He attended public school and in 1902 was admitted to the National Academy of Design in Manhattan. Following his graduation from the Academy, Stahr studied at the Art Students League. Stahr illustrated numerous posters, books, and magazines, including *Life*, the *Elks*, and the *Saturday Evening Post*. As a thirty-five-year-old father, Stahr was not drafted into military service. He contributed artwork for the Red Cross, the Food Administration, Liberty Loans, and other wartime agencies.

"Be Patriotic."

Artist: Paul Stahr; *Printer:* W.F. Powers Co. Litho., New York, New York; *Publisher:* U.S. Food Administration; *Technique:* Lithograph; *Dimensions:* 72 x 51 cm.

This early poster from the U.S. Food Administration reflects Herbert Hoover's reluctance to adopt a strict program of rationing in favor of patriotic appeals to the American people. New York State Archives, A4237-78.

"Food Is Ammunition" (1918).

Artist: J.E. Sheridan; *Printer:* Heywood Strasser and Voight Litho. Co., New York; *Publisher:* U.S. Food Administration; *Technique:* Lithograph; *Dimensions:* 73 x 51 cm.

Americans were encouraged to conserve food, particularly meats, dairy products, and wheat, that were needed to feed the troops in Europe. "Food Is Ammunition" became one of the most popular slogans of the Food Administration during World War I.[1] New York State Museum Collection, H-1975.107.2.

1. Flick, page 333.

"Win the War by Saving Food."

Artist: None; *Printer:* Standard, St. Paul, Minnesota; *Publisher:* U.S. Food Administration; *Technique:* Lithograph; *Dimensions:* 105 x 70 cm.

This U.S. Food Administration poster advertises conservation through reduced consumption and also advocates for "Meatless Tuesdays" and "Wheatless Wednesdays." New York State Library, Manuscripts and Special Collections.

John E. Sheridan (1880–1948).

John E. Sheridan was born in Tomah, Wisconsin, and educated at Georgetown University, graduating in 1901. He was a successful illustrator in New York City and produced numerous covers for the *Saturday Evening Post* and *Collier's Weekly*. He was a member of the Society of Illustrators and was recruited by Charles Dana Gibson to create poster illustrations in support of the war effort.

F. Luis Mora (1874–1940).

Francis Luis Mora was born in Uruguay. His family fled the country when revolution broke out in 1877 and arrived in New York City in 1880. As a student, Mora studied at the School of the Museum of Fine Arts in Boston and with the Art Students League in New York. He became a celebrated artist in New York City and an instructor at the Chase School of Art and the Art Students League. Mora was also an accomplished illustrator, producing works for several books and magazines including *Harper's* and *Colliers Weekly*. During the war, Mora produced posters for the U.S. Food Administration as well as the Third and Fourth Liberty Loans.

"Free Milk for France."

Artist: F. Luis Mora; *Printer:* W.F. Powers Co. Litho., New York, New York; *Publisher:* Unknown; *Technique:* Lithograph; *Dimensions:* 83.5 x 58 cm.

This poster urges conservation of dairy products in order to ship needed foodstuffs to the people of Europe and to American soldiers serving in France. New York State Library, Manuscripts and Special Collections.

"War Rages in France; We Must Feed Them."

Harry Everett Townsend (1879–1941).

Henry Everett Townsend was one of eight official World War I artists employed by the U.S. Army Signal Corps. Born in Wyoming, Illinois, Townsend studied at the Art Institute of Chicago. After studying in Paris and London, he briefly taught art in Chicago before moving to New York City and finding employment as an illustrator for various magazines. Townsend and his family were living in France when war broke out in 1914; they returned to the United States. In 1917, he received a commission in the U.S. Army as a captain. He served with the AEF beginning in May 1918 and contributed numerous works used in various poster campaigns.

Artist: Harry Everett Townsend; *Printer:* Unknown; *Publisher:* U.S. Food Administration; *Technique:* Lithograph; *Dimensions:* 74 x 50 cm.

This poster illustrated by H. E. Townsend implores Americans to limit their consumption of foodstuffs in order to help feed the population of war-ravaged France. New York State Museum Collection, H-1972.7.1.

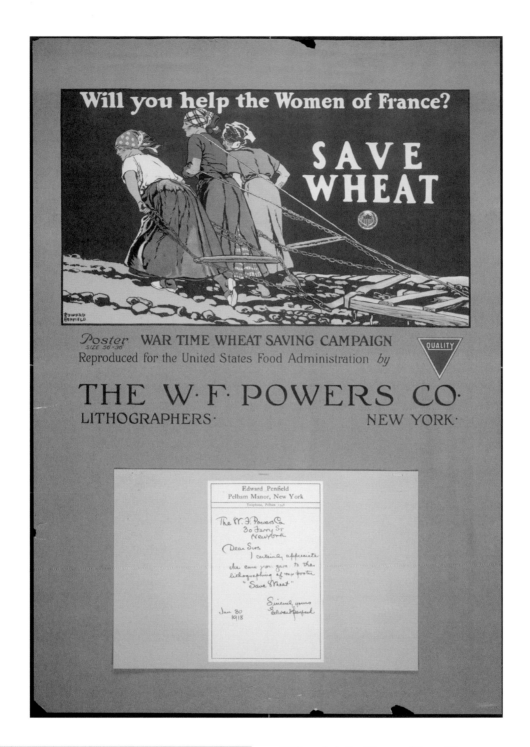

Edward Penfield (1866–1925).

Edward Penfield was born in Brooklyn on June 2, 1866. After studying at the New York Art Students League, he worked for *Harper's Weekly* as an illustrator. He moved to New Rochelle, New York, which by the early twentieth century had become one of the leading artists' colonies in the United States. There, he helped to found the New Rochelle Art Association in 1912. Penfield contributed several posters to the war effort. He is considered the father of the American poster.

"Will you help the Women of France?"

Artist: Edward Penfield; *Printer:* W.F. Powers Co. Litho.; *Publisher:* U.S. Food Administration; *Technique:* Lithograph; *Dimensions:* 78 x 54 cm.

Increased production of wheat in the United States alone was insufficient to meet the needs of the military and the civilian populations in Europe, but rather had to be combined with decreased consumption on the home front. New York State Library, Manuscripts and Special Collections.

WE VIOLATED THE REGULATIONS OF THE FOOD ADMINISTRATION BUT HAVE PLEDGED FULL OBEDIENCE IN THE FUTURE

POSTED BY DIRECTION OF

THE U. S. FOOD ADMINISTRATION

THE ATKINSON PRESS — ITHACA, NEW YORK

This HOME CARD reprinted by the
ALBANY COUNTY HOME DEFENSE COMMITTEE

United States Food Administration

WIN THE WAR BY GIVING YOUR OWN DAILY SERVICE

SAVE THE WHEAT.—One wheatless meal a day. Use corn, oatmeal, rye or barley bread and non-wheat breakfast foods. Order bread twenty-four hours in advance so your baker will not bake beyond his needs. Cut the loaf on the table and only as required. Use stale bread for cooking, toast, etc. Eat less cake and pastry.

Our wheat harvest is far below normal. If each person weekly saves one pound of wheat flour that means 150,000,000 more bushels of wheat for the Allies to mix in their bread. This will help them to save DEMOCRACY.

SAVE THE MEAT.—Beef, mutton or pork not more than once daily. Use freely vegetables and fish. At the meat meal serve smaller portions, and stews instead of steaks. Make made-dishes of all left-overs. Do this and there will be meat enough for every one at a reasonable price.

We are today killing the dairy cows and female calves as the result of high price. Therefore, eat less and eat no young meat. If we save an ounce of meat each day per person, we will have additional supply equal to 2,300,000 cattle.

SAVE THE MILK.—The children must have milk. Use every drop. Use buttermilk and sour milk for cooking and making cottage cheese. Use less cream.

SAVE THE FATS.—We are the world's greatest fat wasters. Fat is food. Butter is essential for the growth and health of children. Use butter on the table as usual but not in cooking. Other fats are as good. Reduce use of fried foods. Save daily one-third ounce animal fats. Soap contains fats. Do not waste it. Make your own washing soap at home out of the saved fats.

Use one-third ounce less per day of animal fat and 375,000 tons will be saved yearly.

SAVE THE SUGAR.—Sugar is scarcer. We use today three times as much per person as our Allies. So there may be enough for all at reasonable price use less candy and sweet drinks. Do not stint sugar in putting up fruit and jams. They will save butter.

If everyone in America saves one ounce of sugar daily, it means 1,100,000 tons for the year.

SAVE THE FUEL.—Coal comes from a distance and our railways are overburdened hauling war material. Help relieve them by burning fewer fires. Use wood when you can get it.

USE THE PERISHABLE FOODS.—Fruits and vegetables we have in abundance. As a nation we eat too little green stuffs. Double their use and improve your health. Store potatoes and other roots properly and they will keep. Begin now to can or dry all surplus garden products.

USE LOCAL SUPPLIES.—Patronize your local producer. Distance means money. Buy perishable food from the neighborhood nearest you and thus save transportation.

GENERAL RULES

Buy less, serve smaller portions.
Preach the "Gospel of the Clean Plate."
Don't eat a fourth meal.
Don't limit the plain food of growing children.
Watch out for the wastes in the Community.
Full garbage pails in America mean empty dinner pails in America and Europe.
If the more fortunate of our people will avoid waste and eat no more than they need, the high cost of living problem of the less fortunate will be solved.

HERBERT HOOVER,
United States Food Administrator.

Copies can be obtained at the FOOD CONSERVATION HEADQUARTERS
ROOM 79, COUNTY COURT HOUSE, ALBANY, N. Y.

"We Violated the Regulations of the Food Administration."

Artist: None; *Printer:* The Atkinson Press, Ithaca, New York; *Publisher:* U.S. Food Administration; *Technique:* Lithograph; *Dimensions:* 60.5 x 40 cm.

Not everyone voluntarily cooperated with rationing. Those individuals or companies who were caught in violation of conservation or rationing efforts often became the object of ridicule and public humiliation. This poster was "Posted by direction of the U.S. Food Administration." New York State Library, Manuscripts and Special Collections.

Albany County Home Defense Committee home card.

This card was distributed by the Albany County Home Defense Committee in order to remind county residents about the wartime food rationing in effect. The card told recipients that their efforts to limit consumption of wheat, meat, milk, fat, sugar, and fuel, would help the Allies win the war. New York State Archives, A3167-78A.

Food riots in New York City, 1917.

On February 21, 1917, nearly 400 women marched on New York City Hall to petition the mayor for assistance with rising food prices. The United States initially attempted to encourage civic mindedness through voluntary rationing. Even in the United States, which had become the bread-basket of the Allied cause, poor families, were threatened with starvation as the cost of basic food items skyrocketed. Demonstrators overturned vendors' carts, smashed windows, and attacked grocers. The government temporarily moved to reduce prices on food items, thereby undercutting the grievances of the protesters and quieting the disturbances in New York City.[1] Courtesy of the Library of Congress.

1. Jaffe, page 193.

Critical Infrastructure

With the opening of the Erie Canal in the 1820s, the subsequent "canal fever," and the rise of railroads by the middle of the nineteenth century, New York State maintained a vital position in the nation in regard to infrastructure when the United States entered World War I. The state's vast transportation network, which included a limited number of highways, enabled large quantities of men and material to be funneled to the battlefields of Europe through the Port of New York, which solidified its place as the country's leading harbor during the war.

New York State Railroads

On the eve of America's entry into World War I, New York State led the nation with more than 9,000 miles of railroad in the state and was home to several of the country's largest carrying companies.[68] With the president's declaration of war,

however, American railroads found themselves ill-prepared for the scope of the task required of them—transporting millions of American soldiers and the materiel needed to supply them. Even prior to the declaration of war, railroad traffic in goods being shipped to the Allies had resulted in a more than 30 percent increase in traffic on American railways.[69] The ensuing traffic jams and shipping delays jeopardized the nation's ability to have an impact in the war in Europe. As a result, President Wilson ordered the creation of the United States Railroad Administration (USRA) in December 1917. The USRA oversaw the nation's railroad operations until March 1920. The USRA established standardized pricing for freight across the nation, adjudicated disputes between railroad management and labor, and ordered standardization of locomotive and freight car design.[70]

A train travels alongside the Ashokan Reservoir in Ulster County, 1916.

Courtesy of the
New York Public Library.

Bush Terminal.

Bush Terminal along Brooklyn's waterfront was a shipping, warehousing, and manufacturing complex first established in the 1890s. Terminals such as this enabled rail freight to be transported directly to New York Harbor to be offloaded and shipped overseas during World War I. Material could be offloaded from arriving trains, stored in one of more than 100 warehouses, and loaded onto ships at one of seven piers. The terminal was commandeered by the U.S. Navy during the war and became part of the New York Port of Embarkation Command in 1918. Courtesy of the Library of Congress.

As the United States prepared to enter World War I, many in the federal government feared that the nation's transportation network was not prepared for the task of moving vast quantities of men and material to Europe. In New York State, workers were rushing to complete the Barge Canal. The new waterway was as yet untested and lacked sufficient boats capable of carrying the needed cargo.[71] Throughout 1917, the Barge Canal lay largely unused.

By the winter, however, the nation's railway system became overburdened by the war effort. As a result, the USRA, under William Gibbs McAdoo, began studying the ability of the nation's inland waterways to alleviate the rail congestion. On April 22, 1918, the USRA assumed control of shipping along the New York State Barge Canal. While the operation and maintenance of the canal remained under state control, all shipping and cargo fell to federal oversight.

While shipping along the canal should have been cheaper, federal rates for the canal were set at the same level as those for the railroads. This created little incentive to use the Barge Canal, which remained underutilized throughout the war. By 1919, only 1.2 million tons of freight destined for American troops in Europe passed through the newly opened canal.[72]

Bush Terminal female workers.

Female workers in front of a locomotive at the Bush Terminal's railroad yard, 1918. With a shortage of manpower resulting from the war, railroads also turned to women to supply the necessary workforce brought about by the war effort. Courtesy of the National Archives and Records Administration.

Concrete barge.

The USRA contracted all available ships that could be used along the Barge Canal, but failed to effectively use them. With all available steel being diverted to the war effort, there was none available to construct additional barges. In response, the federal government ordered concrete boats constructed for use on the canal. These were constructed at Fort Edward, Ithaca, and Tonawanda, New York, as well as Detroit Michigan. In the end, these barges were not well suited for the canals. Although, they could float, one knock into a dock or lock and the concrete could crumble. New York State Museum Collection, 1990.11.253.

As the largest port of embarkation during the war, New York City bore the added burden of housing and supplying the soldiers prior to their sailing for France. Four transient camps were established around New York City—Camp Merritt, Camp Upton, and Camp Mills on Long Island and Camp Dix in New Jersey. Between July 1, 1918, and the Armistice on November 11, 1918, one million troops—50 percent of the entire American Expeditionary Force in Europe—sailed from the Port of New York.[73] This figure does not account for the thousands of soldiers, including the 27th and 77th Divisions, who departed New York prior to July 1918. In total, more than 80 percent of all AEF soldiers set sail from the Port of New York.[74]

We started for France at 2:30 PM the same day, sailing slowly past the Statue of Liberty. . . . I cannot explain to you my feeling as that old statue finally faded out of site [sic].

—Corporal Howard L. Kline, Company C,
51st Pioneer Infantry Regiment,
27th Division[75]

THE YANKS ARE COMING

This Map Illustrates Troop Sailings from American Ports to Great Britain and France

During our 19 months of war more than 2,000,000 American soldiers were carried to France. Half a million of these went over in the first 13 months and a million and a half in the last 6 months.

The highest troop-carrying records are those of July, 1918, when 306,000 soldiers were carried to Europe and May, 1919, when 330,000 were brought home to America.

Most of the troops who sailed for France left from New York. Half of them landed in Great Britain and the other half landed in France.

Among every 100 Americans who went over 49 went in British ships, 45 in American ships, 3 in Italian, 2 in French, and 1 in Russian shipping under English control.

Our cargo ships averaged one complete trip every 70 days and our troop ships one complete trip every 35 days.

The cargo fleet was almost exclusively American. It reached the size of 2,600,000 deadweight tons and carried to Europe about 7,500,000 tons of cargo.

The greatest troop-carrier among all the ships has been the *Leviathan*, which landed 12,000 men, or the equivalent of a German division, in France every month.

The fastest transports have been the *Great Northern* and the *Northern Pacific*, which have made complete turnarounds, taken on new troops, and started back again in 19 days.

LEONARD P. AYRES, Colonel, G. S.,
Chief of the Statistics Branch of the General Staff.

"The Yanks Are Coming!"

This graphic illustrates troop departures from the major ports along the eastern seaboard of North America. Of the nearly 2.1 million men transported to Europe as part of the AEF, 1.65 million sailed from New York Harbor.

From *U.S. Official Pictures of the Great War* (Washington, DC: Pictorial Bureau, 1920), New York State Museum Collection, H-1971.113.11.

U.S. Marines aboard a train of the Pennsylvania Railroad bound for the New York Port of Embarkation.

Courtesy of the Library of Congress.

Loading supplies for shipment to France.

Soldiers on the docks at New York Harbor load supplies onto cargo vessels to be shipped to the AEF. Courtesy of the Library of Congress.

Transports sail past the Statue of Liberty.

Transports sail past the Statue of Liberty in New York Harbor carrying troops and supplies bound for France. Courtesy of the U.S. Army Center of Military History.

Port of Embarkation uniform.

This U.S. Army Medical Corps uniform tunic is adorned with a rare New York Port of Embarkation (POE) insignia on its shoulder. The New York POE became a distinct command during the war. The silver service chevrons on the left sleeve indicate stateside service. Overseas service was denoted by gold service chevrons. William F. Howard Collection.

Financing the War

New York played a crucial role in financing the conflict in Europe in the years leading up to America's entry into the war. By April 6, 1917, New York City banks had secured nearly $2.5 billion in foreign loans, the majority of the funding going to Great Britain and France.[76] Between 1914 and 1917, New Yorkers joined other Americans in contributing generously to the Red Cross and other charities, such as the Committee for the Relief of Belgium.

With America's entry into the war in April 1917, the Wilson administration sought to raise the funds necessary to finance the war through a combination of increased taxation, loans from the Federal Reserve System, and Liberty Bonds and War Savings Stamps from the American people. In March 1917, Congress passed a tax on what were deemed "excessive" corporate profits, which placed an 8 percent tax on profits and income above an established threshold. Congress followed in October with the War Revenue Act of 1917, which mandated a 2 percent increase on incomes over $1,000.[77] Increased taxation proved insufficient for the cost of the war effort. In response, the government turned to borrowing through Liberty Bonds.

Liberty Loans

The American government authorized the first Liberty Bond issue on April 24, 1917. The first Liberty Loan drive raised more than $3 billion in subscriptions from four million participants. Between 1917 and 1919, the United States government authorized four Liberty Loan drives and a fifth, Victory Loan, five months after the Armistice to continue to pay for the two million American soldiers still in Europe in April 1919. Through two years of loans, sixty-six million Americans had pledged more than $24 billion to the war effort. New Yorkers were in the forefront of this endeavor. During the first two loan drives alone, New York State's citizens accounted for one-third of the $2.5 billion subscribed. In Monroe County, the citizens of Rochester raised more than $126 million during the five Liberty Loan drives, as well as an additional $3 million in War Savings Stamps. This contribution was the largest per capita for any county in New York State.[78]

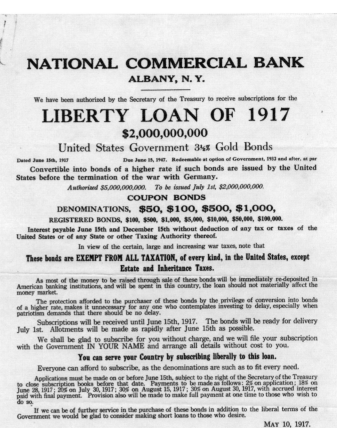

Broadside.

Liberty Bond drives encouraged average citizens to do their part for the war effort. Bonds of various values were available for purchase so that everyone could contribute no matter their financial situation. 30 percent of the Liberty Bond sales during the war were from people earning less than $2,000 per year. New York State Archives, A3167-78A.

Women's Liberty Loan Committee.

This photograph features a group of women from a New York State branch of the National Women's Liberty Loan Committee. This organization, created in 1917, worked with the national War Loan Organization to sell Liberty Bonds and to enlist other women as bond sellers. The National Women's Liberty Loan Committee in New York State boasted 1,491 local committees and 35,000 volunteers.[1] New York State Archives.

    1. Flick, page 325.

"Women! Help America's Sons Win the War" (1917).

Artist: R.H. Porteous; *Printer:* Edwards and Deutsch Litho. Co., Chicago, Illinois; *Publisher:* U.S. Treasury Department; *Technique:* Lithograph; *Dimensions:* 76.25 x 51 cm.

In addition to their contributions to the war effort in the state's industrial factories and in the farmers' fields, New York State's women were invaluable in the effort to raise money for charity and Liberty Bonds. The New York subcommittees for the National Women's Liberty Loan Committee raised $216,675,050 from more than 445,000 New York State residents.[1] Many fundraising posters underscored the importance of the patriotic efforts of the nation's women. This particular poster was intended to target mothers, many of whom had sons serving in the military. New York State Museum Collection, H-1976.149.18.

1. Flick, page 325.

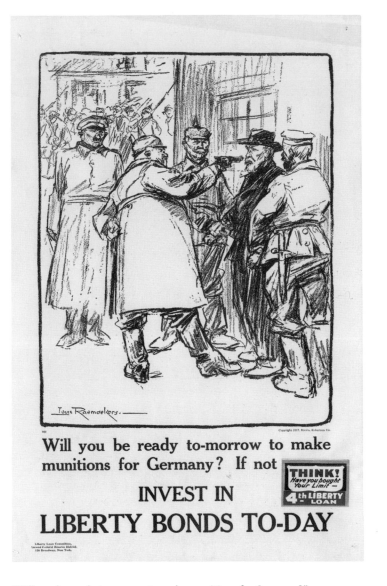

"Will you be ready tomorrow to make munitions for Germany?"

Artist: Louis Raemaekers; *Printer:* Brown Robertson Co., New York; *Publisher:* Liberty Loan Committee, Second Federal Reserve District; *Technique:* Lithograph; *Dimensions:* 48.25 x 30.5 cm.

The image and text of this poster alludes to ultimate German victory—and conquest—should the American people fail to sufficiently support the war effort through the purchase of Liberty Bonds. New York State Museum Collection, H-1992.19.64.

"Have you bought your bond?"

Artist: Adolph Treidler; *Printer:* M. Rusling Wood Litho., New York, New York; *Publisher:* Wells Fargo and Co.; *Technique:* Lithograph; *Dimensions:* 139 x 89.5 cm.

This poster, identified as probably the first Liberty Loan poster to be produced, was illustrated by New York City-based artist Adolph Treidler.[1] New York State Library, Manuscripts and Special Collections.

　1. Rawls, pages 198–200.

"You Buy a Liberty Bond Lest I Perish!" (1917).

Artist: G.R. Macauley; *Printer:* Unknown; *Publisher:* First Liberty Loan Committee; *Technique:* Lithograph; *Dimensions:* 75 x 50.5 cm.

Three posters were initially designed for the first Liberty Loan drive by the DPP. All three featured the Statue of Liberty. In an allusion to James Montgomery Flagg's Uncle Sam, this poster by G.R. Macauley features Lady Liberty pointing admonishingly towards the viewer.[1] New York State Museum Collection, H-1972.112.1 S.

　1. Rawls, page 198.

"You Buy a Liberty Bond Lest I Perish!" (1917).

Artist: Unknown; *Printer:* Unknown; *Publisher:* Liberty Loan of 1917;
Technique: Lithograph; *Dimensions:* 76.25 x 51 cm.

The Statue of Liberty featured prominently in many of the posters of the
period, including this one from the first Liberty Loan drive in 1917. New York
State Museum Collection, H–1972.112.1 A.

"Goodbye Dad, I'm Off to Fight for Old Glory."

Artist: Laurence S. Harris; *Printer:* Sackett and Wilhelms Corp., New York,
New York; *Publisher:* Third Liberty Loan; *Technique:* Lithograph;
Dimensions: 75 x 49.5 cm.

A poster from the Third Liberty Loan drive, which began on April 5, 1918. New
Yorkers subscribed for more than $965 million in Liberty Bonds. New York
State Museum Collection, H–1972.112.1 G.

"That Liberty Shall Not Perish."

Artist: Joseph Pennell; *Printer:* Heywood, Strasser and Voight Litho. Co., New York, New York; *Publisher:* Fourth Liberty Loan; *Technique:* Lithograph; *Dimensions:* 102 x 70.5 cm.

This poster for the fourth Liberty Bond drive shows New York City and the Statue of Liberty in ruins. A U-boat sails into New York Harbor as the city burns. The fourth Liberty Bond drive saw New Yorkers contribute the most to a single effort, subscribing for more than $1.8 million in bonds. New York State Museum Collection, H-1976.145.5.

Joseph Pennell (1857–1926).

Joseph Pennell was born in Philadelphia and attended the Pennsylvania Academy of the Fine Arts. As a young artist, he was employed creating etchings of historic American landmarks for travel articles and publications. In the 1880s, he moved to Europe, where he continued to develop as an artist before returning to the United States at the outbreak of World War I. Pennell's most notable contribution to the war effort was his rendering of New York Harbor in the wake of a German attack for the Fourth Liberty Loan in 1918.

Liberty Bond button.

This pin signified an individual had purchased a Liberty Bond. Pins such as this one were intended to be displayed as a symbol of the wearer's patriotism and as a means to encourage participation from others. As such, they became a visible instrument in the coerced voluntarism of the era.[1] One's failure to display a Liberty Loan pin was frequently viewed as comparable to slackers and traitors. New York State Museum Collection, H-1970.135.57 A.

1. Capozzola, page 10.

Liberty Loan pin.

This pin signified participation in the Fourth Liberty Loan following passage of the Fourth Liberty Bond Act on July 9, 1918.[1] New York State Museum Collection, H-1970.135.57 B.

1. Treasury Department, *Liberty Loan Acts* (Washington, DC: Government Printing Office, 1921), title page (https://books.google.com/books?id=4qFAAAAAYAAJ), accessed May 4, 2016.

"Where's Your 'Liberty Bond' Button?"

Artist: Unknown; *Printer:* Unknown; *Publisher:* Unknown; *Technique:* Lithograph; *Dimensions:* 28 x 53.5 cm.

The Liberty Loan campaigns sought to create an atmosphere of "voluntary coercion" in the American population by instilling a sense of shame or guilt in those individuals who failed to support the war effort through the purchase of bonds.[1] By creating a sense of collective obligation that could be enforced through public coercion, wartime leaders sought to generate popular support for the American war effort. New York State Museum Collection, H-1976.147.5.

    1. Capozzola, page 11.

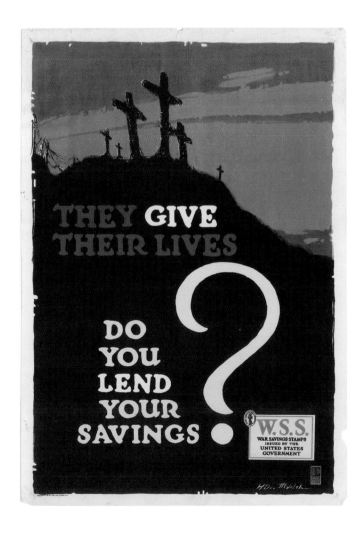

"They Give Their Lives; Do You Lend Your Savings?"

Artist: H. Devitt Welsh; *Printer:* Sackett and Wilhelms Corp., New York, New York; *Publisher:* Committee on Public Information, Division of Pictorial Publicity; *Technique:* Lithograph; *Dimensions:* 76.25 x 51 cm.

As in recruitment, the United States relied on a veiled system of voluntary coercion, shame, and public pressure to encourage support for the war effort. In this poster, the graves of American soldiers killed in France are visible. The viewers are then asked whether they have made a sufficient sacrifice to the cause. New York State Museum Collection, H-1992.19.80.

"Joan of Arc Saved France."

Artist: Haskell Coffin; *Printer:* United States Printing and Lithograph Company; *Publisher:* War Savings Stamps Campaign, U.S. Treasury Department; *Technique:* Lithograph; *Dimensions:* 101 x 75 cm.

In addition to Liberty Bonds, the U.S. government sold War Savings Stamps (WSS). WSS earned four percent interest on the initial investment, compounded quarterly. Stamp owners could redeem the WSS for cash once the stamp reached its maturity date. New York State Museum Collection, H-1992.19.16.

"Boys and Girls!"

Artist: James Montgomery Flagg; *Printer:* American Lithographic Co., New York, New York; *Publisher:* Unknown; *Technique:* Lithograph; *Dimensions:* 102 x 76 cm.

Even children were targeted for support of the war effort. Boy and Girl Scouts were employed in the sale of Liberty Bonds and War Savings Stamps. In this poster, boys and girls are encouraged to use their own money to purchase stamps. New York State Museum Collection, H-1976.56.1.

Haskell Coffin (1878–1941).

William Haskell Coffin, who was better known as artist and illustrator Haskell Coffin, was born in Charleston, South Carolina. As a young man, he studied at the Corcoran School of Art in Washington, DC. He spent much of his early career in New York City. Haskell Coffin became one of his era's most prevalent illustrators of feminine beauty. His work adorned the covers of numerous publications including *McCall's* and the *Saturday Evening Post*. His depiction of Joan of Arc as the savior of France is one of the most recognizable posters of World War I.

COMMUNITY WAR CHESTS

Across New York State in 1918, cities and towns began to raise money for the war effort through community war chests to finance various wartime needs. The practice was first implemented in Syracuse and was soon followed by the establishment of war chests in Rochester, as well as in Yates and Jefferson counties.[79] In general, funds remaining in these community war chests at the end of the conflict were used toward the erection of local monuments and war memorials.

CHARITABLE ORGANIZATIONS

When war broke out in Europe, many Americans sought to alleviate the suffering of civilian populations in war-ravaged nations. New Yorkers responded to their calls for aid with substantial generosity. Existing charitable organizations, such as the American Red Cross and the Salvation Army, sprang into action when the war in Europe erupted in 1914, while others were established as a direct response to the humanitarian crisis caused by the war. When the United States declared war in April 1917, many of these organizations offered their services to the American government. In 1914, New York State citizens had contributed $2.8 million to war relief charities.[80] By June 1918, New York State had contributed nearly $47 million, 2.5 million pounds of clothing for Belgian Relief, 63 million pounds of surgical dressings, and 5.5 million pounds of hospital clothing to the American Red Cross.

In November 1918, the YMCA, YWCA, National Catholic War Council, Jewish Welfare Board, Salvation Army, War Camp Community Service, and American Library Association in New York State joined together to raise funds for their war relief work. Their efforts raised more than $205 million in donations from New Yorkers.[81]

The American Red Cross experienced a period of significant growth during World War I. Nationwide, the number of local chapters increased from 107 in 1914 to more than 3,800 in 1918. Membership rose from 17,000 to 20 million.[82] The Red Cross raised more than $400 million during the war, purchased medical supplies, staffed hospitals both on the home front and in Europe, and recruited more than 20,000 trained nurses for the war effort.

The Salvation Army began its war work in 1914, and volunteered its services to the American

"Will She Find It Filled?" (1918).

Artist: Lillian O. Titus; *Printer:* Unknown; *Publisher:* Unknown; *Technique:* Lithograph; *Dimensions:* 62.25 x 44.5 cm.

The Community War Chest Drive in Rochester in May 1918 raised more than $4.8 million from 117,064 residents of the city.[1] New York State Museum Collection, H-1992.19.3.

1. Flick, page 327.

Pin.

This membership pin signified a person's participation in the War Chest Drive in Albany in 1918. New York State Museum Collection, H-5264.

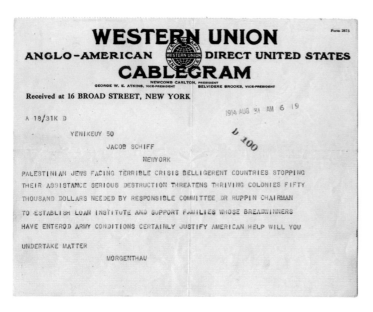

JDC telegram.

When the Ottoman Empire entered the war in Europe in August 1914, more than 50,000 Jewish settlers in Ottoman-ruled Palestine were cut off from humanitarian assistance. With the flow of money and goods from Europe cut off, America's ambassador to Turkey, Henry Morgenthau, sent this telegram to Jewish leaders in New York City urging their assistance. Initially, funds were raised through a variety of existing Jewish charities.[1] As the war continued, however, these organizations combined their efforts to establish the Joint Distribution Committee to provide humanitarian relief.[2] The JDC was formally established on November 27, 1914. Much of the aid went to Jews living in Palestine and on the Eastern Front in Russia. Between 1914 and 1929, the JDC raised more than $75 million from Jews in the United States.[3]

    1. Flick, page 336.

    2. "About JDC," American Jewish Joint Distribution Committee (http://www.jdc.org/about-jdc/?s=global-topnav), accessed November 9, 2016.

    3. "American Jewish Joint Distribution Committee and Refugee Aid," The United States Holocaust Memorial Museum (https://www.ushmm.org/wlc/en/article.php?ModuleId=10005367), accessed November 9, 2016.

Henry Morgenthau, American Ambassador to Turkey, ca. 1916.

Courtesy of the Library of Congress.

government in April 1917. The Salvation Army in the United States had fewer than 1,000 individuals, but their impact far exceeded their numbers. The first group of Salvation Army workers sailed from New York Harbor on August 12, 1917. Their mission was to provide food to American soldiers on the front lines in France. On the home front, the Salvation Army operated respite houses for soldiers in the newly constructed camps across the country.[83]

News of atrocities in Europe sparked the creation of several new agencies as well, such as the Committee for Belgian Relief, the Serbia Relief Committee of America, and the American Committee for Relief in the Near East. Following America's entry into the war, other organizations, such as the YMCA and the Knights of Columbus, sought to provide services to American soldiers of the AEF[84]

America's entry into the conflict prompted the creation of the Jewish Welfare Board on April 9, 1917. One of the organization's first tasks was to recruit and train rabbis to serve as chaplains in the AEF, and to maintain Jewish chapels at military installations.[85]

The expansion of efforts by New York's charitable organizations also provided New York State women with new roles to play in the war. Not only did New Yorkers serve as nurses and canteen girls in military camps on the home front, but many served in the trenches of Europe. Philanthropic endeavors in New York State also saw numerous instances of women leading efforts to organize goods to be sent to soldiers in France and collecting medical supplies for Army hospitals.

"Morale Hastens Victory."

Artist: F. Luis Mora; *Printer:* Unknown; *Publisher:* United War Work Campaign; *Technique:* Lithograph; *Dimensions:* 28 x 53.5 cm.

This trolley card advertisement was created for the 1918 United War Work Campaign. Seven charities—most of which were headquartered in New York City—were selected to provide support and comfort to soldiers in military camps on the home front and in the trenches overseas. The selected organizations included the YMCA and the YWCA, the National Catholic War Council, the Knights of Columbus, the Jewish Welfare Board, the American Library Association, and the Salvation Army. All told, their combined fundraising appeal netted more than $200 million by November 1918. Of this, New York State contributed in excess of $35 million.[1] New York State Museum Collection, H-1975.72.9.

1. Flick, pages 336–337.

Pin.

This celluloid fundraising pin was issued by the Red Cross during its efforts in 1919. New York State Museum Collection, H-1970.135.57 C.

"Keep This Hand of Mercy at Its Work."

Artist: P.G. Morgan; *Printer:* Unknown; *Publisher:* American Red Cross, Second War Fund; *Technique:* Lithograph; *Dimensions:* 69 x 51.5 cm.

This poster depicts the arm of a Red Cross nurse shielding civilians from the fighting taking place at left. The Second War Fund for the American Red Cross took place from May 18 to 27, 1918, and sought to raise $100 million in 10 days. To accomplish this goal, the organization embarked on an intense publicity campaign utilizing posters, mass rallies, schools, churches, and other civic organizations. By the end of the drive, the Red Cross had raised $170 million—$60 million being contributed by New York State residents.[1] New York State Library, Manuscripts and Special Collections.

1. Sullivan, James. Working files for a publication on New York in World War I, 1917–1925. New York State Archives, Series A3166.

"Greatest Mother in the World."

Artist: Alonzo Earl Foringer; *Printer:* Unknown; *Publisher:* American Red Cross; *Technique:* Lithograph; *Dimensions:* 107 x 71 cm.

Artist A.E. Foringer's "Greatest Mother in the World" poster for the American Red Cross became one of the most famous posters of World War I. In the illustration, a Red Cross Nurse cradles a wounded soldier in her arms. The image was intended to evoke Michelangelo's sculpture, *Pieta*, in which Mary is holding Jesus in her arms. The poster encouraged more than 16 million Americans to participate in the December 1918 Christmas drive.[1] New York State Museum Collection, H-1975.85.2.

1. *The American Experience*, Poster Art of World War 1 (http://www.pbs.org/wgbh/amex/wilson/gallery/p_war_09.html), accessed January 22, 2016.

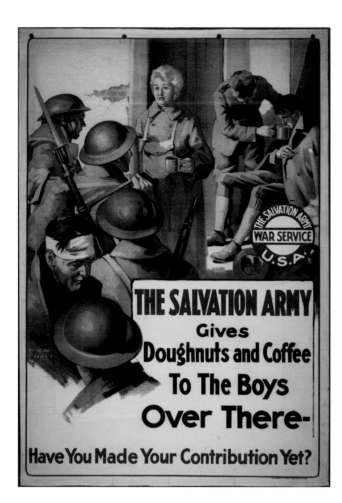

If the Salvation Army Doughnut . . . has brought any little cheer and comfort to the soldier and sailor boys of the great and free nation they have with their blood and brave hearts saved from destruction, I want to say that we "shall in nowise lose our reward."

—Evangeline Booth,
Salvation Army Commander, 1919

"The Salvation Army Gives Doughnuts and Coffee to the Boys Over There."

Artist: William Meade Prince; *Printer:* Illinois Litho. Co., Chicago, Illinois; *Publisher:* Salvation Army; *Technique:* Lithograph; *Dimensions:* 103 x 70 cm.

Salvation Army workers provided hot food and drinks to soldiers in the AEF. Two women serving with the Salvation Army were credited with the popularization of the doughnut while serving the men of the 1st Division in France.[1] New York State Library, Manuscripts and Special Collections.

1. "The History of Donut Day," The Salvation Army Metropolitan Division (http://centralusa.salvationarmy.org/metro/donutdayhistory/), accessed January 22, 2016.

Doughnuts and coffee.

Sylvia Coney, a canteen worker from New York, offers doughnuts and coffee to soldiers on the Italian Front. Courtesy of the Library of Congress.

"His Home Over There."

Artist: Albert Herter; *Printer:* Unknown; *Publisher:* YMCA/YWCA; *Technique:* Lithograph; *Dimensions:* 104 x 71 cm.

During the war, the YMCA and YWCA provided morale and welfare services to soldiers in the U.S. Army through the operation of 1,500 canteens at training camps in the United States and with the AEF in France. The Y also established more than 4,000 recreational facilities and raised more than $235 million for its relief efforts. New York State Museum Collection, H-1973.5.7 D.

YWCA jacket.

This woman's YWCA uniform jacket was worn by Henrietta D'Aran of New York City while in France where she served with the organization, which provided comfort and aid stations to soldiers in the AEF.[1] Courtesy of the New York State Military Museum, Division of Military and Naval Affairs.

1. *The Association Monthly: Official Organ of the Young Woman's Christian Association*, Volume 14, Issues 7–12, page xi. Available via Google Books (https://books.google.com/books?id=R3vOAAAAMAAJ&pg=PR11&lpg=PR11&dq=Henrietta+D%27Aran&source=bl&ots=6CfDi00uXz&sig=vE8z5EhcsPJKmKOO7ZklIUTbN98&hl=en&sa=X&ved=0ahUKEwiSn-vm0-jMAhVHmx4KHejZDzQQ6AEIMTAF#v=onepage&q=Henrietta%20D'Aran&f=false), accessed May 20, 2016. Henrietta D'Aran is listed in the publication as one of the "Workers in Europe" at 33 rue Caumartin, Paris, France.

Albert Herter (1871–1950).

Albert Herter was born in New York City, the son of a prominent interior designer. He studied at the Art Students League in New York and continued his artistic training in Paris in the 1890s. After returning to the United States, Herter and his wife settled in East Hampton on Long Island. Herter contributed to the war effort through illustrations and paintings for the American Red Cross and the United War Work Campaign. His eldest son, Everit, was killed in combat during World War I.[1]

1. Biography of Albert Herter, Wikipedia (https://en.wikipedia.org/wiki/Albert_Herter), accessed January 22, 2016.

"Civilians"(1918).

Artist: Sidney H. Riesenberg; *Printer:* Alco-Gravure, Inc., New York; *Publisher:* Jewish Welfare Board; *Technique:* Lithograph; *Dimensions:* 84 x 56 cm.

The Jewish Welfare Board was formed in New York City under the leadership of Dr. Cyrus Adler, a prominent Jewish scholar and religious leader and founder of the American Jewish Committee.[1] The Jewish Welfare Board coordinated the charitable work of twelve Jewish welfare agencies to provide comfort and support to the approximately 200,000 Jewish servicemen in the U.S. Army, Navy, and Marine Corps, the vast majority of whom came from New York. While headquartered in Manhattan, the board organized charitable drives across the state and nation with major events in Rochester (Monroe County) and Columbia County.[2] New York State Museum Collection, H-1973.94.1 X.

1. "Cyrus Adler," Jewish Virtual Library (http://www.jewishvirtuallibrary. org/jsource/judaica/ejud_0002_0001_0_00426.html), accessed November 9, 2016.

1. Flick, page 340.

Sidney H. Riesenberg (1885–1971).

Sidney Riesenberg was born in Chicago and studied at the Art Institute of Chicago. He moved to New York in 1905, settling in Yonkers, Westchester County. He was employed by several magazines and newspapers in New York City as a cover artist and illustrator.[1] During the war, Riesenberg was recruited to illustrate several posters for the war effort by the Division of Pictorial Publicity.[2] Among these posters was *Civilians*, published by the Jewish Welfare Board in 1918.

1. "Sidney H. Riesenberg Biography," The Vintage Poster (https:// www.thevintageposter.com/artist-biography/?at=SidneyHRiesenberg &InvNo=6139), accessed November 9, 2016.

2. Rawls, pp. 162, 248, and 253.

Millions of homeless and penniless Belgians urgently need our assistance. It is our sacred duty to aid these innocent victims until their cowardly despoilers have been put in their proper place, and Belgium restored to her people and to her brave King. If your wives, your brothers and your children were in a similar plight, how would you feel? Let your response be generous.

"Let Your Response Be Generous."

Artist: Unknown; *Printer:* Unknown; *Publisher:* Belgian Relief Fund;
Technique: Lithograph; *Dimensions:* 31.5 x 24 cm.

The Commission for Relief in Belgium was a charitable organization headed by future President Herbert Hoover. The Commission from 1914 to 1919 raised enough money to feed 11 million Belgian civilians living under German occupation. New Yorkers contributed generously to the aid of Belgium and other civilians caught in the fighting. In New York City alone $783,000 was donated in the first effort.[1] New York State Library, Manuscripts and Special Collections.

    1. Flick, page 336.

"American Ouvroir Funds" (1918).

Artist: Lucien Jonas; *Printer:* Imp. H. Chachoin, Paris, France;
Publisher: American Ouvroir Funds; *Technique:* Lithograph;
Dimensions: 78.75 x 58.5 cm.

The American Ouvroir Funds was a charitable organization established in Paris with its American headquarters at 681 Fifth Avenue in Manhattan. The Ouvroir Funds represented ten French societies caring for French children orphaned by the war. From 1918 to 1922, the organization sent $1.5 million to France.[1] New York State Museum Collection, H-1976.147.21.

    1. Miller, Lina D., *Directory of Social Agencies of New York*, 1922 (New York: The Charity Organization Society, 1922), pages 10–11.

"Save Serbia, Our Ally."

Artist: Théophile Alexander Steinlen; *Printer:* Unknown; *Publisher:* Serbian Relief Committee of America; *Technique:* Lithograph; *Dimensions:* 91 x 60 cm.

This poster for the Serbian Relief Committee of America calls on Americans to contribute to the refugee crisis in Serbia. Following the defeat of the Serbian Army, nearly 700,000 Serbians fled to the mountains of Albania where they faced disease, starvation, and death during the winter of 1915. Similar charitable organizations were established for civilians in other war-torn nations including Poland, Lithuania, Belgium, France, and Russia. New York State Museum Collection, H-1976.145.17.

Théophile Alexander Steinlen (1859–1923).

Théophile Alexander Steinlen was born in Switzerland. After studying at the University of Lausanne, he settled in eastern France and began his career as a painter and printmaker. In the 1880s, he moved to Paris and was soon circulating in the artist community around Montmartre, where he first began to create posters for local cabarets and other businesses. During the war, Steinlen created several posters for various charitable efforts in France, including one for the June 25, 1916, "Journée Serbe" (Serbia Day). Steinlen's art was co-opted by the Serbian Relief Committee of America for its fundraising efforts as well.

Journée Serbe.

Artist: Théophile Alexander Steinlen;
Printer: I. Lapina, Imp., Paris, France; *Publisher:* Unknown;
Technique: Lithograph; *Dimensions:* 120 x 80 cm.
New York State Library, Manuscripts and Special Collections.

"Lest They Perish."

Artist: William Gunning King; *Printer:* Conwell Graphic Companies, New York, New York; *Publisher:* American Committee for Relief in the Near East; *Technique:* Lithograph; *Dimensions:* 46.5 x 30 cm.

The American Committee for Relief in the Near East was founded in 1915 following reports of atrocities being committed against ethnic Armenians in the Ottoman Empire. The reported atrocities being committed against the Armenian Christian minority by the largely Muslim Ottoman authorities aroused American sympathies in ways that similar acts—of Eastern European Jews by Russian and Austrian authorities—did not.[1] The American Committee for Relief in the Near East was among the first charities to solicit funds through a national appeal. The Committee raised money through public rallies, private donations, and cooperation with other charitable organizations in order to purchase food and other necessary items for Armeinian refugees in modern-day Syria. New York State Library, Manuscripts and Special Collections.

1. Miglio, Sarah, "America's Sacred Duty: Near East Relief and the Armenian Crisis, 1915–1930," (South Bend: University of Notre Dame, PhD Candidate, Department of History, 2009), pages 1–2, Rockefeller Archive Center (http://rockarch.org/publications/resrep/miglio.pdf), accessed November 14, 2016.

William Gunning King (1859–1940).

William Gunning King was a British artist and illustrator. King studied at the Royal Academy Schools and became known for his depiction of rural life. During World War I, he created illustrations for posters for several British charitable organizations. His image of an Armenian mother and child was utilized by the American Committee for Relief in the Near East for its fundraising efforts.

"Helping Your Boy through No Man's Land."

Artist: Unknown; *Printer:* J.H. Hooker Litho. Co., New York, New York;
Publisher: Knights of Columbus; *Technique:* Lithograph;
Dimensions: 102 x 70 cm.

This poster advertises a Knights of Columbus event at Coney Island to raise money to provide comfort to soldiers in the AEF. The Knights raised nearly $30 million as a result of its fundraising efforts. New York State Library, Manuscripts and Special Collections.

"See Him Through."

Artist: Burton Rice; *Printer:* American Lithographic Co., New York, New York;
Publisher: Knights of Columbus, National Catholic War Council; *Technique:*
Lithograph; *Dimensions:* 76.25 x 51 cm.

The Knights of Columbus, a Catholic fraternal organization, operated respite centers for American soldiers both at home and abroad. 292 New Yorkers joined the 1,075 Knights sent overseas to care for American troops in France.[1] New York State Museum Collection, H-1973.94.1 J.

1. Flick, page 339.

Uncle Joe.

"Uncle Joe," a member of the Knights of Columbus from Utica, Oneida County, administers care to a wounded refugee in France.

From *U.S. Official Pictures of the Great War* (Washington, DC: Pictorial Bureau, 1920), New York State Museum Collection, H-1971.113.11.

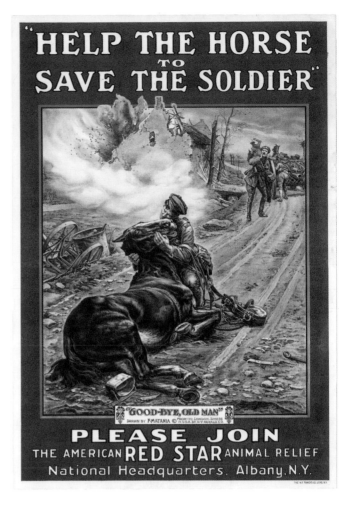

"American Red Star Animal Relief."

Artist: Unknown; *Printer:* Goodwin Lith., Albany, New York;
Publisher: American Red Star Animal Relief; *Technique:* Lithograph;
Dimensions: 81.5 x 56 cm.

In 1916, the American Humane Association, at the request of the United States Army, established the American Red Star Animal Relief Program to raise funds and supplies to care for the animals used by the AEF during World War I. The U.S. armed forces used over 240,000 horses and mules during the war to transport supplies and equipment in France. The Red Star Animal Relief agency was headquartered in Albany, New York, and collected funds, medical supplies, bandages, and ambulances to care for animals injured at the front. New York State Museum Collection, H-1976.158.16.

"Help the Horse to Save the Soldier."

Artist: Fortunino Matania; *Printer:* W.F. Powers Co. Litho., New York, New York;
Publisher: American Red Star Animal Relief; *Technique:* Lithograph;
Dimensions: 76.25 x 51 cm.

This poster for the American Red Star Animal Relief features a heart-wrenching illustration of a soldier cradling his dying horse on the battlefields in France. The illustration was created by Fortunino Matania, an Italian artist who had been living in Paris in 1914. As a war artist, Matania became famous for his realistic images of trench warfare and conditions at the front. This emotional appeal was intended to generate donations to purchase supplies for the horses of the American Expeditionary Force. New York State Museum Collection, H-1975.105.1.

"Help him to help U.S.!"

Artist: James Montgomery Flagg; *Printer:* W.F. Powers Co. Litho., New York, New York; *Publisher:* American Red Star Animal Relief; *Technique:* Lithograph; *Dimensions:* 82.5 x 57.5 cm.

James Montgomery Flagg again enlisted Uncle Sam to spur patriotic zeal during World War I in this poster for the American Red Star Animal Relief. New York State Library, Manuscripts and Special Collections.

"Books Wanted for Our Men!"

Artist: Charles Buckles Falls; *Printer:* Gill Engraving Company, New York, New York; *Publisher:* American Library Association; *Technique:* Lithograph; *Dimensions:* 106 x 70 cm.

This poster was created by artist Charles Buckles Falls for an American Library Association (ALA) book drive in 1918. The association was seeking books and magazines to be sent to respite areas behind the front lines in France. The ALA sought to improve education and recreational facilities for American soldiers at camps in the United States and at rest areas in the AEF. Dr. James I. Wyer, director of the New York State Library, led the association's wartime efforts. New York State Library, Manuscripts and Special Collections.

Charles Buckles Falls (1874–1960).

Charles Buckles Falls was born in Fort Wayne, Indiana, and moved to Chicago as a young man. He was employed as an architect's assistant and an illustrator for the *Chicago Tribune*. In 1900, Falls moved from Chicago to New York City, where he became a protégé of artist Joseph Pennell. He became a member of the Society of Illustrators and produced a number of posters for the Division of Pictorial Publicity for both military recruiting and other efforts.

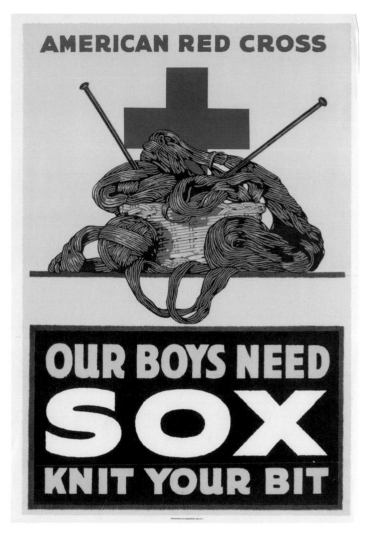

"Hey Fellows!"

Artist: John E. Sheridan; *Printer:* Unknown; *Publisher:* American Library Association; *Technique:* Lithograph; *Dimensions:* 68.5 x 35.5 cm.

During the course of the war, the American Library Association donated more than 3 million books and raised over $1.5 million to purchase more.[1] New York State Museum Collection, H–1973.94.1 0.

    1. Flick, page 341.

"Our Boys Need Sox."

Artist: Unknown; *Printer:* American Lithographic Co.; *Publisher:* American Red Cross; *Technique:* Lithograph; *Dimensions:* 76.25 x 51.5 cm.

Civilians on the home front were encouraged to participate in the war effort by contributing items, such as knit socks, that could be used to improve the comfort of American soldiers on the front lines. In Buffalo alone, the local Red Cross chapter employed nearly 20,000 knitters who produced 395,738 knitted garments for shipment to the AEF. Even the city's fire department was involved in the effort, producing more than 30,000 pairs of socks.[1] New York State Museum Collection, H–1976.147.7.

    1. Sullivan, page 1240.

Cooperstown knitting club.

School-age boys from Cooperstown, Otsego County, knitting for the Cooperstown Chapter of the American Red Cross during the war. In response to the boys' efforts, the Superintendent of Knitting for the Red Cross' Atlantic Division commended Cooperstown High School for their "manly boys."[1] Courtesy of the New York State Archives, A0412-78.

1. Letter, M.E. Baker to Miss M.L. Merchant, March 23, 1918. New York State Archives, New York State Education Department, Division of Archives and History, World War I veterans' service data and photographs, 1917–1938, Series A0412-78, Box 33, Folder 11.

Knitted balaclava, muffler, and wristlets.

This set of garments was hand knit for U.S. soldiers by "school girls or Red Cross Volunteers" during the war. It was donated to the New York State Museum by the widow of Captain George Corby, who served as a training officer at Camp Dix, New Jersey, during the conflict. New York State Museum Collection, H-1972.76.100 A-C.

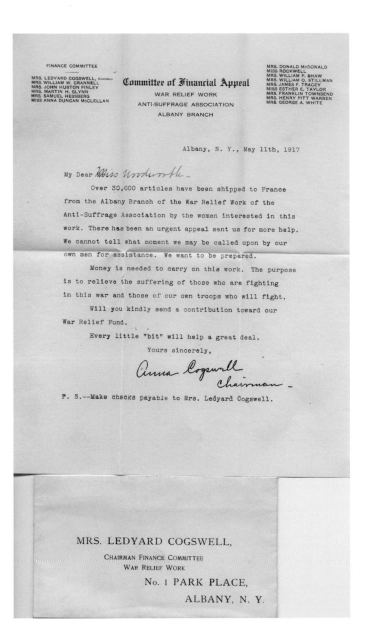

Anti-Suffrage Association.

This May 11, 1917, letter from Anna Cogswell, Chair of the Albany Branch of the Anti-Suffrage Association's War Relief Work Finance Committee, documents the efforts of the organization's membership to raise money and send comfort items to the soldiers of the AEF. New York State Archives, A3167-78A.

Cecil Josephine Cochran (1894–1918)
American Red Cross

Cecil Josephine Cochran was born in LeRoy, Genesee County. She volunteered for service with the American Red Cross at Rochester on May 10, 1918, at the age of twenty-four. After receiving training as a Red Cross nurse, Cochran was sent to Huntsville, Alabama—most likely to the Army training facility at Camp Sheridan. When she arrived there the field agent told her of the terrible epidemic of pneumonia that was raging and gave her the opportunity to turn back, but she insisted on aiding the suffering and dying soldiers. After faithfully nursing for ten days among the soldiers, she contracted the disease and died on October 10, 1918, at Huntsville, Alabama, Cecil Cochran was buried at St. Francis Catholic Cemetery in LeRoy.

Cecil Josephine Cochran.

Courtesy of the Rochester Historical Society.

"Remember Your First Thrill of American Liberty"

Artist: Unknown; *Printer:* Sackett and Wilhelms Corp., New York; *Publisher:* Second Liberty Loan; *Technique:* Lithograph; *Dimensions:* 76 x 51 cm.

The illustration on this poster for the Second Liberty Loan drive features immigrants aboard a ship as it sails past the Statue of Liberty into New York Harbor. The poster exhorts these new arrivals to the United States—many of whom fled in search of freedom and a better life—to contribute money to the war effort. The same poster was printed in Yiddish and Italian as well. In a sadly ironic way, the end of World War I and the restrictive immigration laws that ensued would put a halt to the type of immigration celebrated in the poster. Courtesy of the Library of Congress.

7

New York Divided

The War at Home

I do not think that by taking an oath of allegiance or a constitutional oath an enemy alien ceases to be an enemy alien. A citizen of Germany or Austria-Hungary is a citizen of a country at war with the United States.

—New York State Attorney General Merton E. Lewis[1]

As New Yorkers and other Americans rushed to show support for the war effort, a darker side to this patriotic zeal emerged. Suspicion of foreigners was heightened during the war, particularly of those of German descent, but later toward other groups as well. New repressive laws were enacted and civil liberties came under attack in the name of national security. President Wilson's declaration of war on April 2, 1917, did not immediately dispel the strong isolationist and antiwar sentiment of a large portion of the American population. The Espionage Act (1917) and the Sedition Act (1918) greatly increased the government's ability to suppress dissent. The Sedition Act, in particular, placed great restrictions on freedom of speech and punished disloyalty with imprisonment. Among the groups most frequently targeted under these new repressive laws were pacifists, socialists, labor organizers, and other "radicals."[2] Many of these groups made New York City their headquarters and national base. New Yorkers thus experienced a significant share of the repression of civil liberties during the war—both as the enforcer of that suppression and as the target of it. The New York State Police were frequently dispatched to investigate instances of suspected sedition. On January 2, 1918, troopers from Troop G were sent to Schenectady to investigate reports of a Canadian citizen who was accused of slandering the British government.[3] On February 18, the U.S. Army's Military Intelligence Bureau filed a complaint against Johedore Richert of Hudson Avenue in Albany. Over the next several days the State Police investigated the German immigrant, though nothing apparently came of their investigation.[4]

The State Council of Defense oversaw and investigated questions regarding the loyalty of New York State residents and answered requests for reports on the loyalty of prospective employees (most frequently of foreign birth or descent). The council also monitored several newspapers whose loyalty had been called into question by groups such as the American Defense Society.[5]

The war in Europe resulted in a rise of nationalistic sentiment among many in New York's immigrant communities across the state. Many volunteered to return to Europe to

"Americans All!"

Artist: Howard Chandler Christy; *Printer:* Unknown; *Publisher:* Victory Liberty Loan; *Technique:* Lithograph; *Dimensions:* 103 x 68.75 cm.

During the war, approximately 20 percent of the AEF was from an immigrant family.[1] As a result, the Committee on Public Information recognized the importance of producing posters that highlighted the contributions of immigrants to the American war effort. The CPI also produced several posters in foreign-language versions.[2] This poster, published for the 1919 Victory Liberty Loan drive, features an allegorical feminine America holding a laurel wreath above a "Roll of Honor." The names on this roll are clearly and distinctively ethnic, showing soldiers of Irish, Polish, Russian, Jewish, Italian, and Hispanic heritage, the implication of the poster being that all had served and died as 100 percent Americans. The publication of this poster, however, coincided with the formation of the Joint Legislative Committee to Investigate Seditious Activities in New York State. Under the leadership of State Senator Clayton Lusk, the committee sought to investigate socialist, labor, and ethnic organizations that were deemed a "threat to American democracy and capitalism."[3] The work of this committee and similar activities nationwide led to increased suspicion of immigrants and to restrictive immigration policies enacted by Congress in the 1920s. New York State Museum Collection, H-1972.112.1 Q.

1. Higham, John. *Strangers in the Land: Patterns of American Nativism 1860–1925* (New Brunswick, NJ: Rutgers University Press, 1983), page 216.

2. Keene, Jennifer. "Images of Racial Pride: African American Propaganda Posters in the First World War." In *Picture This: World War I Posters and Visual Culture*, edited by Pearl James (Lincoln, NE: U of Nebraska, 2009), page 210.

3. "The Lusk Committee: A Guide to the Records of the Joint Legislative Committee to Investigate Seditious Activities: A Guide to the Records Held in the New York State Archives" (Albany: New York State Archives, 1992), page 3.

Howard Chandler Christy (1872–1952).

Howard Chandler Christy was born in Morgan County, Ohio. After moving to New York City in 1890, Christy studied at the Art Students League and the National Academy of Art. During the Spanish-American War in 1898, Christy served as a combat artist with American forces in Puerto Rico and provided drawings of the conflict for several publications, including *Harper's Weekly* and *Leslie's Illustrated*. Upon returning to New York, Christy focused his work on female figures, creating the "Christy Girl," a modern American woman.[1] During the war, Christy produced several posters for the United States Navy and Marine Corps, as well as the Motor Corps of America. Even in his wartime work, his "Christy Girl" featured prominently.[2]

1. Biographical Sketch, Howard Chandler Christy Papers, 1873–2001, Lafayette College Special Collections and College Archives (http://academicmuseum.lafayette.edu/special/Christy/Christyonline/bio.html), accessed February 8, 2016.

2. Howard C. Christy Biography, Ohio History Central (http://www.ohiohistorycentral.org/w/Howard_C._Christy), accessed February 8, 2016.

"New York Jews Will Raise $5,000,000."

Artist: Unknown; *Printer:* Unknown; *Publisher:* The Jewish War Relief Committee; *Technique:* Lithograph; *Dimensions:* 28 x 53.5 cm.

Between December 3 and 15, 1917, Jewish business and community leaders in New York City pledged to raise $5 million for war relief efforts by requesting a $3 donation from each member of the Jewish population in New York City.[1] Despite these efforts and the enlistment of more than 50,000 Jewish soldiers and sailors, the loyalty of the Jewish population in New York and across the United States was repeatedly called into question by anti-Semitic politicians and organizations.[2] While New York's Jewish community was seeking to prove its loyalty to the United States, other New Yorkers including Madison Grant, John Trevor, and other wartime anti-Semites, were working to ensure a dramatic reduction in the number of "undesirable" immigrants permitted into the country.[3] New York State Library, Manuscripts and Special Collections.

1. "Jews to Raise $5,000,000," *The New York Times*, November 12, 1917 (http://timesmachine.nytimes.com/timesmachine/1917/11/12/102649223.html), accessed May 24, 2015.

2. Records of the Joint Legislative Committee to Investigate Seditious Activities (Lusk Committee), New York State Archives Series L0039, Investigative Subject Files, 1919–1920, Box 1, Folder 18.

3. Jaffe, pages 214–215.

defend the nations of their birth. Others worked to support their homelands financially. This surge of loyalty for their homelands among New York's immigrant population also caused concern in the government—both state and federal—and within the native-born population over the apparently divided loyalties of a large segment of the populace.[6]

American entry into the war heightened these fears. In Rochester, and presumably elsewhere, the U.S. Marshals undertook a census of foreign-born workers in the city's industries; the Rochester total was more than 40,000 individuals who were either naturalized citizens or resident aliens.[7] The fear and suspicion of foreigners intensified the already prevalent Americanization movement. Newly arrived immigrants were encouraged to learn English and to discard much of the cultural identity of their native lands.

The outbreak of war in Europe resulted in a halt to traditional immigration to the United States. At the same time, the need for wartime labor led to an increased migration of African Americans from the South into New York cities. In Brooklyn, it was estimated that 10,000 African Americans had migrated north between 1917 and 1918 in search of better wages and more humane treatment.[8] Rochester saw an 80 percent increase in its African American population between 1910 and 1920. Much of this migration was due to the rise in wartime manufacturing in the city as companies such as Eastman Kodak and Bausch and Lomb received massive contracts for war materiel.[9] Others found opportunities as farm laborers. This influx of blacks into predominantly white cities and towns frequently resulted in racial tensions.[10] These workers were often given the most menial jobs and were the first to be fired when the wartime contracts ended.[11] At the same time, both of these groups were expected to prove their loyalty through unwavering participation in the war effort. During the war, the U.S. government often produced posters that targeted specific segments or groups in American society to encourage participation in the war effort. This included African Americans and immigrant populations.[12] Perhaps nowhere is this dichotomy and hypocrisy between reality and expectations more readily apparent than in the poster art being produced by the DPP.

Americanism

Americanism and nativism were hardly new ideologies in the United States in 1917. Prior to the outbreak of the American Civil War in 1861, native-born citizens feared the influx of immigrants who spoke different languages, subscribed to different religions, or competed for jobs. This anti-immigrant sentiment coalesced around the Know-Nothing Movement of the 1850s.

In the decades after the Civil War, Americanism and its adherents advocated for the assimilation of immigrant groups into "100 percent Americans." Theodore Roosevelt emerged as one of the leading proponents of this new Americanism. Rather than turning away newly arrived immigrants, Roosevelt advocated that "We must Americanize them in every way, in speech, in political ideas and principles, and in their way of looking at the relations between Church and State. We welcome the German or the Irishman who becomes an American. We have no use for the German or Irishman who remains such."[14] Roosevelt and other adherents to Americanization in the late-nineteenth and early-twentieth centuries believed in creating a unified and culturally homogenous national citizenry by fostering civic Americanism in newly arrived immigrants. They directed their ire toward groups who refused to abandon their cultural

"We Are Doing Our Bit" (1918).

Artist: Jane "Jennie" Toussant; *Printer:* Unknown; *Publisher:* War Savings Stamp Committee; *Technique:* Lithograph; *Dimensions:* 77.5 x 52 cm.

This War Savings Stamp advertisement features an African American soldier in close quarters combat with multiple Germans. The soldier's canteen bears the number "15," likely a reference to the 15th Regiment of the New York National Guard. The regiment, re-designated as the 369th Infantry Regiment during the war, was an African American unit from Harlem in New York City.

The lone African American soldier isolated from the rest of the American forces in the background may have been a symbolic choice by the artist. Most African American soldiers were used in labor battalions and as stevedores. The 369th Infantry and other African American combat troops were assigned to the French Army rather than the AEF. In August 1918, American commanders in the AEF sent a communiqué to the French expressing concern over the treatment of African American troops under French command. According to the circular, American officers were "afraid that contact with the French will inspire in black Americans aspirations which to them [the whites] appear intolerable."[1] Thus, while 200,000 African Americans were serving in the United States Army, and just one month before the war savings stamp drive advertised in this poster called on African American civilians to invest in the American war effort, the United States government was actively working to ensure that African Americans retained their inferior status in American society. New York State Museum Collection, H-1976.147.8.

1. "Documents of the War," *The Crisis*, Volume 18, No. 1, May 1919, pages 16–17.

THE FLAG SPEAKS

I am whatever you make me, nothing more.
But always, I am all that you hope to be,
and have the courage to try for.
I am song and fear, struggle and panic, and
ennobling hope.
I am the days work of the weakest man,
and the largest dream of the most daring.
I am the constitution and the courts,

statutes and the statute makers, soldier and
dreadnaught, drayman and street sweep,
cook, counselor and clerk.
I am no more than what you believe me to be.
My stars and my stripes are your dream
and your labors. For you are the makers of
the flag and it is well that you glory in the
making.

FRANKLIN K. LANE

ISSUED BY NATIONAL AMERICANIZATION COMMITTEE, 20 West 34th St., City of New York

DISTRIBUTED BY DEPARTMENT OF INTERIOR BUREAU OF EDUCATION

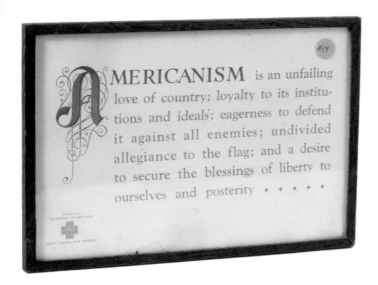

Roosevelt Americanism.

In a 1915 Columbus Day speech at Carnegie Hall, former President Theodore Roosevelt asserted, "There is no place here for the hyphenated American, and the sooner he returns to the country of his allegiance, the better."[1] For Roosevelt—a leading proponent of 100% Americanism—and others in the movement, the failure of immigrant communities to fully assimilate into American society posed a significant threat to American national security.[2] By 1917, Americanism had a wide adherence in New York State and across the nation. Of newly arriving immigrants, Roosevelt argued that the nation must "Americanize them in every way, in speech, in political ideas and principles . . . We welcome the German or Irishman who becomes American. We have no use for the German or Irishman who remains such."[3] While much of Roosevelt's immediate ire was directed towards German Americans during the war years, Americanism and the mistrust of immigrants who retained their ethnic (and racial) identity was applied to all immigrant communities to varying degrees. Such prevailing attitudes among native-born Americans made it very difficult for German Americans—and immigrants of all national origins—to fully "prove" their loyalty above reproach and suspicion during World War I. New York State Museum, H-1998.20.132.

1. "Roosevelt Bars the Hyphenated American," *The New York Times*, October 13, 1915, page 1.

2. Roosevelt, Theodore, *The Great Adventure* (New York: Charles Scribner's Sons, 1918), page 49.

3. Roosevelt, Theodore, "True Americanism," *Forum* Magazine, April 1894 (http://www.theodore-roosevelt.com/images/research/speeches/trta.pdf), accessed November 15, 2016.

"Many Peoples, One Nation."

Artist: Franklin Knight Lane; *Printer:* Ray Greenleaf, New York; *Publisher:* National Americanization Committee, New York City; *Technique:* Lithograph; *Dimensions:* 61 x 143.25 cm.

This poster published by the National Americanization Committee advocated for the Americanization of all under the national flag. New York State Museum Collection, H-1992.19.18.

heritage, who continued to speak in their native languages, and who professed a continued loyalty to their mother country. Those immigrants who assimilated into American society were welcomed by Roosevelt. Roosevelt applauded Americans of German descent, such as Eddie Rickenbacker, the American ace pilot, and others fighting in the American Expeditionary Forces in France. He called on German-language newspapers to suspend publication or to print only in English. To refuse to do so would mean these publications would "cease to be useful to the country."[15]

By 1917, anti-German sentiments combined with a rising fear of socialism—seen by many in America as a foreign threat—after the Bolshevik

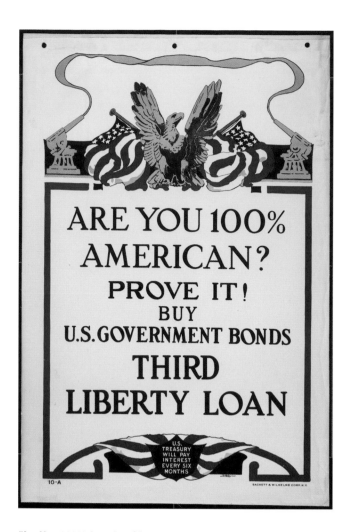

"Are You 100% American?"

Artist: Stern; *Printer:* Sackett and Wilhelms Corp., New York; *Publisher:* Unknown; *Technique:* Lithograph; *Dimensions:* 74 x 49.5 cm.

The U.S. Government's Committee on Public Information became one of the leading proponents of 100 Percent Americanism during World War I, calling for total allegiance to the nation and the war effort. New York State Library, Manuscripts and Special Collections.

Revolution in Russia resulted in a significant shift in the "100 percent American" movement. This ideology advocated total allegiance to the United States, its customs and traditions, symbols, government, and language. Anyone deemed foreign was not welcome. The movement by World War I sought to erase the culture and heritage of immigrant groups. The German immigrant population was the initial focus of the movement's efforts, and later targeted Eastern Europeans and other immingrant groups. After the war, adherents to the Americanism movement were generally strictly anticommunist and proponents of restrictive immigration policies.

The central role occupied by New York State's industrial and agricultural centers, New York Harbor's position as the primary port of embarkation for almost 80 percent of the AEF, and New York City's position as the financial capital of the nation did make the Empire State an inviting target for enemy activities during the war. German agents and sympathizers did indeed plan and attempt numerous plots aimed to thwart the steady flow of materiel to the Allied armies in Europe from the outset of war in 1914. New York City remained a hotbed of German espionage efforts from 1914 until 1917. With the end of diplomatic relations after America's declaration of war, German efforts to undermine the American war effort through espionage and sabotage declined significantly.

Schumann-Heink sewing flag,

German American opera star Ernestine Schumann-Heink photographed here sewing an American flag. Like many lesser known German immigrants, even Schumann-Heink, who frequently performed at the Metropolitan Opera House in New York City, sought to prove her loyalty to her adopted country despite questions of loyalty to their native Germany. Courtesy of the Library of Congress.

Fingerprinting a German.

This 1917 photograph, captioned, "Fingerprinting a German," shows a New York City Police Officer in the process of arresting an unidentified German national or immigrant. Courtesy of the Library of Congress.

Despite the lack of successful attempts at spying and sabotage, large segments of the state's population were placed under increased and often unwarranted suspicion during World War I. Those of German descent, in particular, became the target of private groups such as the American Defense Society. Some of these groups had the unofficial or even the official backing of the state and federal governments during the conflict. The war witnessed a dramatic rise in the use of police and other law enforcement agencies in the observation and investigation of individuals. In New York, the newly established State Police were frequently dispatched at the request of federal agencies to investigate violations of the federal espionage and sedition laws, as well as to enforce the draft. The fear and suspicion that permeated society during World War I would continue well after the Armistice and fell on a broader segment of American society—immigrants, African Americans, labor organizers, and many others.

Foreigners soon became the focus of suspicions, particularly immigrants from the Central Powers. World War I pitted the United States against a nation that had sent one of the largest and most distinctive ethnic populations to the U.S. for decades.[16] Americans struggled with how to deal with this potential danger from within. German-language newspapers became the target of government censorship and New York State schools dropped German from the curriculum.[17] Doubts about the loyalty of some Irish immigrants were also raised. Many supported the nationalist movement in Ireland, then under British rule, and saw a German victory over Great Britain as a means to gain Irish independence. Following the 1917 overthrow of the tsarist government in Russia by the Bolsheviks, many Americans also saw a subversive threat posed by socialism, which was viewed as a foreign movement. Immigrants from Eastern Europe and of Jewish descent in particular were suspected of radical socialist leanings.

These groups and others faced significant repression, censorship, and harassment—both from official government representatives and from private citizens' groups such as the American Protective League. In some cities, German aliens were required to register and to carry identification cards. By 1918, federal law required enemy aliens to do so nationwide.

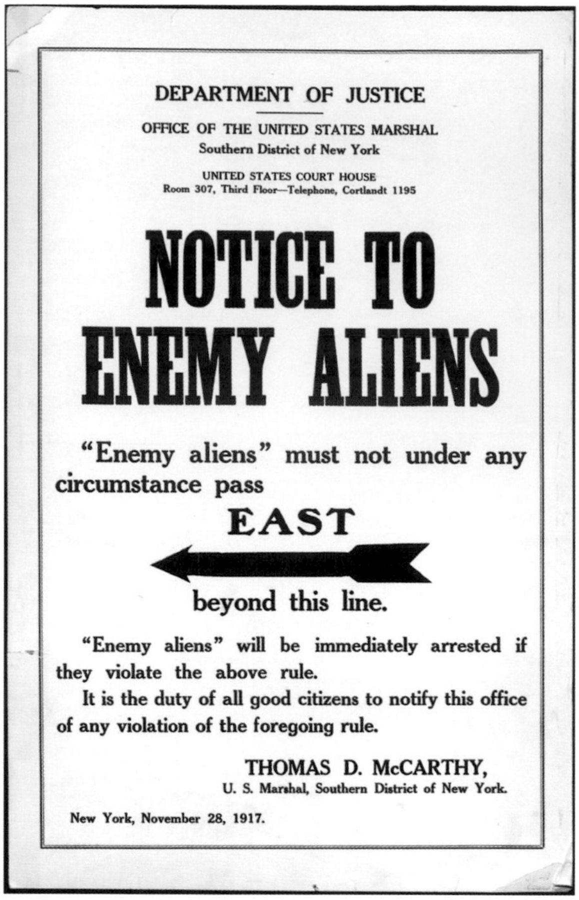

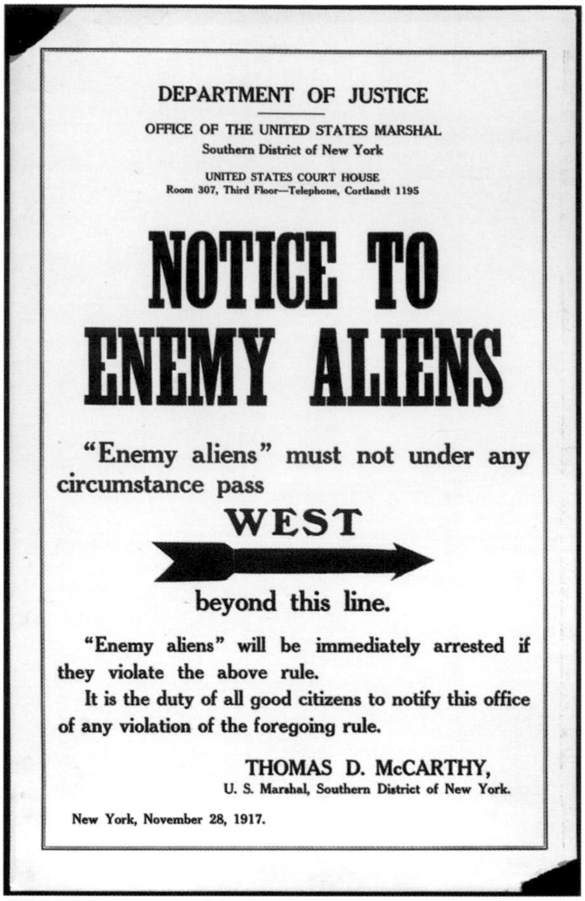

DEPARTMENT OF JUSTICE

OFFICE OF THE UNITED STATES MARSHAL
Southern District of New York

UNITED STATES COURT HOUSE
Room 307, Third Floor—Telephone, Cortlandt 1195

NOTICE TO ENEMY ALIENS

"Enemy aliens" must not under any circumstance pass

EAST

← beyond this line.

"Enemy aliens" will be immediately arrested if they violate the above rule.

It is the duty of all good citizens to notify this office of any violation of the foregoing rule.

THOMAS D. McCARTHY,
U. S. Marshal, Southern District of New York.

New York, November 28, 1917.

DEPARTMENT OF JUSTICE

OFFICE OF THE UNITED STATES MARSHAL
Southern District of New York

UNITED STATES COURT HOUSE
Room 307, Third Floor—Telephone, Cortlandt 1195

NOTICE TO ENEMY ALIENS

"Enemy aliens" must not under any circumstance pass

WEST

→ beyond this line.

"Enemy aliens" will be immediately arrested if they violate the above rule.

It is the duty of all good citizens to notify this office of any violation of the foregoing rule.

THOMAS D. McCARTHY,
U. S. Marshal, Southern District of New York.

New York, November 28, 1917.

"Notice to Enemy Aliens," U.S. Department of Justice.

Artist: None; *Printer:* Unknown; *Publisher:* U.S. Department of Justice; *Technique:* Lithograph; *Dimensions:* 56 x 35 cm.

Enemy aliens were barred from areas near sites of critical infrastructure and factories out of fear for potential sabotage or espionage. Other citizens were encouraged to report any suspicious activity by "enemy aliens" to the government. New York State Library, Manuscripts and Special Collections.

JUSTIZ-ABTEILUNG

BÜRO DES UNITED STATES MARSHALS
Südlicher Bezirk von New York

UNITED-STATES-COURT-GEBÄUDE
Zimmer No. 307, 3. Etage—Telefon: Cortlandt 1195

Warnung für Feindliche Ausländer

Solchen Ausländern (also Feindesange-hörigen) ist der Übergang oder Aufent-halt verboten:

ÖSTLICH

← dieser Linie

Bei Nichtbeachtung dieser Gesetzesbestimmung werden solche Ausländer sofort in Haft genommen.

Es ist die Pflicht eines jeden guten Bürgers, des Marshals Büro in Kenntnis zu setzen bei etwaiger Verletzung obiger Gesetzesbestimmung.

THOMAS D. McCARTHY,
U. S. Marshal, südlicher Bezirk von New York.

New York, 28. November 1917.

"Alien Enemies Take Notice."

Artist: None; *Printer:* Brooklyn Eagle Press; *Publisher:* U.S. Department of Justice; *Technique:* Lithograph; *Dimensions:* 55.5 x 36 cm.

Citizens of Germany, Austria-Hungary, and the Ottoman Empire were forced to register as Enemy Aliens. They were prohibited from entering zones near military installations, ports, railroads, and other infrastructure and industries critical to the war effort. The U.S. Marshal's Office was tasked with the registration of enemy aliens. New York State Library, Manuscripts and Special Collections.

"Vigilance Corps."

Artist: Unknown; *Printer:* Unknown; *Publisher:* American Defense Society; *Technique:* Lithograph; *Dimensions:* 55.5 x 35 cm.

The American Defense Society (ADS) was founded in 1915 in response to the sinking of the *Lusitania*. The organization advocated for American intervention in World War I against Germany and was strongly opposed to Socialism and its potential subversion in the United States. The ADS was also a strong voice for "100% Americanism" and restrictive immigration policies following World War I. The Society's "Vigilance Corps" was created to assist the government with the registration of enemy aliens.[1] New York State Library, Manuscripts and Special Collections.

1. Historical Note, Guide to the Records of the American Defense Society, New-York Historical Society, October 19, 2011 (http://dlib.nyu.edu/findingaids/html/nyhs/americandefsoc/bioghist.html), accessed April 17, 2016.

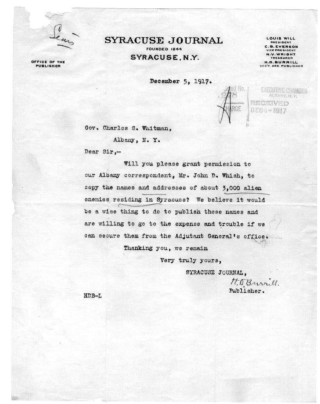

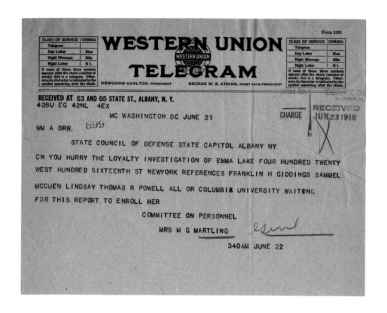

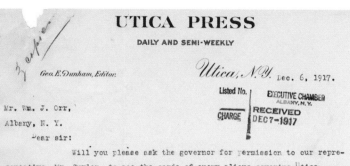

Correspondence files, New York State Council of Defense.

These correspondence to the state's Council of Defense include requests for reports on the loyalty of potential employees. These requests came from companies or organizations such as Columbia University and the American Red Cross. The State Defense Council also received requests from newspapers across the state seeking to publish the names of enemy aliens whose loyalty to the United States was in question—regardless of whether they had committed any act to warrant such suspicion. New York State Archives, A4234-78.

PUBLICATIONS IN THE ENGLISH LANGUAGE

Loyalty Questioned	:	Alleged to be seditious
American Hebrew	:	American Isrealite
Fatherland	:	American Jewish Review
	:	
	:	
	:	
	:	
	:	
	:	

    In addition to the foregoing, the publications checked on the enclosed list of the New York Public Library are questioned. Those marked in pencil with an interrogation mark are alleged to be disloyal, while those marked with a check mark are said to contain seditious articles.

American Defense Society Certificate of Membership.

Artist: Unknown; *Printer:* Unknown; *Publisher:* American Defense Society; *Technique:* Unknown; *Dimensions:* 21.5 x 28 cm.

The ADS called upon Americans to join under the motto, "Serve at the Front, or Serve at Home." Membership fees ranged from $1 to $100.[1] New York State Library, Manuscripts and Special Collections.

1. *Handbook of the American Defense Society*, May 1918, page 8. Google Books (https://books.google.com/books?id=qPE7AQAAMAAJ&printsec=frontcover#v=onepage&q&f=false), accessed May 23, 2016.

Charles Steinmetz (1865–1923)

Charles P. Steinmetz was born in 1865 in Breslau, Germany. Steinmetz's involvement with the Socialist Party while he was a student at the University of Breslau led to suspicion by the German government and caused him to flee his homeland and immigrate to the United States, arriving at Ellis Island in 1888.

Steinmetz eventually made his way to Schenectady and the General Electric Company. His study of alternating electrical currents revolutionized the engineering and manufacture of circuits and machinery. Steinmetz soon earned the nickname "The Wizard of Schenectady."

Steinmetz supported the American policy of neutrality and was initially opposed to the nation's entry into the war. Once war was declared, he supported the war effort and, as chief of General Electric's Consulting Engineering Laboratory, assisted in GE's work for the U.S. Navy. Despite his important work with GE, Steinmetz's German roots and socialist leanings left him open to suspicion. In an August 11, 1917, letter from Lieutenant Colonel Marlborough Churchill, chief of the War Department's Military Intelligence Branch, to Bruce Bielaski of the Bureau of Investigation (the precursor to the FBI), Churchill describes Steinmetz as a "prominent theoretical socialist" and "bitterly pro-German." The Bureau's investigative file on Charles Steinmetz ran to more than eighty pages.[18]

Charles Proteus Steinmetz with Italian inventor Guglielmo Marconi.

Courtesy of the Library of Congress, George Grantham Bain Collection.

195

During the last months, grave doubts have arisen in the minds of many thoughtful citizens of the United States, whether the attitude of our industrial, social and political government is in agreement with the principles laid down by the founders of our nation: to develop our own destiny, without entangling alliances with European interests, but with equal fairness and impartiality to all. A fear is gaining ground, that the mental attitude of our leading classes is more and more becoming that of a British colony rather, than an independent American nation, and that on our present path we are drawing upon us the mutual hatred, which has arisen between European nations, and may even drift into war, in spite of our desire for peace, (by some European nation considering our action while at peace, as more harmful to their interests, than our open warfare could be.)

Whatever America may have become, if it had remained a British Colony, is of no interest today: we know what it is, a new nation, formed by the amalgamation of numerous races and nations, in which none of the races, neither the British nor the Irish, neither the German nor the Mediterranian or Slav, preponderates sufficiently to allow its mental attitude, its allegiance to the Mother Country of their ancestors, to dominate the American policy.

While Dutch and Irish, Scandinavian and French contributed to the early colonisation of the United States, British colonies prevailed, and during the days of Washington, America was essentially an Anglo-Saxon country: probably over 70% of the population being of English descent. Even as late as 1850, the racial composition of the new nation had changed little. Then however came the great streams of immigration: German and Irish, Scandinavians, and later Mediterranians and Slavs came to these shores, became citizens, created America's prosperity and fought its wars, and gradually the Anglo-Saxon contingent fell below 50% (in the early 80's), and in the 90's, the Irish-German contingent passed numerically the Anglo-Saxon. It is significant that from this period dates the more liberal conception of life, as exemplified by the elimination of the blue laws and other remnants of partisanism. Puritanism.

At present, the white population of the United States approximates 35% of Anglo-Saxon descent, 40% of Irish, German, Dutch and Scandinavian descent and 25% of Mediterranian and Slav descent.

It is interesting to note, that since a generation, America has not been an Anglo-Saxon nation any more.

However, American society, American domestic and public life and policy, are still dominated and controlled by the Anglo-Saxon minority, and other races, which merged

Pamphlet, "Neutrality Meeting, April 1915."

This typed document advocating for continued American neutrality features handwritten corrections and notes, presumably made by Charles Steinmetz. While Steinmetz initially opposed American involvement in the war, when President Wilson declared war in April 1917, Steinmetz became a supporter of the American war effort. The Charles P. Steinmetz Collection, Schenectady County Historical Society, Series 3, No. 54.

SUSPICION AND PARANOIA

Once war was declared, immigrants from the Central Powers and other potential sympathizers immediately fell under suspicion as potential threats to the security of New York. A number of measures were taken to defend the state. On May 21, 1917, the state legislature passed the Peace and Safety Act authorizing the attorney general to investigate all cases of suspected disloyalty. A system of surveillance was deployed statewide, including listening in on telephone conversations, inspecting mail, and reporting conversations and public statements of suspects. Volunteers for the American Protective League were organized in virtually every community. The record of the New York State Police, which was established in 1917, indicates that eight individuals were arrested

---

into the American nation, have usually submitted, and tried to adapt their mental attitude to that of the Anglo-Saxons, with the only exception of the Irish, who consistently opposed "British Dominion".

But with the present European war, the difference between the American, and the British-Anglo-Saxon interests have become apparent: America's interest is that of perfect and strict neutrality, that is, non partisanship; to take care and protect our business, our industrial and agricultural production, our commerce, and use all our influence for peace and for an early ending of the terrible slaughter; to avoid any action, however permissible it may appear to us under formal law, which violates international and national morality by prolonging and increasing the slaughter of our European brothers, even if we should go as far as our nation has gone a year ago, when during the Mexican war we placed an embargo on the exportation of arms to Mexico on the high moral ground, that America should not contribute to the slaughter of people, with whom we have no quarrel, especially when - without any fault or responsibility of ours - our exportation of arms would have helped the one Mexican faction and not the other one, since only one had control of harbors and therefore could import arms from us.

CPS-SW   Charles P. Steinmetz
April 22, 1915
Schenectady, N.Y.

August 16, 1915.

Editor New York Press,
New York City.

Dear Sir:-

My answer to the ten questions, which your
representative submitted to me, is as follows:

Question 1). Was the sinking of the Lusitania
justified under any circumstances?

Question 2). Did President Wilson err in either
thought or action in his notes,
following the torpedoing of the
Lusitania?

Question 3). Was he (Pres. Wilson) wise in asking
for an apology and further reparation
from the German Government?

Question 4). Was William J. Bryan wiser or more
practical than the President in his
action on the German notes?

Question 5). Has the general conduct of President
Wilson towards the belligerents been
that of an impracticable administrator,
one out of touch with his countrymen?

"Questions 1) to 5) are difficult to answer, as
their wording suggests a form of criticism of our administrative
officials, which does not appear entirely proper.   For

-3-

In a national editorial published some weeks
ago, I have more fully explained this in reference to
the submarine as factor of our national defense, as
follows:

"The submarine is the newest and most terrible
weapon of naval warfare, and in its short career it has
outraged humanity and made war more inhuman than any
other engine of destruction.

Its first exploit, in sinking the three British
cruisers at the beginning of the war, necessitated the order
to all the ship commanders, never to stop to save life, but
when a ship is struck, to scatter and leave the crew of the
torpedoed ship to its fate: practically certain death. From
then on, the loss of life in naval battle has tremendously
increased.

The defenselessness of the submarine, when seen,
means, that it must strike like the rattle-snake, before it
is discovered, and the laws of civilized warfare, as they
were developed when the nations fought on the water, and not
under the water and in the air above the water, are being
thrown aside, made scraps of paper, like many other things
in the present war.

-2-

instance, the expression "impracticable administrator"
applied in question 5) to our chief executive, would
be most improper.   It would in addition be a
reflection on the millions of citizens, who elected
President Wilson, to which no sane man can subscribe.

In my opinion, as American citizen, the duty
of our nation during the present war is:

1) To protest against any and every violation of
international law by any of the belligerents, even if we
are neither willing nor able to enforce compliance, so
that such violations do not become established as law by
precedent, and that our nation has proper voice and
influence to remodel international law after the war.

2) To carefully guide all our actions, even if it
should result in a temporary inconvenience, so that the
modifications of international law, which, has pointed
out by our President, will result from the war, are in
the interest of humanity and more particularly increase
the efficiency of our national defense.

-4-

Justly humanity is outraged and frantically tries
to stop international lawlessness.   But still all warring nations
without exception overthrow and disregard whatever "international
law" - if such a thing really exists - operates against their
interest.

And still all neutral nations build submarines,
and how they will use them in an emergency when their
national existence is at stake, we fear to think.

The laws of civilized warfare are being changed
with the changing conditions of the engines of war, and so
far the change has not been towards the better, the more human,
and naturally and justly we protest against such a change.

But when doing so, let us look beyond the present
horrors, weigh carefully what we approve, and what we disapprove,
lest by present sentiment we may be carried away to approve
things which may in the future endanger our national safety,
oppose things, on which some time we might have to rely for
our preservation, for after all, war and humanity have never
gone together and never will, but as Sherman said "War is Hell".

The grave question now is before us, whether submarines
can be permitted to destroy merchant ships carrying ammunition
and other supplies of the enemy, when such destruction neces-

---

Typescript.

Typed answers to questions submitted to Charles Steinmetz by the *New York Press* in 1915 regarding Steinmetz's views on war, politics, and the sinking of the *Lusitania*. The Charles P. Steinmetz Collection, Schenectady County Historical Society, Series 3, No. 79.

for violations of the Espionage Act. Three enemy aliens were apprehended by State Troopers and one person was charged with sedition.[19] In a state whose population was more than 9.1 million people in 1910, much of this fear and suspicion proved to be unwarranted or at least greatly exaggerated.[20]

"Warning!"

Artist: None; *Printer:* Unknown; *Publisher:* National Committee of Patriotic Societies; *Technique:* Unknown; *Dimensions:* 74 x 53 cm.

This poster sets out to clarify certain rumors on the home front as German lies, "sent out to keep this Country from putting its whole strength into the War." New York State Library, Manuscripts and Special Collections.

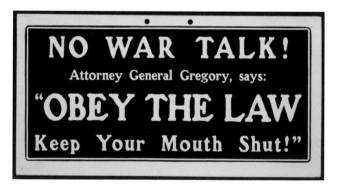

"No War Talk!" (1917).

Artist: None; *Printer:* Unknown; *Publisher:* Unknown; *Technique:* Lithograph; *Dimensions:* 19 x 36 cm.

This text only poster exhorts civilians to keep quiet about their war work out of fear of information being overheard by German spies. New York State Library, Manuscripts and Special Collections.

PROCLAMATION

STATE OF NEW YORK
EXECUTIVE CHAMBER

WHEREAS: Adequate supplies of food, munitions and all other products necessary for the equipment and maintenance of our Army and Navy, and for the maintenance of our people and our allies constitute an immediate and vital necessity in the world war upon which we have entered, and

WHEREAS: Attainment of this end requires first of all conservation of such food and resources as are now in hand as well as the production of new supplies.

NOW, THEREFORE, I, Charles S. Whitman, Governor of the State of New York, do hereby call upon all citizens of the State, particularly those concerned with the production and storage or handling of food, munitions, and all other supplies useful or necessary to the successful conduct of the war, to vigilantly guard against loss by fire or explosion, one great source of waste which is constantly menacing stored or manufactured materials and the plants producing or handling them, the losses from which in New York State exceed thirty millions of dollars a year. Much of this waste is preventable, requiring only care and watchfulness for its elimination. Preventable fire has been characterized by the President of the United States as a "public dereliction."

And I do further call to the attention of our citizens the fact that the National Board of Fire Underwriters in the Nation, and other similar organizations in our State, are engaging in a vigorous campaign for a war-time protection of industries and vital resources from destruction by fire, enlisting for this purpose the services of a large number of trained inspectors, who are acting under the authority of the State Defense Council, through its Industrial Division. It will not be the purpose of these inspectors to find fault, but rather to advise and assist citizens in taking every precaution, by care and constant watchfulness, to prevent to the utmost, loss by fire. In this crisis therefore, it becomes the patriotic duty of every citizen or resident of the State to assist in this most useful work for our country. New York is the foremost industrial State of the Union, and here are manufactured, stored and handled vast supplies vitally needed.

While this is primarily the duty of the owners of the plants and warehouses, it does not stop there. At this time what is ordinarily a matter of private interest becomes an urgent public duty. It becomes, therefore, equally the duty of the workmen, the employers, and of citizens generally, to participate whole-heartedly in the promotion of this campaign. Let there be not only a remedying of dangerous and defective conditions, but let there be also a general and widespread observance of such rules of personal conduct and the exercise of such vigilance in and about places where valuable stores of supplies are made and handled, that the danger of fire may be reduced to the lowest point possible.

This is your patriotic duty. Waste helps only our enemy. Protect our supplies and help win the war.

GIVEN UNDER MY HAND AND THE PRIVY SEAL OF THE STATE, in the Capitol, at the City of Albany, this seventeenth day of July, in the Year of Our Lord, One Thousand Nine Hundred and Seventeen.

(L. S.)

(Signed) CHARLES S. WHITMAN

By the Governor
WILLIAM A. ORR,
Secretary to the Governor

Proclamation (1917).

This proclamation concerns the protection of Rochester's manufactured goods from fire. The fear of saboteurs was a significant concern across New York State in 1917 and 1918. Courtesy of the Rochester Historical Society.

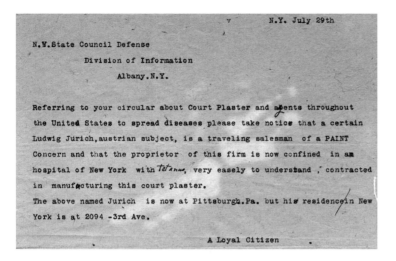

N.Y. July 29th

N.Y.State Council Defense

Division of Information

Albany.N.Y.

Referring to your circular about Court Plaster and agents throughout the United States to spread diseases please take notice that a certain Ludwig Jurich, austrian subject, is a traveling salesman of a PAINT Concern and that the proprietor of this firm is now confined in an hospital of New York with *Tetanus*, very easely to understand , contracted in manufacturing this court plaster.

The above named Jurich is now at Pittsburgh.Pa. but his residence in New York is at 2094 -3rd Ave.

A Loyal Citizen

Letter.

This July 1917 letter was sent to the New York State Defense Council by an anonymous "Loyal Citizen." In the letter, the author implicates Ludwig Jurich, an Austrian immigrant and paint salesman, with contaminating court plaster with tetanus. Unfounded fear and suspicion of enemy aliens was rampant in New York as well as across the nation. New York State Archives Collection, Series A4238-78, Box 1, Folder 5.

Saboteurs

Between 1914 and America's entry into World War I, Germany sought numerous ways to slow the flow of war materials from the United States to the Allies. With the official American policy of neutrality still in effect, German use of submarines threatened to bring America into the war as an active participant. Thus, the German government sought more covert means of impacting shipping: sabotage.

New York City presented several unique vulnerabilities that state and local authorities were tasked with defending. New York was almost wholly dependent on the uninterrupted flow of food, fuel, and water into the city via rail, ship, and aqueduct, as well as a growing highway system. The water system was of particular concern. New York City consumed more than 580 million gallons of water each day. Damage or contamination of the system of reservoirs and aqueducts could not only threaten the city's civilian population, but it would inhibit the nation's ability to use the Port of New York to ship large numbers of soldiers to Europe.[21] Additionally, the ability of the city's fire department to safeguard New York was dependent on the water system. Due to fears of sabotage of Manhattan's water supply, the New York National Guard and Naval Militia were dispatched to guard the critical infrastructure across the state beginning in February, 1917—two months before the nation entered the war.[22]

German saboteurs did have some success in New York. German immigrant chemist Dr. Walter Scheele, aided by crewmembers aboard the German passenger ship *Friedrich der Grosse*, which had been interned in port by U.S. authorities, manufactured incendiary bombs, which were then placed into the holds of cargo ships by Irish longshoremen opposed to English occupation of their homeland. The bombs destroyed tons of material bound for the Allies before detectives of the New York City Police Department discovered the plot.

In the early morning hours of July 30, 1916, an enormous explosion at a munitions depot on Black Tom Island, New Jersey, in New York Harbor, rocked New York City and the surrounding region. Damage from the explosion totaled nearly $20 million and left five people dead. Thousands of tons of munitions set to be shipped to the Allies were destroyed. The blast was quickly blamed on German saboteurs, though subsequent investigation called the theory into question, and the explosion was ruled accidental. Despite this report, New Yorkers were more than willing to accept that a massive web of German intrigue was involved.[23] It was only after the war that U.S. authorities learned that the explosion at Black Tom was, in fact, the work of German saboteurs.[24]

On October 13, 1917, a massive fire at the Dow's storehouse and grain elevators along the East River piers in Brooklyn destroyed more than 800,000 bushels of grain awaiting shipment to Europe and badly damaged a nearby aircraft-manufacturing plant. The New York City fire chief and many in the media immediately blamed the blaze on German saboteurs despite the determination by the city fire marshal and federal investigators that the fire was probably accidental.[25] Despite the questionable cause of the fire, the Brooklyn conflagration was used in an October 31, 1917, circular issued by the New York State Defense Council warning of a "widespread conspiracy to destroy by fire, cattle and grain throughout the state . . . as recently occurred in the barley and wheat fire in Brooklyn."[26]

In response to these perceived threats, the New York State Police were called on repeatedly to provide additional security at upstate stockyards. On October 29, 1917, two New York State troopers were dispatched to the West Albany stockyards in response to a "complaint in regard to [the] conspiracy over killing of cattle and destroying grain."[27] Over the next several months, Troop G in New York's Capital Region responded to fears of German saboteurs at stockyards in Albany and Schenectady. Similar concerns were addressed by troopers at barracks across the state. Whether real or imagined, New Yorkers—and all Americans—viewed potential enemy spies and saboteurs as a significant threat to national security.

The fear of sabotage was not limited to New York Harbor. On October 31, 1917, the New York State Defense Council issued a circular citing a "widespread conspiracy . . . throughout the State."[28] The Council called for vigilance from all New Yorkers in combatting this threat. Governor Whitman issued a ban on boating and fishing on the reservoir and tributary waterways that supplied water to New York City as a means of preventing potential saboteurs from contaminating the drinking water in New York.[29] A security cordon was established along the newly completed New York State Barge Canal to prevent unauthorized access to this vital waterway.[30] In the western part of the state, Buffalo Mayor Louis P. Fuhrmann wrote to the New York State Adjutant General to request National Guardsmen be employed in guarding the grain elevators and milling district in that city. As the second-largest city in the state, Buffalo's security was a major concern; the city was home to several vital industries and critical infrastructure needed for the war effort. In his request, Fuhrmann stated that the grain elevators, "with a storage capacity of twenty-five million bushels of grain; flour and cereal mills with a daily output about twenty-five thousand barrels of flour, and corresponding quantity of feed, feel that their property is in jeopardy

A view of the carnage after the Black Tom explosion.

Because New York Harbor was the largest port for munitions shipments to Europe, it was in New York City that many German plots were centered. Prior to the declaration of war, diplomats and military officers at the German Embassy in Washington worked with local sympathizers to undermine American support for the Allies. Although they had limited success, munitions and equipment continued to flow to Europe. Courtesy of the Library of Congress.

Sorting shells at Black Tom explosion.

Workers sift through debris to recover munitions after the Black Tom explosion. Courtesy of the Library of Congress.

Guarding the Aqueduct.

New York State's infrastructure—including the Erie Canal, railroads, and the Croton Aqueduct—were seen as vulnerable targets for saboteurs during World War I. The New York National Guard was called to defend the aqueduct that runs 41 miles from the Croton River in Westchester County into New York City against German sabotage.[1] When the National Guard entered federal service, the state turned to the New York Guard, an all-volunteer force, for assistance. William F. Howard Collection.

1. O'Ryan, John Francis. *The Story of the 27th Division* (New York: Wynkoop, Hallenbeck, Crawford Co., 1921), page 46.

Standing sentry on the Barge Canal.

A soldier from the New York National Guard or New York Guard stands watch at Lock 3 of the New York State Barge Canal during World War I. New York State Museum Collection.

A LOCKAGE OF OLD-SIZED CANAL-BOATS

Six of these boats and a small tug may be locked through at a single lockage. Not many old boats were available when the new canal was completed and their number is steadily diminishing. The new boats are of larger size.

SEARCHING A SUSPECT AT BRIDGE 4125.3

Naval Militia patrol.

Here, members of the New York Naval Militia assigned to patrol a New York City bridge over the East River in February 1917 stop and search a passerby. The militiamen were tasked with preventing saboteurs from attacking the city's bridges and infrastructure.[1] Courtesy of the Library of Congress.

    1. O'Ryan, pages 46–47.

U.S. Coast Guard Insignia, ca. 1915.

These collar insignia from the Shinnecock and Mecox Coast Guard Stations on Long Island Sound date to the World War I era. The Coast Guard was tasked with protecting merchant shipping from sabotage and, before American entry in to the war, with enforcing American neutrality. Coast Guard stations along Long Island Sound were charged with guarding the shoreline against possible saboteurs—a threat that became a reality in World War II—and scanning the waters for enemy submarines. New York State Museum Collection, H-2010.47.53-.54.

Aqueduct Service Medal.

The Aqueduct Service Medal was awarded to members of the New York National Guard and New York Guard for their defensive service during World War I. They had protected the aqueducts that provide water to New York City from sabotage. New York State Museum Collection, H-2513.

Proclamation.

This proclamation issued by Governor Charles S. Whitman prohibited boating and fishing on waterways that provided water to Croton Aqueduct and the reservoir system for New York City. The state government established a security cordon around these waterways out of concern that the water supply to New York City was vulnerable to sabotage. New York State Archives, 13035-79.

unless given immediate military protection."[31] More often than not, the fear of perceived threats of enemy action far exceeded the success of efforts by German saboteurs.

SPIES

Fear of enemy spies was rampant in New York State. Before April 1917, several German diplomats were accused of espionage in New York City, including the military attaché, Franz von Papen, and were expelled from the United States. Von Papen was discovered attempting to enlist the German American population in New York City to aid in slowing the flow of supplies to the Allied war effort through

sabotage and espionage.[34] New York Harbor, as the port of embarkation for the majority of American troops, was viewed as a prime target for enemy spies, as were New York industries involved in the manufacture of war materiel. A request for photographs of war work by New York State Historian James Sullivan in May 1918 to the New York State Defense Council was rejected due to "the great danger of such information falling into the hands of German agents, who are devoting an immense amount of labor to obtain just these facts." The letter to Sullivan went on, "It seems to us a peculiarly dangerous procedure to start such compilation at this time."[35]

Franz Von Papen in military uniform circa 1915.

Courtesy of the Library of Congress.

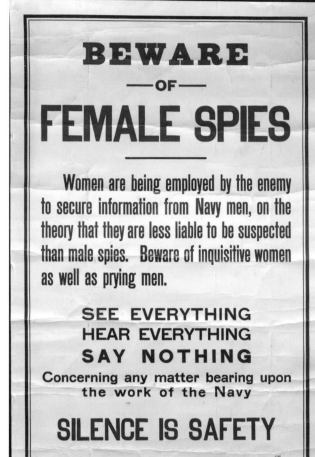

BEWARE
—OF—
FEMALE SPIES

Women are being employed by the enemy to secure information from Navy men, on the theory that they are less liable to be suspected than male spies. Beware of inquisitive women as well as prying men.

SEE EVERYTHING
HEAR EVERYTHING
SAY NOTHING
Concerning any matter bearing upon the work of the Navy

SILENCE IS SAFETY

"Beware of Female Spies."

Artist: None; *Printer:* Unknown; *Publisher:* United States Navy; *Technique:* Lithograph; *Dimensions:* 55.5 x 35.5 cm.

This poster warns sailors to guard against potential female spies. The Navy feared that women would less likely be suspected of being German agents than men. New York State Library, Manuscripts and Special Collections.

To Win This War
German Spies Must Be Jailed

Through the courtesy of the management of this building, the American Defense Society has a booth in the lobby for distribution of important literature.

YOU ARE INVITED
TO VISIT THIS BOOTH AND SECURE WITHOUT CHARGE AS MUCH LITERATURE AS YOU WISH

EVERY PERSON IN THIS OFFICE SHOULD BECOME A MEMBER OF THE AMERICAN DEFENSE SOCIETY

Help us in our fight against the widespread campaign of disloyalty being waged by Pro-Germans, Socialists, Pacifists, Anti-Militarists, Conscientious Objectors, Anarchists, I.W.W.'s, so-called Friends of Irish Freedom and all the forces of treason.

SERVE AT THE FRONT—OR SERVE AT HOME

If you are an American citizen, help to put an end to German activities in this country by joining

The American Defense Society
National Headquarters, 44 East 23d Street, New York

"To Win This War."

Artist: None; *Printer:* Unknown; *Publisher:* American Defense Society; *Technique:* Unknown; *Dimensions:* 35.5 x 28 cm.

Volunteer organizations such as the American Defense Society sought to root out potential enemy spies and often saw potential threats in numerous facets of society. In this poster, the supposed danger is posed not only by enemy aliens, but also Communists, pacifists, and Irish nationalists among others. New York State Library, Manuscripts and Special Collections.

Atlantic Communication Company/ Telefunken Wireless Station, West Sayville, Suffolk County

On April 8, 1917, two days after the United States declared war, Dr. Karl George Frank and fourteen other men were arrested by U.S. Marshals and the Department of Justice's Bureau of Investigation. The suspected spies were incarcerated at the former U.S. Immigration Station at Ellis Island.[36]

Frank was the head of Atlantic Communications Company's wireless radio station at West Sayville, Long Island. Atlantic Communication Co. was the American subsidiary of Telefunken, the German national communications firm, and had constructed the site in 1911 to provide wireless communication between Sayville and Nauen, Germany.[37] The station had the ability to transmit and receive communications from more than 3,000 miles away—including ships at sea and wireless stations in Europe and elsewhere in North America.[38]

When the war began in 1914, the British Navy severed undersea cable communications between the Central Powers and the United States. This left wireless stations such as the one at West Sayville as the primary means of communication between Germany and the United States.[39] To ensure American neutrality, President Wilson censored communications from Sayville and other wireless stations from transmitting war-related messages that could be used by the combatants.[40] Operations at the site were overseen by the U.S. Navy after 1915, when it was suspected that the Sayville station may have played a role in communicating the location of the *Lusitania* to German U-boats. While this charge was never proven, the station did frequently relay ciphered messages between Germany and its consulates and embassy in

New York. Ellis Island. Neg. No.

Ellis Island (1918).

During World War I, the former U.S. Immigration Station at Ellis Island was converted for use as a detention center for enemy aliens and suspected spies and saboteurs. The island's use as a detention facility continued after the war during the "Red Scare" for the detention of suspected socialists and other radicals.[1] Courtesy of the Library of Congress.

1. "Ellis Island History—A Brief Look," The National Park Service (http://www.nps.gov/elis/learn/historyculture/upload/Brief-History-of-Ellis-Island.pdf), accessed February 3, 2016.

"Don't Talk."

Artist: Unknown; *Printer:* Walker Litho. and Pub. Co.; *Publisher:* U.S. Army Intelligence Officer, Northeastern Department; *Technique:* Lithograph; *Dimensions:* 70.5 x 52 cm.

This poster depicts a German soldier with the iconic *Pickelhaube* helmet as a spider who has woven a web of intrigue across the Atlantic. Throughout the war, many feared a vast network of German spies operating in the United States and especially among the German American population in New York and other major cities. While a small number of German immigrants and German Americans did participate in pro-German acts of espionage and sabotage, the vast majority remained patriotically loyal to their adopted country. Despite this fact, German Americans remained the object of fear and suspicion throughout the war. New York State Library, Manuscripts and Special Collections.

the United States.[41] On January 19, 1917, the Telefunken station at West Sayville relayed a coded message from German foreign minister Zimmerman to the German Embassy in Mexico City—the infamous Zimmerman Telegram. The message was intercepted by the British and leaked to the American government in late February, prompting America's declaration of war. With American entry into the war, the West Sayville wireless station was seized by the federal government.[42]

CONSCIENTIOUS OBJECTORS

America's entry into World War I witnessed a new form of "coercive voluntarism" enforced by the federal government. For the first time, regardless of social standing, men were expected to serve in the nation's military or to contribute meaningfully to the war effort.[43] This most notably took the form of the Selective Service Act and the anti-loafing laws that were passed during the war year. Many religious groups were exempt from military service under the Selective Service Act if they served in a noncombatant role. Others refused to fight based on political or social viewpoints. About 2,000 absolutist conscientious objectors refused to accept service as noncombatants, citing their belief that doing so would indirectly aid the war effort that they opposed. Some eventually accepted farm furloughs or other substitute service. Many others remained imprisoned until well after the Armistice in November 1918. Many were subjected to harsh treatment and verbal and physical abuse.

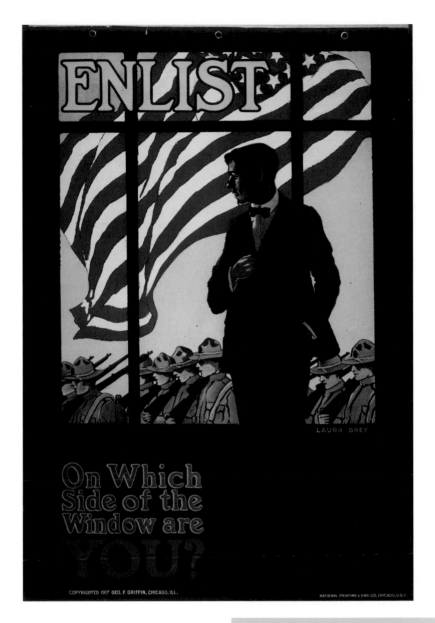

"On Which Side of the Window Are You?" (1917).

Artist: Laura Brey; *Printer:* National Printing and Eng. Co., Chicago, Illinois; *Publisher:* George F. Griffin, Chicago, Illinois; *Technique:* Lithograph; *Dimensions:* 98 x 64 cm.

As this poster illustrates, men who refused to join the army were depicted as shadowy lurkers, hiding from their duty to the nation. Conscientious objectors and "slackers" who refused to fight were treated very harshly by the U.S. criminal justice system, often receiving extended sentences at hard labor in U.S. military prisons. In all, more than 300,000 men successfully avoided the draft despite the efforts of the U.S. Army and local law enforcement.[1] In New York State, the troopers of the State Police were routinely tasked with searching for and detaining suspected deserters, draft evaders, and other "slackers."[2] New York State Library, Manuscripts and Special Collections.

1. Capazzola, pages 9–10.

2. New York State Police, Troop G, Police Blotter Books (1917–1919), New York State Archives, Series 13445-82, Volume 69/261, pages 19, 26–27.

Laura Brey (ca. 1891–1980).

Laura Brey grew up in Elgin, Illinois, and attended the Art Institute of Chicago. Unlike many of her male contemporaries, Laura Brey had not been employed by newspaper or magazine publishers prior to the war. When the United States entered World War I in 1917, Brey was a young artist and recent graduate. Her design for *On Which Side of the Window Are You?* garnered Brey First Honorable Mention at the July 1917 *Exhibition for Posters for National Service* hosted at the Institute.[1] As one of the relatively few female poster artists of the war, Laura Brey's poster was doubly powerful in its challenge to the masculinity of those who refused to fight.

1. Exhibit program, "Exhibition of Posters for National Service," the Art Institute of Chicago, July 2 to July 31, 1917. (http://www.artic.edu/sites/default/files/libraries/pubs/1917/AIC1917Posters_comb.pdf), accessed February 7, 2016.

Howard Moore at Fort Douglas, Utah.

Howard W. Moore (right) and fellow conscientious objectors at the detention camp at Fort Douglas, Utah, in 1919. Moore was sent first to Fort Leavenworth, Kansas, and later at Fort Douglas. He was not released until 1920. Courtesy of the New York State Library, Manuscripts and Special Collections.

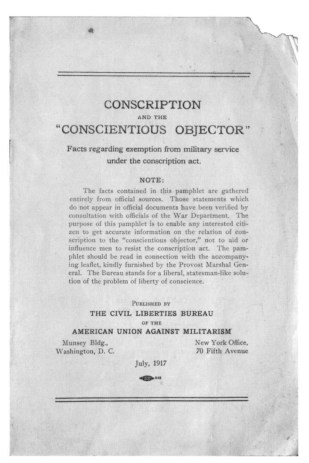

Booklet, "Conscription and the 'Conscientious Objector' Question" (1917).

This pamphlet was published by the Civil Liberties Bureau of the American Union Against Militarism, the predecessor to the American Civil Liberties Union (ACLU). The work of this organization influenced Howard Moore and others opposed to military service. New York State Library, Manuscripts and Special Collections.

Howard W. Moore (1889–1993) ·

Howard W. Moore was born February 9, 1889, in Sing Sing (now Ossining), Westchester County. After age six, Moore grew up in Cherry Valley, Otsego County. Moore moved to New York City at age fourteen and resided there until the outbreak of war in 1914. In New York, Moore was employed by the New York Telephone Company. In 1917, Moore began attending lectures at the Rand School, headquarters of the Socialist Party in Manhattan. While he sympathized with many of the socialists' tenets, Moore never became an active member. He also frequently attended sermons by Rabbi Stephen Wise and Unitarian minister John Haynes Holmes. It was at this time that Moore first developed pacifist leanings.

Witnessing the pro-war propaganda in New York City and the backlash against any who opposed it led Howard W. Moore to declare himself a conscientious objector. Despite harsh treatment and imprisonment, Moore remained resolute in his refusal to serve. He was imprisoned for over three years at military posts across the country.

[I am not a member of] any religious sect or organization whose creed forbids me to participate in war, but the convictions of my own conscience as an expression of my social principles forbid me from so doing and [thus, I] claim the same rights accorded under the law to members of a well-recognized religious sect or organization whose principles forbid their members to take part in war.

—Howard W. Moore, affidavit to local draft board, December 28, 1917

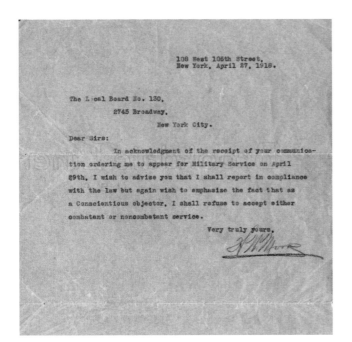

Howard Moore's Letter to Local Draft Board, April 27, 1918.

Rather than evade the draft, Moore opted instead to oppose it directly. He notified his local draft board of his opposition to the war and refusal to serve. When he was drafted on April 20, 1918, Moore again submitted his refusal to serve in either a combatant or noncombatant role. New York State Library, Manuscripts and Special Collections.

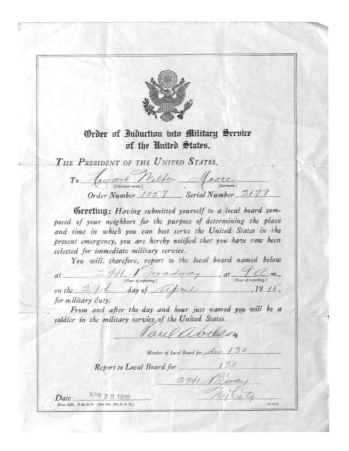

Orders of Induction and Dishonorable Discharge.

Howard Moore received this orders to report for military service. He did so, but refused to comply with the draft. He was imprisoned for three years and given a dishonorable discharge. Following his release in 1920, Moore returned to New York, eventually settling on the family farm in Cherry Valley. New York State Library, Manuscripts and Special Collections.

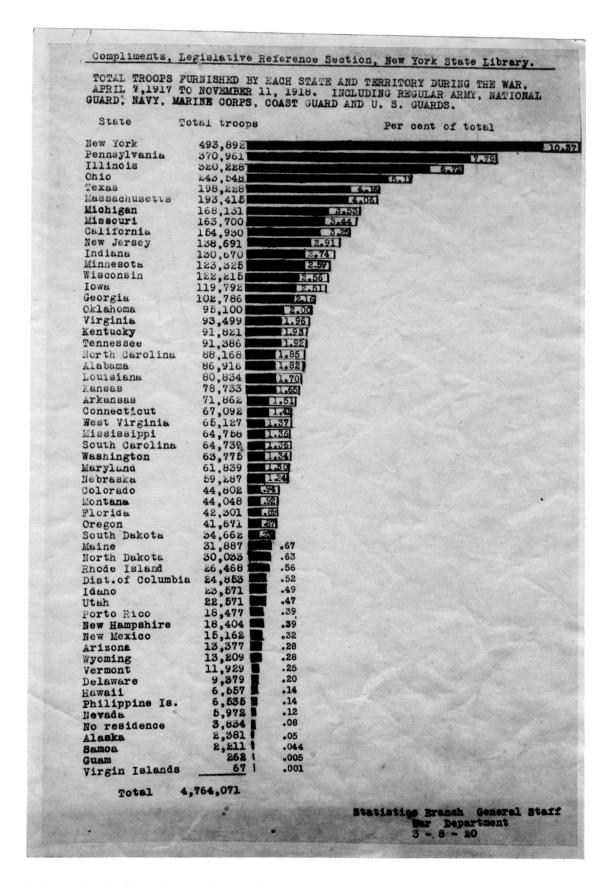

TOTAL TROOPS FURNISHED BY EACH STATE AND TERRITORY DURING THE WAR, APRIL 7,1917 TO NOVEMBER 11, 1918. INCLUDING REGULAR ARMY, NATIONAL GUARD, NAVY, MARINE CORPS, COAST GUARD AND U. S. GUARDS.

State	Total troops	Per cent of total
New York	493,892	10.37
Pennsylvania	370,961	7.79
Illinois	320,228	6.72
Ohio	243,548	5.11
Texas	198,228	4.16
Massachusetts	193,415	4.06
Michigan	168,131	3.53
Missouri	163,700	3.44
California	154,930	3.25
New Jersey	138,691	2.91
Indiana	130,670	2.74
Minnesota	123,325	2.59
Wisconsin	122,215	2.56
Iowa	119,792	2.51
Georgia	102,786	2.16
Oklahoma	95,100	2.00
Virginia	93,499	1.96
Kentucky	91,821	1.93
Tennessee	91,386	1.92
North Carolina	88,168	1.85
Alabama	86,916	1.82
Louisiana	80,834	1.70
Kansas	78,733	1.65
Arkansas	71,862	1.51
Connecticut	67,092	1.41
West Virginia	65,127	1.37
Mississippi	64,755	1.36
South Carolina	64,739	1.36
Washington	63,775	1.34
Maryland	61,839	1.30
Nebraska	59,287	1.24
Colorado	44,802	.94
Montana	44,048	.92
Florida	42,301	.89
Oregon	41,671	.87
South Dakota	34,662	.72
Maine	31,887	.67
North Dakota	30,033	.63
Rhode Island	26,468	.56
Dist.of Columbia	24,853	.52
Idaho	23,571	.49
Utah	22,571	.47
Porto Rico	18,477	.39
New Hampshire	18,404	.39
New Mexico	15,162	.32
Arizona	13,377	.28
Wyoming	13,209	.28
Vermont	11,929	.25
Delaware	9,379	.20
Hawaii	6,557	.14
Philippine Is.	6,535	.14
Nevada	5,972	.12
No residence	3,834	.08
Alaska	2,381	.05
Samoa	2,211	.044
Guam	263	.005
Virgin Islands	67	.001
Total	4,764,071	

Statistics Branch General Staff
War Department
3 - 8 - 20

Total troops furnished by each state and territory during the war.

New York State Archives, A3166-78.

8

"Somewhere in France"

New Yorkers in the American Expeditionary Force[1]

When President Woodrow Wilson asked for a declaration of war on April 2, 1917, the United States Army totaled only 121,707 enlisted soldiers and 5,791 officers.[2] By contrast, in the Battle of Verdun (February–December 1916) nearly 300,000 French and German soldiers were killed and another 770,000 wounded.[3] The Battle of the Somme would total 1.3 million casualties. The American Army of 1917 was ill prepared for war on this scale. In Washington, DC, and across the nation, military planners embarked on a rapid expansion of the U.S. military, calling for four million American men to enter military service during the crisis.

The wartime organization of the army consisted of divisions of 30,000 men, including infantry, artillery, and supply units. This was about twice the strength of British or French divisions.[4] Divisions 1 to 20 were assembled from the Regular Army and volunteer enlistees. Divisions 26 to 42 were designated for the National Guard units from across the country, and 76 to 93—designated the National Army—were composed of draftees.[5] In addition to the National Guard units from New York, New Yorkers could be found in nearly every Regular Army and National Army division.[6]

Governor Whitman and the War Council established a military census and began preparations to send the New York National Guard into federal service. As in the American Civil War (1861–1865), New York State was called on to furnish large numbers of men to fill the ranks of a rapidly expanded American Army. On July 10, 1917, President Wilson issued a proclamation calling for the federalization of the National Guard.[7] By August 5, 1917, all of the 40,780 officers and men of the New York National Guard were formally drafted into the service of the United States Army.[8] New York became one of only three states to furnish an entire division of National Guardsmen to the war effort; Pennsylvania and Illinois were the other two. The majority of New York's National Guard served with the 27th Division under the command of Major General John Francis O'Ryan. The 69th Infantry Regiment was assigned as New York's contribution to the 42nd Division as the 165th Infantry, and the 15th New York would serve as the 369th Infantry Regiment.[9] The Germans gave this African American regiment the nickname "Hellfighters" because of their tenacity in combat. More than 5,000 members of the New York National Guard were commissioned as officers in the United States Army.[10]

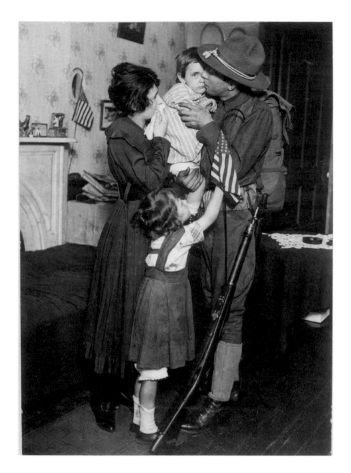

In addition to its National Guardsmen, New York State furnished a second full division—the 77th—composed almost entirely of men drafted from New York City. Sizable numbers from western New York State also served with the 78th and 81st Divisions.[11] By the end of the war, New York State had contributed over 500,000 of its citizens to military service, serving in all branches of service. This was the largest contribution of men from any state in the nation. More than ten percent of the soldiers in the American Expeditionary Force hailed from New York State.[12] An unknown number of others enlisted with the Canadian or British forces prior to America's entry into the war.

Major General John Francis O'Ryan

John Francis O'Ryan was born August 21, 1874, in Manhattan. The son of an Irish immigrant, O'Ryan grew up in Westchester County. While a student at the College of the City of New York, O'Ryan enlisted as a private in the 7th Regiment of the New York Militia. After graduating from New York University in 1898, he embarked on a legal career in New York

Departing for service.

Private T.P. Loughlin of the 69th Regiment, New York National Guard bids his wife and children farewell before departing for service in World War I. Courtesy of the National Archives and Records Administration.

Departure of the 69th Infantry Regiment.

The famed "Fighting Irish" of the 69th Infantry Regiment, New York National Guard, was selected as New York State's contribution to the 42nd Division. The regiment departed New York City for Camp Mills on Long Island on August 24, 1917.[1] Once in Federal Service, the regiment was redesignated as the 165th Infantry Regiment. Courtesy of the Library of Congress.

1. Hogan, page 9.

MAJOR GENERAL JOHN FRANCIS O'RYAN

General John F. O'Ryan, Commander 27th Division

The shoulder sleeve insignia of the division features the constellation Orion, a subtle homage to the unit's leader. William F. Howard Collection

City. O'Ryan continued to serve in the militia, rising through the ranks. In 1899, he was commissioned an officer in the New York State Militia, which was redesignated the National Guard in 1903.[13] O'Ryan was promoted to major general and given command of the New York National Guard in 1912.[14] He was appointed to the U.S. Army War College by General Leonard Wood in 1914—a rare event for National Guardsmen of the era.[15] In 1916, he led the New York National Guard Division when it was ordered to the Mexican border. Before World War I, O'Ryan became a proponent of the Preparedness Movement and the Plattsburgh Training Camps. He led the New York National Guard Division throughout the war.

Following World War I, O'Ryan returned to civilian life as an attorney and held a variety of civilian and government positions. In World War II, O'Ryan again returned to the service of his state, serving as director of civil defense.

Steel helmet.

This steel combat helmet belonged to Major General John F. O'Ryan, commander of the 27th Division during World War I. The helmet's interior is marked, "MAJ GEN J.F. O'RYAN 27th DIV USA. New York State Military Museum, Division of Military and Naval Affairs.

Major General John F. O'Ryan, 1917.

Courtesy of the Library of Congress.

New York's Contribution to the AEF

According to New York State Historian James Sullivan in 1928, "To review adequately the military part taken by New York State in the World War, one would have to sketch the history of the American Expeditionary Forces as a whole, for New Yorkers were to be found in every American division that served in France."[16] The artifacts presented here offer only a small sampling of the units in which men and women from New York State served while in the American Expeditionary Forces. These soldiers, sailors, nurses, and Marines, served in the National Guard, in the Regular Army, and in National Army units, aboard ships at sea, and in hospitals in the United States and across the globe.

Painted helmet, 27th "Empire" Division.

The New York State National Guard Division was designated the 27th Division on July 20, 1917. When it sailed for France, the 27th numbered 991 officers and 27,114 enlisted men. The size of U.S. Army infantry regiments in World War I increased dramatically. During the American Civil War (1861–1865), regiments had totaled approximately 1,000 officers and men. Infantry regiments during World War I would number more than 3,000. This required a dramatic reorganization of New York's National Guard as existing regiments were combined and consolidated into four regiments—the 105th through the 108th. The old First and Seventh Regiments of the New York National Guard, for example, were combined to create the 107th Infantry Regiment. The loss of their unit history and tradition initially caused much stir among the National Guardsmen. Colonel Willard Fisk, commander of the newly reorganized 107th Infantry Regiment addressed his men with the statement, "We are still the 1st and the 7th, but with *Nothing* in between."[1] The 1st Regiment of the New York National Guard was headquartered in Albany, and drew much of its strength from upstate farm towns and villages, including Newburgh, Utica, and Ogdensburg. The 7th Regiment—the vaunted Silk Stocking Regiment—drew its men from New York City and included a number from the upper echelons of Manhattan society (Vanderbilt, Van Rensselaer, etc).[2] The combination of farm boys and financiers epitomized the diversity of the Empire State at the outbreak of war, but also highlighted the involvement of New Yorkers from all walks of life and all regions of the state during the war. New York State Museum Collection, H-1985.63.13 and H-2010.47.24.

1. Harris, Stephen L. *Duty, Honor, Privelege: New York's Silk Stocking Regiment and the Breaking of the Hindenburg Line* (Washington, DC: Potomac Books, Inc., 2001), page 82.

2. Harris, *Duty, Honor, Privilege*, pages 72–82.

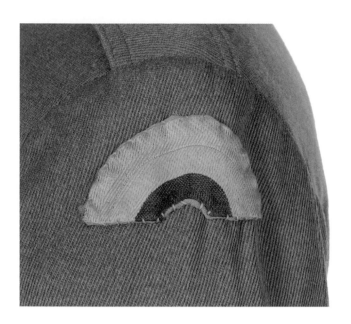

Shoulder sleeve insignia, 165th Infantry Regiment, 42nd Division.

According to New York State Historian James Sullivan, "Although the Rainbow Division cannot be claimed as wholly of New York . . . that a whole regiment of irrepressible Irish Americans of New York City came into the personnel of the 42nd Division, one can be sure that New York City was not long in making its presence known and felt."[1] The old "Fighting 69th" became the 165th Infantry Regiment of the 42nd "Rainbow" Division. While the core of the regiment was comprised of the old 69th New York, nearly two-thirds of the men had been "purloined" from the other infantry regiments of the New York National Guard in order to bring the 69th up to wartime strength.[2] Under orders from the War Department, 346 men from each of New York City's other infantry regiments were transferred to the 69th Infantry Regiment rather than affording the regiment enough time to recruit enough soldiers to bring it to wartime strength. According to General O'Ryan, the mass transfer of Guardsmen from one regiment to another threatened to be a drain on morale throughout New York's National Guard.[3] The new arrivals to the 69th were quickly welcomed into the Irish Regiment and were described by Father Francis Duffy, the regimental chaplain, as " . . . Irish by adoption, Irish by association, or Irish by conviction."[4] New York State Military Museum, Division of Military and Naval Affairs.

1. Sullivan, James S. *History of New York State, 1523–1927*, Volume IV (New York: The American Historical Society, Inc., 1928), page 1299.

2. Sullivan, Volume IV, pages 1301–1302.

3. O'Ryan, page 85.

4. Harris, *Duffy's War*, page 36.

Shoulder sleeve insignia, 369th Infantry Regiment.

The 15th Regiment, New York National Guard was an all African American unit raised primarily in Harlem, New York City. During the war, many of the regiment's black officers were replaced by whites as the U.S. Army prohibited black field grade officers.[1] Due to racial tensions between the African American 15th and white units primarily from southern states, the New Yorkers from Harlem were rushed overseas.[2] While the average American soldier received approximately six months of training in the U.S. and an additional two months behind the lines in France, the men of the 369th had spent less than two weeks in camp before sailing for Europe.[3] The regiment became the only unit to arrive in Europe still bearing its state designation. It was only after its arrival in France that the 15th received its new federal designation.[4]

The regiment was not permitted to serve as a combat infantry regiment alongside white units in the segregated U.S. Army of World War I. Rather, they were not even allowed to fight in the U.S. Army at all. Instead, the soldiers from Harlem were lent to the French Army by AEF commander General John Pershing. The 15th New York would earn glory as the 369th Infantry Regiment, the "Harlem Hellfighters," in the American Press. The men would refer to themselves as "Harlem's Rattlers," and selected the rattlesnake for their regimental insignia.[5] New York State Military Museum, Division of Military and Naval Affairs.

1. Slotkin, page 137.

2. Sammons and Morrow, pages 160–169.

3. Harris, Stephen L., *Harlem's Hellfighters: The African American 369th Infantry in World War I* (Washington DC: Potomac Books, Inc., 2003), page 150.

4. Slotkin, page 125.

5. Sammons and Morrow, page 2.

Painted helmet and shoulder sleeve insignia, 78th Division.

While the 78th Division originally was comprised of soldiers from New Jersey and Delaware, a significant number of the men in the division came from Western New York. This insignia belonged to a soldier from Geneseo, Livingston County.

After assembling at Camp Dix, New Jersey, in August 1917, the 78th Division arrived in the trenches in France in June 1918. The "Lightning Division" fought during the St. Mihiel Offensive and in the battle for the Argonne Forest. During the war, the 78th Division suffered 1,384 killed and 5,861 wounded.[1] New York State Museum Collection, H–1976.105.2 and H–1972.76.178.1–.2.

1. Sullivan, Volume IV, page 1363.

Enlisted tunic and helmet, 77th "Liberty" Division.

The 77th Division was raised almost entirely from conscripted soldiers from the New York City region. The division was applauded as a true "cross section of the city and state, and contained "almost every race and creed under the sun."[1] After being organized at Camp Upton, Long Island, the division became the first National Army division to arrive in Europe in April 1918.

The 77th was both the archetype example of the nation's pluralistic, immigrant society as well as the "dubious experiment" in transforming men from all ethnicities, languages, and backgrounds into an effective fighting unit.[2] Just as New York's immigrant communities were attempting to prove their loyalty to their adopted country on the home front, so too were they expected to demonstrate their allegiance in the trenches of the Western Front.

During its service, the division also became the first National Army division to be given responsibility for a sector of the front lines, and it was the first to be placed in active combat operations in the trenches.[3] New York State Military Museum, Division of Military and Naval Affairs, New York State Museum Collection, H–1976.98.1.

1. Sullivan, Volume IV, page 1333.

2. Sullivan, Volume IV, page 1333.

3. Adler, Major J.O., ed. *A History of the Seventy-Seventh Division: August 25th, 1917 to November 11th, 1918* (New York: Wynkoop Hallenbeck Crawford Company, 1919), page 7.

Collar insignia, U.S. Army Nurses Corps.

Hundreds of New Yorkers volunteered with the U.S. Army and the American Red Cross to serve as nurses at hospitals in France and in the United States. More than 21,000 women joined the service as nurses during the war. Forty nurses from New York State were killed in the conflict.[1] New York State Museum Collection, H-1972.97.15.

    1. Flick, page 320.

United States Marine Corps tunic.

The 2nd Division, U.S. Army included a brigade of United States Marines. This uniform belonged to Private A. William Fremd of Rye, Dutchess County. Private Fremd served with 49th Company, 5th Marine Regiment in the 2nd Division of the AEF. The Marines were heavily involved in the fighting at Chateau Thierry, Belleau Woods, and the St. Mihiel Offensive. New York State Museum Collection, H-1970.119.1 A.

"Strike Now! He's Fighting for You."

Artist: John A. Coughlin; *Printer:* Robert Gair Co., Brooklyn, New York; *Publisher:* Liberty Bond Committee; *Technique:* Lithograph; *Dimensions:* 76.25 x 51 cm.

This Liberty Bond poster by the Robert Gair Company of Brooklyn, New York, depicts an American soldier in combat. Stylized versions of attacks across No Man's Land seldom conveyed the true horror of the conflict. New York State Museum Collection, H-1976.149.10.

Enlisted soldier's uniform.

An example of a World War I—era enlisted soldier's uniform with tunic, trousers, wrap puttees, and overseas cap. The tunic bears the insignia of the 27th Division, which was composed of men from the New York National Guard. The tunic was worn by Private Harry Schinnerer, of Albany, who was a medic with the 27th Division during its service in World War I. New York State Museum Collection, H-1976.220.1 [tunic]; H-1972.74.3 [trousers]; H-1972.61.2 A–B [puttees]; H-1970.160.8 A–B [boots]; H-1972.74.4 [Overseas Cap]..

Fiorello LaGuardia.

The caption to this July 14, 1918 *New York Times* photograph reads, "Captain F.H. La Guardia, member of Congress from the Fourteenth Manhattan District, with Signor Caproni, one of the Caproni Brothers, airplane inventors, in Milan [Italy]. Captain La Guardia is now flying with the American Forces on the Italian Front."[1] New York State Museum Collection, H-1972.76.NN [dup 13].

1. Photo Caption, *New York Times,* Sunday, July 14, 1918 Rotogravure Photo Section 7, page 5, New York State Museum Collection.

Joint Legislative Resolution regarding the 332nd Regiment of the American Expeditionary Force, 1919.

The 332nd Infantry Regiment was the only American Army combat unit to serve on the Italian Front. Attached to the Italian Army, the regiment participated in the Vittorio-Veneto Offensive in October 1918. After driving the Austrian Army from its positions, the regiment pursued the enemy northward. An armistice between Austria-Hungary and Italy took effect on November 4, 1918. The 332nd was stationed in Austria along the Dalmatian Coast until February 1919, when it sailed for New York, arriving on April 14. This resolution recognizes the "conspicuous services and devotion to duty" of the regiment. Among its most notable members was U.S. Congressman and future mayor of New York City, Major Fiorello LaGuardia, who was attached to the 332nd as a pilot. New York State Archives, B0303-84.

STATE OF NEW YORK

In Senate

Albany

April 16, 1919

By Mr. Cotillo:

WHEREAS, the three hundred and thirty-second regiment of the American expeditionary force is returning to this country from the Italian front whither it was sent by the American Government to be a token to the Italian people that the great American Republic was engaged in the struggle with its gallant armies as well as with its economic wealth, and

WHEREAS, Such regiment is about to be decorated by the Italian government in New York in recognition of its conspicuous services and devotion to duty throughout the course of the war,

BE IT RESOLVED. (the Assembly concurring) that the Legislature thus express its welcome to the officers and men of such regiment and its hearty congratulation at the safe return and the distinction they have merited at the hands of the Italian government.

By order of the Senate.

Ernest A Fay
Clerk.

IN ASSEMBLY.
April 17th 1919.
Concurred in without amendment

By order of the Assembly
Fred W. Hammond
Clerk.

Form No. 84

"Join the Army Air Service."

Artist: Charles Livingston Bull; *Printer:* Alpha Litho Co. Inc., New York, New York; *Publisher:* U.S. Army Recruiting (Air Service); *Dimensions:* 69 x 51 cm.

Recruitment poster for the U.S. Army Air Service. New York State Library, Manuscripts and Special Collections.

Air Service coat and scarf.

This three-quarter-length aviator's coat and silk scarf was worn by Anderson Bowers Sr., who served as an American Army pilot during World War I. New York State Military Museum, Division of Military and Naval Affairs.

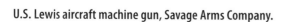

U.S. Lewis aircraft machine gun, Savage Arms Company.

This variation of the Lewis machine gun was designed to mount to an American airplane. Savage Arms produced this weapon at its factory in Utica. New York State Military Museum, Division of Military and Naval Affairs.

U.S. naval mine.

In 1918, the American and British navies began the North Sea Mine Barrage. The U.S. Navy laid more than 50,000 mines in the North Sea in an effort to bottle up German U-boats in port. The operation sank at least 6 submarines and damaged several more. This mine was manufactured at Norfolk, Virginia, and sent to the U.S. Naval Weapons Depot at Iona Island, New York. The island, situated in the Hudson River estuary near Stony Point, Rockland County, was purchased by the navy in 1899 and served as one of the nation's largest ammunition depots. Naval mines such as this were charged with explosives and loaded aboard naval ships at Iona Island, which distributed a large portion of naval ammunition throughout World War I. The island remained a naval arms depot through World War II until its closure in 1947. Courtesy of Timothy Whitten and Marlinsespike Chandlery.

U.S. Naval ships lay mines in the North Sea in 1918.

Courtesy of the U.S. Naval History and Heritage Command.

"The U.S. Navy Needs Men."

Artist: Raymond Bannister; *Printer:* Louis Roesch Co., San Francisco, California.; *Publisher:* U.S. Navy; *Dimensions:* 101.5 x 70 cm.

U.S. Navy Recruiting Poster. New York State Library, Manuscripts and Special Collections.

Private Herbert H. Taber (1899–1960)
Esperance, Schoharie County

Herbert Taber attended Delanson High School in Duanesburg, Schenectady County, where he played for the school's baseball team. Immediately upon graduation, Taber enlisted in the United States Army following President Wilson's declaration of war in April 1917. Like many other New Yorkers, Herbert Taber was not assigned to one of the several units being raised within the Empire State for the American Expeditionary Force. Rather, the Schoharie County native was assigned to Battery A, 7th Field Artillery, 1st Division. Taber arrived with the rest of the 1st Division in June 1917. It was Taber's battery of the 7th Field Artillery Regiment that fired the first American artillery in combat operations during the war.[17] Through a regular stream of correspondence with his mother in Esperance, Private Taber documented his wartime experiences and his time in the trenches, where, he wrote, the "mud is ankle deep." Taber also wrote of being in a gas attack and having

Private Herbert Taber, ca. 1917.

Courtesy of the Brandoline Family

"The First Three!"

Artist: Kidder; *Printer:* Unknown; *Publisher:* American Red Cross; *Technique:* Lithograph; *Dimensions:* 69.75 x 52 cm.

Soldiers of the 1st Division arrived in France in June 1917. By late October, they had completed their training and were sent to a relatively quiet sector of the Lorraine front. In the early morning hours of November 2, the German Army attacked positions held by Company F, 16th Infantry Regiment. Three men were killed, three were wounded, and eleven taken prisoner.[1] The three men killed—Corporal James Gresham, Private Merle Hay, and Private Thomas Enright—were memorialized in recruitment and liberty loan campaigns throughout the United States. New York State Museum Collection, H- 1976.31.6.

1. Stewart, Volume II, page 26.

Captain Wendell Curtis Jr.

Courtesy of the Rochester Historical Society.

Captain Wendell Joseph Curtis Jr.
Company A, 309th Machine Gun Battalion,
78th Division

Wendell Joseph Curtis Jr. was born in Rochester. He enlisted in the New York National Guard on April 16, 1912, as a private assigned to Troop H, 1st New York Cavalry. He was promoted to sergeant and sent with his regiment to the Mexican border from June 1916 to January 1917. With U.S. entry into the war in April 1917, Curtis was sent to the Officers' Training Camp at Madison Barracks in Sackets Harbor, Jefferson County, on June 12, 1917. He was commissioned in the U.S. Army Reserve on August 29, 1917, and sent to Camp Dix, New Jersey. Curtis was assigned to Company A, 309th Machine Gun Battalion, 78th Division, and sailed for France on May 27, 1918. The division participated in the Allied offensive in the Meuse-Argonne in September–October 1918. Captain Curtis returned to the United States after the Armistice and was discharged on June 10, 1919.

"Hitches in Hell": Life in the Trenches[20]

By the time American troops began to arrive in the trenches of the Western Front, the front lines had remained relatively stagnant for more than two years. The system of trenches ran "twisting and turning" across the countryside—along hillsides and even through villages and towns.[21] Many of the dugouts and fortifications had begun to have an air of permanence to them. When members of the 165th Infantry Regiment were placed in the trenches in the line in the Baccarat sector, the men were housed in dugouts that were forty feet underground, with as many as thirty-five rooms, each with a stove, wooden walls, and floors.[22] The trenches themselves, however, were exposed to the cold and rain and mud, as well as enemy fire. The conditions in the trenches presented unforeseen enemies. Disease, vermin, mud, and the stench of thousands of men living and dying in close quarters tormented soldiers in the trenches. Dysentery, typhus, cholera, gangrene, and "trench fever" were as great a threat as combat.

artillery shells "drop about 50 ft from me." His early letters assure his mother that he is not in significant danger, and that he would rather "be on the front than back of the lines for we have lots of excitement here." [18] Later letters describe his participation in the Battle of Cantigny—the first combat operations for any American units during the war in May 1918—as well as during the Second Battle of the Marne (July 15–August 6).[19] By the end of the war, Taber's letters frequently indicate his longing for home. Private Herbert Taber survived the war and returned to the United States with the 1st Division. After his discharge, he returned to Esperance.

It is a miserable life to be condemned to, shivering in these wretched holes, in the cold and the dirt and semidarkness. . . . The increasing cold will make this kind of existence almost insupportable, with its accompanying vermin and dysentery. . . . The real courage of the soldier is not in facing the balls, but the fatigue and discomfort and misery.

—Alan Seeger, November 14, 1914[23]

Life in the trenches was an endless cycle of nighttime maneuvers and raids. Snipers and artillery fire during the day often separated long periods of boredom. At dawn and dusk, soldiers were ordered to "stand to" in case of an enemy assault. Chores, inspections, writing letters, or playing cards filled the day. Soldiers slept when they could. The tedium of this routine was abandoned when the order came to go "over the top."

When you picture the war, the dugouts, the trenches, etc., you think of shells bursting three feet to one side of you and then two feet to the other. And then you think that it is constantly boom-booming! 'Taint so—that's all—it ain't so. For hours at a time we never hear or see a thing.

—Lieutenant Basil Beebe Elmer, April 4, 1918[24]

There are nights in the trenches when there is no noise but the squealing of rats.

—Corporal Garwood Dains, May 1918[25]

[T]he hour from three-thirty to four-thirty is "stand-to," the hour when most attacks start, and the time at which all soldiers are expected to be armed, awake and at their posts.

—Sergeant Peyton Randolph Campbell, May 26, 1918[26]

Mealtime in the American trenches.

Courtesy of the New York State Library, Manuscripts and Special Collections.

Soldiers of the American Expeditionary Force in the training trenches near Verdun, France, 1918.

From the New York Public Library.

Comfort bag with comb, razors, tootbrush, shaving brush, shaving strop.

Comfort kits were supplied to U.S. soldiers by the American Red Cross. Such kits could include mundane items such as toiletries, matches, and even chewing gum. These were often coveted by troops in the trenches. The linen bag and toiletries pictured were found at the New York National Guard's Kingsbridge Road Armory in the Bronx. The matchbook and chewing gum were found inside the pocket of a World War I uniform. The gum was produced by the Beech-Nut Packing Company, formerly located in Canajoharie, Montgomery County. New York State Military Museum, Division of Military and Naval Affairs.

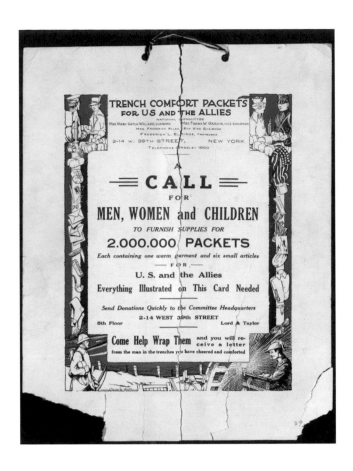

Trench Comfort Packets Committee.

Artist: Stacy H. Wood; *Printer:* Unknown; *Publisher:* Trench Comfort Packets Committee; *Technique:* Lithograph; *Dimensions:* 35 x 27 cm.

The Trench Comfort Packets Committee was headquartered at Lord and Taylor on Fifth Avenue in New York City. It was founded by Mary Hatch Willard following a trip to France during which she witnessed the deplorable conditions experienced by soldiers in the trenches. The packets included warm clothing and other comforts for the soldiers.[1] New York State Library, Manuscripts and Special Collections.

1. Clarke, Ida Clyde Gallagher. *American Women and the World War* (New York: D. Appleton and Company, 1918), page 434. Available via Google Books (https://books.google.com/books?id=lvDOAAAAMAAJ&pg=PA434&lpg=PA434&dq=trench+comfort+packets+committee&source=bl&ots=XC0NJOLk7f&sig=2HVLKcCDAvqXRzDJiPzRFs2BX5s&hl=en&sa=X&ved=0CCkQ6AEwBGoVChMlIMm-qMr5yAIVxSsmCh1QWwBH#v=onepage&q=trench%20comfort%20packets%20committee&f=false), accessed January 14, 2016

Condiment can.

The M1910 Condiment Can was designed to carry a soldier's ration of sugar, salt, and coffee in watertight compartments. The can contains two compartments within the main body with a divider in the center. Each compartment is accessible with a screw-on cap. One cap contains a small compartment—presumably intended for the soldier's salt ration—with a pry-off lid on the end.[1]

New York State Museum Collection, H-1972.76.38.

1. "World War I Field and Mess Equipment," U.S. Army Center for Military History.

Periscope.

Soldiers in the trenches developed numerous variations of the trench periscope, allowing them to peer over the top of the trench without exposing themselves to sniper fire. New York State Museum Collection, H-1979.36.1

Meat can, fork, spoon, and knife.

A U.S. Army field mess kit included a "meat can" and utensils. This meat can and canteen was carried by Captain Rutherford Ireland of Brooklyn.[1] New York State Military Museum, Division of Military and Naval Affairs, and New York State Museum Collection, H-1972.76.190 A-C (utensils).

1. Norton, Frank H., Colonel. *A Short History and Illustrated Roster of the 106th Infantry United States* (Philadelphia: Edward, Stern and Co., Inc., 1918), page 110.

Wristwatch band.

This leather band is an early form of what eventually became the wristwatch. These types of bands were originally used by women. During World War I, they became popular with soldiers because it was easier to tell time with a watch on your wrist than with a pocket watch. A man's pocket watch would insert into the leather band and then be strapped to the wrist for easy view. New York State Museum Collection, H-2010.27.1.

Wristwatches.

World War I saw the dramatic rise in the use of wristwatches. Traditionally, men wore pocket watches as a sign of masculinity and social standing.[1] By contrast, wristwatches were delicate pieces of jewelry worn by women. The rise of modern warfare involving complex coordination and timing between infantry, artillery, and other elements of the army heightened the need for accurate timekeeping. Under these circumstances, the pocket watch was no longer a convenient option for troops in the trenches.[2] As a result, the wristwatch became popular among soldiers in the American Expeditionary Forces and quickly lost its gender identification. The wristwatch remained in vogue in the United States after the Armistice and beyond.[3] New York State Museum Collection, H-1972.76.129 and H-1987.1.24.

1. Fangboner, Donald, "The Wristwatch Comes of Age," *Journal of the Company of Military Historians*, Vol. XXXVI, No. 1, Spring 1984, pages 31–32.

2. Mulligan, Robert, " 'Real Men' Didn't Wear Wrist Watches," *New York Alive,* July/August 1989, page 12.

3. Fangboner, page 32.

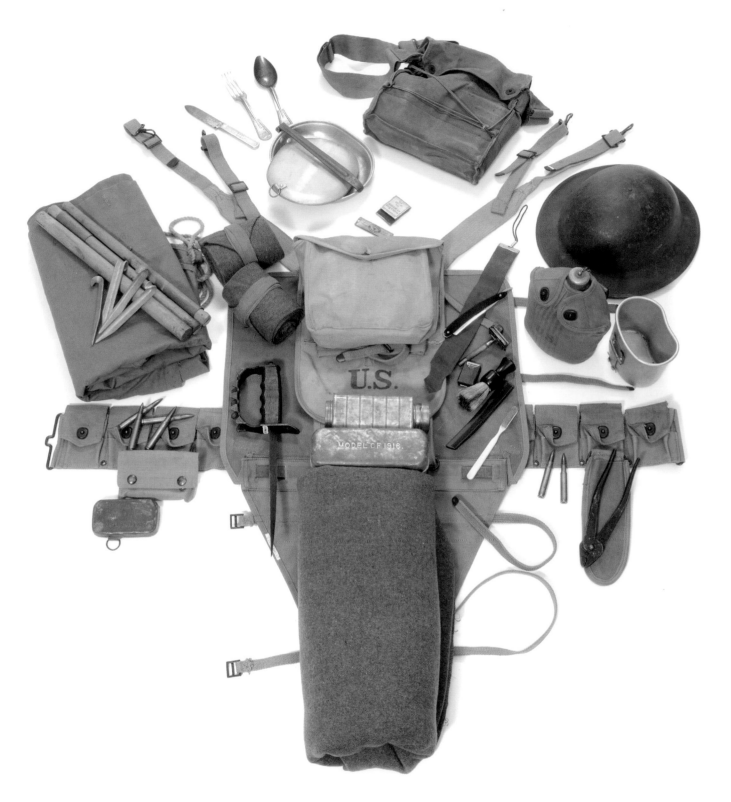

Model 1910 rucksack and accoutrements.

In 1909, the United States Army adopted new models for all of the field equipment issued to U.S. soldiers. The Model 1910 equipment included a rucksack, haversack, meat can, condiment can, mess utensils, canteen with cover, entrenching tool, first aid pouch, wool blanket, and a web cartridge belt. The M1910 system was designed to be disassembled prior to combat so as to lighten the soldier's load.[1] Courtesy of the New York State Military Museum, Division of Military and Naval Affairs.

1. "World War I Field and Mess Equipment," U.S. Army Center for Military History.

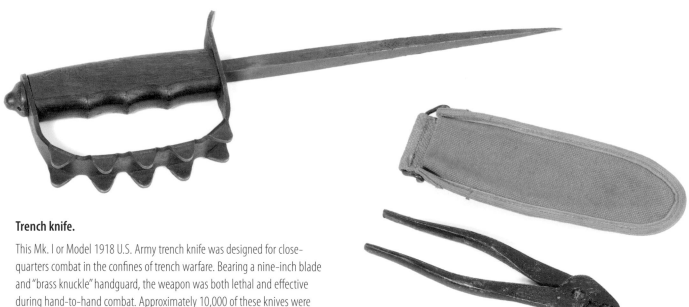

Trench knife.

This Mk. I or Model 1918 U.S. Army trench knife was designed for close-quarters combat in the confines of trench warfare. Bearing a nine-inch blade and "brass knuckle" handguard, the weapon was both lethal and effective during hand-to-hand combat. Approximately 10,000 of these knives were manufactured by the Oneida Flatware Company.[1] This particular knife was removed from the Oneida Armory. New York State Military Museum, Division of Military and Naval Affairs.

　1. Crowell, Benedict, Assistant Secretary of War. *America's Munitions, 1917–1918* (Washington, DC: Government Printing Office, 1919), page 228.

Wire cutters.

The U.S. Army equipped its infantrymen with the Model 1910 wire cutters, which were used to cut through enemy barbed wire defenses. These cutters were removed from the New York National Guard's Oneida Armory. New York State Military Museum, Division of Military and Naval Affairs.

"Do Your Bit, Save the Pit"

Artist: Unknown; *Printer:* Unknown; *Publisher:* United States Army, Gas Defense Division, Chemical Warfare Services; *Technique:* Photochemical Print; *Dimensions:* 35.5 x 28 cm.

American civilians were tasked with collecting peach pits and other materials that could be used in the manufacture of activated charcoal, the key component in Allied gas masks during World War I. The American Red Cross was one of the organizations tasked with collecting this material. New York State Library, Manuscripts and Special Collections.

Poison Gas

Poison gas was first introduced to the battlefield in 1915 by the German Army at the Second Battle of Ypres. Gas could kill quickly or cause permanent damage. The Germans had first used chlorine gas. Soon, armies were making use of phosgene and mustard gas. Mustard gas caused severe burnlike blisters when inhaled or in contact with the skin. Since the gas was denser than air, those most affected were nearer the ground, in the trenches or wounded and unable to move.

On March 20–21, 1918, the Germans fired approximately 400 mustard gas shells into the American lines. Tragically, the men of the 42nd Division had received little training in how to deal with gas attacks and suffered 417 casualties. Overall in the American Expeditionary Force, gas attacks resulted in over 25 percent of all American battlefield casualties during the war.[27]

U.S. Army gas mask.

U.S. Army-issued gas mask with box respirator. The charcoal filter of the mask prevented soldiers from inhaling deadly poison gases. New York State Museum Collection, H-1970.124.1.

"The Final Inspector."

Artist: W.G. Thayer; *Printer:* Alco-Gravure, Inc., New York, New York; *Publisher:* Gas Defense Division, United States Army[1]; *Technique:* Lithograph; *Dimensions:* 75 x 50 cm.

This poster was designed by Lieutenant W.G. Thayer of the Army's Gas Defense Division. The poster's graphic imagery was intended to reinforce the need for care in the manufacture and use of gas masks during World War I.[2] New York State Library, Manuscripts and Special Collections.

1. Auld, S.J.M. *Gas and Flame in Modern Warfare* (New York: George H. Doran Company, 1918), frontispiece (https://books.google.com/books?id=F X46AAAAMAAJ&pg=PR2&lpg=PR2&dq=The+Final+Inspector+W.G.+Th ayer&source=bl&ots=RUyg1J0mEc&sig=a1ebX1GA--fNWOkHYwahWipY9A I&hl=en&sa=X&ved=0ahUKEwjB_uTyw97MAhUJHD4KHXS8Ax4Q6AEIITAB #v=onepage&q=The%20Final%20Inspector%20W.G.%20Thayer&f=false), accessed May 16, 2016.

2. Auld, frontispiece.

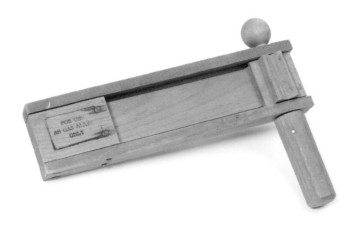

Gas alarm.

Soldiers developed several means of sounding the alarm for gas, including this rattle device. When the alarm sounded, soldiers often had only seconds to don their protective masks. New York State Museum Collection, H-1974.153.1.

Eye glasses.

These eye glasses were specifically designed and issued for use inside soldiers' gas masks. William F. Howard Collection.

27th Division

On August 30, 1917, the New York National Guard Division marched down Fifth Avenue in New York City and embarked for training at Camp Wadsworth in Spartanburg, South Carolina. In mid-April 1918, General O'Ryan received orders for the 27th Division to sail for France.

By 1918, the armies of France and Britain were exhausted and desperate for reinforcements. The situation coincided with the collapse of the Imperial Russian Army following the Bolshevik Revolution and the defeat of the Italian Army at the Battle of Caporetto in November 1917, which freed up large numbers of German troops for a spring offensive on the Western Front. Both the British and French wanted American troops to become part of their armies rather than wait for the American Army to be brought entirely up to strength. American Expeditionary Force Commander General John Pershing, however, insisted that the U.S. Army remain independent. In the spring of 1918, a new German offensive threatened Paris. Though the assault was stopped along the Marne River with the help of American divisions, the British and French armies were badly weakened in the effort.[28] General Pershing allowed two divisions to be assigned to the British Army, though as distinctly American divisions with American officers. The 27th and the 30th Divisions were selected.[29]

After training with the British, the 27th Division entered the trenches in Belgium. For nearly two months, the New Yorkers worked to fortify their position against an anticipated enemy attack. On August 31, 1918, the 27th Division assaulted Mont Kemmel, capturing the hill on September 2. After this initial combat experience, the 27th was sent to the rear in preparation for the Somme Offensive, and an assault on the German Hindenburg Line in the fall of 1918.[30]

BATTLE FOR THE HINDENBURG LINE

The Hindenburg Line was a system of trenches, barbed wire, and concrete fortifications near the St. Quentin Canal Tunnel east of Peronne, France.[31] The 27th and 30th Divisions were selected to lead the attack on the Hindenburg Line.[32] On September 27, 1918, the two American divisions began the assault, supported by British artillery and two Australian divisions. During the initial advance across No Man's Land, many of the officers and NCOs of the 27th were killed or wounded. In his recollection of the attack on the Hindenburg Line, General O'Ryan noted the bravery of his men as "[t]hey assaulted by common impulse, every man getting through the best way he could. This was done with a recklessness, valor, and determination that proved irresistible. They rushed forward in small groups and as individuals. . . . A moment later they were in the [enemy] trenches."[33] In addition to the deadly fire from the German defenders, the men of the 27th Division encountered land mines as they attempted to advance. These mines had been laid by the British Army, which had held the

"The Glorious 27th."

An artistic rendering of the 27th Division's assault on the Hindenburg Line. This particular drawing was produced in 1952 by the *New York World-Telegram and Sun* as part of a series of illustrations titled, "The Battlefields of France."[1] New York State Museum Collection, H-1971.89.1.

1. "The 27th Division on the Hindenburg Line," Catalog Record, Library of Congress Online Catalog (https://www.loc.gov/item/2010645781/), accessed April 25, 2016.

territory before the German offensive in the spring of 1918. Inexplicably, the British never informed General O'Ryan or the officers and men of the 27th of the existence of these mines.[34] The fighting was brutal and frequently in close quarters. The massed formations used by the attacking soldiers quickly fell apart under withering machine gun fire from the entrenched Germans. The 107th Infantry Regiment, which led the charge, suffered more men killed in a single day of combat than any other regiment in American history.[35] Soon, advances were made by small groups or individuals moving from shell hole to shell hole and trench to trench. It was only through such initiatives that the attack continued to push the enemy from their positions.[36] On October 1, the men of the 27th were relieved by the 3rd Australian Division, which continued the advance. The New Yorkers had succeeded in breaking through the Hindenburg Line, once believed by the Germans to be impregnable. During the fighting, six members of the division earned the Medal of Honor.[37] Over the next twenty-four days, the New Yorkers struggled alongside the 30th Division and their British and Australian allies to drive the German defenders from their fortifications. By the end of the offensive, the 27th Division had advanced more than ten miles and captured 6,000 enemy prisoners.[38]

> I desire to express to you the great pleasure that it has been to me and to the troops of the Australian Army Corps to have been so closely allied to you in the recent very important battle operations which have resulted in the breaking through of the HINDENBURG LINE."
>
> —Major General John Monash, Commander Australian Army Corps, British Fourth Army, to the commanders of the 27th and 30th American Divisions, October 2, 1918[39]

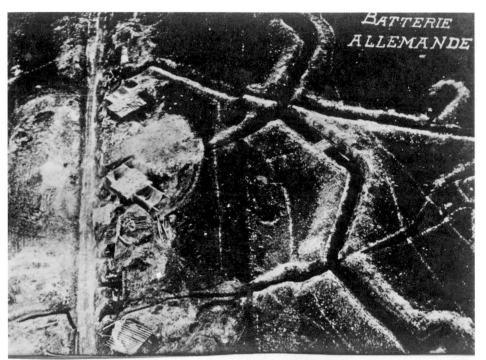

BATTERIE ALLEMANDE

trenches in the Hindenburg section taken from a french plane
Allies troops had broken through the lines

Aerial view of the Hindenburg Line.

Aerial cameras such as those developed by Eastman Kodak of Rochester enabled military planners to gain bird's-eye views of the battlefield in order to plan military operations. This image features an aerial view of a sector of the Hindenburg Line through which the 27th Division penetrated on September 29–30, 1918. The Hindenburg Line was situated almost halfway between the North Sea and the Swiss border. The position formed a pivot point that needed to be overcome before French and American forces to the south and the British to the north could begin an overall advance. New York State Museum Collection, H-1981.25.10.4.

German MG1908 bi-pod mounted machine gun.

This MG1908 with a bi-pod mount was lighter and more maneuverable than the sled-mounted version. The weapons could fire between 500 and 600 rounds per minute using 250-round belts. Its range was approximately 2,000 yards making it highly effective against attacking infantry soldiers attempting to cross No Man's Land. It was weapons such as this that awaited the New Yorkers of the 27th during their attack on the Hindenburg Line. New York State Museum Collection, H-1977.200.2.

Fragment of the Hindenburg Line.

This piece of stone was taken from the German fortifications near Bony, France, following the successful breakthrough on October 1, 1918. This example of "Trench Art" was carved by a soldier in the 105th Infantry Regiment. It was purchased by New Yorker John Walter Strauss on the dock in Brest as the 27th awaited transport home. New York State Museum Collection, H-1978.81.1.

Corporal Thomas E. O'Shea
(April 18, 1895–September 29, 1918)
Machine Gun Company, 107th Infantry, 27th Division

Thomas O'Shea was born in New York City, but spent his childhood years in Summit, New Jersey, where he sang in the choir of the Calvary Church.[40] When war was declared, O'Shea and several of his friends from Summit enlisted in the 7th Regiment of the New York National Guard, which was later redesignated the 107th Infantry Regiment. Assigned to the regiment's machine gun company, Corporal O'Shea accompanied the unit during its assault on the Hindenburg Line in late September 1918. During the attack, O'Shea and two other soldiers—Sergeants Alan Louis Eggers and John C. Latham—were separated from their platoon and took cover in a shell hole within German lines. "Upon hearing a call for help from an American tank, which had become disabled 30 yards from them, the three soldiers left their shelter and started toward the tank under heavy fire from German machine guns and trench mortars."[41] When Eggers was stunned by a German bullet, O'Shea

Soldiers of the 107th.

In this U.S. Army photograph, soldiers of the 107th are seen training alongside British tanks in preparation for the assault on the Hindenburg Line. Corporal O'Shea was killed in action while coming to the aid of a disabled tank similar to this one on September 29, 1918. New York State Military Museum, Division of Military and Naval Affairs.

27th Division Cemetery.

During the Somme Offensive, the 27th suffered 1,237 men killed and 5,327 wounded. The division's losses for the entire war totaled 8,209. Many were laid to rest at this American cemetery in France, the Bony National Cemetery, near the Hindenburg Line. This 1920 photograph features the welcome cottage erected by the American Red Cross and operated by the YWCA at the edge of the cemetery. Courtesy of the Library of Congress.

continued on while Latham tended to their comrade. As he proceeded toward the tank, enemy soldiers fired from three sides at a distance of fewer than 300 yards.[42] "In crossing the fire-swept area Corporal O'Shea was mortally wounded and died of his wounds shortly afterwards."[43] For their actions, all three men were cited for "conspicuous gallantry and intrepidity above and beyond the call of duty." Sergeants Eggers and Latham and Corporal O'Shea (posthumously) were awarded the Medal of Honor. Corporal Thomas O'Shea is buried in the Bony National Cemetery, an American cemetery near Bony, France, alongside his fellow soldiers of the 27th Division who fell in the assault on the Hindenburg Line.

> [I]t was the barbed wire which formed the groundwork of the defense. It was everywhere, and ran in all directions, cleverly disposed so as to herd the attackers into the very jaws of the machine guns.
> —J. Walter Strauss, Company F, 102nd Engineer Battalion, 27th Division[44]

First Sergeant Charles Adrean
(October 1877–October 1, 1918)
107th Infantry Regiment, 27th Division

Charles H. Adrean was born in Utica, New York, in October 1877. He first enlisted in the New York National Guard in 1898 and served with the New York Volunteers in the Spanish-American War. In Utica, he was a gas meter reader and collector for the Utica Gas and Electric Company.[45] By 1916, Adrean was a sergeant in Company A, 1st Regiment. He served with the unit along the Mexican border. On August 5, 1917, Sergeant Adrean and the rest of the 1st Regiment were drafted into federal service and merged with the 7th Regiment, New York National Guard into the newly redesignated 107th Infantry Regiment.

During the assault on the Hindenburg Line, Sergeant Adrean led his unit against German fortifications near Vandhuile, France, on September 29, 1918. In the attack, he was wounded in the head by an enemy bullet. Refusing to be evacuated, Adrean remained with his men, where he was wounded a second time. He was carried to a field hospital in the rear, where he died of his wounds on October 1.[46] For his action, Sergeant Charles Adrean was awarded the Distinguished Service Cross, the nation's second-highest award for valor. Sergeant Adrean was buried in the American Cemetery near Bony, France. After the war, his body was returned to Utica for reburial. The American Legion Post in Utica is named in his honor.

Charles Adrean and his wife.

Sergeant Adrean and his wife, Regina, on their tenth wedding anniversary, June 27, 1916. Oneida County Historical Society.

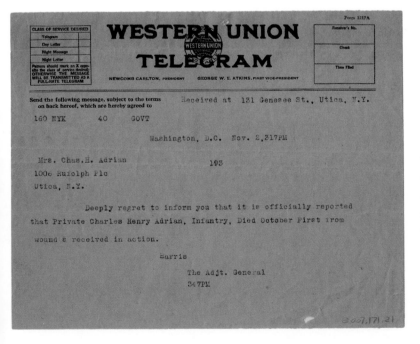

Telegram.

This telegram from the United States War Department to Mrs. Charles H. Adrean, informs his widow that Sergeant Adrean had succumbed on October 1, 1918, to wounds received in combat. The telegram is dated November 2, 1918—more than one month after his death. Oneida County Historical Society.

Private James R. Civitillo.

Courtesy of the Rochester Historical Society.

*Private James R. Civitillo
(1902–September 29, 1918)
Company G, 108th Infantry Regiment,
27th Division*

Born in Rochester in 1902, fifteen-year-old James Civitillo lied about his age and enlisted in the New York National Guard on May 28, 1917, as a private in Company G, 3rd Infantry Regiment. In August, Civitillo and the rest of his regiment were drafted into federal service as part of the newly redesignated 108th Infantry Regiment of the 27th Division. After training at Camp Wadsworth in Spartanburg, South Carolina, the division embarked for France on May 17, 1918.

Private Civitillo and the 108th Infantry participated in the 27th Division's assault on the Hindenburg Line between Cambrai and the St. Quentin Canal. James Civitillo was killed in action on September 29, 1918. He was buried alongside the other fallen men of the 27th Division at the American Cemetery near Bony, France.

Private James R. Civitillo.

This multiple exposure photograph shows Private Civitillo seemingly sitting at a table with himself. Courtesy of the Rochester Historical Society.

Private Peter Schaming Jr.
106th Infantry Regiment, 27th Division

Sixteen-year-old Peter Schaming Jr. dropped out of Curtis High School on Staten Island and enlisted in the New York National Guard on April 12, 1917, just one week after the declaration of war. Schaming was assigned to the 106th Infantry Regiment of the 27th Division. At the start of the war, the 106th had a total effective strength of 3,003 officers and men.

Schaming and the 106th Infantry Regiment were assigned to the initial wave of the attack on the Hindenburg Line. The 106th Infantry Regiment comprised the old 14th and 23rd Regiments of the New York National Guard from Brooklyn and Manhattan.[47] The 106th was tasked with capturing the outer defenses of the Hindenburg Line before the main assault. On September 27, 1918, the New York Regiment attacked. At the close of the day, the 106th had lost 910 men and had not fully succeeded in driving the Germans from their defenses.[48] The remainder of the objectives would be achieved in the following days by the 106th as well as the rest of the 27th Division. During its service in World War I, the 106th sustained 1,955 casualties, including 1,496 wounded, 376 killed, and 83 who later died of their wounds.

Private Schaming survived the assault on the Hindenburg Line. Many of his comrades were not so lucky. In a letter to his parents on October 1, 1918, Schaming wrote, "My Seargent [sic], my corporal, my squad all got it but me, even my Lieutenant was wounded three times."[49]

Peter Schaming survived the war and returned to New York City. He continued his service with the 102nd Observation Squadron, the aerial unit of the New York National Guard. He was employed as a traveling salesman for the American Thread Company. When the United States entered World War II, Schaming again volunteered for service, but was turned down due to his age. He died in 1973.

> I have been in the trenches again and I am one of the very few who is still alive and haven't a scratch on me. My regiment the 106th Infantry is wiped out. How I ever got out alive is more than I can tell.
> —Private Peter Schaming,
> October 1, 1918

Private Peter Schaming Jr.

Courtesy of the Schaming Family.

Steel helmet.

This helmet belonged to Private Peter Schaming Jr., 106th Infantry Regiment, 27th Division. New York State Museum Collection, H-2015.21.1.

Tombstone.

As part of the 27th Division, the 105th Infantry Regiment helped to break the Hindenburg Line. After a very brief rest, the 27th Division was ordered to dislodge the German Army from its positions along the Selle River. With the 105th in the lead, the division attacked on October 17, 1918. Despite heavy casualties, the 27th swept the enemy from its positions.

Among those killed was twenty-three-year-old Corporal John A. Higgins of Troy, New York. Higgins had enlisted in the New York National Guard on February 11, 1915. He is buried in Oakwood Cemetery in Troy. This tombstone, bearing the date 19 October 1918, was removed and replaced with one bearing the proper date of October 17. New York State Museum Collection, H–1994.24.3

Steel helmet, canteen, and mess kit.

These items belonged to Captain Rutherford Ireland of Brooklyn, who served with the Company L, 106th Infantry Regiment, 27th Division.[1] During the 27th Division's attack along the Le Selle River in October 1918, Ireland was severely wounded, but he refused to leave his men. When ordered to go to the medical station, Captain Ireland obeyed long enough to have his wounds bandaged. He then returned to the front lines with pieces of shrapnel still in his body. For his heroism, Captain Ireland was awarded the Distinguished Service Cross, the Army's second highest award for valor.[2] New York State Military Museum, Division of Military and Naval Affairs

1. Norton, page 110

2. "Ireland, Rutherford," Home of Heroes (http://www.homeofheroes.com/members/02_DSC/citatons/01_wwi_dsc/dsc_05wwi_Army_IJ.html), accessed May 20, 2016

Trench Art

Soldiers often expressed their creativity to pass the time. While the practice existed before World War I, it is today often referred to as "Trench Art."

Aluminum canteen engraved with the 27th Division insignia.

New York State Military Museum, Division of Military and Naval Affairs.

Meat can lid engraved with 27th Division insignia.

William F. Howard Collection.

Shell casing vase.

New York State Museum Collection, H–1972.61.21.

Shell casing vases.

These French 75 mm artillery casings have been polished, fluted, and embossed with a morning glory floral design. Each is engraved with the name of a major battle in which the U.S. Army played a critical role—the Marne and St. Mihiel. New York State Military Museum, Division of Military and Naval Affairs.

369th Infantry Regiment

The men of the 15th New York Infantry were overlooked for inclusion in the 42nd Division in favor of the Irishmen of the 69th New York. The soldiers from Harlem faced another slight when the regiment was omitted from New York's National Guard Division, the 27th. Following their hurried departure from stateside, the men of the regiment again confronted racism in the segregated United States Army; the men of the newly federalized 369th Infantry were put to work digging latrines and serving as stevedores unloading ships at harbor. General John Pershing, commander of the American Expeditionary Force, intended to use African American soldiers as laborers and pioneer troops, not as combat units.[50] It was the looming German offensive in the spring of 1918

and the French Army's lack of troop strength that prompted a change in the situation. The regiment's commander, Colonel William Hayward, and officers such as Hamilton Fish III and Arthur Little eventually convinced the American command to allow the men to fight—but under French Army command. On March 12, 1918, the regiment was assigned to the 16th Division of the French Fourth Army.[51] The men arrived at Givry in Bourgogne to begin training on March 18.[52] By April 10, the men from Harlem entered the French trenches.[53]

During the Allied Meuse-Argonne Offensive in September–October 1918, the 369th was tasked with spearheading an assault on the French village of Sechault in support of the assault on the Hindenburg

Line. The 369th thus went into combat at the same time as their fellow New Yorkers in the 27th Division, but remained under French command.[54] In eight days of fighting, the regiment suffered 144 officers and men killed and more than 1,000 wounded.[55] By the time the Armistice was announced on November 11, 1918, the 369th had spent more days in combat—191—than any other regiment in the United States Army. In recognition of its gallantry, the French Army selected the men from Harlem to lead the crossing of the Rhine River into Germany on November 17.[56]

The Battle of Henry Johnson

On the night of May 14, 1918, then-Privates Henry Johnson and Needham Roberts of the 369th Infantry Regiment were stationed at a listening outpost in No

French Army style "Adrian" helmet.

The 15th New York was the only American unit to arrive in France with its state designation. The regiment was re-designated the 369th Infantry Regiment and was assigned to the 93rd Division, a proposed all-black division in the segregated U.S. Army. The division was never formed; the 369th was instead assigned to the French Army, which was depleted from four years of war and eager to employ able-bodied fighters regardless of color. For many in the unit, the assignment of the 369th to the French was "liberation."[1] The French had utilized African colonial soldiers as shock troops throughout the war. Many saw the French as "color blind" and more accepting of black soldiers than their American counterparts.[2]

As the 369th served with and was supplied by the French Army, the men were equipped with French Adrian helmets and Berthier rifles rather than the steel helmets and 1917 Enfields used by other American forces. New York State Museum Collection, H-1978.137.23.

1. Slotkin, page 136.

2. Harris, *Harlem's Hellfighters,* page 179.

Man's Land to detect enemy movements. At approximately 3:30 a.m., they were attacked by a German raiding party estimated at between twenty and thirty enemy soldiers.[57] Roberts was quickly incapacitated, but he continued to hand grenades to a wounded Johnson. The Germans attempted to drag Roberts back to their trenches, but Johnson pursued them. Firing his rifle until it jammed and then using it as a club until it broke, Johnson drew a bolo knife and continued to fight. After reinforcements arrived, Johnson collapsed from twenty-one wounds. Henry Johnson and Needham Roberts became the first Americans of any color to be awarded the French Croix de Guerre with palms for bravery in action.[58]

Colonel William Hayward (second from left) with officers and men of the 369th Infantry Regiment.

New York State Museum Collection, H-1971.113.11.

"Our Colored Heroes," lithograph 1918.

This 1918 lithographic print was sold throughout the United States, likely targeting the African American population on the home front, honoring Johnson and Roberts as heroes. The shield at the lower left includes a May 19, 1918, communique from General John Pershing to the War Department in which Pershing cites "a notable instance of bravery and devotion shown by two soldiers of an American colored regiment operating in a French Sector." Despite this and other acknowledgments of his heroism, Johnson did not receive official commendation for his actions until 1996 when President Bill Clinton bestowed the Purple Heart for Johnson's wounds in combat. In 2002, Johnson was awarded the Distinguished Service Cross, and in May 2015, President Barrack Obama posthumously presented the Medal of Honor to Sergeant Henry Johnson. New York State Museum Collection, H-1976.31.10.

This bolo knife is similar to the type used by Henry Johnson on May 14–15, 1918.

New York State Museum Collection.

The Hellfighters' Band

Colonel William Hayward raised $10,000 with which he tasked Lieutenant James Reese Europe to enlist a regimental band befitting of the Harlem Regiment.[59] In addition to Europe, the band of the 369th included renowned jazz artist Noble Sissle. Europe recruited talented musicians from New York City, Puerto Rico, and across the country. When the 15th New York—later reorganized as the 369th Infantry—arrived in France, the men were assigned as laborers on the docks at St. Nazaire rather than as combat troops.[60]

It was at St. Nazaire that Lieutenant Europe's band began to earn its reputation, as "[t]he morale of the regiment at this time was getting very low. At daybreak every morning the entire regiment would be awakened to the martial strains of our band." As the men marched to and from their assigned labors, the band played "a good ragtime tune to try to cheer the boys up."[61] Word of James Reese Europe and his band as "an organization of the very highest quality, trained and led by a conductor of genius," spread quickly through the American Expeditionary Force.[62] On February 12, the band boarded a train for the American respite center at Aix-les-Bains where they entertained white American soldiers to rave reviews.[63] During their journey to Aix-les-Bains, the band made several stops to play for both American soldiers and French citizens.[64] Following the war, Colonel Hayward commended Europe and the regimental band, stating "without the band of the 369th U.S. Infantry the regiment could never have performed the long and difficult service it did both in America and in the AEF, and without Lieutenant Europe, there would have been no band."[65]

> [T]here has never been such an organization of Negro men that will bring together all classes of men for a common good. And our race will never amount to anything, politically or economically, in New York or anywhere else, unless there are strong organizations of men who stand for something in the community.
>
> —James Reese Europe to Noble Sissle from Sissle's memoirs

Lieutenant James Reese Europe

Europe was born February 22, 1880, in Mobile, Alabama, and moved to Washington, DC, where his

Lieutenant James Reese Europe.

Lieutenant James Reese Europe and the Harlem Hellfighters' Regimental Band perform for wounded American soldiers and French civilians at a U.S. Army hospital in Paris. Courtesy of the Library of Congress.

Hellfighters' Regimental Band.

The Harlem Hellfighters' Regimental Band on board a transport ship en route to New York City from France, 1919. Courtesy of the National Archives.

Sheet music, "On Patrol in No Man's Land."

James Reese Europe was a leading figure in American jazz and ragtime in Harlem when he joined the New York National Guard. As the bandleader for the Harlem Hellfighters, Europe and his band are largely credited with the introduction of jazz to France during World War I. He composed this song while recovering from a gas attack in France. New York State Museum Collection, H-1978.206.1.

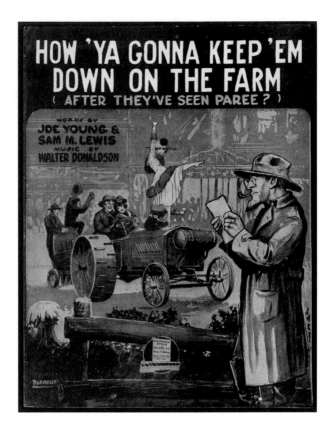

Sheet music, "How Ya Gonna Keep 'em Down on the Farm (After They've Seen Paree?)"

Lieutenant James Reese Europe's 369th Infantry Band recorded this song, published by Waterson, Berlin and Snyder Co. in New York, in 1919. The lyrics of the song likely resonated strongly with African American veterans of World War I. Many of the men in the 369th and other black veterans returned to civilian life determined not to accept the racial status quo.[1] New York State Library, Manuscripts and Special Collections.

1. Memorandum, Special Agent M.J. Driscoll to C.L. Converse, July 13, 1919, Subject: "Protest Meeting, Rush A.M.E. Zion Church, West 138th St., City," page 2. Joint Legislative Committee to Investigate Seditious Activities, Investigations Files, 1918–1920, New York State Archives, L0038, Box 1, Folder 19.

mother taught him to play the violin and piano.[66] Following the death of his father in 1899, the teenaged Europe moved to New York City to pursue a career in music.[67] His arrival in New York was not without challenges, for few clubs or theaters would hire black musicians. Europe persevered and began to establish himself in the New York music world.[68] In 1910, he formed the African American Clef Club and led its 125 members at a concert at Carnegie Hall in 1912.[69] Shortly after this history-making performance, Europe partnered with famed dancers Vernon and Irene Castle and composed numerous numbers for them.[70]

James Reese Europe joined the New York National Guard on September 18, 1916, as a member of the 15th New York Infantry Regiment.[71] He was already established as one of the leading conductors of jazz and ragtime in the nation. He was tasked by the regimental commander, Colonel William Hayward, with assembling the unit's marching band. Europe agreed under the condition that the colonel allow him to recruit "the best band in the country."[72]

He was one of the only African American commissioned officers in a combat unit and was the first to come under enemy fire when he accompanied a French patrol in No Man's Land. He was injured in a German gas attack in April 1918. While in the hospital, he penned "On Patrol in No Man's Land."[73]

After the war, Europe and the Hellfighters Band embarked on a nationwide tour. Europe was killed on May 9, 1919, in Boston, Massachusetts, by one of his drummers, Herbert Wright, after an argument.[74] He is buried in Arlington National Cemetery.

In February 1918, the band was ordered to travel to Aix-Les-Bains, France, a resort town in the southern Alps that had been converted to a respite area for the AEF As the Hellfighters' Band made the 400-mile trip, they played a series of concerts in cities such as Nantes and Tours along the route. In late August, the band played for a crowd of 50,000 in the Tuileries Gardens in Paris alongside some of the most renowned military bands of the Allied armies, to raucous applause.[75] One of the band's performances was described by a correspondent from the *St. Louis Post-Dispatch*: "it seemed the whole audience began to sway, dignified French officers began to pat their feet, along with the American General, who, temporarily had lost his style and grace." The reporter continued, "Lieut. Europe was no longer the Lieut. Europe of a moment ago but Jim Europe, who had rocked New York with his syncopated baton."[76] For many French civilians, this was the first introduction to ragtime and jazz.[77]

165th Infantry Regiment, 42nd Division, American Expeditionary Force

The 42nd Division arrived in France in November 1917. Shortly after Christmas, the men of the 165th undertook an eighty-mile march through the Vosges Mountains to Longeau, where the regiment was placed in the line. The 165th first saw combat in March 1918 in the Chausilles sector near the village of Baccarat when one of its battalions was selected by the French to raid German trenches across No Man's Land.[78]

The 42nd joined 300,000 other newly arrived American soldiers in halting the German offensive along the Marne River in July 1918.[79] During the enemy onslaught, the men endured intense German bombardments in which "the sky and the earth seemed just one conglomerate of fire" as hundreds of guns on both sides sent "screaming shells" into the trenches.[80] During this defensive, the 165th repelled five separate German attacks on July 15 alone.[81] The New York regiment also fought with distinction at the Battle of Chateau-Thierry, as well as in the American offensive against the St. Mihiel Salient, and during the final Meuse-Argonne Offensive. Three members

of the regiment earned the Medal of Honor, including Lieutenant Colonel William Donovan on October 14–15, 1918, for his actions near Landres-et-St. Georges, France.

By the time the Armistice was signed on November 11, 1918, the 165th Infantry Regiment had spent 164 days in combat and had suffered 844 men killed in action.[82] On November 16, the 42nd Division departed the Argonne as part of the Allied Army of Occupation. The 165th was stationed in Remagen, Germany.[83] The regiment remained there until March 1919.

Window banner.

This window banner bears the rainbow insignia of the 42nd Division and lists the battles in which the unit—including New York's 165th Infantry Regiment—fought during the war. New York State Museum Collection, H-1988.72.2.

Collar disk insignia, Company A, 165th Infantry Regiment.

When war was declared, the 69th like all other New York Regiments, sought to bring its numbers to wartime strength. As the nation rushed to mobilize, individual states competed to be the first to send their National Guard units to France. In response, the War Department announced the formation of the 42nd Division, which would include units from twenty-six states and the District of Columbia. The 69th New York, later redesignated the 165th Infantry Regiment, was named as New York's contribution to the division. Courtesy of the New York State Military Museum, Division of Military and Naval Affairs.

Collier's New Photographic History of the World's War, 1918, pg. 60.

Tunic, 165th Infantry Regiment.

This tunic belonged to a soldier in the 165th Infantry Regiment.

William F. Howard Collection.

Sergeant Richard O'Neill.

Sergeant Richard O'Neill shown with the Medal of Honor around his neck. Courtesy of The Disabled American Veterans of the World War. Chicago via Wikimedia Commons.

Sergeant Richard O'Neill
(August 28, 1898–April 9, 1982)
Company D, 165th Infantry Regiment, 42nd Division

Richard O'Neill was born in New York City in August 1898 and grew up in Harlem. He joined the 69th Infantry Regiment of the New York National Guard and was a sergeant in the unit at the outbreak of war. O'Neill was assigned to Company D, 165th Infantry when the regiment was rushed into the line in the face of the German Army's major offensive in July 1918. After forcing the enemy into retreat on July 15, the 42nd Division joined in the pursuit of the German Army.[84]

On July 30, 1918, during the Aisne-Marne Offensive, O'Neill earned the Medal of Honor for

"extraordinary heroism" at the Ourcq River in France. According to the Medal's citation: "In advance of an assaulting line, Sergeant O'Neill attacked a detachment of about 25 of the enemy. In the ensuing hand-to-hand encounter he sustained pistol wounds, but heroically continued in the advance, during which he received additional wounds; but, with great physical effort, he remained in active command of his detachment. Being again wounded, he was forced by weakness and loss of blood to be evacuated, but insisted upon being taken first to the battalion commander in order to transmit to him valuable information relative to enemy positions and the disposition of our men."

O'Neill's actions reportedly caused confusion among the German defenders and forced them into retreat.[85] Sergeant Richard O'Neill was awarded the Medal of Honor in 1921 by President Warren G. Harding. He emerged from World War I as one of New York State's most decorated soldiers.[86]

Rouge Bouquet

After arriving in France in November 1917, the 165th was placed in the "quiet" Rouge Bouquet sector of the trenches. On March 7, 1918, a German shell struck a dugout of the 165th Infantry Regiment. Two men were rescued, five bodies were recovered, and fifteen remained buried. Acclaimed poet and sergeant in the 165th, Joyce Kilmer penned a tribute for their memorial service at Rouge Bouquet. On March 12, 1918, regimental chaplain Father Francis Duffy read the services of the dead and blessed their "tomb."[87]

> In a wood they call Rouge Bouquet
> There is a new-made grave today,
> Built by never a spade nor pick
>   Yet covered with earth 10 meters thick.
> There lie many fighting men,
> Dead in their youthful prime,
> Never to laugh nor love again
>   Nor taste the Summertime.
> For Death came flying through the air
> And stopped his flight at the dugout stair,
> Touched his prey and left them there,
>   Clay to clay.
> He hid their bodies stealthily
> In the soil of the land they fought to free . . .
>   —Excerpt from
>   "Rouge Bouquet" by Joyce Kilmer,
>   Sergeant, 165th Infantry Regiment[88]

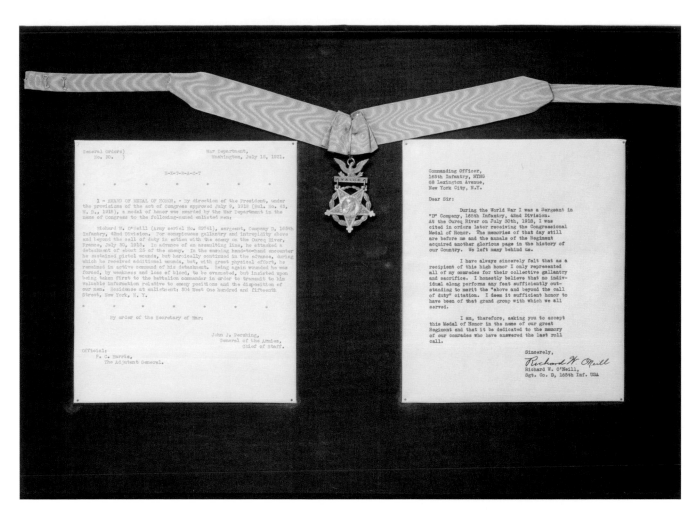

Medal of Honor.

Sergeant Richard O'Neill presented his Medal of Honor to the 69th Regiment's armory at Lexington Avenue in New York City. In the letter framed alongside the Medal, O'Neill honors his fallen comrades by asking that the award be hung in the unit armory in their honor. New York State Military Museum, Division of Military and Naval Affairs and the Veterans of the 69th Infantry Regiment Association, Lexington Avenue Armory, New York, NY.

Sergeant Joyce Kilmer (December 6, 1886–July 30, 1918)
Intelligence Section, 165th Infantry Regiment,
42nd Division

Alfred Joyce Kilmer grew up in New Brunswick, New Jersey. He spent two years at Rutgers University before attending Columbia University. After graduating in 1908, he worked as an editor for various publications before being hired by the *New York Times*. In 1914, Joyce Kilmer published his most famous poem, "Trees," which reflected his love of nature and his deeply held religious beliefs. Age thirty-one when war was declared, Kilmer, with a wife and four children, was not obligated to serve, but he enlisted in the 7th Regiment. Kilmer requested a transfer to join the 69th Regiment—the "Fighting Irish"—when it was selected to be the first New York unit sent to France.

Kilmer was initially assigned to regimental headquarters, where he had clerical duties. When Lieutenant Basil Elmer was assembling the regiment's intelligence section, Kilmer begged Father Duffy, the regimental chaplain, to assist him in getting "out in the line."[89] As a member of Elmer's intelligence section, Kilmer was tasked with leading patrols into No Man's Land and gathering intelligence. During the Aisne-Marne Offensive, he volunteered to scout for enemy machine-gun positions ahead of the regiment's advance. Kilmer was killed on July 30, 1918. He was posthumously awarded the French Croix de Guerre for bravery. He was buried alongside his comrades "at the edge of a wood overlooking a brook" which had just recently been won by the regiment.[90]

Sergeant Joyce Kilmer.

Courtesy of the Library of Congress.

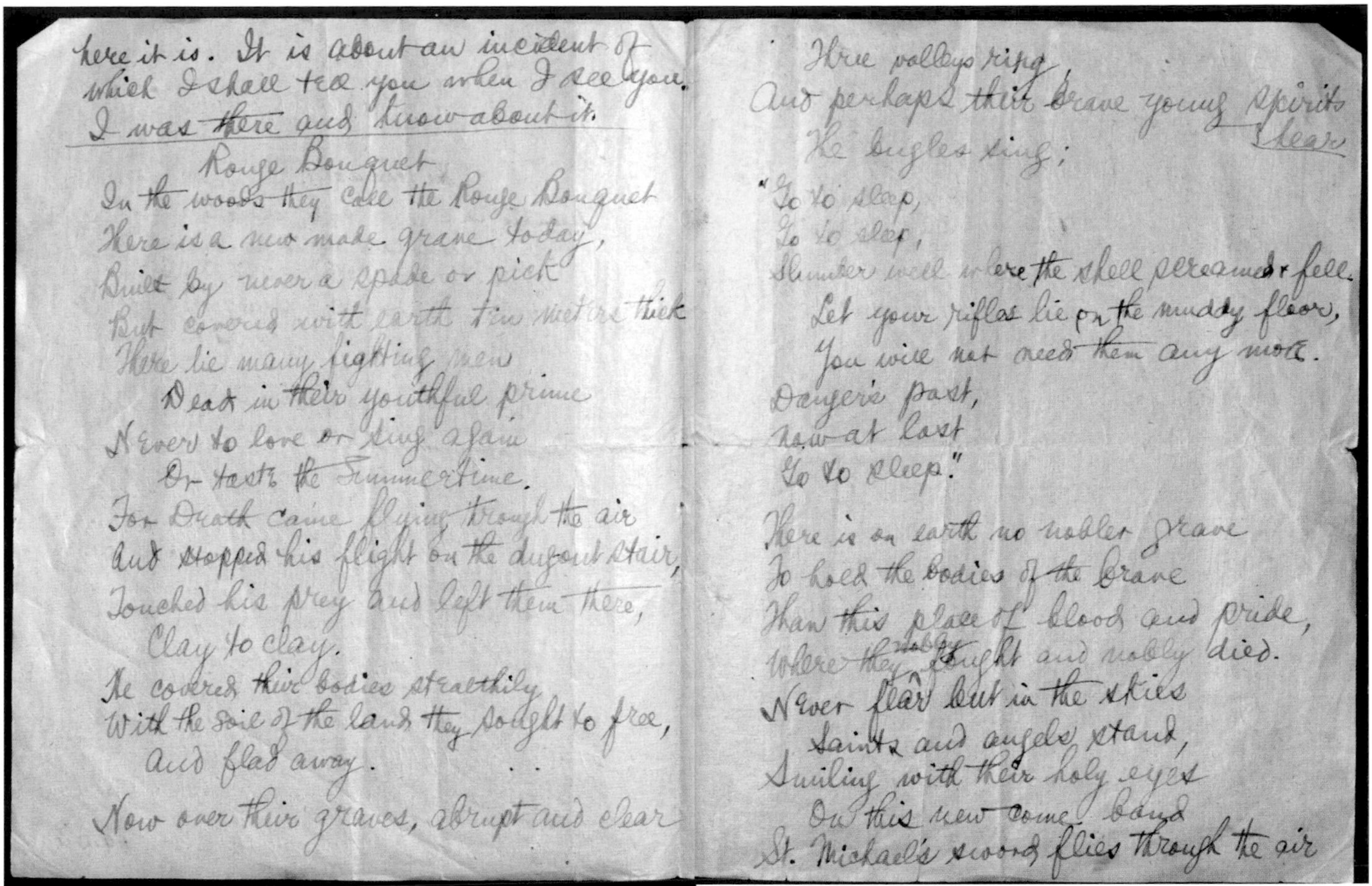

here it is. It is about an incident of
which I shall tell you when I see you.
I was there and know about it.

Rouge Bouquet

In the woods they call the Rouge Bouquet
Here is a new made grave today,
Built by never a spade or pick
But covered with earth ten meters thick
There lie many fighting men
    Dead in their youthful prime
Never to love or sing again
    Or taste the Summertime.
For Death came flying through the air
And stopped his flight on the dugout stair,
Touched his prey and left them there,
    Clay to clay.
He covered their bodies stealthily
With the soil of the land they sought to free,
    And fl ad away.

Now over their graves, abrupt and clear

Three valleys ring
And perhaps their brave young spirits
    the bugles sing;   hear
"Go to sleep,
Go to sleep,
Slumber well where the shell screamed & fell.
    Let your rifles lie on the muddy floor,
    You will not need them any more.
Danger's past,
now at last
Go to sleep."

Here is on earth no nobler grave
To hold the bodies of the brave
Than this place of blood and pride,
Where they nobly fought and nobly died.
Never fear but in the skies
    Saints and angels stand,
Smiling with their holy eyes
    On this new come band
St. Michael's sword flies through the air

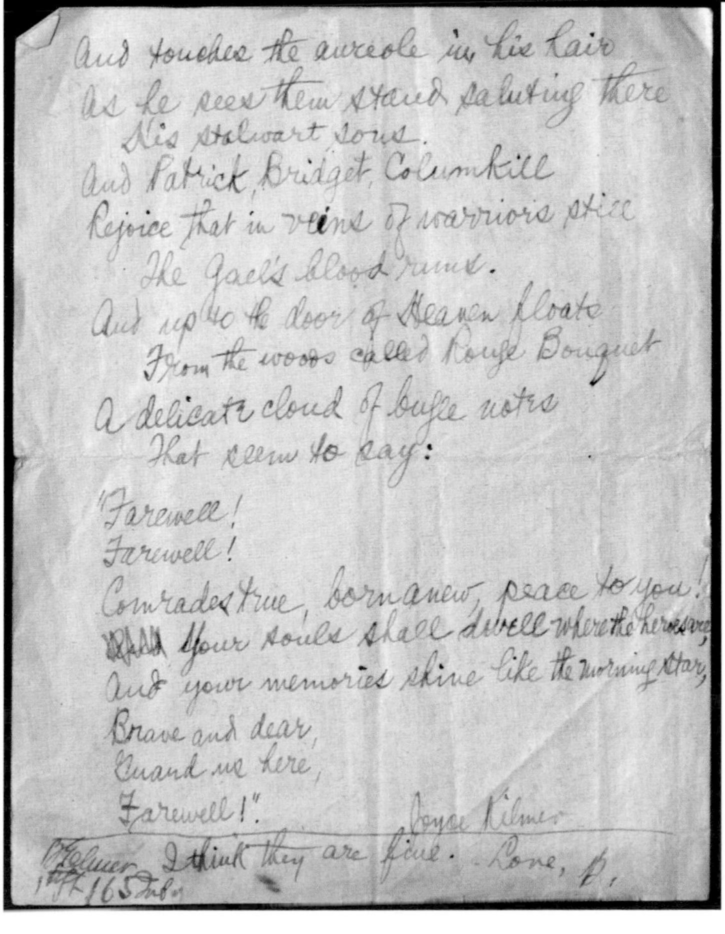

And touches the aureole in his hair
As he sees them stand saluting there
    His stalwart sons.
And Patrick, Bridget, Columkill
Rejoice that in veins of warriors still
    The Gael's blood runs.
And up to the door of Heaven floats
    From the woods called Rouge Bouquet
A delicate cloud of bugle notes
    That seem to say:

"Farewell!
Farewell!
Comrades true, born anew, peace to you!
Your souls shall dwell where the heroes are
And your memories shine like the morning star,
Brave and dear,
Guard us here,
Farewell!"
                    Joyce Kilmer

Elmer   I think they are fine.   Rone, B,
165th Inf.

Letter, June 14, 1918.

Lieutenant Basil Beebe Elmer was Joyce Kilmer's commanding officer
with the Intelligence Section of the 165th Infantry Regiment. In his
correspondence with his parents, Elmer makes frequent mention of the
"famous poet" Joyce Kilmer. In this June 1918 letter, he tells his parents
in Ithaca that Kilmer will have a poem published in an upcoming edition
of *Scribner's* magazine and requests that they save a copy for him. That
poem, which is transcribed in the letter, was "Rouge Bouquet." New York
State Library, Manuscripts and Special Collections.

Father Francis Duffy in uniform.

Courtesy of the U.S. Army Chaplain Center and School.

Father Francis Duffy (May 2, 1871–June 27, 1932)
Chaplain, 165th Infantry Regiment, 42nd Division

Father Francis Duffy was born May 2, 1871, in Cobourg, Ontario, Canada. After attending St. Michael's College in Toronto, Duffy immigrated to New York City. He was ordained as a Catholic priest in the archdiocese of New York in 1896. While serving at Our Savior Church in the Bronx, Duffy joined the predominantly Irish 69th Regiment of the New York National Guard. He served as regimental chaplain during the unit's service in the Spanish-American War in 1898.[91]

When the United States went to war in April 1917, Father Duffy marched with the 165th Infantry Regiment as part of the 42nd Division. While in Europe, Father Duffy served with distinction, ministering to the sick, wounded, and dying, counseling, and consoling the soldiers in his charge. In combat, Father Duffy "was always near the heaviest fighting, exposing himself to constant danger as he moved from unit to unit" without regard to his own well-being.[92]

By the time of the Armistice, Duffy had earned the Distinguished Service Cross, the Distinguished Service Medal, the Conspicuous Service Cross, the Legion d'Honneur, and the Croix de Guerre. He left Europe as the most decorated chaplain in the American Army.[93] After the war, Duffy returned to his ministry in New York City. He died of colitis in June 1932. A statue in his memory was erected at Times Square in 1937.

Last rites kit.

This last rites—or extreme unction—kit was carried by Father Francis Duffy, Chaplain of the 165th Infantry Regiment during World War I. The kit includes a purple stole, two small crucifixes, and a tin container that held oil or water used in the rites. New York State Military Museum, Division of Military and Naval Affairs and the Veterans of the 69th Infantry Regiment Association, Lexington Avenue Armory, New York, NY.

Father Francis Duffy presides over the funeral services for Quentin Roosevelt, youngest son of President Theodore Roosevelt.

Quentin was an aviator in the U.S. Army Air Service. He was killed when his plane was shot down near Chamery, France on July 14, 1918. New York State Library, Manuscripts and Special Collections.

77th Division

The conscripted soldiers who would eventually make up the 77th Division began arriving at Camp Upton, Long Island, on September 10, 1917. Even as immigrants fell under suspicion at home, the 77th Division reflected New York City's cosmopolitan character: "Many could not speak English. There were Italians, Jews, Chinese, Irish, Armenians, Syrians and other nationalities, rubbing elbows with the native born."[94] For the next six months, the men were trained to become soldiers. On March 27, 1918, the first elements of the division set sail for Europe. The entire 77th Division arrived in France in April 1918.[95] It was the first division of drafted soldiers to arrive in France and was the seventh division of the American Expeditionary Force in Europe.

On June 24, the Germans attacked the untested men of the division with gas, resulting in 180 casualties.[96] This pattern would be repeated in American trenches across the Western Front as the inadequacy of training in gas warfare by the U.S. Army became readily apparent. The soldiers of the 77th continued to hold a series of trenches in the Baccarat sector in the Lorraine region of Eastern France throughout July. During this period, the division completed its training in anticipation of offensive operations.

Between July 15 and 20, Allied forces halted a final German offensive along the Marne River. In early August, the 77th Division joined the American counterattack as part of the Aisne-Marne Offensive. After this baptism by fire, the 77th was withdrawn from the front lines in preparation for the larger and far more deadly Meuse-Argonne Offensive in late September. During its time in the AEF the 77th Division suffered 10,194 casualties, including 1,486 killed and 8,708 wounded. The 77th Division was credited with making the furthest gains of any division in the AEF by General Pershing's chief of staff, Major General Peyton March.[97]

During the Allied Meuse-Argonne Offensive (September 26–November 11, 1918), the 77th Division was tasked with clearing a three-mile-wide portion of the Argonne forest against "an enemy posted in an indescribable tangle of wooded hills, marshy bottoms, and deep ravines."[98] As the division advanced over the rugged, forested terrain, communication between units quickly broke down. One battalion of the 308th Infantry Regiment advanced beyond both of its flanking units and found itself surrounded behind enemy lines. Under the command of Major Charles Whittlesey, the "Lost Battalion" held out under murderous German fire for six days with little food, fresh water, or ammunition. Their stalwart defense forced the German Army to expend resources to dislodge them and aided other American units to force a breakthrough.

Hill 240.

American soldiers advancing up the slope of Hill 240 during the opening days of the Meuse-Argonne Offensive. From the New York Public Library.

Steel helmet.

This artifact was worn by Joseph A.C. Kennedy of the 77th Division, who reportedly served as part of the "Lost Battalion" in which 554 members of the division were isolated for five days during the Meuse-Argonne Offensive in October 1918. Of the men who entered "The Pocket," on October 2, fewer than 200 survived the battle.[1] Courtesy of the New York State Military Museum, Division of Military and Naval Affairs.

1. Slotkin, page 362.

Lost Battalion.

Survivors of the "Lost Battalion" of the 77th Division after their rescue from behind enemy lines. New York State Museum Collection, H-1971.113.11.

Captain Lewis F. Harder.

Captain Lewis F. Harder, from *A History of Columbia County in the Great War*. Courtesy of Robert H. Stitham.

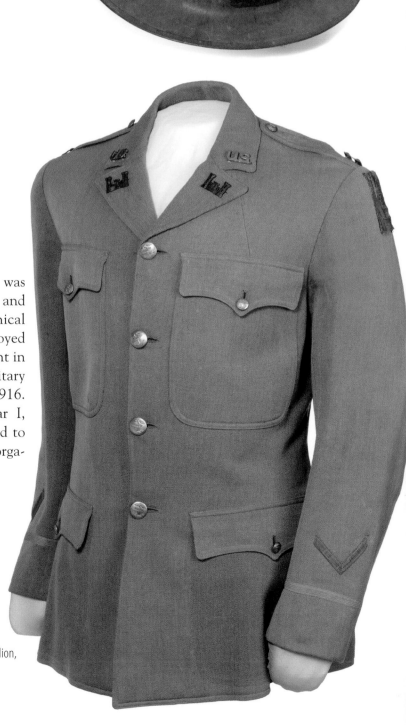

Captain Lewis F. Harder

Lewis F. Harder of Philmont, Columbia County, was born in 1892. He attended Hudson High School and later Yale University, where he studied mechanical engineering. Upon graduation, Harder was employed at the High Rock Knitting Company in Philmont in 1914. Lewis Harder attended the Citizens Military Training Camp at Plattsburgh in 1915 and 1916. When the United States entered World War I, Harder volunteered for service and was assigned to Company C, 302nd Engineers, 77th Division, organizing at Camp Upton.[99]

Tunic and helmet.

This steel helmet and postwar U.S. Army uniform coat belonged to Captain Lewis F. Harder during his service with the 302nd Engineer Battalion, 77th Division during the war. Courtesy of Robert H. Stitham.

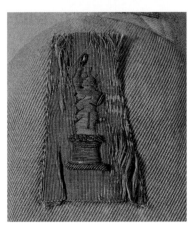

302nd Engineer Battalion pin and shoulder patch.

Pin and shoulder patch from postwar U.S. Army uniform coat that belonged to Captain Lewis F. Harder. Courtesy of Robert H. Stitham.

While in France, Harder was promoted to the rank of captain and given command of Company C. The unit participated in combat operations in support of the 77th Division along the Vesle River in August 1918 before being withdrawn from the front lines in preparation for the Allied Meuse-Argonne Offensive. On September 28, Captain Harder was severely wounded in the opening of the assault in the Argonne Forest.[100] Having suffered compound fractures in both legs and multiple lesser wounds, Harder was evacuated to an Army field hospital and invalided back to the United States, arriving in February 1919. After recovering from his wounds, he resumed working at the High Rock Knitting Co., rising to company vice president and treasurer. In 1923, Harder was elected to a single term in the New York State Assembly. He continued to work at the Knitting Company until his retirement. Lewis Harder died in 1964.

"Argonne Conquerors."

Artist: Lt. Augustus Kaiser; *Printer:* Wynkoop, Hallenbeck, Crawford Co., New York, New York; *Publisher:* 77th Division Association; *Technique:* Lithograph; *Dimensions:* 56 x 35 cm.

This poster was created as an advertisement for the 1919 publication of the History of the 77th Division, which was produced by the newly formed 77th Division Association for the division's return to the United States. The poster depicts Mars, the Roman god of war, leading the fight in the Argonne. The glorified and allegorical battle scene depicted in the illustration in no way resembled the horrifying conditions that existed during the fighting in the Argonne Forest as is evidenced by the fact that someone wrote, "a typical war picture by the artists who were never there" on the poster. This juxtaposition is even more interesting due to the fact that the poster's artist, Lieutenant Augustus Kaiser, was himself a veteran of the 77th Division and served with Company A of the 302nd Engineer Battalion. During the Argonne Offensive, soldiers of Company A were among the engineers advancing alongside the infantry of the division.[1] New York State Library, Manuscripts and Special Collections.

1. Crawford, Ellet, and Hyland, page 85.

Lieutenant Augustus Kaiser.

Augustus Kaiser served as a lieutenant in Company A, 302nd Engineer Battalion, 77th Division during the war. Following the Armistice, Lieutenant Kaiser was among the officers tasked with compiling a published history of the 77th Division.[1] Kaiser, who had been an illustrator in Minneapolis before the war, served as the art editor for the final publication of the history in 1919. He also made numerous drawings and sketches of the men of the 77th Division while serving in France with the AEF.[2]

RESPONSE OF NEW YORK'S OWN

"Response of New York's Own."

This drawing titled, "Response of New York's Own" by Lieutenant Augustus Kaiser was published in *A History of the Seventy-Seventh Division: August 25th, 1917 to November 11th, 1918*.[3] New York State Library

1. "Compile History of the 77th," *New York Times*, April 13, 1919, p. 19 (http://timesmachine.nytimes.com/timesmachine/1919/04/13/96292793.html), accessed February 22, 2016.

2. "History of 77th Division Unique," *Brooklyn Standard Union*, April 12, 1919, p. 4 (http://fultonhistory.com/Newspaper%2014/Brooklyn%20NY%20Standard%20Union/Brooklyn%20NY%20Standard%20Union%201919/Brooklyn%20NY%20Standard%20Union%201919%20-%201487.pdf), accessed February 22, 2016.

3. Adler, page 10.

Captain Edward "Eddie" Leslie Grant (1883–1918)
307th Infantry Regiment, 77th Division

Edward Grant was born in Franklin, Massachusetts, and educated at Harvard University. After graduation, he became a professional baseball player with the Cleveland Indians, the Philadelphia Phillies, the Cincinnati Reds, and the New York Giants from 1913 to 1915, playing on the 1913 World Series champion team. Grant retired after the 1915 season and became a lawyer in Manhattan. In the summer of 1916, he attended the Plattsburgh Citizens Military Training Camp, where he befriended Charles Whittlesey. When war was declared, Eddie Grant volunteered for military service despite the fact that at age thirty-four he was beyond draft age.[101] He became a company commander in the 307th Infantry Regiment, 77th Division.

When word of the Lost Battalion reached Captain Grant, he and his men had been in constant combat for four days. Despite their exhaustion, Grant's men pressed forward in an attempt to reach the men under Whittlesey's command.[102] Eddie Grant was killed on October 5, 1918, leading an effort to rescue Major Whittlesey and the Lost Battalion in the Argonne Forest. He was one of eight major-league baseball players to be killed in action in the World War.[103]

> . . . The final box score of a Player who
>   Gave
> The flag that he fought for, his ghost,
> —and his grave . . .
>   —Excerpt from "Eddie Grant's Last
>   Game" by Grantland Rice, ca. 1921[104]

Eddie Grant.

Edward Leslie Grant in his New York Giants baseball uniform in 1914. In 1921, the New York Giants erected a memorial plaque in Grant's honor at center field at the New York Polo Grounds. Courtesy of the Library of Congress.

Tobacco felt.

This 1914 felt square features the likeness of New York Giants infielder Eddie Grant. These "tobacco felts" were produced by several companies and would have been fastened to tobacco products as a collectible item.[1] Women were often encouraged to sew the felts together to create quilts. New York State Museum Collection, H-2016.11.1.

1. "1914 Felt Blanket/B-18 Blanket," Keymancollectibles.com (http://keymancollectibles.com/miscellaneous/1914feltblanket.htm), accessed January 25, 2016.

Nurses in the AEF

In April 1917, the U.S. Army Nurses Corps included 403 nurses. In cooperation with the American Red Cross, the Army was prepared to call 8,000 reservists into military service.[105] By the time the AEF sailed for Europe, the Army had 33 base hospitals nearly ready for service. Six sailed for France within a month. Each base hospital was staffed with a full complement of medical personnel, including 65 nurses. This number would prove inadequate and was increased to 100 within six months. By December 1918, 21,480 nurses had enlisted and more than 10,000 were in service overseas.[106] This number was wholly inadequate to tend to the wounded, but nurses were given a lower priority than combat troops by military planners on the limited shipping available for the AEF

During the war, over 200 nurses were killed. Of that 200, forty—or 20 percent—hailed from New York State.[107] Most of these succumbed to the influenza epidemic of 1918 and other diseases contracted as they sought to care and comfort the men in their charge.[108]

Nurse's smock, sleeve protectors, and apron.

The smock, sleeve protectors, and apron displayed here were issued to American Red Cross nurses in France during World War I. New York State Museum Collection, H-1985.56.4-.5 and .12 A-B.

"Five Thousand by June."

Artist: C. Rakeman; *Printer:* Rand McNally and Co., New York, New York; *Publisher:* American Red Cross; *Technique:* Lithograph; *Dimensions:* 69.5 x 49.5 cm.

With entry into World War I, the U.S. Army coordinated with the American Red Cross in order to bolster its Nursing Corps and bring it to wartime strength under the newly formed Department of Military Relief. New York State Library, Manuscripts and Special Collections.

The Influenza Pandemic of 1918

In the spring of 1918, soldiers training at Camp Funston in Haskell County, Kansas, began falling ill with fever. Initially, few deaths were reported and patients recovered after several days.[3] By September, an influenza pandemic had spread worldwide. The spread of the disease was aided by the large number of men at military camps in the United States and in Europe. The movement of these men from Army camps on the home front through cities and towns along the nation's railways and overseas also helped to spread influenza on a global scale.

The influenza epidemic targeted people of all ages, races, and social classes. Soldiers in the American Army—men in the prime of their health—were not immune. In an October 1, 1918, letter to his sister from Fort Hancock, New Jersey, Private Roy W. Edgett of Pulaski, Jefferson County, who was serving with the 56th Infantry Regiment, noted that four men

Private Frank Dolan.

This photograph of Frank Dolan and his dog was likely taken at Camp Wadsworth, South Carolina, prior to transport overseas. He enlisted in Company F, 12th Infantry and was later assigned to the 52nd Pioneer Infantry Regiment of the 27th Division. Originally from Utica, Oneida County, Private Dolan died of influenza March 12, 1919, while awaiting return to the U.S. New York State Archives.

Service record, James Reid Robinson.

This military service record for Seaman 2nd Class James Reid Robinson, originally of Livingston Manor, Sullivan County, indicates that Robinson enlisted in the U.S. Navy in April 1918. He was stationed at Great Lakes Naval Training Station "during the 'flu' epidemic of August to September of 1918." Military training camps in the United States witnessed the horrific spread of the influenza epidemic as large numbers of men in close quarters proved an ideal condition for the disease's spread. New York State Archives.

in his unit had died from the flu in the past week.[4] Forty-three thousand soldiers and sailors mobilized for the war effort would die of influenza. Half of the soldiers in the AEF who died in Europe fell to influenza rather than on the battlefield.[5]

Between September 1918 and spring 1919, an estimated 50 million people died of the disease, more than three times as many as were killed in four years of fighting during the war. In New York State, the first cases of influenza were reported in early September.[6]

By September 21, dozens of people in New York City had fallen ill. By October 4 the state's health authorities were reporting cases from Manhattan to Buffalo. In six weeks, from mid-September to the end of October, more than 30,000 people in New York City died from influenza. More than 12,000 died during the week of November 1.[7] Large public gatherings were banned statewide in an effort to curb the disease. Nationwide, more than 675,000 Americans died during the pandemic.

John Hendrickson.

John Hendrickson enlisted in the U.S. Navy from Huntington, Suffolk County, in 1912. He participated in the American landing at Vera Cruz, Mexico, in March 1914, during the Mexican Civil War. He reenlisted on April 11, 1917, and was stationed aboard the battleships *U.S.S. New York* and *U.S.S. Wisconsin* operating out of Norfolk, Virginia. Hendrickson died during the influenza epidemic at the base hospital at Hampton Roads, Virginia, on September 30, 1918. New York State Archives.

Gold Star Roll of Honor.

This service record was completed by the parents of Private Felix Patzold of White Plains, Westchester County. Patzold enlisted in the Army on September 9, 1918, and was sent to Camp Jackson, Mississippi for training. He died there due to influenza just seventeen days later on September 26. New York State Archives.

Esther A. Denison
U.S. Army Nurses Corps
Base Hospital #41, Paris (St. Denis)

Esther Denison grew up in the Albany area and attended nursing school at Albany Hospital. When the United States entered the war, Denison enlisted in the U.S. Army Nurses Corps. After training at Fort Dix, New Jersey, she was assigned to a unit in Virginia in preparation for overseas service. Once in France, Denison was assigned to Base Hospital #41 just outside Paris.

After the war, Esther Denison married Walter Haswell, of Colonie, in a New York City wedding. The couple eventually moved to Syracuse and raised two sons. Esther worked at the Onondaga Pottery Company, Stickley Manufacturing Company, and Niagara Mohawk Power Corporation in Syracuse.

> The first few weeks were very dramatic—we could hear the firing and battlefield casualties were coming in day and night.
>
> —Esther Denison,
> December 17, 1980

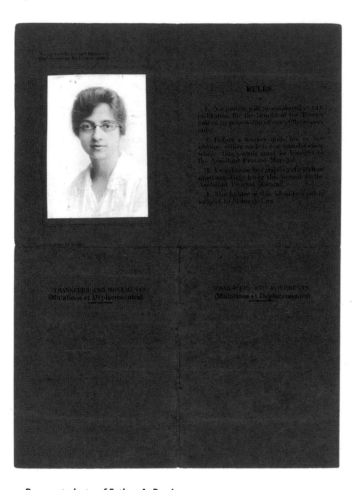

Passport photo of Esther A. Denison.

New York State Museum Collection, H-1979.95.11.

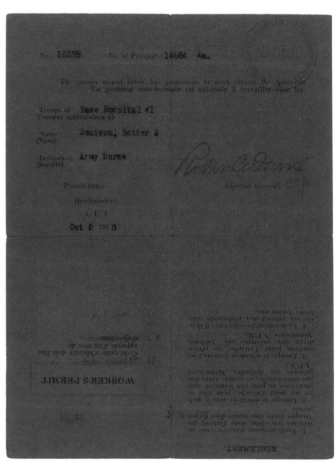

Dog tags.

These identification tags belonged to Esther A. Denison, a nurse in the U.S. Army Nurses Corps in France. New York State Museum Collection, H-1993.50.1.

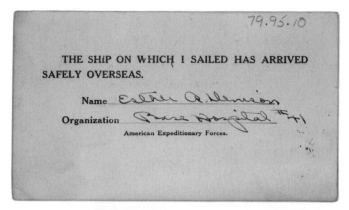

Postcard.

Pre-printed postcards like the one shown here were issued to nurses and soldiers prior to their sailing for France. The cards were then collected as the soldiers or nurses were boarding the ships and mailed to the family after the transports arrived in Europe.[1] New York State Museum Collection, H-1979.95.10.

1. Schmitz, Andrew, Letter to Sabyna E. Copper, May 5, 1918. World War I Letters and Memorabilia Collection, New York State Library, Manuscripts and Special Collections, SC21813.

Patch and pins, U.S. Army Nurses Corps uniform.

New York State Museum Collection.

U.S. Army Nurses Corps uniform worn by Esther A. Denison.

The entry of women into the U.S. military saw the creation of uniforms for women. Patterned after male service uniforms, the Army Nurses Corps uniforms included a skirt in lieu of trousers. Dennison wore this uniform as her wedding dress on March 17, 1919, to Walter Haswell—the day following her discharge from military service. New York State Museum Collection, H-1979.95.2-.5, H-1972.61.3 B (necktie)

Motor Corps recruits receiving vaccines.

The Women's Motor Corps of America provided a way for women to participate in World War I. Women volunteered as drivers and provided transport services at home and in Europe. Courtesy of the Library of Congress.

Women's Motor Corps at Armory.

Recruits for the Motor Corps of America assembled at the 71st Regiment Armory in New York City prior to their departure for France. Courtesy of the Library of Congress.

"The Motor Corps of America."

Artist: Howard Chandler Christy; *Printer:* Unknown; *Publisher:* Motor Corps of America; *Technique:* Lithograph; *Dimensions:* 107.5 x 80 cm.

The women of the Motor Corps of America served as ambulance and transport drivers both on the home front and in Europe as members of the American Expeditionary Forces. Courtesy of the Library of Congress.

"Yes sir—I am here!"

Artist: Edward Penfield; *Printer:* Carey Print Litho; *Publisher:* Motor Corps of America; *Technique:* Lithograph; *Dimensions:* 100 x 67.5 cm.

Recruiting poster featuring a woman, in the uniform of the Motor Corps of America, saluting. New York State Library, Manuscripts and Special Collections.

THE MOTOR CORPS OF AMERICA

During the war, the American Red Cross began training women to serve as mechanics and ambulance drivers as well as nurses. This led to the establishment of the Motor Corps of America. For the first time, women were able to serve in the U.S. Armed Forces in roles other than nurses. The purpose of the organization was to provide a ready pool of trained drivers to free male soldiers for service in combat roles.[109]

"My Boy, You Certainly Made Good!"

Artist: N.B.T.; *Printer:* Unknown; *Publisher:* United Cigar Stores; *Technique:* Lithograph; *Dimensions:* 84 x 46 cm.

Variations on this "Welcome Home!" poster were distributed by United Cigar Stores, one of the largest retail chain stores in the United States in the first quarter of the twentieth century. New York State Museum Collection, H–1976.147.27.

9

The Welcome Home

[B]elieve me it will be the happiest day I have ever seen when the boat comes to New York Harbor.   —Private Herbert Taber, November 11, 1918[1]

Beginning in February 1919, the United States began the process of transporting two million troops in France back home. As troop ships arrived in New York Harbor, the doughboys were welcomed by throngs of cheering citizens along parade routes through the city. To celebrate the end of World War I, Mayor John Hylan ordered a "Victory Arch" constructed over Fifth Avenue at Madison Square to honor the city's war dead. The temporary arch was designed by Thomas Hastings at a cost of $80,000 and was modeled after the Arch of Constantine in Rome, Italy. Tens of thousands of doughboys marched beneath the arch on their return from the battlefields of France.

Official sketch of the temporary memorial arch.

Artist: Chesley Bonestell; *Printer:* Alco-Gravure, Inc., New York, New York; *Publisher:* Unknown; *Technique:* Lithograph; *Dimensions:* 54 x 73 cm

This sketch of the "Victory Arch" was published by the Mayor's Committee in order to solicit donations from the public for the construction of the Arch, eventually constructed on Fifth Avenue at Madison Square. New York State Library, Manuscripts and Special Collections.

U.S.S. *Arizona*.

The U.S. Navy's battleship, U.S.S. *Arizona* leads the parade of nine battleships and their twenty-eight escort vessels during the Naval Review in New York Harbor on December 26, 1918. The ship had just returned from France where the fleet had escorted President Woodrow Wilson to attend the Paris Peace Conference at Versailles.

The ship was constructed and outfitted at the Brooklyn Navy Yard before being commissioned in late 1916. The U.S.S. *Arizona* served in U.S. waters during the war, but was tasked with escorting President Wilson and the American delegation to France following the Armistice. The *Arizona* was transferred to the Pacific Fleet in the 1920s. The ship was sunk during the Japanese surprise attack on the U.S. fleet at Pearl Harbor, Hawaii, on December 7, 1941, sparking American involvement in a Second World War. Courtesy of the National Archives and Records Administration.

Batavia homecoming.

Recently returned soldiers march down a street in Batavia, Genesee County. New York State Archives, A0412-78.

Elmira homecoming.

Homecoming celebration welcoming Elmira's soldiers and sailors. New York State Archives, A0412-78.

Coffins laid out in Elmira, New York.

Not all homecomings were joyous affairs. This photograph shows a group of soldiers standing watch in Elmira, Chemung County, in a room full of coffins of New Yorkers who had been killed in Europe. New York State Archives, A0412-78.

World War I Victory Parade, 28th Infantry Regiment, 1st Division.

This photograph features soldiers of the U.S. Army's 1st Division marching in New York City upon their return from France in September 1919. New York State Museum Collection, H-2010.33.189.

Rochester Victory Medal.

Many cities across New York commissioned medals and held parades and ceremonies to welcome home their local heroes. This medal was struck for veterans in Rochester, Monroe County. New York State Museum Collection, H-1972.74.10.

Albany County Victory Medal.

New York State Museum Collection, H–1987.3.1.

Watervliet Victory Medal.

New York State Museum Collection, H–1987.3.2.

City of Albany Victory Medal.

New York State Museum Collection, H–1987.3.3.

NYAC Medal.

This medal was presented by the New York Athletic Club (NYAC) to Colonel Nathan K. Averill, commanding officer of the 308th Infantry Regiment during the Meuse-Argonne Offensive. New York State Museum Collection, H–1971.113.16 A.

Putnam County Victory Medal.

New York State Museum Collection, H-1971.113.16 B.

Dutchess County World War I Service Medal.

New York State Military Museum, Division of Military and Naval Affairs.

Mechanicville Service Medal.

This medal was presented by the city of Mechanicville, Saratoga County. New York State Military Museum, Division of Military and Naval Affairs.

Whitesborough Medal.

World War I Service Medal issued by the Village of Whitesborough, Oneida County. New York State Military Museum, Division of Military and Naval Affairs.

Program.

A program from a welcome home ceremony in Oneida, Madison County, for the men and women from the county who served during World War I. New York State Archives, A0412-78.

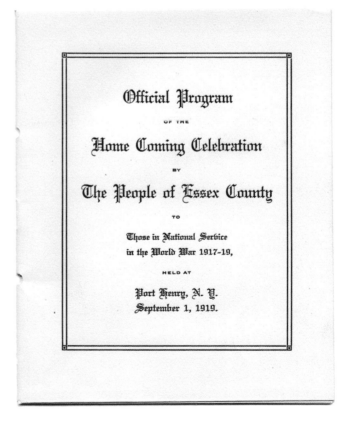

Broadside.

This poster was created as an advertisement for a homecoming celebration for the returning veterans of Nassau County, Long Island. New York State Archives Collection.

Program.

A program for the World War I veterans of Essex County. The welcome home celebration was held September 1, 1919, at Port Henry. New York State Archives Collection.

Pin.

This celluloid button was produced for welcome home festivities in Geneseo, Livingston County, on June 28, 1919. New York State Museum Collection, H-1972.76.178 G.

Souvenir program.

A program for a two-day celebration in Cohoes, Albany County, welcoming home the city's World War I veterans. New York State Archives, A0412-78.

27th Division

On March 25, 1919, the 27th "Empire" Division, Major General John F. O'Ryan at its head, marched along a five-mile route in New York City thronged with cheering crowds. In May of the previous year, the division had marched the same route on its way to Europe. The New York National Guardsmen had left 1,800 of their comrades on the battlefields of France and Belgium.

"Welcome Home Our Fighting 27th O'Ryan's 'Roughnecks'"

Artist: Unknown; *Printer:* Acme Litho. Co., New York; *Publisher:* Unknown; *Technique:* Lithograph; *Dimensions:* 71 x 53.5 cm.

Posters welcoming home the state's National Guard Division plastered storefronts and walls all along the parade route. New York State Museum Collection, H-1975.185.2.

27th Division Parade.

Courtesy of the Library of Congress.

"Welcome Home to the Land of Liberty."

Artist: Unknown; *Printer:* Unknown;
Publisher: Unknown; *Technique:* Lithograph;
Dimensions: 35.5 x 53.5 cm.

New York State Museum Collection, H–1975.185.1.

"The *Leviathan* Bringing Home Some of the 27th Division."

Artist: Unknown; *Printer:* New York Tribune;
Publisher: New York Tribune; *Technique:* Newsprint;
Dimensions: 57.25 x 42 cm.

This full-page graphic from the April 6, 1919, *New York Tribune* celebrates the return of New York's National Guard Division. New York State Museum Collection.

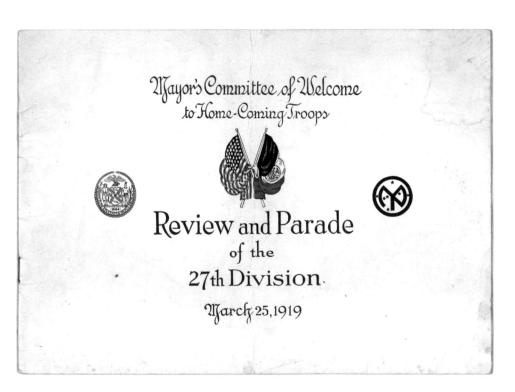

Program.

Program from the March 25, 1919, welcome home parade for the Empire Division. New York State Museum Collection, H-1970.119.6.

New York State Victory Medal.

New York State Museum Collection, H-3513.

World War I and New York State Victory Medals.

These medals were awarded to Peter Schaming Jr. Two of the bronze clasps on the ribbon indicate that Schaming and his 106th Infantry Regiment, 27th Division were involved in the Ypres-Lys Offensive and the Somme Offensive of 1918, and the Defensive Sector clasp acknowledges service with the British Army. New York State Museum Collection, H-2015.21.1-.2.

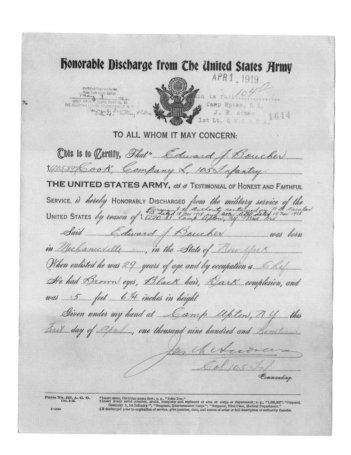

Honorable Discharge, Edward J. Boucher, Company L, 105th Infantry.

After the parade, the 27th Division returned to Camp Upton on Long Island, where it was mustered out of federal service in April 1919. New York State Museum Collection, H-1983.122.6.

369th Infantry Regiment

On February 17, 1919, one million New Yorkers gathered to welcome home the first of the state's returning National Guardsmen—the 369th Infantry, Harlem's Hellfighters. The 369th Infantry had seen more combat than any other American unit: 191 days. Five hundred members of the regiment were awarded the French Croix de Guerre for gallantry, and the unit suffered 1,500 casualties. The regiment became the first to return to the United States from France after American commanders refused to allow the African American combat troops to march in the Allied victory parade in Paris.

369th Infantry Parade.

Courtesy of the National Archives.

Ribbons.

Veterans of the war frequently sought to continue their association with their comrades in arms. Members of the 27th Division formed the 27th Division Association and held reunions of the New York Division. These commemorative ribbons are from the first reunion in 1920 at Saratoga Springs and the third reunion in 1924 at Troy. New York State Museum Collection, H-1982.128.10 and H-1987.28.52.

165th Infantry Regiment

After completing occupation duty at Remagen, Germany, the 165th Infantry Regiment returned to New York on April 21, 1919.[2]

165th Infantry Parade.

The 165th Infantry Regiment passes beneath the Victory Arch in New York City. The famed Flatiron Building is visible in the background. Courtesy of the Library of Congress.

77th Division

The 77th Division returned to New York City on May 6, 1919. During the parade, the "Melting Pot" Division was cheered by nearly one million spectators as they marched along Fifth Avenue.

"Welcome 77th New York's Own."

Artist: Unknown; *Printer:* New York Tribune; *Publisher:* New York Tribune; *Technique:* Newsprint; *Dimensions:* 57.25 x 42 cm.

This full-page graphic welcoming home the 77th Division was published in the May 4, 1919, issue of the *New York Tribune.* The image appeared two days before the division made its triumphal march through New York City. New York State Museum Collection, H-1979.95.15 A-G.

"Welcome to the Heroic 77th Division" (1919).

Artist: Unknown; *Printer:* Grayzel Press, Inc.; *Publisher:* Jewish Welfare Board; *Technique:* Lithograph; *Dimensions:* 70 x 53 cm.

This poster, published by the Jewish Welfare Board, illustrates the cosmopolitan make-up of the 77th Division. New York State Library, Manuscripts and Special Collections.

Pin.

This celluloid button was produced for the welcome home parade for the 77th Division. New York State Museum Collection, H-1975.2.1.

"Well Done, 77th!"

Artist: Lawrence Wilbur; *Printer:* W.F. Powers Co. Litho., New York, New York; *Publisher:* 77th Division Association; *Technique:* Lithograph; *Dimensions:* 50 x 33 cm.

This welcome home poster for the 77th Division features throngs of cheering well-wishers as a lone soldier marches down the street. The Victory Arch and Statue of Liberty are visible in the background. New York State Library, Manuscripts and Special Collections.

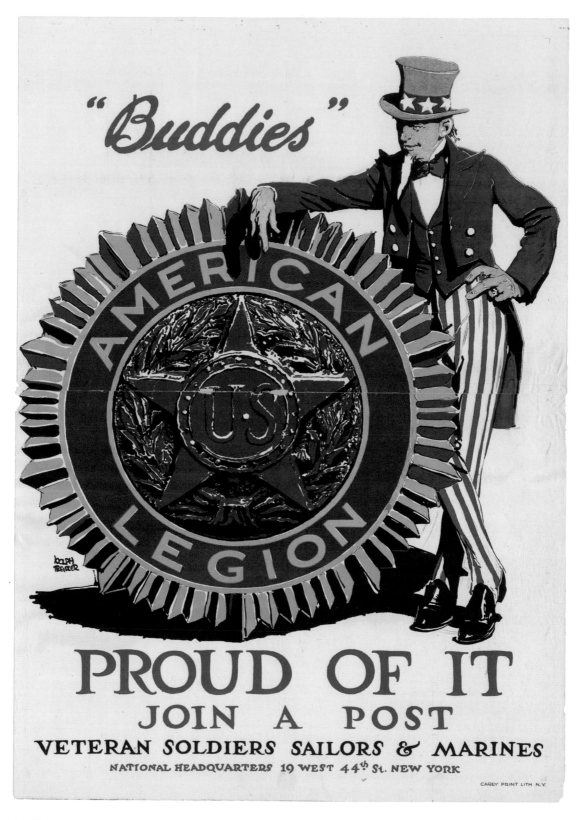

"Buddies."

Artist: Adolph Treidler; *Printer:* Carey Print Lith.; *Publisher:* American Legion; *Technique:* Lithograph; *Dimensions:* 101 x 71 cm.

The American Legion was to be a strictly non-partisan, fraternal organization that promoted issues central to the AEF veterans, including permanent disability pay and soldiers' bonuses. The Legion was also a forceful advocate for 100% Americanism and anti-Bolshevism. New York State Museum Collection, H-1976.149.3.

10

"I have done my part over here"

Postwar New York[1]

As troop ships arrived in New York Harbor, the doughboys were welcomed by throngs of cheering citizens along the parade routes through the city. The reception these soldiers received was often in sharp contrast to the realities of returning to civilian life. As the war receded, new fears and problems pervaded New York State—and American—society.

With the end of the war, the military contracts that had bolstered the New York State economy for nearly half a decade came to an end. As industries reverted to a peacetime economy, a period of retrenchment led to layoffs of factory workers and a lack of employment opportunities for returning veterans. Newly elected New York governor Alfred E. Smith established a commission to oversee postwar reconstruction, veterans' care, and other pressing issues.[2] Economic unease frequently led to labor tensions and strikes. The rise of activism within American labor stoked fears of a communist revolution in the United States. In New York, a "red scare" permeated the government. Radical conspiracy was seen everywhere.

Many of the problems experienced by New Yorkers in the years following World War I would linger throughout the 1920s. Promised benefits to the nation's veterans were slow to materialize. The difficulties were only exacerbated during the stock market crash in 1929 and the ensuing Great Depression, prompting a march on the nation's capital in 1932.

The American Legion

Following the Armistice, a group of American Army officers, including Theodore Roosevelt Jr. and Hamilton Fish III of New York, proposed the formation of a new veterans' organization for those who had served in the AEF. After an initial meeting in Paris in March 1919, and a larger congress in St. Louis, Missouri, in May, the American Legion was formed at a founding convention in November in Minneapolis, Minnesota. Hamilton Fish III, formerly an officer of the 15th New York/369th Infantry, helped draft the preamble to the Legion's constitution. The American Legion was intended as a fraternal organization of AEF veterans that would advocate on their behalf. The Legion's founders also believed that the organization could help to prevent veterans from gravitating toward radical groups in the economic strife of the postwar years.

"Join! American Legion."

Artist: None; *Printer:* Unknown; *Publisher:* War Camp Community Service; *Technique:* Lithograph; *Dimensions:* 23 x 18 cm.

This broadside encourages soldiers to join the newly formed American Legion. New York State Library, Manuscripts and Special Collections.

"4,800,000 of us."

Artist: Adolph Treidler; *Printer:* Carey Print Lith.; *Publisher:* American Legion; *Technique:* Lithograph; *Dimensions:* 101 x 71 cm.

This recruitment poster for the American Legion encourages the nation's 4.8 million new veterans to join the organization. Opportunity for some of these veterans, including members of New York's 369th Infantry Regiment and the 370,000 African American soldiers who had answered the nation's call, was limited. The official position of the American Legion left the question of African American membership up to individual states or to individual Legion posts. This resulted in the formation of segregated posts or the exclusion of African American members in many instances. New York State Library, Manuscripts and Special Collections.

American Legion lapel button.

Bronze American Legion lapel pin, circa 1919. New York State Museum Collection, H-1972.61.23.

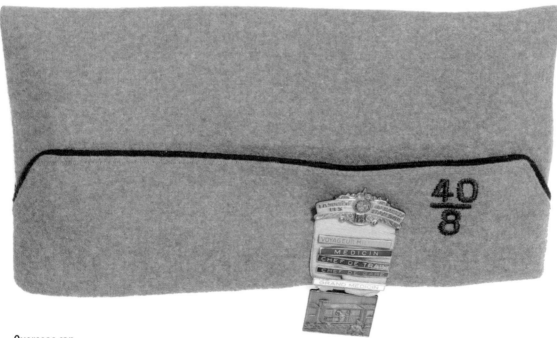

Overseas cap.

La Société des 40 Hommes et 8 Cheveaux (the Society of 40 Men and 8 Horses) was formed as a distinct level of membership within the American Legion in 1920. The term "40 and 8" referred to the maximum capacity of the French railroad boxcars that transported the soldiers to the front and became identified with the experience in the AEF. The Société's local units were called "Voitures" (cars) and its members were called "Voyageurs" (travelers). Levels of membership reflected the French railroad theme.[1] New York State Museum Collection, H-1982.105.2.

1. "History and Highlights of the Forty and Eight," *La Societe des Quarante Hommes et Huit Cheveaux* (www.fortyandeight.org/history-of-the-408), accessed May 4, 2016.

MILO RIBBON & CARBON CORPORATION

PERFECT CARBONS
TYPEWRITER PAPERS

NON-FILLING, NON-DRYING
TYPEWRITER RIBBONS

CABLE ADDRESS,
"MILO," PENN YAN

GENERAL OFFICES,
PENN YAN, NEW YORK

TRADE MARK

ORGANIZATION OF THE AMERICAN LEGION IN YATES COUNTY.

Shortly after the Armistice on Nov.11,1918 a group of soldiers in the American Expeditionary Forces assembled in Paris for the purpose of organizing a society to be composed of veterans of the World War. The movement to establish an organization for the common welfare of every soldier, sailor and marine who had served in the Great War quickly gained momentum and out of the nucleus which met in Paris was born what is now known as the American Legion.

The organization grew apace with demobilization of service men and by the early part of the year of 1919 National Headquarters had been set up at Indianapolis, Indiana and shortly thereafter active State organizations were established everywhere in the United States. To-day the American Legion is the largest organization composed of World War Veterans and numbers more than three quarters of a million members.

In the late summer of 1919 the majority of service men from Yates County had been demobilized. Fifteen veterans met at an informal meeting in Penn Yan for the purpose of making application for a temporary charter of a local Post of the American Legion. Dr.E.C.Foster was elected temporary County Chairman and Harold F.Tuthill temporary County Secretary, both of whom where later elected as permanent officers in their respective capacities. The first regular meeting of the Penn Yan Post was called at Wendia Hall, Penn Yan on September 24,1919. At this meeting the following officers were elected for the first year:
Commander: Ray C.Harter,
1st Vice Commander, Francis P.Reilly
2nd Vice Commander, Paul Stark
3rd Vice Commander, William B.Welch
Secretary, Joseph P.Craugh
Treasurer, Parmele Johnson
Executive Committee: In addition to the above officers,
Rev.C.K.Imbrie, Harold F.Tuthill, Thomas F.Carroll, George Morse, Howard Sprague, and John J.Hyland.

A permanent charter was later secured for the Post and 79 members who joined the organization during the first month were entitled to charter membership. The Post has since been

MILO RIBBON & CARBON CORPORATIO

PERFECT CARBONS
TYPEWRITER PAPERS

NON-FILLING, NON-DRY
TYPEWRITER RIBBONS

CABLE ADDRESS,
"MILO," PENN YAN

GENERAL OFFI
PENN YAN,

TRADE MARK

2

designated as the Johnson-Costello Post No.355 in honor of Charles E.Costello the first soldier from Yates County to die in the service and Harold Johnson of Benton the first Yates County soldier to die in action.

Since its inception the Post has been active in every civic and patriotic movement in Penn Yan and is to-day a flourishing organization of about 170 members.

Two other Posts in the County have likewise been established, one at Dundee with a membership of about 50 and the other at Middlesex with a membership of about the same size.

Joseph P.Craugh.

American Legion Post letter.

This document outlines the formation of an American Legion Post in Yates County, New York. New York State Archives, A0412-78.

Hamilton Fish III (1888–1991)

Hamilton Fish III's family had long been active and influential in New York State and national politics. Fish served as a white company commander with the African American 369th Infantry Regiment during the war. Following the war, in 1920, Fish was elected as a Republican to the House of Representatives, where he would serve for nearly 25 years. He was an ardent supporter of veterans' causes and a founding member of the American Legion. He spearheaded the effort to establish the Tomb of the Unknown Soldier at Arlington National Cemetery. His experiences during the war led him to be an ardent anticommunist and a staunch isolationist. He was also a leading opponent of President Franklin Roosevelt and the New Deal. He was defeated for re-election in 1944. He died at Cold Spring New York at age 102.

Hamilton Fish Jr. Identity Card.

Identification papers of Captain, and later Major, Hamilton Fish Jr. during his service in France with the Harlem Hellfighters. New York State Library, Manuscripts and Special Collections.

Veterans' "Benefits"

If the United States was ill equipped for war in 1917, it was even less prepared for peace in 1918. Few in Washington had anticipated the collapse of the German Army and the abdication of Kaiser Wilhelm II. No mechanism was established to demobilize the millions of men in military service, to care for the wounded, or to address the difficulties of reintegrating these men into civilian life. Veterans' bonuses and pensions were often insufficient, and for returning veterans unable to resume their civilian careers, little aid was available.

> In a great war for the right, the one great debt owed by the nation is that to the men who go to the front and pay with their bodies for the faith that is in them.
> —Former President Theodore Roosevelt, 1919[3]

Souvenir photograph (1919).

Private Guilford Roy Howard (second from left) poses with fellow Marines next to a statue of French author René de Chateaubriand at St. Malo, France. In his diary, Howard noted that the statue reminded him of a statue of James Fenimore Cooper in Cooperstown, Otsego County. William F. Howard Collection

Demobilization

> I got my final pay and my discharge . . . and if you had seen me beating it toward New York State—why I went so fast my shadow was ½ mile behind me.
> —Warren Spicer, January 1, 1919[4]

The administrative machinery that had been created to organize the war effort was quickly disbanded. The State Industrial Commission allocated $50,000 to open employment offices in cities around the state. Statewide, municipalities and charitable organizations attempted to aid in the re-employment of soldiers. Governor Alfred E. Smith appointed a Reconstruction Commission in March 1919 to replace the defunct Council of Defense, but most of the agencies under the commission ceased operations by December 1919. More than 930,000 American soldiers applied for some form of disability benefits by 1923. Of these, more than 200,000 were permanently disabled. New York State and the nation struggled to meet the needs of these veterans.

Private Guilford Roy Howard in his U.S. Marine Corps uniform, ca. 1918.

William F. Howard Collection

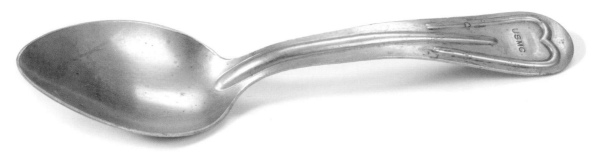

A U.S. Marine Corps–issued spoon used by Private Guilford Roy Howard.

William F. Howard Collection

U.S.M.C. tunic and overseas cap.

Guilford Roy Howard was born in Union Center, Broome County, on June 29, 1897. He was a student at Syracuse University when he was drafted for service in World War I. Inspired by stories of ace fighter pilots, Howard wanted to join the Air Service but was rejected for poor vision. He joined the United States Marine Corps at Syracuse on August 18, 1918. He was sent to Parris Island, South Carolina, for basic training and then to Quantico, Virginia, for embarkation to France. He arrived in France on November 10, 1918—just one day before the Armistice took effect. Private Howard served as a machine gunner in Company C, 5th Marine Brigade, guarding in a camp for German POWs before returning to the United States and being discharged from service at Hampton Roads, Virginia on August 13, 1919. Arriving in Albany by train, he walked up State Street hill for overnight lodging. He was denied a room at a hotel because the clerk did not want soldiers in uniform bringing lice into their establishment. Howard tried to return to his studies at Syracuse University but found it difficult to settle into an academic routine. He went to work for the A and P supermarket chain and enjoyed a long career with the company in Buffalo, Syracuse, and Albany. Howard died in February 1970, his uniform still carefully preserved as a remembrance of his military service. William F. Howard Collection

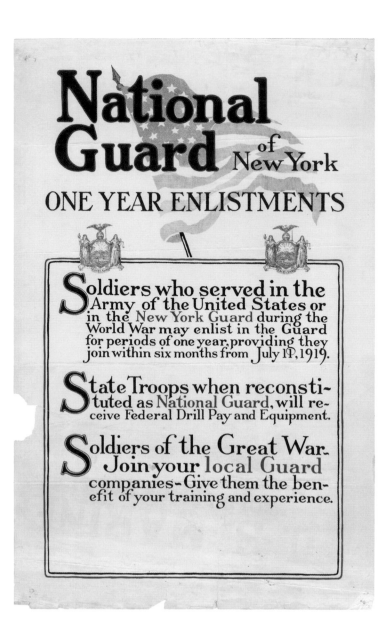

"National Guard of New York: One Year Enlistments."

Artist: None; *Printer:* Unknown; *Publisher:* New York National Guard;
Technique: Lithograph; *Dimensions:* 96.5 x 61 cm.

Following the return of the 27th Division, 165th Infantry, and 369th Infantry Regiments, the New York National Guard embarked on a mission to bring itself back to the levels called for in the National Defense Act of 1920. Veterans of World War I were encouraged to re-enlist in the National Guard—and many did. Others had seen enough of military service and opted to return to civilian life. While the National Guard across the nation—including New York State— struggled to reach levels called for by Congress throughout the 1920s and 1930s, the National Guard was better funded and trained when it was again called into federal service in 1940 than it had been in 1917.[1] New York State Museum Collection, H-1992.19.30.

1. Stewart, Volume II, page 60.

NATIONAL DEFENSE ACT OF 1920

In June 1920, Congress enacted significant reforms to the nation's military organizations. Under the National Defense Act of 1920, many of the mechanisms that had been adopted to expand the Army to meet the needs of a global war were codified into law. In addition to the Regular Army and the National Guard, the legislation established an Army Reserve. For the first time, national leaders acknowledged the need for a system to rapidly expand military forces in times of crisis and that the Army should oversee training for the reserve components. While the law called for a National Guard of 436,000, the actual numbers averaged approximately 180,000 between the end of World War I and the start of World War II.[5] The National Defense Act of 1920 governed America's military structure until after World War II.

VETERANS BUREAU

After the war, programs for disability compensation, veterans insurance, and vocational rehabilitation training were under the operation of several government agencies. Through extensive lobbying by the American Legion, Congress established the U.S. Veterans Bureau in 1921 to combine these operations. The bureau established a system of regional offices and hospitals. The Veterans Bureau was again reorganized in 1930 as the Veterans Administration.

REHABILITATION

The Veterans Bureau established programs focusing on physical rehabilitation for wounded veterans and vocational training to give returning soldiers the skills to find employment. This focus was based on the progressive ideal that job training and employment were the best ways to reintegrate veterans as members of society, rather than relying on a system of "public dependency." Rehabilitation schools were established across the country, including several cities across New York State. While many veterans were indeed aided by this program—approximately 53 percent of those who applied received some form of rehabilitation training—nearly half were not. In 1919, New York State authorized $100,000 for vocational training of returning soldiers.

The focus on rehabilitation and vocational training failed to address the fact that many wounded veterans suffered from physical injuries that prevented their return to full employment. Other veterans returned bearing unseen scars of their wartime experiences. The phenomenon called "melancholy" during the Civil War came to be called "shell shock" in the trenches of World War I. Today, such battle wounds are frequently diagnosed as post traumatic stress disorder and traumatic brain injury. There was little understanding of the suffering endured by these veterans, and returning soldiers had few avenues for assistance; they were expected to return to their pre-war lives and rejoin civil society. An unknown number of the nation's World War I veterans struggled with these unaddressed traumas.

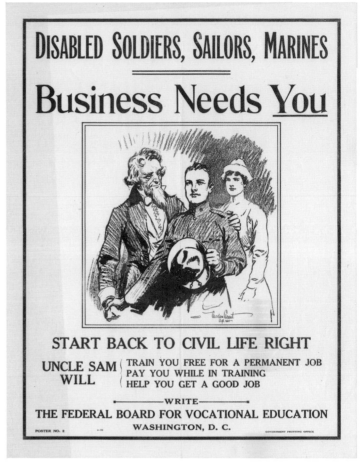

"Disabled Soldiers, Sailors, Marines, Business Needs You! Federal Board for Vocational Education."

Artist: W. Pain; *Printer:* Government Printing Office;
Publisher: Federal Board for Vocational Education;
Technique: Lithograph; *Dimensions:* 26.5 x 20.5 cm.

This poster was part of a series printed to encourage disabled veterans to seek vocational training. Courtesy of the Rochester Historical Society.

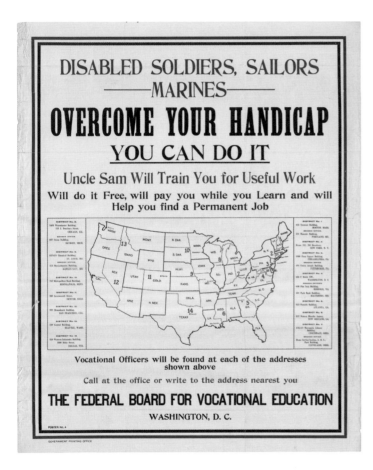

"Overcome Your Handicap."

Artist: Unknown; *Printer:* Government Printing Office;
Publisher: Federal Board for Vocational Education; *Technique:* Lithograph;
Dimensions: 48 x 30.5 cm.

This poster, published by the Federal Board for Vocational Education, offers wounded and disabled soldiers, sailors, and marines, training in job skills to assist their return to civilian life. Courtesy of the Rochester Historical Society.

Diploma.

This diploma was issued to Wm. George Steinbrecker of Binghamton, Broome County, for completion of the United States Veterans Bureau's vocational training course on September 15, 1921. By completing this course, Steinbrecker was declared "rehabilitated." New York State Museum Collection, H-2010.33.174.

Facts of Interest to the Disabled Soldier or Sailor

THE military and naval authorities will provide him, not only with ordinary medical care, but also with special treatment to put him in the best condition possible to return to work.

WHILE he is under treatment in reconstruction hospitals maintained by the Surgeon-General, U. S. Army, and the Surgeon-General, U. S. Navy, he will be offered educational advantages, which will promote his recovery, put his time to good use, and improve his chances for the future.

IF he has lost an arm or a leg, a temporary artificial limb will be furnished him at as early a date as possible, while he is still in the hospital. Later a permanent artificial limb of the most modern type will be provided by the Bureau of War Risk Insurance. It will be kept in repair and replaced when worn out, as long as he lives, at government expense.

AFTER completion of treatment and discharge from the army or navy, if he remains permanently disabled, the Bureau of War Risk Insurance will pay him until the end of his life disability compensation, which is intended as an aid in working out his future plans.

THIS compensation for disability is paid whether or not he has taken out a policy of War Risk insurance.

AFTER discharge from the service, if he is disabled to any considerable degree—so as to be entitled to compensation for disability—he is offered training for a skilled job in which his injury will not prevent his earning good wages. Experience of our Allies has shown this to be entirely practicable.

COMPENSATION for permanent disability will not be reduced or in any way be affected by what he may be able to earn. It is determined by his physical injury alone. He may have earned before enlistment $20 a week and be able after disability, by reason of having taken a course of training, to earn $40 a week, yet his compensation will be paid him just the same.

TRAINING after discharge will be provided him at government expense by the Federal Board for Vocational Education, charged by Congress with the responsibility of restoring him to self-support.

DURING the course of training, in order that he may have no financial worries, he will receive either the same pay as during his last month in the service or his compensation for disability, whichever is larger. His family will continue to receive the same allotment and allowances as when he was in the service.

IT is greatly to his advantage to avail himself of all opportunities of training, either before or after discharge. While it may be easy now for even a disabled man to get a well-paid but temporary job, the labor situation will be different in the years after the war when normal conditions return. If he wants to be independent and self-supporting in the future he must prepare now so that later on he will be a skilled worker and his services will be in demand.

WHEN training is completed the government will find for him a desirable job. This service will be performed for him by the Federal Board for Vocational Education in cooperation with the United States Employment Service.

DURING the period of training and after, the American Red Cross, through its home service sections, will look after the needs of his family, and advise on any points in connection with which it can be helpful.

AFTER he returns home and enters on employment the home service section of the American Red Cross will stand by as a big brother to help in any possible way to make successful his change from the world of the soldier back to the world of industry and commerce. In all this work the Red Cross recognizes the leadership of the government.

EMPLOYERS are giving careful thought to the selection of jobs in which his services can be used to the best advantage—in which he can be paid good wages and earn them. The employers realize that what he wants is not charity, but the opportunity of self-support.

LABOR unions are giving thought to the ways in which he may best be replaced in his trade, and are prepared to assist the readjustment to the greatest possible degree.

THE people of the United States are resolved that he shall have every advantage within their resource and every chance to make good and get back on his feet.

AMERICA is looking to her men disabled in the splendid job overseas to "carry on" after their return home, to continue into civilian life the standards of self-respect, honor, and courage of the A. E. F. She is looking to her disabled men to take rank among the most useful and respected members of the community.

Information regarding the opportunities described may be obtained in the larger centers from offices of the Federal Board for Vocational Education and the Bureau of War Risk Insurance and in all centers from the local Home Service Section of the American Red Cross

Poster issued and distributed by the Red Cross Institute for Crippled and Disabled Men, New York

"Facts of Interest to the Disabled Soldier or Sailor."

Artist: None; *Printer:* Unknown; *Publisher:* Red Cross Institute for Crippled and Disabled Men; *Technique:* Lithograph; *Dimensions:* 42 x 26 cm.

This poster, published by the American Red Cross, outlines the programs for compensation and rehabilitation vocational training offered to wounded veterans following the war. The Institute for Crippled and Disabled Men was established by the Red Cross and headquartered in New York City to assist the government in establishing rehabilitation centers for returning veterans. New York State Library, Manuscripts and Special Collections.

BONUSES

In 1924, New York State authorized a bonus fund of more than $49 million. Between 1924 and 1934, nearly 96 percent of these monies were paid to veterans of the war. In addition a federal bonus was passed by Congress that same year. The Federal World War Adjusted Compensation Act authorized payments based on the veteran's length of service. The law, however, only permitted immediate payment of up to $50. The remainder was awarded as a bond certificate that could not be collected until 1945.

Bonus Army on the lawn of the U.S. Capitol.

In 1932, in the midst of the Great Depression, tens of thousands of World War I veterans marched on the nation's capitol to demand early payment of their bonuses. When Congress failed to act, the veterans clashed with local police and two protesters were killed. The U.S. Army was called in to dislodge the "Bonus Army" from its encampment. During the confrontation, 55 veterans were injured and 135 were arrested. The forcible removal of the Bonus Army by the Hoover Administration strengthened the campaign of New York Governor Franklin D. Roosevelt during the presidential election in 1932. Courtesy of the Library of Congress.

SCHOLARSHIPS

New York State sent more than 500,000 men to war in 1917–1918. After the war, the state offered 450 state scholarships of $100 annually in tuition and an additional $100 to cover expenses to help young men continue their education at colleges, universities, and technical schools in New York State. These scholarships, awarded by the Commissioner of Education, were determined by an annual competitive examination. Colleges and technical schools were flooded with returning veterans for years following the war. It would not be until near the end of World War II that a federal education benefit—the

"Enlist for College" (1917).

Artist: Maud Petersham; *Printer:* Latham Litho. and Ptg. Co., Brooklyn, New York; *Publisher:* United States War Department Public Relations; *Technique:* Lithograph; *Dimensions:* 71.25 x 51 cm.

Private charitable organizations joined federal efforts to provide funding for college education for the nation's veterans. New York State Museum Collection, H-1977.141.5.

G.I. Bill—was established, in 1944. Such limited spending efforts illustrate the struggle of government leaders to address the needs of returning veterans while at the same time rolling back wartime big government.

Re-Employment Bureau of New York City

The end of the war brought an end to the wartime economy as weapons and materiel for the war effort were no longer needed. The U.S. economy in the early 1920s slowed and the nation entered a severe but short-lived economic recession.

As demobilization commenced, leaders in New York City feared a massive influx of demobilized soldiers would be discharged and saturate the employment market. Efforts were made to ensure that soldiers from inland communities and states were not discharged from military service in coastal port cities, but rather were returned to camps closer to their homes. New York City established a Re-Employment Bureau to assist returning soldiers and sailors in finding gainful employment.

As the nation's economy stabilized, a period of economic growth and prosperity emerged. The "Roaring Twenties" saw an unprecedented level of prosperity in the United States. The average wage of American workers increased by approximately 25 percent and the standard work week dropped to just over 44 hours.[6] Spending on consumer goods and leisure activities dramatically increased. The economic resurgence, however, masked underlying problems with the national economy. Unemployment remained high, particularly among veterans. Large segments of the nation's population struggled with persistent poverty. The period of expansion came to an abrupt end with the stock market collapse of 1929 and the ensuing Great Depression.[7]

"The Past is Behind Us; the Future is Ahead."

Artist: Unknown; *Printer:* Unknown; *Publisher:* U.S. Department of Labor; *Technique:* Lithograph; *Dimensions:* 51 x 38 cm.

This postwar poster depicts a factory laborer and an American soldier shaking hands in a congratulatory gesture following the Armistice. Relations between workers and returning soldiers would often be strained in the years after the war as workers were often displaced by veterans. At the same time, many ex-soldiers were unable to gain meaningful employment after their discharge, which created resentment towards workers who had stayed on the home front rather than enlisting. New York State Museum Collection, H-1992.19.68.

"And They Thought We Couldn't Fight; He Can Work as Well as Fight" (1919).

Artist: Y.D.E.; *Printer:* Unknown; *Publisher:* Re-Employment Bureau of New York City; *Technique:* Lithograph; *Dimensions:* 103 x 76 cm.

With the rapid end to the war, the government found itself dealing with the demobilization of hundreds of thousands of soldiers into an economy not prepared to absorb them into the workforce. The haphazard nature of this effort is illustrated by the repurposing of this 1918 Victory Loan poster and replacing the "Victory Liberty Loan" text with a pasted strip advertising New York City's Re-Employment Bureau. New York State Library, Manuscripts and Special Collections.

"For Home and Country He Wants Work" (1919).

Artist: Alfred Everett Orr; *Printer:* Unknown; *Publisher:* Re-Employment Bureau of New York City; *Technique:* Lithograph; *Dimensions:* 100 x 75 cm.

Again this Victory Loan poster has been repurposed in order to advertise for New York City's Re-Employment Bureau. By September 1919, the Bureau employed 125 people and was placing an average of 1,000 veterans per week. Despite these efforts, unemployment among returning veterans remained high. New York State Library, Manuscripts and Special Collections.

"The 27th—New York's Own Division."

Artist: Unknown; *Printer:* Unknown; *Publisher:* United Cigar Stores Co.; *Technique:* Lithograph; *Dimensions:* 96 x 64 cm.

With the return and demobilization of the 27th Division in late March 1919, the bulk of New York State's National Guardsmen were at once returned to civilian life. This poster, published by the United Cigar Stores Company, assures the Guardsmen that their former employer would welcome them back to their pre-war occupations. While this was often the case, in 1919 there was no legal mandate for employers to hold positions for members of the National Guard called into Federal Service. In many instances, the re-employment of these Guardsmen meant the firing of another employee. New York State Library, Manuscripts and Special Collections.

Alfred Everett Orr (1886–1927).

Alfred Everett Orr was born in New York City. He studied at the Art Students League in Manhattan as well as under W. M. Chase, and at London's Royal Academy. His most noted contribution to the war effort came with his *For Home and Country* illustration for the Victory Liberty Loan drive in 1919. After the war, Orr moved to California and eventually settled in London, England.

"After the Welcome Home—a Job."

Artist: Edmund Marion Ashe; *Printer:* Heywood, Strasser and Voight Litho. Co., New York, New York; *Publisher:* U.S. Department of Labor Employment Service; *Technique:* Lithograph; *Dimensions:* 104 x 70 cm.

The U.S. government established an employment service to assist returning veterans. The effort was plagued by political infighting. On March 14, 1919, an article in the *Schenectady Gazette* announced that the agency was closing 700 offices nationwide. Only 56 offices remained open to assist the nearly four million men who had joined the military during the war. New York State Library, Manuscripts and Special Collections.

"U.S. Employment Service."

Artist: Gordon Grant; *Printer:* Thomsen-Ellis Co., Baltimore, Maryland; *Publisher:* U.S. Department of Labor; *Technique:* Lithograph; *Dimensions:* 56 x 37 cm.

This poster by Gordon Grant depicts a recently returned Doughboy entering a U.S. Employment Service office. New York State Library, Manuscripts and Special Collections.

Edmund Marion Ashe (1867–1941).

Edmund Marion Ashe was born on Staten Island, New York, and studied at the Metropolitan Art School and the Art Students League. Early in his career, Ashe worked as an illustrator for several publications in New York City and illustrated numerous books. From 1896 to 1909, Ashe worked as an artist and correspondent for *Leslie's Weekly*, the *New York Tribune*, and the *New York World*, covering the McKinley and Roosevelt administrations. He became one of the first members of the Society of Illustrators in 1901. Like other members of the Society, Ashe was recruited to design illustrations for the Division of Pictorial Publicity during World War I.

Henry Johnson (1897–1929)

Henry Lincoln Johnson was born in 1897 in Alexandria, Virginia, and spent his early years in Winston-Salem, North Carolina. As a young man, Johnson arrived in New York's Capital Region, where he became a redcap porter at Albany's Union Station. Shortly after the United States entered World War I, Henry Johnson enlisted in the all-black 15th New York Infantry Regiment. His heroic actions while serving with the French Army in May 1918 left him severely wounded.

Immediately after the war Henry Johnson's heroic efforts were well publicized and celebrated. Johnson led the regiment's homecoming parade up Fifth Avenue in New York City on February 17, 1919. In Albany, at a dinner hosted by Governor Al Smith and Mayor James Watt, promises were made to honor Johnson by naming an Albany street after him; he was also promised a monetary award.

For Henry Johnson, like many other African Americans who had answered the nation's call in the Great War, returning home to the status quo was unacceptable. At a Liberty Bond rally in St. Louis, Missouri, Johnson decried the racism and prejudice of white soldiers in the American Army, including what the *St. Louis Argo* called, "a haranguing of the white soldiers' valor and bravery." Johnson left the city that evening, just hours before a warrant was issued for his arrest.[8]

The tragedy surrounding Henry Johnson epitomized the widespread failure of the nation to adequately address veterans' needs for returning soldiers of all races, but the fact that he was African American made his situation worse. Despite being welcomed home as a hero, Henry Johnson was quickly forgotten by his nation. Following the event in St. Louis, Henry Johnson largely disappeared from American memory. The severity of his wounds prevented his return to the physical work required of a redcap porter. The lack of educational opportunities afforded to Johnson as a black youth growing up in the South meant that he was unequipped for employment in more white-collar jobs—especially given the scarcity of such jobs for African Americans. As a largely uneducated African American veteran, Johnson was unable to take advantage of the few programs available to wounded veterans. His outspokenness after the war about racism in the AEF alienated him from erstwhile white supporters. Johnson and other African Americans often found it difficult to take advantage of the job-training opportunities offered by the Veterans Bureau, due to the intransigence of southern leaders in the government bureaucracy. It is also likely that Henry Johnson suffered from the invisible wounds of war, which were unknown and untreated by medical professionals of the time.

The scars of war apparently led to an estrangement between Johnson and his wife, Edna. The monies and accolades promised to Johnson never materialized. Unable to find gainful employment and suffering from the pain from his wounds, Henry Johnson died impoverished and alone on July 10, 1929, at the age of thirty-two. To add insult to his story, he was buried at Arlington National Cemetery under an incorrect name—an error that went undiscovered for more than half a century.

The racial climate in the nation at the time also meant that official recognition from the U.S. Army of Johnson's bravery would not be forthcoming. It would not be until 1996 that Henry Johnson was awarded the Purple Heart—an award presented to every American service man or woman wounded in combat. In 2002, Johnson was posthumously awarded the Distinguished Service Cross, the nation's second-highest award for valor. Finally, on June 2, 2015, ninety-seven years after Johnson was wounded, President Barrack Obama presented the Medal of Honor to Sergeant Johnson in a White House ceremony.

> Take care of the boys who did their bit.
> —Henry Johnson to the New York State
> Senate Judiciary Committee,
> March 5, 1919

Sergeant Henry Johnson.

After the war, Johnson advocated for veterans' benefits and lobbied unsuccessfully with the New York State Legislature for a bill that would have given World War I veterans preference in civil service hiring. According to the *Dallas Express*, Johnson gave a short but "forcible" speech to the legislature, "I do not know rightly just what to say to you gentlemen. You know we went over there and did our bit. Only a few of us came back. Now, what are you going to do for us?"[1] Others, including the *New York Sun*, were less impressed by Johnson's speech, noting that Johnson had "stage fright in its worst form." Nonetheless, the *Sun* lauded Johnson's efforts on behalf of his fellow veterans.[2] Courtesy of the U.S. Army Center for Military History.

1. "Sergeant Henry Johnson Addresses New York Legislature," *The Dallas Express*, Saturday, March 22, 1919, page 1 (http://chroniclingamerica.loc.gov/lccn/sn83025779/1919-03-22/ed-1/), accessed April 29, 2016.

2. "As an Orator, Henry is a Good Soldier," *The New York Sun*, Thursday, March 6, 1919, page 7 (http://chroniclingamerica.loc.gov/lccn/sn83030431/1919-03-06/ed-1/seq-7/), accessed April 29, 2016.

Croix de Guerre.

This Croix de Guerre is similar to the one that was awarded to Henry Johnson in 1918. The bronze star device shown here would have been replaced by a bronze palm to denote the award was presented for Johnson's heroic actions on May 14–15. New York State Museum Collection, H-2012.23.8.

World War I service card for Henry Johnson.

Despite the notation that he was "severely wounded," Johnson never received the Purple Heart, nor was he able to collect benefits as a wounded veteran. It is not clear whether Henry Johnson sought assistance through vocational training or "rehabilitation," or whether the fact that he was classified as "0% disabled" upon discharge ultimately barred him from seeking this aid due to a man that Theodore Roosevelt Jr. labeled one of the five bravest soldiers of the Great War.[1] New York State Archives, B0808-85.

    1. Roosevelt, Theodore Jr. *Rank and File: True Stories of the Great War* (New York: C. Scribner's Sons, 1928), pages 91–116.

SOLDIERS' MONUMENT, BELFAST, N. Y.

Soldiers' Monument, Belfast, New York.

Communities across New York State erected monuments and memorials to the local men and women killed during World War I. New York State Archives, A0412-78.

11

Legacy

The legacy of World War I is substantial. In terms of the human cost, 48,909 Americans were killed in battle and an additional 63,523 died from disease. More than 230,000 were wounded. Nearly 14,000 men from New York State were killed.[1] Globally, more than seventeen million people were killed, including over seven million civilians. Twenty million others were wounded.

The legacy of the war extended far beyond the battlefields of Europe. World War I gave rise to a period of expansion of the federal government. Even during the nation's most preeminent crisis, the Civil War, much of the responsibility for raising and equipping troops, contracting for war materiel, and enforcing the wartime draft were left to state governments. World War I witnessed the end of this reliance on the states for the supply of troops. No longer would soldiers go into battle under the flag of their state regiment, but rather as part of a new National Army. Though a draft had been enacted during the Civil War, conscripted soldiers comprised only a small percentage of total Union forces. By contrast, more than 70 percent of the National Army were men inducted into the Army through the federal draft.[2] This massive conscription represented compulsory service on a scale never seen before in the United States. Contracts for weapons and material would be signed by the War Department rather than by quartermasters in each state. Funding the war effort was no longer the responsibility of the state governments. A new federal income tax, national liberty loan drives, and other nationwide efforts emanated from Washington to be carried out in New York State and elsewhere. The national debt, which had totaled one billion dollars in 1917, had swelled to $26.6 billion by 1919.[3] World War I also gave significantly increased authority to the executive branch of the federal government. The War Department during the conflict oversaw the mobilization and subsequent demobilization of four million men. Federal agencies such as the Justice Department's Bureau of Investigation were given increased authority to investigate claims of sedition and disloyalty.[4] Efforts to care for and provide benefits to the nation's veterans also contributed to an expansion of the government.[5] This expansion laid the foundation for the government's response to the Great Depression in the 1930s and its efforts at the outbreak of World War II in 1941.[6]

Many of the nation's leaders in the decades following World War I gained experience during the conflict. Herbert Hoover was head of the U.S. Food Commission and Franklin D. Roosevelt was assistant secretary of the Navy; both played significant administrative roles in the wartime government. In the years following the war, their experiences informed their policies. Colonel William Donovan, of the 165th Infantry Regiment, and Theodore Roosevelt Jr., son of the late president, both entered the political fray in unsuccessful bids to become governor of New York in the 1920s. Despite their defeats, both men remained active in public service. During World War II, Donovan headed the Office of Strategic Services, the precursor to the CIA. Roosevelt became a general in the Army during the war and commanded troops at Utah Beach during the invasion of Normandy on June 6, 1944. For his actions, he was posthumously awarded the Medal of Honor. Major Hamilton Fish, III, was elected to

Grave marker.

This 1950s-era grave marker was produced to honor a soldier of Battery C, 104th Field Artillery, 27th Division. The New York National Guard Artillery Regiment served with the New York Division from the Mexican Border in 1916 through the end of World War I.[1] New York State Military Museum, Division of Military and Naval Affairs.

1. Bakker, Pamela. *The 104th Field Artillery Regiment of the New York National Guard, 1916–1919: From the Mexican Border to the Meuse-Argonne* (Jefferson, NC: McFarland and Company, Inc., 2014).

Chemung County Memorial.

New York State Archives, A0412-78.

Hero Park, Staten Island.

The citizens of Staten Island dedicated Hero Park to the "splendid sons of Staten Island who so nobly gave their lives in the World War 1917–1919." New York State Archives, A0412-78.

Map of Europe (1923).

The end of World War I resulted in a dramatic transformation of the world map. The Austro-Hungarian, Ottoman, and German empires were dismantled, resulting in new nations such as Poland, Czechoslovakia, and Yugoslavia. The Middle East was carved up between Great Britain and France. South Africa, Australia, and New Zealand received Germany's former colonies in Africa and the South Pacific.[1] Courtesy of the Library of Congress.

1. Kitchen, Martin. *Europe Between the Wars: A Political History* (New York: Longman Group, Ltd., 1994), pages 3–13.

Congress in 1920 and served as a representative from New York for more than two decades. Initially a progressive adherent of Theodore Roosevelt, Fish became a staunchly conservative anticommunist, isolationist, and a leading opponent of the New Deal in the 1930s.

The end of World War I also initiated the beginning of the end of German American culture as a significant presence in New York State and across the nation. Many German language newspapers that had been boycotted during the war years failed to resume printing after the Armistice. In the 1920 federal census, fewer than 5 percent of American households listed German as a primary language. German language remained off the curriculum in many public schools.[7]

A World Transformed

The Great War dramatically transformed America's place in the world. The horrors of war led to a reversion to American isolationism and the abandonment of President Wilson's new world order. Fear of communism and foreign influence led to increasingly restrictive immigration policies and a push toward "100% Americanism." Adherents of this perspective called for "universal conformity organized through total national unity."[8] This entailed full assimilation into American cultural and social norms—and abandonment of one's ethnic or cultural identity. It was demanded that English be the primary language for all "true" Americans.[9] The fear of enemy aliens that had emerged during the war in the United States became a broader fear of all

Deutschland und der Friedensvertrag **(Germany and the Peace Treaty).**

Artist: Stefan; *Printer:* W. Bükenstein, Berlin, Germany; *Publisher:* Liga zum Schutze der Deutschen Kultur (League for the Protection of German Culture); *Technique:* Lithograph; *Dimensions:* 70 x 93 cm.

The harsh conditions imposed by the Treaty of Versailles were extremely unpopular in Germany, as is evidenced by this poster illustration depicting the German state shackled by chains. It was largely due to the popular backlash against the treaty that aided the rise of the National Socialists and Adolf Hitler in the 1920s.[1] New York State Library, Manuscripts and Special Collections.

1. Taylor, A.J.P. *The Origins of the Second World War* (New York: Atheneum, 1961), pages 42–43.

aliens—particularly those from Eastern and Southern Europe. The immediate postwar years witnessed a significant rise and strengthening of the American nativist movement.[10] The demands for conformity also led to immigrants being targeted for suspected radical beliefs. Association with socialist or anarchist organizations in the Old World was viewed as evidence of radicalism in the U.S.[11]

The Treaty of Versailles attempted to punish Germany for the war. The harsh conditions of the treaty

contributed to the rise of Adolf Hitler and the Nazis less than a decade later. The Bolshevik takeover in Russia and the Western response led to decades of tension and a Cold War that lasted half a century.

Perhaps the most significant legacy of the Great War, however, was how much the conflict left unresolved. World War I was not the "War to End All Wars," and in fact, it created the conditions that led to a larger and more deadly conflict just twenty years later. America did not emerge as a world leader after the war, but rather shrank back within the apparent safety of its two oceans. The care of the millions of young men and women who answered the call to arms was left largely unaddressed until after World War II. The legacy of World War I remains visible today as borders drawn in 1918 continue to influence conflicts in Europe, the Middle East, and Africa. It is important to remember World War I as much for the things it left unresolved as for what the conflict decided.

New York State and the Red Scare

The Great War has shaken the foundation of European Civilization. The same forces which promote civil strife in many of the countries of Europe are at work on this side of the ocean seeking to create a division in our population, stimulating class hatred and contempt for government.

—*Final Report of the Joint Committee for the Investigation of Seditious Activities*[12]

In October 1917, Bolshevik forces in Russia succeeded in overthrowing the Provisional Government that replaced Tsar Nicholas II in March. The communist takeover in Russia was followed in 1919 by revolution in Hungary in which communists under leader Béla Kun seized power.[13] At the same time, large swaths of Germany teetered on the verge of civil war as communists attempted to seize power from more moderate forces in the fledgling republican government. Britain, France, and the other allied democracies feared communist revolutions in their own nations.

In 1919, as the American economy retracted with the loss of wartime contracts, the fragile peace that had remained relatively intact throughout the war between industry and labor came to an end. That year, labor strikes erupted across the nation. In May 1919, a mob of soldiers and sailors attacked a meeting of garment-trade union members at Madison Square.[14] In September 1919, more than 300,000 steelworkers walked off the job—including those at the Lackawanna Steel Company in western New York—demanding unionization. Opponents of organized labor, often aided by government officials, blamed this labor unrest on communist agitators.

The "red scare" had reached the United States. U.S. Attorney General A. Mitchell Palmer led a nationwide effort to suppress radical agitation in the United States. Raids, arrests, and deportations of suspected radicals took place across the country.[15] American officials were convinced that socialist and communist agitators were part of a vast international conspiracy and that suspected radicals in the United States were "so closely interlocked and so governed by the same group of men."[16] In New York, the mistrust of foreigners that had emerged during the war once again manifested in the postwar years. Jews and other Eastern European immigrants were suspected of being Bolshevik agents. The institutions established during the war years persisted in the years of the red scare as federal and state governments continued to support a surveillance state to monitor suspected radicals within American society.[17] In New York State, the Joint Committee for the Investigation of Seditious Activities, led by State Senator Clayton Lusk of Cortland County, was tasked with investigating "a large number of persons within New York State engaged in circulating propaganda calculated to set in motion forces to overthrow the government of this State and the United States."[18] The Lusk Committee, as it came to be known, targeted groups that advocated Marxist, socialist, and anarchist philosophies and doctrines. The Committee's investigations focused on labor unions, immigrants (particularly those of Eastern European and Jewish backgrounds), and African Americans as groups "susceptible" to radical influences. Between 1918 and 1920, seventy-six individuals were arrested and indicted on various charges, most frequently criminal anarchy. Raids and arrests took place in New York, Utica, Buffalo, Rochester, and elsewhere across the state.[19] The rampant fear of communist revolution in New York coincided with economic turmoil resulting from the end of a wartime economy. As wartime contracts were terminated, workers in factories faced layoffs. Tens of thousands of returning soldiers and sailors found themselves unable to get jobs. Workers witnessed their wartime wages plummet while manufacturers sought to suppress the organization of labor, which had progressed during the war years.[20] This economic displacement led to numerous strikes across the nation, including those in Buffalo and New York City.[21] This rise in labor unrest was seen by the Lusk Committee and others as a sign of impending communist revolution. In his *Communist Manifesto*,

Wall Street bombing.

This photograph shows the aftermath of the September 16, 1920, bombing on Wall Street in New York City. Fear of socialists, anarchists, and other radicals was rampant in 1919 and 1920 in New York State and across the nation. Through acts of terrorism such as the bombing of Wall Street, a relatively small group of radical extremists served to taint the entire American Left and labor movements. The overriding fear of communist radicals was utilized by the government to continue the pattern of suppression of dissent and freedom of speech that had been established during the war in New York State and elsewhere. Courtesy of the Library of Congress.

Karl Marx asserted that, "the more or less veiled civil war, raging within existing society" would eventually erupt in "open revolution."[22] To members of the Lusk Committee, the general strikes breaking out across the state were the first salvos in this revolution.[23]

As a result of the Lusk Committee report, four laws were passed by the New York State legislature aimed at curbing revolutionary activity through the state's educational system. These bills established loyalty certification criteria for teachers, expanded Americanization efforts in adult education to bring educational opportunities into factories, and required schools to be licensed and answerable to the Board of Regents. The laws were vetoed by Governor Smith, who cited his commitment to the nation's founding principles and the rule of law in his veto message.[24] While the laws were eventually adopted in the term of Governor Nathan L. Miller in 1921, they were again overturned when Alfred E. Smith resumed the governor's office in 1924. Indeed, it was the efforts of politicians such as Smith and journalists in questioning the "Americanism" of the tactics employed during the red scare that ultimately brought this dark period to a close.[25]

"Tretet der Antibolschewistischen Liga bei "(**Join the Anti-Bolshevist League**).

Artist: Krotowski; *Printer:* Unknown; *Publisher:* Propaganda Verlag; *Technique:* Lithograph; *Dimensions:* 69 x 96 cm.

This image graphically depicts the widespread fear in Germany—and elsewhere—of the danger posed by the Communists and other radical organizations. Such fear was not limited to war-torn Europe. In the United States, a Red Scare permeated the government in New York State and suspected communist plots were seen in all facets of society. New York State Library, Manuscripts and Special Collections.

"Die Heimat ist in Gefahr!" (The Homeland is in Danger!) (1919).

Artist: N. Arnaud; *Printer:* R. Barnick, Berlin, Germany; *Publisher:* Die Freiwillige Wirschaftschilfe fur den Ostschutz; *Technique:* Lithograph; *Dimensions:* 93.5 x 69 cm.

This poster depicts dead and dying German civilians. The skeletal figure in the background wears a Russian Cossack-style hat. The poster's text translates as, "The Bolshevist wave threatens to flood over our eastern borders from Russia." With communist revolts in numerous German cities after the collapse of the imperial government, Germans feared a Bolshevik takeover of the entire nation. The threat of Communist takeover in Germany and elsewhere in Europe aided the rise of far-right political organizations, particularly Adolf Hitler's National Socialist German Workers Party in the 1920s. New York State Library, Manuscripts and Special Collections.

State of New York.

Nos. 40, 1331. Int. 39.

In Assembly,

January 9, 1919.

Introduced by Mr. WILSON — read once and referred to the Committee on Codes — committee discharged, bill amended, ordered reprinted as amended and recommitted to said committee.

AN ACT

To amend the penal law, in relation to displaying the red flag as a symbol or emblem of any organization.

The People of the State of New York, represented in Senate and Assembly, do enact as follows:

1   Section 1. The penal law is hereby amended by inserting

2   therein, after section two thousand and ninety-five, a new section,

3   to be section two thousand and ninety-five-a, to read as follows:

4   § 2095-a. *Display of red flag. A person, who shall display or*

5   *expose to view the red flag in any public assembly or parade as*

6   *a symbol or emblem of any organization or association, or in fur-*

7   *therance of any political, social or economic principle, doctrine or*

8   *propaganda, is guilty of a misdemeanor.*

9   § 2. This act shall take effect immediately.

EXPLANATION — Matter in *italics* is new; matter in brackets [ ] is old law to be omitted.

New York State Senate Act, January 9, 1919.

In January 1919, the New York State Legislature passed legislation to amend the State Penal Code banning the use of a red flag as the "symbol or emblem of any organization." Red was the color associated with the Communists in Russia. Following the Bolshevik Revolution, many Americans feared that communist revolutions would spread worldwide. Courtesy of the New York State Archives, A3166-78.

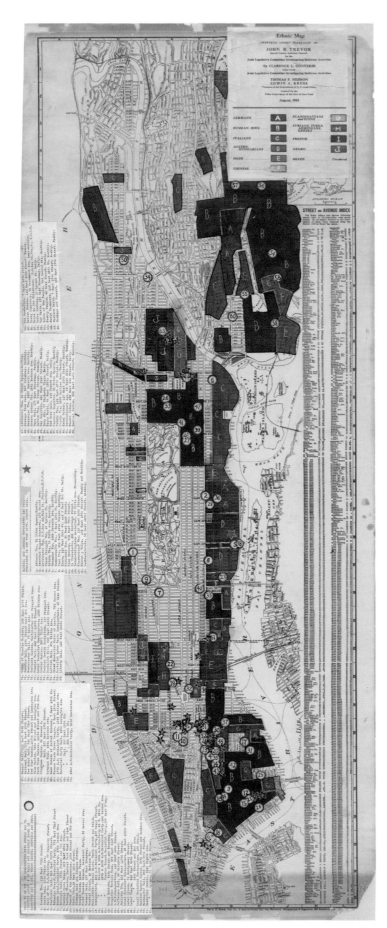

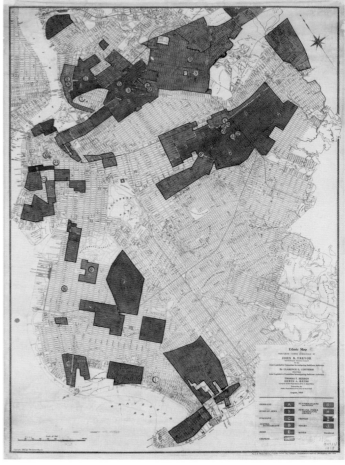

Ethnic maps of Manhattan and Brooklyn.

This "Ethnic Map" was created for the NYS Joint Legislative Committee to Investigate Seditious Activities in August 1919. The maps were likely created in conjunction with Captain John B. Trevor and the War Department's Military Intelligence Division. The map highlights neighborhoods in Manhattan and Brooklyn based upon their ethnic and racial compositions. The map was used by the committee to identify areas within both boroughs that might have been more "susceptible" to radical influences. An ally of noted anti-Semite Madison Grant, Trevor and others were convinced that the Bolshevik and Communist movements were under the control of Jews and that the large concentrations in New York City presented a significant threat to American security. Trevor argued that the city was poised to become the epicenter of a massive radical revolution in the United States.[1] New York State Archives, L0041-78.

1. Jaffe, page 214.

Demonstrating the hollow formation.

Soldiers of the 2nd Battalion, IX Coast Artillery Corps demonstrated the hollow formation devised by the Military Intelligence Division to be implemented in the event of an uprising in New York City or other urban center during the unrest following the end of World War I. In the photograph, soldiers in the front lines of the formation cover the street while those in the interior aim towards the surrounding windows and rooftops. Captain Trevor and the MID developed a plan to utilize machine guns in order to control the mob.[1] Courtesy of the National Archives and Records Administration.

    1. Jaffe, page 214.

Springfield rifle.

In anticipation of a potential communist uprising in New York City, the War Department shipped 6,000 Model 1903 Springfield Rifles similar to this one to Captain John Trevor and the Military Intelligence Division in New York City.[1] New York State Museum Collection, H-1972.76.1.

    1. Jaffe, page 214.

CIVIL RIGHTS

Even after the signing of the armistice, men have been sent to jail for violating the Espionage Act, a law ostensibly framed to prevent the giving of aid to Germany, but in practice used to jail radical protestants against social injustice.

—Final Report of the Joint Committee for the Investigation of Seditious Activities[26]

World War I gave rise to an intense debate over civil liberties and rights. Many New Yorkers were among the most vocal—on all sides. The United States has experienced periods of crisis throughout its history in which civil liberties were impinged on in times of national crisis: the Alien and Sedition Acts of the 1790s, suppression of free speech and habeas corpus during the Civil War, and the McCarthy-era red scare in the 1950s to name but a few. The years during and immediately following World War I marked another such episode in American history.[27]

The passage of the federal Espionage Act in 1917 and the Sedition Act in 1918 resulted in much debate in New York State over the role of the government and the right of freedom of speech. The Espionage Act empowered the government to regulate any speech deemed helpful to the enemies of the United States, while the Sedition Act made it a crime to make disloyal statements against the U.S. government or its allies.[28] In a series of court cases, the U.S. Supreme Court upheld convictions of several New Yorkers for the act of distributing revolutionary material.[29] In *Abrams v. United States* (1919), Jacob Abrams, a Russian immigrant living in Manhattan, was convicted of distributing socialist and anarchist literature. While the courts upheld Abrams's conviction, Justices Oliver Wendell Holmes and Louis Brandeis wrote dissenting opinions that called for limits on the government's ability to restrict free speech.[30]

In New York, the Joint Legislative Committee Investigating Seditious Activities specifically cited the use of the state's criminal anarchy law to "punish only that license of speech which exists in the advocacy of the doctrine that organized government should be overthrown by force, violence, or any unlawful means."[31] The committee also cited the decisions of the U.S. Supreme Court upholding the government's limits on speech in times of crisis.

Across the United States, the federal government initiated a policy of forcible deportation of alien residents who espoused radical philosophies.[32] Many of these "unwanted aliens" were detained at Ellis Island in New York Harbor before being returned to their homelands. All of these debates over civil liberties prompted the formation of the American Civil Liberties Union in New York City in 1920.[33]

END OF MASS IMMIGRATION

World War I marked the end of widespread, unrestricted immigration to the United States. Racial and ethnic fears, combined with fear of communist subversion, resulted in a sharp curtailment of immigrants permitted to enter the United States. Beginning in May 1917, the United States Congress passed legislation to limit entry into the United States of those immigrants deemed undesirable.[34] The legislation initially applied to enemy aliens from Germany and Austria-Hungary. In October 1918, these new immigration policies were expanded to include those suspected of being adherents to socialist, communist, or anarchist political groups.[35] These laws disproportionately targeted immigrants from Russia and Eastern Europe. Jewish immigrants were also often turned away for suspected radical affiliations.[36] Such new policies dramatically transformed the demographic makeup of cities and towns across New York State. In Rochester, for example, the city's population from the Civil War era until the outbreak of war in 1914 was nearly 70 percent foreign-born or descendants of immigrants. This figure began to steadily decline in 1920 with the enactment of restrictive immigration policies.[37]

In 1921, legislation drafted under the guidance of men such as Madison Grant and John Trevor was passed in the U.S. Congress establishing strict federal quotas on the number of immigrants from Eastern and Southern Europe permitted to enter the United States each year.[38] The laws targeted Jews, Catholics, and other groups deemed racially inferior to Americans of northern European heritage.[39] A revised Immigration Act in 1924 limited immigration to 2 percent of the foreign-born residents of each nationality already residing in the United States.[40] These laws remained in effect through the 1930s and ultimately prevented the escape of an unknown number of Jews from Germany and Europe following the rise of the Nazi Party.

In addition to restrictions on immigrants entering the United States, the government enacted a program of deportation as a weapon against foreign-born radicals. No longer was it necessary to violate American law to be expelled from the United States. Rather, by the end of the war, the tinge of radical association would be enough to warrant deportation.[41] In New York, suspected radicals, including Emma Goldman and Alexander Berkman, were among those forcibly deported from the United States.[42]

It was not until 1965 that New York Congressman Emanuel Celler succeeded in introducing legislation that began to reverse the trends of restrictive immigration. The Hart-Celler Act abolished the quota system and permitted immigration regardless of national origin.[43]

Emma Goldman (1869–1940)

Emma Goldman was born in the Russian Empire in Kovno in present-day Lithuania. At age thirteen, she moved with her family to St. Petersburg. Rising anti-Semitism in imperial Russia prompted the family to immigrate to the United States. Goldman and her sister Helena arrived in 1885, when Emma was fifteen, and settled with relatives in Rochester.[44] In Rochester, Goldman got a job in a clothing factory, where she was first exposed to ideas about socialism and labor organization.

After moving to New York City in 1889, Goldman became an adherent of anarchism and was active in political organization, labor disputes, and other activities. She also became a staunch supporter of women's rights and freedom of speech. When the U.S. government initiated the military draft after the nation's declaration of war in 1917, Goldman vocally encouraged men to refuse to register. She was a founding member of the No-Conscription League in May 1917. The following month, Goldman was imprisoned for conspiring against the draft. Under the 1917 Espionage Act, any action or speech deemed subversive and "potentially injurious" to the war effort was a criminal offense. After being convicted, she was sentenced to two years in prison.[45]

Following her release from prison in December 1919, she was again arrested under orders from J. Edgar Hoover, director of the General Intelligence Division at the Justice Department. Under authority of the Immigration Act of 1918, also known as the Anarchist Exclusion Act, Goldman's citizenship was denied and she was deported to the Soviet Union. The legislation eliminated due process and

Emma Goldman's deportation photograph, 1919.

Courtesy of the Library of Congress.

Goldman received no hearing to determine her guilt, nor did the law provide any mechanism for appeal.[46] She lived in exile for the remainder of her life, but remained active in political causes across the globe. She died in Canada in 1940.[47]

Harlem Renaissance— the New Negro Movement

> I think that a new era will arise on our nation as I do not think that the old conditions can prevail long without trouble.
> —John C. Ross to Augustus Dill, February 25, 1919[48]

In New York State, the combat record of the soldiers of the 369th Infantry Regiment afforded these veterans a sense of pride in their accomplishments and instilled a belief that their service to the nation warranted an improvement in race relations in postwar society.[49] The welcome home experienced by Harlem's Rattlers differed drastically from that of other African American units. Correspondence among the Military Intelligence Division prior to the return home of several black units warned of a secret organization being established with the stated purpose "to gain all rights of American Citizens. No more to be subjected to the Southern prejudice."[50] In response, many African American units were unceremoniously discharged in camps and the soldiers dispersed as individuals.

According to historian Steven Watson, the return of the Harlem Hellfighters on February 17, 1919, led by the band of James Reese Europe, marked a celebration of the return of "cultural nationalist" icons.[51] To residents of New York's African American population, the soldiers of the 369th had provided indisputable evidence of their community's commitment as American citizens and placed them firmly on equal footing with white veterans. W. E. B. Du Bois, editor of *The Crisis* and leader of the National Association for the Advancement of Colored People, wrote in May 1919, "But today we return! We return from the slavery of uniform which the world's madness demanded us to don to the freedom of civilian garb. We stand again to look American squarely in the face and call a spade a spade" and called for black veterans to "marshal every ounce of our brain and brawn to fight a sterner, longer, more unbending battle against the forces of hell in our own land."[52]

The renewed sense of self-confidence experienced by Harlem's returning veterans coincided with the emergence of a cultural awakening of African American art, music, and literature known as the Harlem Renaissance.[53] The Renaissance marked an "unprecedented artistic and creative output by African Americans."[54] Several veterans of the 369th emerged as leading figures in the Harlem Renaissance, including Noble Sissle, who in partnership with jazz composer and pianist Eubie Blake produced in 1921 *Shuffle Along*, the first Broadway musical by African Americans and featuring blacks on stage. Their second major hit, *Chocolate Dandies*, opened in 1924.[55] Bill "Bojangles" Robinson, also a veteran of the 369th band, became a tap-dancing star on the stages of New York City in the 1920s and popularized the dance form for widespread audiences.[56] Corporal Horace Pippin (1888–1946) of the regiment went on to a career as a creator of "primitive," nonacademic

NAACP flag.

A flag flies outside the NAACP headquarters on Fifth Avenue in New York City announcing a lynching, 1936. Courtesy of the Library of Congress.

art. As a young man, Pippin had enjoyed success as an amateur sketch artist. After enlisting in the 15th New York and while serving in the trenches of France with the 369th Infantry, Pippin created a visual journal of his experiences during the war. He was wounded in combat and lost the use of his right arm. After returning home, Pippin taught himself to paint and draw again, exhibiting his work across the nation.[57] The experiences of these black veterans not only influenced the development of their artistic works—particularly in Pippin's case—but also gave them confidence in their abilities.[58]

This confidence was evident in African Americans not only in Harlem, but across the nation. Asserting that the World War was a turning point in race relations, leaders of the NAACP and others called forth a "New Negro"—a philosophy born of the experiences of black troops in World War I and their determination to "achieve fuller participation in American Society"—civil rights leaders pushed for the passage of anti-lynching legislation in Congress and sought to ensure equal access to benefits for black veterans.[59]

While progress was painfully slow, and setbacks were numerous, the NAACP and the New Negro Movement persevered in the years following World War I. The Harlem Renaissance flourished and established the New York City neighborhood as the undisputed center of black culture. Though the civil rights movement did not reach its zenith until the 1960s, the violation of an implied social contract by white America that exchanged loyalty to the nation for promised improvements in race relations following the war greatly influenced the growing movement in New York and across the nation.

James Reese Europe and Noble Sissle

After their homecoming, Europe, Sissle, and the 369th Regimental band embarked on a nationwide tour on March 16, 1919. On May 9, the band performed at Mechanic's Hall in Boston to mark the end of the ten-week tour.[60] During the intermission, drummer Herbert Wright went to Europe's dressing room, where an argument ensued. In the scuffle, Wright drew a penknife and fatally stabbed Europe. News of Europe's death spread across the nation, and many mourned the loss of this "master of the art of ragtime."[61]

Shuffle Along.

Shuffle Along, by Noble Sissle and Eubie Blake, 1921. Courtesy of the New York Public Library.

Noble Sissle assumed leadership of the Hellfighters Band following the death of his mentor and friend. He partnered with songwriter and former Jim Europe protégé Eubie Blake, and as mentioned earlier, in 1921 the pair released *Shuffle Along*, the first Broadway hit musical written by African Americans. Sissle remained active with veterans of the 369th Infantry Regiment up to his death in December 1975.[62]

The death of Europe before the age of forty cut short a flourishing career in its prime. Not only did New York and the nation lose one of the leading figures in jazz music, but the African American community lost a growing voice in their continued struggle for civil rights.[63] The African American weekly, *The New York Age*, called Europe "the Roosevelt of the Negro musicians—a dynamic force that did things—big things." His funeral was "one of the largest ever held in New York for a member of the race."[64]

Lieutenant James Reese Europe Funeral.

Pallbearers carry the casket of Lieutenant James Reese Europe from St. Mark's Church in Harlem. Courtesy of the New York Public Library.

A Spirit of Sacrifice

While World War I was not the "war to end all wars" and tested the limits of President Wilson's claim to "make the world safe for democracy," the response of the men and women of New York State in industry, charity, and military service was preeminent among the states. For all of its horror and bleakness, World War I highlighted many positive aspects of New York society. The war effort engendered a sense of unity and duty in many of the state's citizens. This drive toward a common purpose created that "spirit of sacrifice" toward which Governor Whitman encouraged all New Yorkers to strive in 1918. Regardless of their motivations for doing so, New Yorkers answered the nation's call to arms—either through voluntary enlistments or registration for the wartime draft. Tens of thousands of New Yorkers entered work in state industries manufacturing

for the war effort. The war gave women opportunities outside their traditional spheres and contributed toward the state's passage of women's suffrage in 1917. Their contributions to the public cause gave many immigrants and African Americans an increased sense of pride and self-worth. In so doing, they sought to take advantage of the rights owed to them as citizens. Many felt that their wartime service entitled them to feel American and to seek to take advantage of these rights. While postwar reversions and retrenchment limited these efforts, early tenets of the civil rights movement were laid in the shadow of World War I. Equally important, New York State served as a center of the debate and discussion surrounding the war, its meaning, the role of government, and the limitations of civil rights in times of national crisis.

Notes

Introduction

1. Whitman, Governor Charles S., Proclamation announcing the Third Liberty Loan Drive, April 6, 1918, New York State Archives, Series 13035-79, Box 2, Folder 50.

2. Rawls, Walton. *Wake Up, America! World War I and the American Poster* (New York: Abbeville Press, 1988), pp. 13–14.

3. Letter, James Sullivan to Karl Singewald, December 1, 1920. Sullivan, James, Working Files for a Publication on New York in World War I, 1917–1925, New York State Archives Series A3166, Box 1, Folder 10. Flick, Alexander C., ed. *History of the State of New York*, vol. VII (Port Washington, NY: National University Publications, 1978), pp. 353–354.

5. Letter, Sullivan to Singewald, December 1, 1920.

6. Ibid.

Chapter 1

1. Barton, Bruce, "I am New York and This Is My Creed" (New York: Bankers Trust Company, 1919), New York State Library, Manuscripts and Special Collections, World War I Poster Collection, U.S. GEN 1053.

2. Whitman, Charles S., *Public Papers of Charles Seymour Whitman, Governor (1915–1918)* (Albany: J. B. Lyon Co., 1919), p. 684.

3. Capozzola, Christopher. *Uncle Sam Wants You: World War I and the Making of the Modern American Citizen* (New York: Oxford University Press, 2008), pp. 6–7.

4. Jaffe, Steven H., *New York at War: Four Centuries of Combat, Fear, and Intrigue in Gotham* (New York: Basic Books, 2012), pp. 180–182.

5. Ibid., p. 185.

6. Ibid., p. 180.

7. Ibid., pp. 180–186.

8. "Roosevelt Bars the Hyphenated," *New York Times*, October 13, 1915, p. 1.

9. Jaffe, p. 185.

10. Slotkin, Richard, *Lost Battalions: The Great War and the Crisis of American Nationality* (New York: Henry Holt and Company, 2005), p. 15.

Chapter 2

1. Letter, George S. McMartin to the Committee of Public Information. Sullivan, James, Working Files for a Publication on New York in World War I, 1917–1925, New York State Archives Series A3166.

2. Rawls, pp. 133–135.

3. Jaffe, pp. 201–202.

4. Rawls, p. 149.

5. Van Schaack, Eric, "The Division of Pictorial Publicity in World War I," *Design Issues* 22, no. 1 (Winter 2006): p. 45.

6. Flick, Alexander C., ed. *History of the State of New York* Volumes VII, VIII, IX, and X (Port Washington, NY: Ira J. Friedman, Inc., 1962), p. 283.

7. Letter, Cuyler Reynolds to James I. Wyer Jr., May 23, 1917; Letter, James I. Wyer Jr. to Cuyler Reynolds, May 24, 1917, Wyer, James I. Jr., New York State Librarian, Correspondence files, New York State Library, Manuscripts and Special Collections.

8. Letter, Reynolds to Wyer, February 15, 1918.

9. Letter from Benjamin Walworth Arnold to Miss Mary Ellis of the New York State Library, April 29, 1927, Wyer, James I., Jr., New York State Librarian, Correspondence files, New York State Library, Manuscripts and Special Collections.

10. Memorandum to Peter Nelson from James I. Wyer Jr., re: [Arnold's] Posters, April 18, 1922, Wyer, James I., Jr., New York State Librarian, Correspondence files, New York State Library, Manuscripts and Special Collections.

11. *Albany Evening News*, November 25, 1930, Wyer, James I., Jr., New York State Librarian, Correspondence files, New York State Library, Manuscripts and Special Collections.

12. Bielinski, Stefan, "Cuyler Reynolds," *The People of Colonial Albany Social History Project* (https://www.nysm.nysed.gov/albany/bios/r/cureynolds.html).

Chapter 3

1. Persico, Joseph, *11th Month, 11th Day, 11th Hour: Armistice Day 1918: World War I and Its Violent Climax* (New York: Random House Books, 2004), p. 119.

2. National Park Service, "Civil War Facts" (https://www.nps.gov/civilwar/facts.htm), accessed October 20, 2016.

3. Jaffe, pp. 180–186.

4. Black, Sylvia R., and Harriett Julia Naylor, "Rochester and World War I," *Rochester History* V, no. 4 (October 1943) (Rochester, NY: Rochester Public Library, 1943), http://www.libraryweb.org/~rochhist/v5_1943/v5i4.pdf, accessed April 1, 2016.

Chapter 4

1. Flick, pp. 287–288.

2. Ibid., p. 285.

3. Ibid., pp. 287–288.

4. "U.S. Merchant Ships, Sailing Vessels, and Fishing Craft Lost from all Causes during World War I," The American Merchant Marine at War (www.usmm.org/ww1merchant.html), accessed November 4, 2016.

5. Flick, p. 289.

6. Moore, Howard W., *Plowing My Own Furrow* (New York: W. W. Norton and Company, 1985), p. 85.

7. Hatch, Alden. *Remington Arms in American History* (New York: Rinehart and Company, 1956), pp. 213–214.

8. Mercaldo, Luke, "Remington's Allied Rifle Contracts During World War I," The Remington Society of America (http://www.remingtonsociety.org/remingtons-allied-rifle-contracts-during-wwi/), accessed November 4, 2016.

9. MeasuringWorth.com (https://www.measuringworth.com/uscompare/relativevalue.php), accessed November 4, 2016.

10. Jaffe, pp. 190–192.

11. Ibid., p. 191.

12. Ibid., p. 192.

13. Chatfield, Charles, "World War I and the Liberal Pacifist in the United States," *American Historical Review* 75, no. 7 (Dec. 1970), p. 1920 (http://www.jstor.org/stable/1848023), accessed November 10, 2016.

14. Carnegie Endowment for International Peace (http://carnegieendowment.org/about/), accessed November 10, 2016.

15. Kotzin, Daniel P., *Judah L. Magnes: An American Jewish Nonconformist* (Syracuse: Syracuse University Press, 2010), p. 145.

16. Kotzin, p. 145.

17. Chatfield, p. 1923.

18. Ibid., pp. 1921–2.

19. Ibid., p. 1924.

20. Kotzin, p. 145.

21. Chatfield, p. 1920.

22. Capozzola, p. 115.

23. Wilson, Woodrow, Second Annual Message to Congress, December 8, 1914, *The American Presidency Project*, University of California, Santa Barbara (http://www.presidency.ucsb.edu/ws/index.php?pid=29555).

24. Hutner, Gordon, *Selected Speeches and Writings of Theodore Roosevelt* (New York: Knopf Doubleday Publishing Group, 2013), "National Preparedness—Military—Industrial—Social;" Speech at Kansas City, May 30, 1916.

25. Roosevelt, Theodore, *The Great Adventure: Present Day Studies in American Nationalism* (London: John Murray, 1919), pp. 143–145.

26. Dickon, Chris. *Americans at War in Foreign Forces: A History, 1914–1945* (Jefferson, NC: McFarland and Company, Inc., 2014), p. 1.

27. Letter, James Sullivan to Brigadier General Charles W. Berry, Adjutant General of New York State, July 31, 1919, Working Files for a Publication on New York in World War I, 1917–1925, New York State Archives Series A3166.

28. Dickon, p. 39.

29. Black and Naylor, p. 3.

30. Urbanic, Kathleen, "Seeking Prosperity: A Brief History of Rochester's Polish American Community, Part One," *Rochester History* LVII, no. 1 (Winter 1995), pp. 12–13.

31. Seeger, Alan, Letter to his mother, October 23, 1914, *Letters and Diary of Alan Seeger* (Toronto: S. B. Gundy, 1917), p. 12. Accessed at Hathitrust.org (http://hdl.handle.net/2027/aeu.ark:/13960/t87h47k7r).

32. Martin, David A., "Dual Nationality: TR's "Self-Evident Absurdity," Chair Lecture, October 27, 2004, *UVA Lawyer*, Spring 2005 (http://www.law.virginia.edu/html/alumni/uvalawyer/sp05/martin_lecture.htm).

33. Dickon, p. 22.

34. Seeger, p. 6.

35. Ibid., p. 29.

36. Seeger, Alan, "Partie à Remplir Par le Corps" in "Mort Pour La France" (http://www.memoiredeshommes.sga.defense.gouv.fr/), accessed May 11, 2016.

37. Seeger, p. 211.

38. Winter and Baggett, p. 209.

Chapter 5

1. Roosevelt, p. 147.

2. Husted, James W., Speech at New Rochelle, Decoration Day 1917, Husted Family Papers, New York State Library, Manuscripts and Special Collections, SC23259, Box 3, Folder 1

3. Ibid.

4. Flick, pp. 295–296.

5. Elmer, Basil Beebe, October 27, 1917, Letter to Parents. The Basil Beebe Elmer Letters, 1917–1919, New York State Library, Manuscripts and Special Collections, SC23224 (Letters from an Ithaca, New York, Soldier in Company A, intelligence section, 165th Infantry Regiment (69th Infantry, New York National Guard) during World War I). Elmer was born in 1892 in Ithaca, Tompkins County. He graduated Cornell University and was a banker in New York City. His correspondences are filled with insights and opinions not only of life in the A.E.F, but also on matters pertaining to American politics and economics.

6. Flick, p. 315.

7. Ibid., p. 297.

8. Ibid., pp. 314–315.

9. Sullivan, *History*, p. 1232.

10. The divisions within the Resource Mobilization Bureau were Military Census; Finance; Publicity and Information; Defense and Security (including enrollment of men not eligible for the National Guard, on account of age or disability, for home defense); Information and Intelligence; Transportation; Food Production and Conservation; Division of Co-Operating Agencies (coordinating organizations and individuals for war work); Division of Aliens (supervising and registering aliens, and dealing with treasonable activities); Instruction (in such areas as personal hygiene, first aid, and economical cooking in the home); Health and Hospital; and Industrial.

11. Elkus, Abram I., and Felix Adler, *Americanization: Report of the Committee on Education of Governor Smith's Reconstruction Commission* (Albany, NY: J. B. Lyons Company, 1919), pp. 4–7.

12. Capozzola, p. 18.

13. Ibid., pp. 6–15.

14. Mitchell, Harold W., Letter to Parents, June 1917, "En route for Somewhere," Harold W. Mitchell Papers, New York State Library, Manuscripts and Special Collections, SC20960, Box 1, Folder 1.

15. Sullivan, *History*, p. 1229.

16. Hogan, Martin J., *The Shamrock Battalion of the Rainbow: A Story of the "Fighting Sixty-Ninth"* (New York: D. Appleton and Company, 1919), p. 7. The author served as a corporal with Company K, 3rd Battalion, 165th Infantry Regiment during the war.

17. Sullivan, *History* pp. 1230–1231.

18. Flick, p. 307.

19. Ibid., pp. 310–311.

20. Ibid., pp. 311–312.

21. Sullivan, *History*, pp. 1229–1230.

22. Flick, p. 311.

23. Sullivan, *History*, p. 1229.

24. Flick, p. 311.

25. Clark, Alton, April 15, 1918, Letter to his Mother. The Alton Clark Letters, 1918–1919, New York State Library, Manuscripts and Special Collections, SC21218. Alton Clark was a soldier from Moravia, New York, serving in the 312th Engineer Battalion, 87th Division.

Chapter 6

1. Mitchell, Harold W., Letter to Parents, June 27, 1918, Harold W. Mitchell Papers, New York State Library, Manuscripts and Special Collections, SC20960, Box 1, Folder 3.

2. Husted, James W., Speech at New Rochelle, Decoration Day 1917, Husted Family Papers, New York State Library, Manuscripts and Special Collections, SC23259, Box 3, Folder 1.

3. Whitman, Charles S., Proclamation, New York State Archives, Series 13035–79, Box 2.

4. New York State Police, "Annual Reports of the Department of State Police for the Years 1918 to 1924 Inclusive" (Albany: J. B. Lyon Company, 1925), pp. 12, 22.

5. Flick, p. 351.

6. Ibid., p. 335–336.

7. Ibid., p. 351.

8. Roosevelt, Theodore. *The Great Adventure*, p. 4.

9. Noble, Henry George Stebbins, *The New York Stock Exchange in the Crisis of 1914* (New York: The Country Life Press, 1915), pp. 7–8.

10. Taylor, Bryan. "World War I Impact on Markets, *Business Insider*, August 1, 2014 (http://www.businessinsider.com/world-war-i-impact-on-markets-2014-8), accessed November 8, 2016.

11. Martin, Andrew D. "The Great War, the NYSE and a Legacy of Strength" (New York: Advisor Perspectives, 2014).

12. Wilkins, Mira. *The History of Foreign Investment in the United States, 1914–1945* (Cambridge, MA: Harvard University Press, 2004), pp. 9–10.

13. Taylor (http://www.businessinsider.com/world-war-i-impact-on-markets-2014-8), accessed November 8, 2016.

14. Noble, p. 4.

15. Flick, p. 323.

16. Taylor (http://www.businessinsider.com/world-war-i-impact-on-markets-2014-8), accessed November 8, 2016.

17. Flick, p. 348.

18. Ibid.19. Ibid., pp. 349–350.

20. Elmer, Basil Beebe. Letter to Parents, December 24, 1917.

21. Hatch, p. 215.

22. Ibid., p. 225.

23. Swantek, John, and James Murray, *Watervliet Arsenal: History of America's Oldest Arsenal* (Watervliet, NY: Watervliet Arsenal Public Affairs Office, 2009), pp. 153–154.

24. Ibid., p. 164.

25. Ibid., p. 167.

26. "Savage Arms," Oneida County Historical Society (http://www.oneidacountyhistory.org/momentsintime/exploringhistory.asp).

27. Swinney, H. J., *The New York State Firearms Trade*, vol. 4 (Rochester, NY: Rove Publications, 2003), pp. 1443–1444.

28. Peterson, Patrick, "Griff Jones, Savage Arms," Transcript and article based on oral history interviews, Oneida County Historical Society Files.

29. Black and Naylor, p. 15.

30. Flick, p. 349.

31. Finding Aid, School of Aerial Photography Collection, Eastman House Museum Archives, 1981:1702.

32. "Pierce-Arrow History," The Buffalo Transportation Pierce-Arrow Museum (www.pierce-arrow.com/history).

33. "History of Aluminum," The Aluminum Association of America (http://www.aluminum.org/aluminum-advantage/history-aluminum), accessed November 9, 2016.

34. Carr, Charles C., *Alcoa: An American Enterprise* (New York: Rinehart and Company, 1952), p. 147.

35. Ibid., p. 148.

36. Ibid., p. 154.

37. Smith, George David, *From Monopoly to Competition: The Transformation of Alcoa, 1888–1986* (New York: Cambridge University Press, 2003), pp. 126–131.

38. Eisenstadt, Peter, ed. *The Encyclopedia of New York State* (Syracuse: Syracuse University Press, 2005), p. 61.

39. Carr, pp. 154–155.

40. Flick, p. 349.

41. Sullivan, Working Files, A3166, Box 1, Folder 5.

42. Sullivan, A3166, Box 1, Folder 5.

43. Zahavi, Gerald, "The Endicott-Johnson Corporation: 19th Century Origins" (http://www.albany.edu/history/ej/origins.html), accessed September 22, 2016.

44. McGuire, Randall H., "Building Power in the Cultural Landscape of Broome County, New York, 1880 to 1940," in *Material Culture: Critical Concepts in Social Sciences*, ed. Victor Buchli, vol. 2 (New York: Routledge, Taylor and Francis Group, 2004), pp. 10–11.

45. Eisenstadt, pp. 965–966.

46. Sullivan, James. Working files, New York State Archives, Series A3166.

47. Couture, Lisa, "The History of Canned Food" (2010). Academic Symposium of Undergraduate Scholarship. Paper 4 (http://scholarsarchive.jwu.edu/ac_symposium/4), accessed January 22, 2016.

48. Flick, pp. 346–347.

49. Ibid., p. 350.

50. Ellis, David M., James A. Frost, Harold C. Syrett, and Harry J. Carman, *A History of the State of New York* (Ithaca: Cornell University Press, 1967), p. 551.

51. Flick, pp. 327–328.

52. Ibid., pp. 329–330.

53. New York State Food Commission, *Report of the New York State Food Commission for Period October 18, 1917 to July 1, 1918* (Albany, NY: J. B. Lyon Company, 1919), p. 104.

54. New York State Food Commission, pp. 103–104.

55. Ibid., p. 118.

56. Ibid., p. 103.

57. Ibid., pp. 23–24.

58. Flick, p. 331.

59. New York State Food Commission, pp. 111–112.

60. Ibid., p. 113.

61. Ibid., p. 14.

62. Ibid., p. 13.

63. Ibid., p. 13.

64. Ibid., p. 115.

65. Ibid., p. 11–12.

66. Rawls, p. 113.

67. Flick, pp. 331–333.

68. Grant, H. Roger, "Railroads," *The Encyclopedia of New York State* (Syracuse: Syracuse University Press, 2005), pp. 1282–1284.

69. Huddleston, Eugene, *Uncle Sam's Locomotives: The USRA and the Nation's Railroads* (Bloomington: University of Indiana Press, 2002), p. 2.

70. Ibid., pp. 2–5.

71. Riley, Mike, "Federal Control: The NYS Barge Canal During World War I," *The New York History Blog*, March 5, 2014 (http://newyorkhistoryblog.org/2014/03/05/federal-control-the-nys-barge-canal-duirng-workld-war-i), accessed March 6, 2014.

72. Smith, Alfred E., *Progressive Democracy: Addresses and State Papers of Alfred E. Smith* (New York: Harcourt, Brace, and Company, 1928), p. 152.

73. Flick, p. 318.

74. Gillett, Mary C., *The Army Medical Department 1917–1941* (Washington, DC: United States Army Center of Military History, 2009), p. 174.

75. Kline, Harry L., "Father's Letter," November 23, 1918. Harry L. Kline Letters, New York State Library, Manuscripts and Special Collections, 21159. This letter, though dated after the war, is part of a compilation written to Kline's family about his experiences *during* the war. Corporal Kline of Newburgh, Orange County, served with Company C, 51st Pioneer Infantry Regiment, 27th Division.

76. Flick, p. 323.

77. "The Income Tax Arrives," The Tax History Museum (http://www.taxhistory.org/), accessed May 5, 2016.

78. Black and Naylor, pp. 7–8.

79. Flick, p. 327.

80. Ibid., p. 335.

81. Ibid., pp. 336–337.

82. "A Brief History of the Red Cross," The American Red Cross (http://www.redcross.org/about-us/who-we-are/history), accessed May 5, 2016.

83. Flick, p. 341.

84. Flick, pp. 335–343.

85. Bridger, David, "National Jewish Welfare Board," *The New Jewish Encyclopedia* (West Orange, NJ: Behrman House, 1962), pp. 339–340.

Chapter 7

1. Lewis, Merton E., Attorney General. Letter to John C. Birdseye, Secretary, New York State Civil Service Commission, December 14, 1917. New York State Museum Collection, H-2007.32.9.

2. Fairman, Matthew D., "The Restriction of Civil Liberties during Times of Crisis: The Evolution of America's Response to National Military Threats" (2009). Government Honors Papers. Paper 7. http://digitalcommons.conncoll.edu/govhp/7, p. 69.

3. New York State Police, Troop G, Police Blotter Books (1917–1919), New York State Archives, Series 13445–82, vol. 69/261, pp. 27–28.

4. New York State Police, Troop G, Police Blotter Books (1917–1919), New York State Archives, Series 13445–82, vol. 69/261, p. 44.

5. State Council of Defense Records, Correspondence Files, 1917–1918, New York State Archives Series A4234.

6. McKelvey, Blake. "Rochester's Ethnic Transformations," *Rochester History* XXV, no. 3, July 1963, pp. 16–17.

7. Ibid., p. 17.

8. *The Crisis* 17, no. 2 (December 1918), p. 86.

9. Lemak, Jennifer, "Advancement Comes Slowly: African-American Employment in Rochester, New York During the Great Migration," *New York History* 92, 1,2 (Winter/Spring 2011), pp. 84–85.

10. McKelvey, Blake. "Lights and Shadows in Local Negro History," *Rochester History* XXI, no. 4 (October 1959), pp. 19–20.

11. Lemak, p. 85.

12. Keene, p. 207.

13. Ross, John C., Letter to Augustus Dill, February 25, 1919. World War I Letters and Memorabilia Collection, New York State Library, Manuscripts and Special Collections, SC21813. Based on the content of his correspondence, it can be presumed that John Ross was an African American soldier serving with the AEF In his letter of February 25, he speaks of his hope for improved conditions for African Americans in the United States as a result of his and other black soldiers' service in the United States Army.

14. Roosevelt, Theodore. "True Americanism," *The Forum Magazine* (April 1894) (https://hudson.org/content/researchattachments/attachment/1216/theodore_roosevelt_true_americanism.pdf), accessed May 24, 2016.

15. Roosevelt, Theodore. *The Great Adventure*, pp. 46–47.

16. Higham, John. *Strangers in the Land: Patterns of American Nativism, 1860–1925* (New Brunswick, NJ: Rutgers University Press, 1983), p. 195.

17. Jaffe, pp. 206–208.

18. Churchill, Lieutenant Colonel Marlborough, Letter to Bruce Bielaski, August 11, 1917, Records of the Federal Bureau of Investigation, Published as part of an article by Paul Grondahl in the Albany *Times Union*, "Secret, prying eyes were on the "Wizard,"" October 23, 2013 (http://www.timesunion.com/local/article/SecretpryingeyeswereontheWizard4918219.php), accessed October 16, 2015.

19. New York State Police. "Annual Reports of the Department of State Police for the Years 1918 to 1924 Inclusive" (Albany: J. B. Lyon Company, 1925), pp. 12–13.

20. Forstall, Richard L., ed.. *Population of States and Counties of the United States: 1790 to 1990* (Washington, DC: U.S. Department of Commerce, Bureau of the Census, 1996), p. 3.

21. O'Ryan, John F., *The Story of the 27th Division* (New York: Wynkoop Hallenbeck. Crawford Co., 1921), p. 45.

22. Ibid., pp. 46–47.

23. Jaffe, pp. 194–197.

24. Ibid., pp. 197–199.

25. "Allies' Grain Feeds Big Fire in Brooklyn," *New York Sun*, October 14, 1917, p. 8 (FultonHistory.com), accessed February 12, 2016.

26. Administrative and Correspondence Files, 1917–1918, New York Council of Defense, New York State Archives, Series A4242.

27. New York State Police, Troop G, Police Blotter Books (1917–1919), New York State Archives, Series 13445-82, vol. 69/261, p. 15.

28. New York State Council of Defense Records, Administrative and Correspondence Files, 1917–1918, New York State Archives Series A4242.

29. Whitman, Charles S., Proclamation, New York State Archives, Series 13035-79, Box 2, Folder 40.

30. New York State Council of Defense Records, Administrative and Correspondence Files, 1917–1918, New York State Archives Series A4242.

31. Sweeney, Daniel J. *History of Buffalo and Erie County, 1914–1919* (Buffalo: Committee of One Hundred, 1919), p. 63.

32. "Safety Engineering," vols. 33–34 (New York: American Society of Safety Engineers, 1919).

33. "Allies' Grain Feeds Big Fire in Brooklyn," p. 8.

34. Neiberg, Michael S., "World War I Intrigue: German Spies in New York!" (2013), HistoryNet (http://www.historynet.com/world-war-i-intrigue-german-spies-in-new-york.htm).

35. Sullivan, James. "Frederick E. Foster, Assistant Secretary to the New York State Defense Council to New York State Historian James Sullivan, August 17, 1918," Working Files for a Publication on New York in World War I, 1917–1925, New York State Archives Series A3166.

36. "19 More Taken as German Spies," *New York Times*, April 8, 1917, p. 1 (http://timesmachine.nytimes.com/timesmachine/1917/04/08/102329999.html), accessed May 23, 2016.

37. Currie, Constance Gibson,"The Telefunken Radio Station in Sayville," *Long Island Forum*, Winter 1996, pp. 4–7.

38. Ibid., p. 10.

39. Wilkins, p. 14.

40. Currie, p. 11.

41. Jones, John Price, and Paul Merrick Hollister, *The German Secret Service in America* (Boston: Small Maynard and Company, 1918), pp. 191–192. The role played by the Sayville Station is discussed in detail by Jones and Hollister. Subsequent investigation has revealed that the signal may have originated from a sister site on the Jersey shoreline. Nonetheless, the West Sayville transmitter was utilized by the German government to relay other pieces of information prior to U.S. entry into the war.

42. McMaster, John Bach. *The United States in the World War* (New York: D. Appleton and Co., 1918), p. 169.

43. Capazzola, p. 8.

Chapter 8

1. Clark, Alton, October 11, 1918. The phrase, "Somewhere in France," was commonly used in correspondence between soldiers in the AEF and their loved ones in the United States. Censorship restrictions in the Army prohibited soldiers from divulging the location of their unit. Letters were strictly censored for any information that was deemed potentially valuable if in enemy hands.

2. Yockelson, Mitchell A. *Borrowed Soldiers: Americans Under British Command, 1918* (Norman: University of Oklahoma Press, 2008, p. 3.

3. Winter and Baggett, p. 157.

4. Stewart, Richard W., ed. *American Military History*, vol. II (Washington, DC: United States Army Center of Military History, 2005), p. 14.

5. Ibid., p. 1.

6. Flick, p. 316.

7. Sullivan, James S., *History of New York State, 1523–1927*, vol. III (New York: The American Historical Society, 1928), p. 1259.

8. O'Ryan, p. 60.

9. Flick, pp. 315–316.

10. Sullivan, vol. III, p. 1262.

11. Flick, pp. 317–318.

12. "Total Troops Furnished by Each State and Territory During the War, April 7, 1917 to November 11, 1918. Including Regular Army, National Guard, Navy, Marine Corps, Coast Guard and U.S. Guards." From Sullivan, James. Working Files for a Publication on New York in World War I, 1917–1925, New York State Archives Series A3166, Box 1, Folder 16.

13. Stewart, Richard W., ed. *American Military History*, vol. II (Washington, DC: United States Army Center of Military History, 2005), p. 373.

14. O'Ryan, p. 15.

15. Yockelson, p. 6.

16. Sullivan, vol. III, p. 1247.

17. Taber, Herbert H., The Private Herbert H. Taber Letters, 1918–1919, Private Collection, November 10, 1918. It deserves to be noted that the Battery C, 6th Field Artillery Regiment—also of the First Division—claims credit for firing this first American shot of the war (from the Hoosier State Chronicles: Indiana's Digital Newspaper Program, http://blog.newspapers.library.in.gov/americas-first-shot/). Accessed April 12, 2016.

18. Taber, Herbert H., March 7, 1918.

19. Taber, Herbert H., September 16, 1918, and November 10, 1918.

20. Dube, Henry, Letter to Thelma Bishop, May 18, 1918. Thelma Bishop Correspondence, New York State Library, Manuscripts and Special Collections, SC20799. Henry Dube was one of two soldiers to correspond with Thelma Bishop of Elmira, Chemung County, during the war. In this May 1918 letter, Dube reports that he had "been in the trenches twice, or in other words have done two hitches in hell as we call it."

21. Elmer, Basil Beebe, Letters to Parents, April and May, 1918. The Basil Beebe Elmer Letters, 1917–1919, New York State Library, Manuscripts and Special Collections SC23224. Elmer was a first lieutenant in the 165th Infantry. Originally from Ithaca, Tompkins County, Elmer first served with Company A before being transferred to the Intelligence Section and appointed the regimental intelligence officer. According to Father Duffy, Elmer assembled and trained "a group of scouts, observers, map-makers and snipers [who were] expert in detecting and hindering the movement of the enemy" (Duffy, *Father Duffy's Story*, p. 345).

22. Elmer, Basil Beebe, Letter to Parents, March 12, 1918 and April 2, 1918.

23. Seeger, Alan, November 10, 1914, pp. 19–20.

24. Elmer, Basil Beebe, Letter to Parents, April 4, 1918.

25. Dains, Garwood, Letter to Thelma Bishop, May 1918. Corporal Dains, who hailed from Elmira, Chemung County, was one of two soldiers who corresponded with Thelma Bishop, also of Elmira. Dains served in Company G, 102nd Infantry Regiment, 26th Division during the war.

26. Campbell, Peyton Randolph. *The Diary-letters of Sergt. Peyton Randolph Campbell* (Buffalo: Pratt and Lambert, 1919), p. 45, HathiTrust.org (http://hdl.handle.net/2027/loc.ark:/13960/t1xd1qh9q), accessed April 27, 2016. Sergeant Peyton Campbell, of Buffalo, was drafted and assigned to Company D, 306th Machine Gun Battalion, 77th Division. He was killed by enemy artillery on September 4, 1918. His letters home were published by the Pratt and Lambert Company. Prior to his military service, Campbell had been an advertising manager for the company.

27. Stewart, vol. II, p. 26.

28. Sullivan, vol. III, pp. 1266–1270.

29. Yockelson, pp. 16–20.

30. O'Ryan, pp. 243–246.

31. Yockelson, pp. 112–113.

32. Ibid., pp. 114–115.

33. O'Ryan, p. 310.

34. Ibid., p. 326.

35. Harris, *Harlem's Hellfighters*, p. 255–256.

36. O'Ryan, pp. 312–321.

37. Persico, pp. 280–281.

38. "Report of Operations of II Army Corps, September 29th to October 20th 1918," Husted Family Papers, New York State Library, Manuscripts and Special Collections, SC23259, Box 3, Folder 4. Lieutenant James Husted Jr. served as the artillery liaison for the U.S. Army's II Corps, which was comprised of the 27th and 30th Divisions. Husted was responsible for coordinating the American infantry offensive with British Artillery units.

39. "Congratulatory Messages, etc. Concerning Operations of Second Corps Sept. 27th–Oct 21st, 1918," Husted Family Papers, New York State Library, Manuscripts and Special Collections, SC23259, Box 3, Folder 4.

40. Harris, *Duty, Honor, Privilege*, p. 70

41. O'Ryan, p. 894.

42. Harris, *Duty, Honor, Privilege*, pp. 255–256.

43. O'Ryan, p. 894.

44. Strauss, Walter J., Diary of J. Walter Strauss, New York State Museum Collection, H-1976.243.2.

45. Slaski, Lisa, "First Sergeant Charles Henry Adrean," Oneida County Gen Web (http://oneida.nygenweb.net/military/aldean.html), accessed June 8, 2016.

46. Jessup, J. B., Lieutenant, Commander, Company A, 107th Infantry Regiment, Letter to Mrs. Adrean, February 17, 1919. Collection of the Oneida County Historical Society, 2007.171.17.

47. Norton, pp. 1–8.

48. Harris, *Duty, Honor, Privilege*, p. 221.

49. Schaming, Peter, Letter to Parents, October 1, 1918. Transcript in Vital Information File, New York State Museum Collection, H-2015.21.

50. Sammons and Morrow, pp. 195–196.

51. Harris, p. 175.

52. Journaux des Marches et Operations (J.M.O.) des Grandes Unités, Divisions d'infanterie et d'infanterie territoriale, 16e division d'infanterie, 1er janvier 1917–23 aout 1918, 18 Mars 1918 (http://www.memoiredeshommes.sga.defense.gouv.fr/fr/arkotheque/inventaires/ead_ir_consult.php?&ref=SHDGR__GR_26_N_I), accessed May 11, 2016.

53. Journaux des Marches et Operations (J.M.O.) des Grandes Unités, Divisions d'infanterie et d'infanterie territoriale, 16e division d'infanterie, 1er janvier 1917–23 aout 1918, 10 Avril 1918

54. Harris, *Harlem's Hellfighters*, p. 240.

55. Ibid., p. 259.

56. Ibid., p. 260.

57. Journaux des Marches et Operations (J.M.O.) des Grandes Unités, Divisions d'infanterie et d'infanterie territoriale, 16e division d'infanterie, 1er janvier 1917–23 aout 1918, 15 Mai 1918.

58. Norder, Akum. "The Battle of Henry Johnson," *518Life* Magazine, November 21, 2014, pp. 22–23.

59. Harris, *Harlem's Hellfighters*, pp. 70–72.

60. Sammons and Morrow, pp. 192–194.

61. Sissle, Noble, *Memoirs of Lieutenant "Jim Europe"* (unpublished, circa 1942), p. 113. From the collections of the Library of Congress Music Division (https://memory.loc.gov/cgi-bin/query/r?ammem/aaodyssey:@field(NUMBER+@band(musmisc+ody0717))), accessed October 14, 2016.

62. Ames, Winthrop, Letter to Noble Sissle, February 10, 1920, in *Memoirs of Lieutenant "Jim Europe,"* p. 125.

63. Harris, *Harlem's Hellfighters*, pp. 166–175.

64. Ibid., pp.167–176.

65. Hayward, William, Letter to Noble Sissle in *Memoirs of Lieutenant "Jim Europe,"* p. 32.

66. Badger, Reid, *A Life in Ragtime: A Biography of James Reese Europe* (New York: Oxford University Press, 1995), p. 10. It should be noted that Europe's sister indicated his year of birth as 1882 in a letter to Noble Sissle included as part of his unpublished memoirs, and the Library of Congress's website gives a date of 1881 (https://blogs.loc.gov/music/2010/02/james-reese-europe/), accessed October 14, 2016.

67. Sissle, pp. 7–8.

68. Badger, pp. 25–40.

69. Harris, *Harlem's Hellfighters*, pp. 1–4.

70. Finding Aid, James Reese Europe Collection, Schomburg Center for Research in Black Culture, The New York Public Library (http://archives.nypl.org/scm/20906), accessed October 17, 2016.

71. Harris, *Harlem's Hellfighters*, p. 47.

72. Ibid., pp. 43–46.

73. Ibid., pp. 219–220.

74. Ibid., pp. 266–267.

75. Ibid., pp. 167–176.

76. Kimball, Robert, and William Bolcom, *Reminiscing with Sissle and Blake* (New York: Viking Press, 1973), p. 68.

77. Slotkin, p. 127.

78. Harris, *Duffy's War*, pp. 182–183.

79. Sullivan, vol. IV, pp. 1305–1307.

80. Elmer, Basil Beebe, Letter to Parents, April 12, 1918.

81. Duffy, Francis P. *Father Duffy's Story* (New York: George H. Doran Company, 1919), pp. 133–135.

82. Harris, *Duffy's War*, p. 373.

83. Duffy, pp. 314–315.

84. Willbanks, James H, ed., *America's Heroes: Medal of Honor Recipients from the Civil War to Afghanistan* (Denver, CO: ABC-CLIO, LLC, 2011), pp. 248–250.

85. Duffy, pp. 194–195.

86. Willbanks, p. 250.

87. Duffy, p. 65.

88. Kilmer, Alfred Joyce, "Rouge Bouquet," *Scribner's* Magazine, September 1918, p. 351 (https://www.unz.org/Pub/Scribners-1918sep-00351), accessed May 25, 2016. A reference to the publication of Kilmer's poem was made in Lt. Basil Beebe Elmer's May 20, 1918, letter to his parents. Elmer was Joyce Kilmer's commanding officer in the Intelligence Section, 165th Infantry Regiment.

89. Duffy, pp. 96–97.

90. Elmer, Letter to Parents, August 5, 1918.

91. Harris, *Duffy's War*, pp. 3–5.

92. Grayson, SK Lawrence P., "Fr. Francis Duffy: The Doughboy Chaplain," Knights of Columbus, Archdiocese of Washington District, 2012 (http://www.awddistrict.org/index.php/catholic-patriotism/military-chaplains/fr-francis-duffy-the-doughboy-chaplain), accessed May 20, 2016.

93. "The U.S. Army Chaplain Corps: Providing Care and Comfort to Soldiers for 239 Years," *Soldiers* Magazine, July 29, 2014 (http://soldiers.dodlive.mil/tag/father-francis-duffy/), accessed May 20, 2016.

94. Sullivan, vol. IV, p. 1333.

95. Sullivan, vol. IV, p. 1335.

96. Sullivan, vol. IV, p. 1339.

97. Crawford, Gilbert H., Thomas Harlan Ellet, and John J. Hyland, eds. *The 302nd Engineers: A History* (n.p.: n.pub., 1919), p. 140 (https://babel.hathitrust.org/cgi/pt?id=mdp.39015027341661;view=1up;seq=7), accessed November 17, 2016.

98. Miles, L. Wardlaw. *History of the 308th Infantry, 1917–1919* (New York: G. P. Putnam's Sons, 1927), p. 113. The author served as a captain with the 308th Infantry Regiment, 77th Division. Miles was awarded the Medal of Honor for heroic actions on September 14, 1918, near Revillon, France. He was wounded five times by machine gun fire and subsequently was not a part of the Meuse-Argonne offensive. He was selected by Colonel Nathan K. Averill to compile the history of the 308th Infantry Regiment. Colonel Averill's copy of this history, which has been signed by several surviving members of the regiment including Major George McMurtry, himself a Medal of Honor Recipient and survivor of the Lost Battalion, resides in the collections of the New York State Museum (H-1971.113.8).

99. "Harder's First Year of Service: His Important Work at Albany," *Chatham Courier*, October 16, 1924, p. 1 (http://fultonhistory.com/Fulton.html), accessed November 17, 2016.

100. Crawford, Ellet, and Hyland, p. 91.

101. Coyne, Kevin, "Ultimate Sacrifice," *Smithsonian Magazine*, October 2004 (http://www.smithsonianmag.com/history/ultimate-sacrifice-180728112/?all), accessed May 16, 2016.

102. Slotkin, pp. 339–340.

103. "Baseball's Greatest Sacrifice," http://www.baseballsgreatestsacrifice.com/biographies/grant_eddie.html, accessed May 16, 2016.

104. Coyne, http://www.smithsonianmag.com.

105. Gillett, p. 19.

106. "Military Nurses in World War I," Women in Military Service for American Memorial Foundation, History and Collections (http://chnm.gmu.edu/courses/rr/s01/cw/students/leeann/historyandcollections/history/lrnmrewwinurses.html), accessed May 19, 2016.

107. Flick, p. 320.

108. "Military Nurses."

109. "The Civilian War Effort in New York City During World War I and World War II," MCNY Blog: New York Stories Museum of the City of New York (https://blog.mcny.org/2015/02/03/the-civilian-war-effort-in-new-york-city-during-world-war-i-and-world-war-ii/), accessed May 19, 2016.

Chapter 9

1. Taber, Herbert, Letter to mother, November 11, 1918.

2. Harris, *Duffy's War*, p. 379.

3. "The Deadly Virus: The Influenza Epidemic of 1918," National Archives and Records Administration Online Exhibit (www.archives.gov/exhibits/influenza-epidemic).

4. Edgett, Roy W., October 1, 1918, Letter to Sister. The Roy W. Edgett Letters, 1917–1918, New York State Library, Manuscripts and Special Collections, SC21234.

5. Billings, Molly, "The Influenza Pandemic of 1918." Department of Human Virology, Stanford University (https://virus.stanford.edu/uda/), 1997.

6. Eisenstadt, pp. 773–774.

7. "The Great Pandemic: The United States in 1918–1919."United States Department of Health and Human Services (http://www.flu.gov/pandemic/history/1918/your_state/northeast/newyork/index.html).

Chapter 10

1. Taber, Herbert H., Letter to mother, November 10, 1918. In the letter, Private Taber awaits word of the Armistice. He tells his mother of his pride in his artillery unit, including firing the first artillery round by American forces in the war, and indicates that the casing was sent to President Wilson.

2. Sullivan, vol. V, p. 25.

3. Roosevelt, *The Great Adventure*, p. 9.

4. Spicer, Warren, Letter to Mother, January 2, 1919, Spicer Family Papers, New York State Library, Manuscripts and Special Collections, SC19560, Box 3.

5. Stewart, vol. II, pp. 57–60.

6. Zeitz, Joshua, "The Roaring Twenties," the Gilder Lehrman Institute of American History (https://www.gilderlehrman.org/history-by-era/roaring-twenties/essays/roaring-twenties), accessed November 21, 2016.

7. Zeitz, Joshua, "The Roaring Twenties," the Gilder Lehrman Institute of American History (https://www.gilderlehrman.org/history-by-era/roaring-twenties/essays/roaring-twenties), accessed November 21, 2016.

8. "Johnson Too Loose with His Jaw," *Ocala Evening Star*, Monday, March 31, 1919, p. 1 (http://chroniclingamerica.loc.gov/lccn/sn84027621/1919-03-31/ed-1/), accessed April 29, 2016.

Chapter 11

1. Flick, p. 319.

2. Capazzola, p. 18.

3. Wickens, Aryness Joy, "The Public Debt and National Income," *American Economic Review* 37, no. 2, pp. 184–185.

4. "A Brief History of the FBI" (https://www.fbi.gov/about-us/history/brief-history), accessed April 16, 2016.

5. Holcombe, Randall G., "The Growth of the Federal Government in the 1920s," *Cato Journal* 16, no. 2 (Fall 1996), p. 178.

6. Capozzola, p. 210.

7. Ibid., pp. 197–201.

8. Ibid., p. 205.

9. Ibid., pp. 205–207.

10. Ibid., p. 204.

11. Ibid., pp. 218–219.

12. "General Introduction," *Final Report of the Joint Committee for the Investigation of Seditious Activities*, part I, vol. I (Albany: J. B. Lyon Company, 1920), p. 7.

13. Lee, Stephen J. *The European Dictatorships 1918–1945* (New York: Routledge, 1998), pp. xi–xiii.

14. Jaffe, p. 215.

15. Eisenstadt, p. 1725.

16. "General Introduction," *Final Report* p. 38.

17. Capozzola, p. 201.

18. "Concurrent Resolution Authorizing the Investigation of Sedition Activities," *Final Report*, p. 1.

19. *Final Report*, pp. 24–26.

20. Ibid., pp. 710–711.

21. Eisenstadt, p. 1725.

22. Marx, Karl, and Friedrich Engels, *The Communist Manifesto* (New York: Penguin Group, 1967), p. 93.

23. *Final Report*, pp. 11–12.

24. Sullivan, volume V, p. 1822.

25. Jaffe, pp. 214–215.

26. *Final Report*, p. 1108.

27. Braeman, John, "World War One and the Crisis of American Liberty," *American Quarterly* 16, no. 1 (Spring 1964) (http://www.jstor.org/stable/2710832), p. 104.

28. Capozzola, pp. 149–160.

29. Eisenstadt, p. 603.

30. Konkoly, Toni, "Famous Dissents: Abrams v. United States (1919), *The Supreme Court: Law, Power, and Personality* (http://www.pbs.org/wnet/supremecourt/personality/landmark_abrams.html), accessed May 6, 2016.

31. *Final Report* p. 2024.

32. *Final Report*, p. 2075.

33. Eisenstadt, p. 603.

34. *Final Report*, p. 2089–2090.

35. Higham, p. 202.

36. Slotkin, pp. 382–385.

37. McKelvey, "Rochester's Ethnic Transformations," pp. 19–20.

38. Higham, p. 311.

39. Jaffe, p. 215.

40. Higham, p. 324.

41. Ibid., pp. 220–221.

42. Capozzola, p. 204.

43. Kammer, Jerry, "The Hart-Celler Immigration Act of 1965" (Center for Immigration Studies, September 2015), http://cis.org/Hart-Celler-Immigration-Act-1965, accessed November 28, 2016.

44. Frank, Meryl, and Blake McKelvey, "Some Former Rochesterians of National Distinction," *Rochester History* XXI no. 3 (July 1959), p. 12.

45. Fairman, p. 74.

46. Ibid. pp. 75–76.

47. "Emma Goldman," Women of Valor exhibition, Jewish Women's Archive (http://jwa.org/womenofvalor/goldman), accessed April 12, 2016.

48. Ross, John C. Letter to Augustus Dill, February 25, 1919, World War I Letters and Memorabilia Collection, New York State Library, Manuscripts and Special Collections, SC21813, Folder 4. Given the content of the letters from John Ross, it is assumed that he was an African American soldier in the AEF This letter is to Augustus Dill, an associate of W.E.B. Du Bois, a business manager for *The Crisis* Magazine, and a member of the NAACP.

49. Slotkin, pp. 46–50.

50. Dunn, John H., Memorandum, "Negro Post-Demobilization Activities," March 4, 1919. "Correspondence of the Military Intelligence Division Relating to "Negro Subversion" 1917–1941," Records of the War Department General and Special Staffs, Record Group 165, Reel 5, 10218-506.

51. Watson, Steven. *The Harlem Renaissance: Hub of African-American Culture 1920–1930* (New York: Pantheon Books, 1995), p. 14–15.

52. Du Bois, W. E. B. "Returning Soldiers," *The Crisis* 18, no. 1 (May 1919), pp. 13–14.

53. Watson, pp. 8–9.

54. Koslow, Philip, ed. *The New York Public Library African American Desk Reference* (New York: Stonesong Press, 1999), p. 13.

55. Koslow, pp. 379, 405.`

56. Ibid., p. 410.

57. West, Aberjhani, and Sandra L. *Encyclopedia of the Harlem Renaissance* (New York: Checkmark Books, 2003), p. 264.

58. Slotkin, p. 545.

59. "NAACP: A Century in the Fight for Freedom," Library of Congress Exhibition (https://www.loc.gov/exhibits/naacp/the-new-negro-movement.html), accessed November 29, 2016.

60. Sissle, pp. 220–222.

61. "Jim Europe Killed by Band Drummer," *New York Sun*, May 10, 1919, p. 1.

62. Fish, Hamilton, Letter to Noble Sissle, April 25, 1973. The Hamilton Fish Papers, New York State Library, Manuscripts and Special Collections, SC21149, Box 73, Folder 23.

63. Slotkin, Richard, *Lost Battalions: The Great War and the Crisis of American Nationality* (New York: Henry Holt and Company, 2005), p. 409.

64. "Lt. James Reese Europe Buried with Honors," *New York Age*, May 17, 1919, pp. 1 and 6 (http://fultonhistory.com/Newspaper%2011/New%20York%20NY%20Age/New%20York%20NY%20Age%201919-1921%20%20Grayscale/New%20York%20NY%20Age%201919-1921%20%20Grayscale%20-%200163.pdf), accessed October 18, 2016.

Bibliography

The exhibition and accompanying publication were built on the scholarship of countless historians and experts. To tell the story of New York State in World War I, the exhibition's curators relied heavily on this foundation of research and to that added primary research of their own from the vast collections of the New York State Museum, the New York State Library, and the New York State Archives, as well as repositories from across New York State and the nation, both in person and digitally.

"19 More Taken as German Spies," *New York Times*, April 8, 1917, p. 1 (http://timesmachine.nytimes.com/timesmachine/1917/04/08/102329999.html), accessed May 23, 2016.

"1914 Felt Blanket/B-18 Blanket," Keymancollectibles.com (http://keymancollectibles.com/miscellaneous/1914feltblanket.htm), accessed January 25, 2016.

1915 Top 40 Songs (http://playback.fm/charts/top-100-songs/1915/); "1915 in Music" (https://en.wikipedia.org/wiki/1915_in_music#Hit_recordings), accessed April 1, 2016.

"The 27th Division on the Hindenburg Line," Catalog Record, Library of Congress Online Catalog (https://www.loc.gov/item/2010645781/), accessed April 25, 2016.

Adler, Major J. O., ed. *A History of the Seventy-Seventh Division: August 25th, 1917 to November 11th, 1918* (New York: Wynkoop Hallenbeck Crawford Company, 1919), p. 10.

Allam, Lorena. "Cooee: The History of a Call," (http://www.abc.net.au/radionational/programs/hindsight/cooee-the-history-of-a-call/3162216), accessed March 3, 2016.

"Allies' Grain Feeds Big Fire in Brooklyn," *The New York Sun*, October 14, 1917, p. 8 (FultonHistory.com), accessed February 12, 2016 .

The American Experience. Poster Art of World War 1 (http://www.pbs.org/wgbh/amex/wilson/gallery/p_war_09.html), accessed January 22, 2016.

American Red Cross. "A Brief History of the Red Cross" (http://www.redcross.org/about-us/who-we-are/history), accessed May 5, 2016.

Anderson, M. S. *The Ascendancy of Europe: 1815–1914* (Essex, England: Pearson Education Limited, 1985), pp. 1–61, 224–239, and 293–330.

"Artist Biography: William Allen Rogers (1854–1931)." Smithsonian Libraries (http://www.sil.si.edu/ondisplay/caricatures/bio_rogers.htm), accessed April 1, 2016.

"As an Orator, Henry Is a Good Soldier." *The New York Sun*, Thursday, March 6, 1919, p. 7 (http://chroniclingamerica.loc.gov/lccn/sn83030431/1919-03-06/ed-1/seq-7/), accessed April 29, 2016.

The Association Monthly: Official Organ of the Young Woman's Christian Association 14, nos. 7–12, p. xi. Available via Google Books (https://books.google.com/books?id=R3vOAAAAMAAJ&pg=PR11&lpg=PR11&dq=Henrietta+D%27Aran&source=bl&ots=6CfDi00uXz&sig=vE8z5EhcsPJKmKOO7ZklIUTbN98&hl=en&sa=X&ved=0ahUKEwiSn-vm0-jMAhVHmx4KHejZDzQQ6AEIMTAF#v=onep.&q=Henrietta%20D'Aran&f=false), accessed May 20, 2016.

Auld, Major S. J. M. *Gas and Flame in Modern Warfare* (New York: George H. Doran Company, 1918), frontispiece (https://books.google.com/books?id=FX46AAAAMAAJ&pg=PR2&lpg=PR2&dq=The+Final+Inspector+W.G.+Thayer&source=bl&ots=RUyg1J0mEc&sig=a1ebX1GA--fNWOkHYwahWipY9AI&hl=en&sa=X&ved=0ahUKEwjB_uTyw97MAhUJHD4KHXS8Ax4Q6AEIITAB#v=onep.&q=The%20Final%20Inspector%20W.G.%20Thayer&f=false), accessed May 16, 2016.

Badger, Reid. *A Life in Ragtime: A Biography of James Reese Europe* (New York: Oxford University Press, 1995) .

Bakker, Pamela. *The 104th Field Artillery Regiment of the New York National Guard, 1916–1919: From the Mexican Border to the Meuse-Argonne* (Jefferson, NC: McFarland and Company, 2014) .

Barton, Bruce. "I Am New York and This Is My Creed" (New York: Bankers Trust Company, 1919), New York State Library, Manuscripts and Special Collections, World War I Poster Collection, U.S. GEN 1053.

"Baseball's Greatest Sacrifice." http://www.baseballsgreatestsacrifice.com/biographies/grant_eddie.html, accessed May 16, 2016.

Berry, Brigadier General Charles W., The Adjutant General. *Annual Report of the Adjutant General for the Year 1919* (Albany: J. B. Lyon Company, 1921) .

Bielinski, Stefan. "Cuyler Reynolds," *The People of Colonial Albany Social History Project* (https://www.nysm.nysed.gov/albany/bios/r/cureynolds.html), accessed March 5, 2016.

Billings, Molly. "The Influenza Pandemic of 1918." Department of Human Virology, Stanford University (https://virus.stanford.edu/uda/), 1997.

Biographical Sketch. Howard Chandler Christy Papers, 1873–2001, Lafayette College Special Collections and College Archives (http://academicmuseum.lafayette.edu/special/Christy/Christyonline/bio.html), accessed February 8, 2016.

"Biography of Albert Herter." Wikipedia (https://en.wikipedia.org/wiki/Albert_Herter), accessed January 22, 2016.

"Biography of H. J. Weston (1874–1938)." National Library of Australia (http://trove.nla.gov.au/people/604315?c=people), accessed February 2, 2016.

Bishop, Thelma L. The Thelma L. Bishop Correspondence, 1916–1919, New York State Library, Manuscripts and Special Collections, SC20799 (Correspondence to Thelma Bishop of Elmira, Chemung County, from two soldiers during World War I).

Black, Sylvia R., and Harriett Julia Naylor. "Rochester and World War I." *Rochester History* V, no. 4 (October 1943) (Rochester: Rochester Public Library, 1943), http://www.libraryweb.org/~rochhist/v5_1943/v5i4.pdf .

Braeman, John. "World War One and the Crisis of American Liberty." *American Quarterly* 16, no. 1 (Spring 1964), pp. 104–112 (http://www.jstor.org/stable/2710832), accessed February 17, 2016.

"A Brief History of the FBI." (https://www.fbi.gov/about-us/history/brief-history), accessed April 16, 2016.

Bruce, Robert. *Machine Guns of World War One* (London: Crowood Press, 1997) .

Capozzola, Christopher. *Uncle Sam Wants You: World War I and the Making of the Modern American Citizen* (New York: Oxford University Press, 2008) .

Carleton, Simon Jr. The Simon Carleton Jr., Papers, 1916–1957, New York State Library, Manuscripts and Special Collections, SC18941 (Collection of papers including letters between Carleton and his mother while serving with the 102nd Infantry Regiment, 26th Division during World War I).

Carnegie Endowment for International Peace (http://carnegieendowment.org/about/), accessed November 10, 2016.

Carr, Charles C. *Alcoa: An American Enterprise* (New York: Rinehart and Company, 1952), pp. 174–163.

Chatfield, Charles. "World War I and the Liberal Pacifist in the United States," *The American Historical Review* 75, no. 7 (Dec. 1970), p. 1920 (http://www.jstor.org/stable/1848023), accessed November 10, 2016.

"The Civilian War Effort in New York City During World War I and World War II." MCNY Blog: New York Stories Museum of the City of New York (https://blog.mcny.org/2015/02/03/the-civilian-war-effort-in-new-york-city-during-world-war-i-and-world-war-ii/), accessed May 19, 2016.

Clark, Alton. The Alton Clark Letters, 1918–1919, New York State Library, Manuscripts and Special Collections, SC21218 (Letters from a soldier from Moravia, New York, serving in the 312th Engineer Battalion, 87th Division, to his mother).

Clarke, Ida Clyde Gallagher. *American Women and the World War* (New York: D. Appleton and Company, 1918), p. 434. Available via Google Books (https://books.google.com/books?id=lvDOAAAAMAAJ&pg=PA434&lpg=PA434&dq=trench+comfort+packets+committee&source=bl&ots=XC0NJOLk7f&sig=2HVLKcCDAvqXRzDJiPzRFs2BX5s&hl=en&sa=X&ved=0CCkQ6AEwBGoVChMIlMm-qMr5yAIVxSsmCh1QWwBH#v=onep.&q=trench%20comfort%20packets%20committee&f=false), accessed January 14, 2016.

Clarke, William F. *Over There with O'Ryan's Roughnecks* (Seattle: Superior Publishing Company, 1966).

"Compile History of the 77th." *New York Times*, April 13, 1919, p. 19 (http://timesmachine.nytimes.com/timesmachine/1919/04/13/96292793.html), accessed February 22, 2016.

"Cornell Founding and the Morrill Act." Cornell University ROTC (http://www.goarmy.com/rotc/schools/cornell-university/history.html), accessed March 30, 2016.

"Correspondence of the Military Intelligence Division Relating to 'Negro Subversion' 1917–1941." Records of the War Department General and Special Staffs, Record Group 165.

Couture, Lisa. "The History of Canned Food" (2010). Academic Symposium of Undergraduate Scholarship. Paper 4 (http://scholarsarchive.jwu.edu/ac_symposium/4), accessed January 22, 2016.

Coyne, Kevin. "Ultimate Sacrifice," *Smithsonian Magazine*, October 2004 (http://www.smithsonianmag.com/history/ultimate-sacrifice-180728112/?all), accessed May 16, 2016.

Crawford, Gilbert H., Thomas H. Ellet, and John J. Hyland, eds. *The 302nd Engineers: A History* (Ann Arbor: The University of Michigan Library, 1920), Hathi Trust (https://babel.hathitrust.org/cgi/pt?id=mdp.39015027341661;view=1up;seq=7), accessed November 17, 2016.

Crowell, Benedict, Assistant Secretary of War. *America's Munitions, 1917–1918* (Washington, DC: Government Printing Office, 1919), p. 228, Available via archive.org (https://archive.org/details/cu31924030744068), accessed May 23, 2016.

Currie, Constance Gibson. "Section 5, West Sayville's World War I Navy Base," *Long Island Forum* (Winter 2000), pp. 4–11.

———. "The Telefunken Radio Station in Sayville." *Long Island Forum* (Winter 1996), pp. 4–16.

Darracott, Joseph, ed. *The First World War in Posters* (New York: Dover Publications, 1974) .

"The Deadly Virus: The Influenza Epidemic of 1918." National Archives and Records Administration Online Exhibit (www.archives.gov/exhibits/influenza-epidemic), accessed April 21, 2016.

Degenhart, William M. The William M. Degenhart Diary, 1918–1919, New York State Library, Manuscripts and Special Collections, 23005 (Diary of a World War I soldier from Lackawanna, Erie County).

DeHaas, David D. "Victor Clyde Forsythe—Art of the West," historynet.com (http://www.historynet.com/victor-clyde-forsythe-and-the-gunfight-at-o-k-corral-a-new-perspective.htm), accessed May 19, 2016.

Dickon, Chris. *Americans at War in Foreign Forces: A History 1914–1945* (Toronto: McFarland, 2014) .

Dowling, Timothy C., ed. *Personal Perspectives: World War I* (Santa Barbara, CA: ABC Clio, 2006). "Service for Soldiers: The Experience of American Social Welfare Agencies in World War I, pp. 205–258.

Du Bois, W. E. B., ed. *The Crisis* 17, no. 2 (December 1918).

———, ed. "Documents of the War," *The Crisis* 18, no. 1 (May 1919).

———. "Returning Soldiers," *The Crisis* 18, no. 1 (May 1919), pp. 13–14.

Duffield, Thomas. *Protected Native Birds of South Australia* (Adelaide, Australia: Rogers, 1910), title p., archive.org (https://archive.org/details/protectednativeb00duff), accessed March 3, 2016.

Duffy, Francis P. *Father Duffy's Story* (New York: George H. Doran Company, 1919).

Edgett, Roy W. The Roy W. Edgett Letters, 1917–1918, New York State Library, Manuscripts and Special Collections, SC21234 (Group of letters written by Roy Edgett to his sister in Pulaski, New York).

Eisenstadt, Peter, ed. *The Encyclopedia of New York State* (Syracuse: Syracuse University Press, 2005).

Elkus, Abram I., and Felix Adler. *Americanization: Report of the Committee on Education of Governor Smith's Reconstruction Commission* (Albany: J. B. Lyons Company, 1919), pp. 4–7.

Ellis, David M., James A. Frost, Harold C. Syrett, and Harry J. Carman, *A History of the State of New York* (Ithaca: Cornell University Press, 1967), pp. 390–392, 462, 514, 517, 524, 545, 547, 549–550, 564, 587, 636, 650, 658.

"Ellis Island History—A Brief Look." The National Park Service (http://www.nps.gov/elis/learn/historyculture/upload/Brief-History-of-Ellis-Island.pdf), accessed February 3, 2016.

Elmer, Basil B. The Basil Beebe Elmer Letters, 1917–1919, New York State Library, Manuscripts and Special Collections SC23224 (Letters from an Ithaca, New York, soldier in Company A, intelligence section, 165th Infantry Regiment [69th Infantry, New York National Guard] during World War I).

Elston, Roy T. The Roy T. Elston Papers, 1916–1919, New York State Library, Manuscripts and Special Collections, SC22718 (Letters from Ellston from Unionville, New York, to his family during war).

"Emma Goldman." Women of Valor exhibition, Jewish Women's Archive (http://jwa.org/womenofvalor/goldman), accessed April 12, 2016.

Evans, Lamonte R. The Lamonte R. Evans Diary, 1918, New York State Library, Manuscripts and Special Collections, BD23126 (Diary detailing the World War I service of Lamonte Evans of Utica, Herkimer County).

Exhibit Program. "Exhibition of Posters for National Service," Art Institute of Chicago, July 2 to July 31, 1917. (http://www.artic.edu/sites/default/files/libraries/pubs/1917/AIC1917Posters_comb.pdf), accessed February 7, 2016.

"Extension Teaching Announcement." *Columbia University Bulletin of Information, 1916–1917*, p. xiii (https://books.google.com/books?id=GrfOAAAAMAAJ&pg=PR13&dq=Vojtech+Preissig&lr=&ei=c5E9S6-bK4LklQS21_HJAQ&cd=99#v=onep.&q=Vojtech%20Preissig&f=false), accessed April 11, 2016.

Fairman, Matthew D. "The Restriction of Civil Liberties during Times of Crisis: The Evolution of America's Response to National Military Threats" (2009). Government Honors Papers. Paper 7 (http://digitalcommons.conncoll.edu/govhp/7), accessed February 17, 2016.

Fangboner, Donald. "The Wristwatch Comes of Age," *Journal of the Company of Military Historians*. XXXVI, no. 1 (Spring 1984), pp. 31–32.

Federal Bureau of Investigation. "A Brief History of the FBI" (https://www.fbi.gov/about-us/history/brief-history), accessed April 16, 2016.

Finding Aid. James Reese Europe Collection, Schomburg Center for Research in Black Culture, The New York Public Library (http://archives.nypl.org/scm/20906), accessed October 17, 2016.

Finding Aid, School of Aerial Photography Collection, Eastman House Museum Archives, 1981:1702.

FirstWorldWar.com: A Multimedia History of World War One (http://www.firstworldwar.com/), accessed April 2015–April 2016.

Fish, Hamilton Jr. The Hamilton Fish Jr. Papers, 1913–1988, New York State Library, Manuscripts and Special Collections, SC21149 (Collection includes papers from Fish's service as an officer for the 369th Infantry Regiment, an African American combat unit during World War I).

Flick, Alexander C., ed. *History of the State of New York*, vols. VII–X (Port Washington, NY: Ira J. Friedman, 1962).

Forstall, Richard L., ed. *Population of States and Counties of the United States: 1790 to 1990* (Washington, DC: U.S. Department of Commerce, Bureau of the Census, 1996).

Frank, Meryl, and Blake McKelvey. "Some Former Rochesterians of National Distinction," *Rochester History* XXI, no. 3 (July 1959).

"Frank Vincent DuMond papers, 1866–1982." Archives of American Art, Smithsonian Institution (http://www.aaa.si.edu/collections/frank-vincent-dumond-papers-7453), accessed January 25, 2016.

Fussell, Paul. *The Great War and Modern Memory* (New York: Oxford University Press, 2013).

Gable, John Allen. *The Bull Moose Years: Theodore Roosevelt and the Progressive Party* (Port Washington, NY: National University Publications, 1978).

"German Expressionism: Works from the Collection." The Museum of Modern Art, New York (http://www.moma.org/explore/collection/ge/index), accessed February 3, 2016.

Gildea, Robert. *Barricades and Borders: Europe 1800–1914*, 2nd ed. (New York: Oxford University Press, 1996), pp. 300–325, 334–343, and 389–420.

Gillett, Mary C. *The Army Medical Department 1917–1941* (Washington, DC: United States Army Center of Military History, 2009).

"Give Your Country Your Vacation." *The Crimson* (Cambridge: Harvard University, June 4, 1918) (http://www.thecrimson.com/article/1918/6/4/give-your-country-your-vacation-pit/), accessed March 30, 2016.

Grayson, Lawrence P. "Fr. Francis Duffy: The Doughboy Chaplain," Knights of Columbus, Archdiocese of Washington District, 2012 (http://www.awddistrict.org/index.php/catholic-patriotism/military-chaplains/fr-francis-duffy-the-doughboy-chaplain), accessed May 20, 2016.

"The Great Pandemic: The United States in 1918–1919." United States Department of Health and Human Services (http://www.flu.gov/pandemic/history/1918/your_state/northeast/newyork/index.html), accessed April 21, 2016.

Greenwald, Maurine Weiner. *Women, War, and Work: The Impact of World War I on Women Workers in the United States* (Westport, CT: Greenwood Press, 1980).

Handbook of the American Defense Society. May 1918, p. 8. Google Books (https://books.google.com/books?id=qPE7AQAAMAAJ&printsec=frontcover#v=onep.&q&f=false), accessed May 23, 2016.

"Harder's First Year of Service: His Important Work at Albany." *The Chatham Courier*, October 16, 1924, p. 1 (http://fultonhistory.com/Fulton.html), accessed November 17, 2016.

Harris, Stephen L. *Duffy's War: Fr. Francis Duffy, Wild Bill Donovan, and the Irish Fighting 69th in World War I* (Washington, DC: Potomac Books, 2008).

———. *Duty, Honor, Privilege: New York's Silk Stocking Regiment and the Breaking of the Hindenburg Line* (Washington, DC: Potomac Books, 2001).

———. *Harlem's Hellfighters: The African-American 369th Infantry in World War I* (Washington, DC: Potomac Books, Inc., 2003).

Hatch, Alden. *Remington Arms in American History* (New York: Rinehart and Company, 1956), pp. 210–225.

Higham, John. *Strangers in the Land: Patterns of American Nativism, 1860–1925* (New Brunswick, NJ: Rutgers University Press, 1983), pp. 194–330.

Hill, Harold B. The Harold B. Hill Papers, 1918, New York State Library, Manuscripts and Special Collections, SC21236 (Collection of letters and memorabilia from Hill, of Goshen, New York, during his service in the 491st Aero Squadron during World War I).

"Histoire des Arts les Affiches." Musée de la Grand Guerre, Péronne, France (www.historial.org), accessed February 3, 2016, p. 2.

Historical Note. Guide to the Records of the American Defense Society, New York Historical Society, October 19, 2011 (http://dlib.nyu.edu/findingaids/html/nyhs/americandefsoc/bioghist.html), accessed April 17, 2016.

"History and Highlights of the Forty and Eight." *La Société des Quarante Hommes et Huit Cheveaux* (www.fortyandeight.org/history-of-the-408), accessed May 4, 2016.

"The History of Donut Day." The Salvation Army Metropolitan Division (http://centralusa.salvationarmy.org/metro/donutday-history/), accessed January 22, 2016.

"History of 77th Division Unique." *The Brooklyn Standard Union*, April 12, 1919, p. 4 (http://fultonhistory.com/Newspaper%2014/Brooklyn%20NY%20Standard%20Union/Brooklyn%20NY%20Standard%20Union%201919/Brooklyn%20NY%20Standard%20Union%201919%20-%201487.pdf), accessed February 22, 2016.

Hobsbawm, E. J. *Nations and Nationalism since 1780* (New York: Cambridge University Press, 1990), pp. 101–130.

Hogan, Martin J. *The Shamrock Battalion of the Rainbow: A Story of the "Fighting Sixty-Ninth"* (New York: D. Appleton and Company, 1919). Accessed via archive.org (https://archive.org/details/shamrockbattalio00hogarich).

Holcombe, Randall G. "The Growth of the Federal Government in the 1920s," *The Cato Journal* 16, no. 2 (Fall 1996), pp. 175–199.

Holden, Edward. The Edward Holden Papers, 1917–1922, New York State Library, Manuscripts and Special Collections, 20790 (Collection of personal narratives of World War I soldiers).

Howard C. Christy Biography. Ohio History Central (http://www.ohiohistorycentral.org/w/Howard_C._Christy), accessed February 8, 2016.

Hume, John R. Captain John R. Hume Diary, September 6, 1917–February 4, 1918, State Historical Society of Missouri (http://shsmo-tc1.missouri.edu/cdm/ref/collection/wwi/id/178), accessed May 16, 2016.

Hume, Sara. *The Great War: Women and Fashion in a World at War, 1912–1922*, Exhibition Catalog (Kent, Ohio: Kent State University Museum, 2014).

Husted, James W. The Husted Family Papers, 1853–1943, New York State Library, Manuscripts and Special Collections, SC23259 (Letters from James W. Husted Jr. to his father, Congressman Husted of Peekskill, New York).

Hutner, Gordon, ed. *Selected Speeches of Theodore Roosevelt* (New York: Knopf Doubleday Publishing Group, 2013).

"The Income Tax Arrives." The Tax History Museum (http://www.taxhistory.org/), accessed May 5, 2016.

"Ireland, Rutherford." Home of Heroes (http://www.homeofheroes.com/members/02_DSC/citatons/01_wwi_dsc/dsc_05wwi_Army_IJ.html), accessed May 20, 2016.

Jackson, Kenneth. "But it was in New York," lecture at the New York State Museum, November 19, 2009 (https://www.youtube.com/watch?v=McDXIC2UH7s), accessed October 19, 2016.

Jaffe, Steven H. *New York at War: Four Centuries of Combat, Fear, and Intrigue in Gotham* (New York: Basic Books, 2012), pp. 177–216.

"J. Allen St. John" Biography. Pulptartists.com (http://www.pulpartists.com/StJohn.html), accessed April 15, 2016.

Jessup, J. B. Lieutenant, Commander, Company A, 107th Infantry Regiment, Letter to Mrs. Adrean, February 17, 1919. Collection of the Oneida County Historical Society, 2007.171.17.

"Jews to Raise $5,000,000." *New York Times*, November 12, 1917 (http://timesmachine.nytimes.com/timesmachine/1917/11/12/102649223.html), accessed May 24, 2015.

"Johnson Too Loose with His Jaw." *The Ocala Evening Star*, Monday, March 31, 1919, p. 1 (http://chroniclingamerica.loc.gov/lccn/sn84027621/1919-03-31/ed-1/), accessed April 29, 2016.

Joint Legislative Committee to Investigate Seditious Activities. *Final Report of the Joint Committee for the Investigation of Seditious Activities* (Albany: J. B. Lyon Company, 1920).

———. National Civil Liberties Bureau Subpoenaed Files, 1917–1919, New York State Archives Series L0031.

———. Suspected Radical Propaganda Files, 1890–1919, New York State Archives Series L0036.

———. Investigative Subject Files, New York State Archives Series L0039.

———. *Revolutionary Radicalism: Its History, Purpose and Tactics with an Exposition and Discussion of the Steps Being Taken and Required to Curb It* (Albany: J. B. Lyons Company, 1920), vols. I–III.

Joint Legislative Resolution Regarding the 332nd Regiment of the American Expeditionary Force, 1919, New York State Archives Series B0303.

Joll, James. *Europe since 1870*. 4th ed. (New York: Penguin Books, 1990), pp. 169–323.

———. *The Origins of the First World War* (New York: Pearson Education Limited, 1992) .

Jones, John Price, and Paul Merrick Hollister. *The German Secret Service in America* (Boston: Small Maynard and Company, 1918), available via archive.org (https://archive.org/details/germansecretser00hollgoog), accessed February 3, 2016.

Journaux des Marches et Operations (J.M.O.) des Grandes Unités. Divisions d'infanterie et d'infanterie territoriale, 16e division d'infanterie, 1er janvier 1917–23 aout 1918 (http://www.memoiredeshommes.sga.defense.gouv.fr/fr/arkotheque/inventaires/ead_ir_consult.php?&ref=SHDGR__GR_26_N_I), accessed May 11, 2016.

Kammer, Jerry. "The Hart-Celler Immigration Act of 1965" (Center for Immigration Studies, September 2015), http://cis.org/Hart-Celler-Immigration-Act-1965, accessed November 28, 2016.

Keene, Jennifer. "Images of Racial Pride: African American Propaganda Posters in the First World War." In *Picture This: World War I Posters and Visual Culture*, edited by Pearl James (Lincoln: University of Nebraska, 2009), pp. 207–240.

Keitch, Charlie. "First World War Recruitment Posters," The Imperial War Museums (http://www.iwm.org.uk/learning/resources/first-world-war-recruitment-posters), accessed February 1–3, 2016.

Kennedy, David M. *Over Here: The First World War and American Society* (New York: Oxford University Press, 1980).

Kilmer, Alfred Joyce. "Rouge Bouquet," *Scribner's* Magazine, September 1918, p. 351 (https://www.unz.org/Pub/Scribners-1918sep-00351), accessed May 25, 2016.

Kimball, Robert, and William Bolcom. *Reminiscing with Sissle and Blake* (New York: The Viking Press, 1973).

Kinder, John M. *Paying with Their Bodies: American War and the Problem of the Disabled Veteran* (Chicago: University of Chicago Press, 2015).

Kitchen, Martin. *Europe Between the Wars: A Political History* (New York: Longman Group, 1994).

Kline, Harry L. *The Henry C. Kline Letters, 1918–1919*, New York State Library, Manuscripts and Special Collections, 21159 (Group of letters from Harry Kline to his mother, Clara, of Newburgh, New York).

Konkoly, Toni. "Famous Dissents: Abrams v. United States (1919)," *The Supreme Court: Law, Power, and Personality* (http://www.pbs.org/wnet/supremecourt/personality/landmark_abrams.html), accessed May 6, 2016.

Koslow, Philip, ed. *The New York Public Library African American Desk Reference* (New York: The Stonesong Press, 1999).

Kotzin, Daniel P. *Judah L. Magnes: An American Jewish Nonconformist* (Syracuse: Syracuse University Press, 2010).

Laemlein, Tom. *The Yanks Are Coming! Firepower of the American Doughboy in World War I* (East Rochester, NY: Armor Plate Press, 2010).

Lee, Stephen J. *The European Dictatorships, 1918–1945* (New York: Routledge, 1998), pp. 1–23.

Lemak, Jennifer. "Advancement Comes Slowly: African-American Employment in Rochester, New York During the Great Migration," *New York History* 92, nos. 1, 2 (Winter/Spring 2011), pp. 79–98.

Lewis, Merton E., Attorney General. Letter to John C. Birdseye, Secretary, New York State Civil Service Commission, December 14, 1917. New York State Museum Collection, H-2007.32.9.

"Lt. James Reese Europe Buried with Honors." *The New York Age*, May 17, 1919, pp. 1 and 6 (http://fultonhistory.com/Newspaper%2011/New%20York%20NY%20Age/New%20York%20NY%20Age%201919-1921%20%20Grayscale/New%20York%20NY%20Age%201919-1921%20%20Grayscale%20-%200163.pdf), accessed October 18, 2016.

Lydecker, Leigh. The Lydecker Family Papers, 1860–1983, New York State Library, Manuscripts and Special Collections, SC19048 (Collection of family papers including correspondence from Leigh Lydecker, 149th Field Artillery, 42nd Division during World War I).

Magnani, Edward. "Detour at Lonelyville," *Long Island Forum*, Summer 1998, pp. 5–19.

Mancini, Al. "Women on the Homefront," "Rochester During World War One," *Rochester History* LI no. 3 (Summer 1989).

Martin, Andrew D. "The Great War, the NYSE and a Legacy of Strength" (New York: Advisor Perspectives, 2014).

Martin, David A. "Dual Nationality: TR's 'Self-Evident Absurdity,'" Chair Lecture, October 27, 2004, *UVA Lawyer*, Spring 2005 (http://www.law.virginia.edu/html/alumni/uvalawyer/sp05/martin_lecture.htm), accessed April 21, 2016.

Marx, Karl, and Friedrich Engels. *The Communist Manifesto* (New York: Penguin Group, 1967), p. 93.

McGuire, Randall H. "Building Power in the Cultural Landscape of Broome County, New York, 1880 to 1940," in *Material Culture: Critical Concepts in Social Sciences*, edited by Victor Buchli. Vol. 2 (New York: Routledge, Taylor and Francis Group, 2004), chapter 61.

McKelvey, Blake. "Lights and Shadows in Local Negro History," *Rochester History* XXI, no. 4 (October 1959), pp. 19–20.

———. "Rochester's Ethnic Transformations," *Rochester History* XXV, no. 3 (July 1963), pp. 16–17.

McMaster, John Bach. *The United States in the World War* (New York: D. Appleton and Co., 1918).

MeasuringWorth.com (https://www.measuringworth.com/uscompare/relativevalue.php), accessed January–November, 2016.

Mémoire des Hommes. The Digital Archives of the First World War, Ministère de la Defense, République Francaise (http://www.memoiredeshommes.sga.defense.gouv.fr/en/article.php?larub=78).

Mercaldo, Luke. "Remington's Allied Rifle Contracts During World War I," The Remington Society of America (http://www.remingtonsociety.org/remingtons-allied-rifle-contracts-during-wwi/), accessed November 4, 2016.

Miles, L. Wardlaw. *History of the 308th Infantry, 1917–1919* (New York: G. P. Putnam's Sons, 1927).

"Military Nurses in World War I." Women in Military Service for American Memorial Foundation, Inc., History and Collections (http://chnm.gmu.edu/courses/rr/s01/cw/students/leeann/historyandcollections/history/lrnmrewwinurses.html), accessed May 19, 2016.

Miller, Lina D. *Directory of Social Agencies of New York*, 1922 (New York: The Charity Organization Society, 1922), pp. 10–11.

Mitchell, Harold W. The Harold W. Mitchell Papers, 1917–1921, New York State Library, Manuscripts and Special Collections, SC20960 (Primarily letters from Mitchell to his parents relating to his World War I military service as chief health officer and sanitary inspector).

Moore, Howard W. The Howard W. Moore Papers, 1915–1993, New York State Library, Manuscripts and Special Collections, SC20795 (Papers from a World War I conscientious objector from Cherry Valley, New York).

———. *Plowing My Own Furrow* (New York: W.W. Norton and Company, 1985).

Moore, William E., and James C. Russell. *U.S. Official Pictures of the Great War: Selected from the Official Files of the War Department* (Washington, DC: Pictorial Bureau, 1920).

More, Ellen. "Rochester Over There: Rochester During World War One," *Rochester History* LI, no. 3 (Summer 1989).

"The Most Famous Poster." Online Exhibit: American Treasures at the Library of Congress (www.loc.gov/exhibits/treasures/trm015.html), accessed April 29, 2016.

Mulligan, Robert. "'Real Men' Didn't Wear Wrist Watches," *New York Alive*, July/August 1989, p. 12.

"NAACP: A Century in the Fight for Freedom." Library of Congress Exhibition (https://www.loc.gov/exhibits/naacp/the-new-negro-movement.html), accessed November 29, 2016.

National Park Service. "Civil War Facts" (https://www.nps.gov/civilwar/facts.htm), accessed October 20, 2016.

New York State Bonus Commission. World War I Veterans Bonus Cards, ca. 1920–1937. New York State Archives Series B1357.

New York State Boys' Working Reserve. Farm Cadet Essays, 1918, New York State Archives Series A4436.

New York State Food Supply Commission. Enlistment Papers and Reports of the New York State Boys' Working Reserve (Farm Cadet Program), 1918, New York State Archives Series A3112.

New York State National Guard. Abstracts of National Guard Service in World War I, 1917–1919, New York State Archives Series 13721.

———. Muster Rolls of New York National Guard Units that Served in the United States Army During World War I, 1917–1918. New York State Archives Series B0814.

New York State Police. "Annual Reports of the Department of State Police for the Years 1918 to 1924 Inclusive" (Albany: J. B. Lyon Company, 1925), pp. 6–13.

———. Troop G, Police Blotter Books (1917–1919), New York State Archives, Series 13445-82.

New York Times. Sunday, July 14, 1918, Rotogravure Photo Section 7, p. 5, New York State Museum Collection, H-1972.77.NN [dup 13].

"Nicholas Murray Butler." *C250 Celebrates Columbians Ahead of Their Time* (http://c250.columbia.edu/c250_celebrates/remarkable_columbians/nicholas_butler.html), accessed November 10, 2016.

Noble, Henry George Stebbins. *The New York Stock Exchange in the Crisis of 1914* (New York: The Country Life Press, 1915).

Nolan, Cathal J. "POV: The Legacy of World War I," *BU Today* (http://www.bu.edu/today/2014/pov-the-legacy-of-world-war-i/), November 11, 2014.

Norder, Akum. "The Battle of Henry Johnson," *518 Life* Magazine, November 21, 2014, p. 22–23.

Norton, Frank H., Colonel. *A Short History and Illustrated Roster of the 106th Infantry United States* (Philadelphia: Edward, Stern and Co., Inc., 1918), p. 110.

O'Ryan, John Francis. *The Story of the 27th Division* (New York: Wynkoop, Hallenbeck, Crawford Co., 1921).

Perry, Ralph Barton. *The Plattsburg Movement, A Chapter of America's Participation in the World War* (New York: E. P. Dutton and Company, 1921).

Persico, Joseph E. *11th Month, 11th Day, 11th Hour: Armistice Day, 1918: World War I and its Violent Climax* (New York: Random House, 2004).

"Pierce-Arrow History." The Buffalo Transportation Pierce-Arrow Museum (www.pierce-arrow.com/history), accessed April 5, 2016.

"Pour la liberté du monde. Souscrivez à l'emprunt national à la Banque Nationale de Crédit," Bibliothèque Numerique Mondial (http://www.wdl.org/fr/item/4613/), accessed February 3, 2016.

Rawls, Walton. *Wake Up, America! World War I and the American Poster* (New York: Abbeville Press, 1988).

Resnick, Mark. *The American Image: U.S. Posters from the 19th to the 21st Century* (Rochester: RIT Cary Graphics Art Press, 2006).

Rickards, Maurice, ed. *Posters of the First World War* (New York: Walker and Company, 1968).

Roosevelt, Theodore. *The Great Adventure: Present Day Studies in American Nationalism* (London, John Murray, 1919).

———. "True Americanism," *The Forum Magazine* (April 1894) (https://hudson.org/content/researchattachments/attachment/1216/theodore_roosevelt_true_americanism.pdf), accessed May 24, 2016.

Roosevelt, Theodore, Jr. *Rank and File: True Stories of the Great War* (New York: C. Scribner's Sons, 1928), pp. 91–116.

Rose, Sarah Frances. *No Right to Be Idle: The Invention of Disability, 1850–1930* (Chicago: University of Illinois at Chicago, 2008).

Rumer, Thomas A. *The American Legion: An Official History 1919–1989* (New York: M. Evans and Company, 1990), pp. 5–170.

Ruskoski, David Thomas. "The Polish Army in France: Immigrants in America, World War I Volunteers in France, Defenders of the Recreated State in Poland." Dissertation, Georgia State University, 2006, pp. 73–75 (http://scholarworks.gsu.edu/history_diss/1), accessed February 3 and April 7, 2016.

Salleck, Lawrence M. The Lawrence M. Salleck Letters, 1916–1919, New York State Library, Manuscripts and Special Collections, SC21734 (Correspondence between a World War I Soldier from Buffalo, Erie County, to his parents during his service on the Mexican Border [1916] and with the A.E.F [1917–1919]).

Sammons, Jeffrey T., and John H. Morrow Jr. *Harlem's Rattlers and the Great War: The Undaunted 369th Regiment and the African American Quest for Equality* (Lawrence: University of Kansas Press, 2014).

Sarnecky, Mary T. *A History of the U.S. Army Nurses Corps* (Philadelphia: University of Pennsylvania Press, 1999), chapter 3.

Schaming, Peter. Letter to Parents, October 1, 1918. Transcript in Vital Information File, New York State Museum Collection, H-2015.21.

Seeger, Alan. *Letters and Diary of Alan Seeger* (Toronto: S. B. Gundy, 1917), p. 12. Accessed at Hathitrust.org (http://hdl.handle.net/2027/aeu.ark:/13960/t87h47k7r), accessed May 10, 2016.

———. "Partie à Remplier Par le Corps" in "Mort Pour La France" (http://www.memoiredeshommes.sga.defense.gouv.fr/), accessed May 11, 2016.

Seigfred, Guy, and Elbert Seigfred. The Seigfred Family Letters, 1917–1919, New York State Library, Manuscripts and Special Collections, SC19814 (Letters from Guy and Elbert, of Seneca Falls, New York, detailing service during World War I).

"Sergeant Henry Johnson Addresses New York Legislature." *The Dallas Express*, Saturday, March 22, 1919, p. 1 (http://chroniclingamerica.loc.gov/lccn/sn83025779/1919-03-22/ed-1/), accessed April 29, 2016.

Shields, Joseph W., Jr. *From Flintlock to M1* (New York: Coward-McCann, 1954), pp. 161–171.

Sissle, Noble. *Memoirs of Lieutenant "Jim Europe"* (unpublished, circa 1942). From the collections of the Library of Congress Music Division, https://memory.loc.gov/cgi-bin/query/r?ammem/aaodyssey:@field(NUMBER+@band(musmisc+ody0717)), accessed October 14, 2016.

Slaski, Lisa. "First Sergeant Charles Henry Adrean," Oneida County Gen Web (http://oneida.nygenweb.net/military/aldean.html), accessed June 8, 2016.

Slotkin, Richard. *Lost Battalions: The Great War and the Crisis of American Nationality* (New York: Henry Holt and Company, 2005).

Smith, George David. *From Monopoly to Competition: The Transformation of Alcoa, 1888–1986* (New York: Cambridge University Press, 2003), pp. 126–131.

Spicer, Warren. The Spicer Family Papers, 1870–1932. New York State Library, Manuscripts and Special Collections, SC19560 (Family correspondence including that between the parents, Frank E. and Nellie, and their son, Warren, who served in the military from 1917–1923).

Stewart, Richard W., ed. *American Military History*, vol. I (Washington, DC: United States Army Center of Military History, 2005), pp. 365–386.

———., ed. *American Military History*, vol. II (Washington, DC: United States Army Center of Military History, 2005).

Stoller-Conrad, Jessica. "Canning History: When Propaganda Encouraged Patriotic Preserves," National Public Radio, August 3, 2012 (http://www.npr.org/sections/thesalt/2012/08/02/157777834/canning-history-when-propaganda-encouraged-patriotic-preserves), accessed January 22, 2016.

Strauss, Walter J. Diary of J. Walter Strauss, New York State Museum Collection, H-1976.243.2.

Sullivan, James, ed. *History of New York State 1523–1927*, vols. III and IV (New York: The American Historical Society, 1927), pp. 1225–1413.

Sullivan, James. Working Files for a Publication on New York in World War I, 1917–1925, New York State Archives Series A3166.

Swantek, John, and James Murray. *Watervliet Arsenal: History of America's Oldest Arsenal* (Watervliet, NY: Watervliet Arsenal Public Affairs Office, 2009).

Sweeney, Daniel J. *History of Buffalo and Erie County, 1914–1919* (Buffalo: Committee of One Hundred, 1919).

Swinney, H. J. *The New York State Firearms Trade*, vol. 4 (Rochester, NY: Rove Publications, 2003), p. 1443–1444.

Taber, Herbert H. The Private Herbert H. Taber Letters, 1918–1919, private collection (Private Taber was a soldier in Battery A, 7th Field Artillery, 1st Division, AEF, during World War I).

Taylor, A. J. P. *The Origins of the Second World War* (New York: Atheneum, 1961), pp. 7–60.

———. *The Struggle for Mastery in Europe, 1848–1918* (New York: Oxford University Press, 1954).

Teall, Maynard C. The Maynard C. Teall Letters, 1918–1919, New York State Library, Manuscripts and Special Collections, 21239 (Letters from Captain Maynard Teall, 311th Field Artillery, to his family in Sodus, New York).

Theofiles, George. *American Posters of World War I: A Price and Collector's Guide* (New York: Dafran House Publishers, 1975).

Thomas, Louisa. *Conscience: Two Soldiers, Two Pacifists, One Family—A Test of Will and Faith in World War I* (New York: Penguin Books, 2011).

Treasury Department. *Liberty Loan Acts* (Washington, DC: Government Printing Office, 1921), title page (http://books.google.com/books?id=4qFAAAAAYAAJ), accessed May 4, 2016.

United States Department of Labor, Bureau of Industrial Housing and Transportation. *War Emergency Construction (Housing War Workers): Report of the United States Housing Corporation*, vol. II (Washington, DC: Government Printing Office, 1919), pp. 185–188.

Urbanic, Kathleen. "Seeking Prosperity: A Brief History of Rochester's Polish American Community, Part One," *Rochester History* LVII, no. 1 (Winter 1995).

"The U.S. Army Chaplain Corps: Providing Care and Comfort to Soldiers for 239 Years," *Soldiers* Magazine, July 29, 2014 (http://soldiers.dodlive.mil/tag/father-francis-duffy/), accessed May 20, 2016.

"U.S. Merchant Ships, Sailing Vessels, and Fishing Craft Lost from all Causes during World War I," The American Merchant Marine at War (www.usmm.org/ww1merchant.html), accessed November 4, 2016.

Van Schaack, Evan. "The Division of Pictorial Publicity in World War I," *Design Issues* 22, no. 1 (Winter 2006), pp. 32–45.

Walker, William Ray. *Only the Heretics Are Burning: Democracy and Repression in World War I America* (Madison: University of Wisconsin, 2008), pp. 236–237.

Ward, Gary. "Engaged in Glory Alone: Yanks in French Foreign Legion Were First to Fight," *VFW Magazine* 102, no. 1 (September 1914), p. 36.

"The War Years," The Pierce-Arrow Society (www.pierce-arrow.org/history/history3.php), accessed April 5, 2016.

West, Aberjhani, and Sandra L. West. *Encyclopedia of the Harlem Renaissance* (New York: Checkmark Books, 2003).

Whitman, Charles Seymour. *Public Papers of Charles Seymour Whitman, Governor, 1915–1918*, vol. 3 (Albany: J. B. Lyon Company, Printers, 1919).

Whitman, Governor Charles S. "Proclamation announcing the Third Liberty Loan Drive, April 6, 1918," Official Proclamations by the Governor, 1893–2010, New York State Archives, Series 13035.

Wickens, Aryness Joy. "The Public Debt and National Income," *The American Economic Review* 37, no. 2, pp. 184–191.

Wilkins, Mira. *The History of Foreign Investment in the United States, 1914–1945* (Cambridge, MA: Harvard University Press, 2004), pp. 33–34.

Willbanks, James H, ed. *America's Heroes: Medal of Honor Recipients from the Civil War to Afghanistan* (Denver, CO: ABC-CLIO, LLC, 2011), pp. 248–250.

Wilson, Captain Dale E. *The American Expeditionary Forces Tank Corps in World War I: From Creation to Combat*. Submitted as a Master's thesis, History Department, College of Arts and Sciences, Temple University, Philadelphia (1988).

Wilson, Woodrow. Second Annual Message to Congress, December 8, 1914, *The American Presidency Project*, University of California, Santa Barbara (http://www.presidency.ucsb.edu/ws/index.php?pid=29555), accessed February 16, 2016.

Winter, Jay, and Blaine Baggett. *The Great War and the Shaping of the 20th Century* (New York: Penguin Studio, 1996).

Wood, Leonard. *Plattsburg Training Camp, July 1916* (Poughkeepsie, NY: Thompson Illustragraph Co., 1916).

"World War I Field and Mess Equipment." U.S. Army Center for Military History, http://www.history.army.mil/html/museums/messkits/Field_Mess_Gear(upd_Jul09).pdf, accessed May 17, 2016.

World War I Letters and Memorabilia Collection. New York State Library, Manuscripts and Special Collections, SC21813 (Letters written by New York State residents during their military service in World War I).

World War I Veterans' Service Data and Photographs, 1917–1938. New York State Archives Series A0412.

Wyer, James I., Jr. New York State Librarian, Correspondence files, 1917–1919, New York State Library, Manuscripts and Special Collections, SC23360 accession file.

Yockelson, Mitchell A. *Borrowed Soldiers: Americans Under British Command, 1918* (Norman: University of Oklahoma Press, 2008).

Zahavi, Gerald. "The Endicott-Johnson Corporation: 19th Century Origins" (http://www.albany.edu/history/ej/origins.html), accessed September 22, 2016.

Zeitz, Joshua, "The Roaring Twenties," the Gilder Lehrman Institute of American History (https://www.gilderlehrman.org/history-by-era/roaring-twenties/essays/roaring-twenties), accessed November 21, 2016.

Index